T0366556

DUMBARTON OAKS
MEDIEVAL LIBRARY

Daniel Donoghue, General Editor

SAINTS AT THE LIMITS

DOML 78

Saints at the Limits

Seven Byzantine Popular Legends

Edited and Translated by

STRATIS PAPAIOANNOU

DUMBARTON OAKS
MEDIEVAL LIBRARY

HARVARD UNIVERSITY PRESS
CAMBRIDGE, MASSACHUSETTS
LONDON, ENGLAND
2023

First Printing

Library of Congress Cataloging-in-Publication Data available from the Library of Congress at https://lccn.loc.gov/2022038046
ISBN 978-0-674-29079-2 (cloth : alk. paper)

Contents

Introduction vii

PASSION OF BONIPHATIOS 1

LIFE OF THE MAN OF GOD, ALEXIOS 23

LIFE OF MARKOS THE ATHENIAN 47

LIFE OF MAKARIOS THE ROMAN 77

PASSION OF CHRISTOPHER 129

GEORGE, THE GREAT MARTYR 171

PASSION OF NIKETAS 249

Abbreviations 279
Note on the Texts 281
Notes to the Texts 293
Notes to the Translations 305
Bibliography 347
Index 349

Introduction

The texts in this volume were never gathered together in a single collection in Byzantium. The connecting threads, however, that unite these popular legends are multiple. All of them, often with cross-references and in mutual influence, tell stories that configure various dimensions of the "limits" as experienced or conceived in Byzantium: the borders, that is, which separated cultural insiders from outsiders. These borders take, as we shall see, different forms, designating the powerful and the outcasts, the real and the imaginary, the human and the beyond human. They also point to a spectacular reversal of expectations, since what stands at first glance outside borders is projected as the ideal.

The stories, with their interlocking themes, will speak for themselves to the modern reader. Yet the texts that follow were to some extent linked also in Byzantine ritual culture and in their textual forms and modes of transmission. In short, they are connected by the usually low-register Greek in which they are told; by the manuscripts (often provincial and usually liturgical) in which they were transmitted, sometimes in proximity with one another and other similar legends; and by the implied suspicion or straightforward rejection that they often received from those pro-

moting official orthodoxy. All these texts thus gesture toward local and what we sometimes call the "apocryphal," as opposed to canonical, Christian traditions, and the "popular," as opposed to more learned, religious expression.

The following brief presentation of the texts offers the reader a starting point for pursuing these connections further, without, however, covering the subject in depth.

PASSION OF BONIPHATIOS

The tale of Saint Boniphatios, commemorated on December 19, is set at an unspecified time in the pre-Byzantine past. The story begins with Aglaïs, a prominent and wealthy noblewoman in Rome, who has a licentious lover: her slave Boniphatios, a witty man, "addicted to drinking and sex," but nevertheless distinguished for his "hospitality, generosity, and charity." The promiscuous couple decides to abandon their wicked ways, and Boniphatios is sent to the East so as to gather relics of holy martyrs. In the city of Tarsos (in Cilicia, Asia Minor), Boniphatios witnesses the tortures of martyrs and eventually suffers martyrdom himself. His fellow companions then purchase and bring his relics back to Rome, where he is buried by Aglaïs. She in turn abandons her status and properties, becomes a nun, and, with her ascetic discipline, achieves sainthood herself, dying peacefully thirteen years later.

As is the case with all the stories included in this volume, it is impossible to know exactly when, where, by whom, and for whom the legend of Boniphatios was first created. By the eighth century, we find mentions of a charitable institution that was located at the Aventine Hill in Rome and hon-

ored Boniphatios as its patron saint. This foundation was probably already a century old and was, as has been convincingly argued by Maya Maskarinec, most probably created by Greek-speaking refugees fleeing Cilicia due to the Persian, and then Arab, invasions that transformed the Mediterranean world over the course of the seventh century.[1]

It is likely, as Maskarinec also claims, that the legend of Boniphatios was first written down in the context of this community of immigrants. However this might be, the story, or elements of the story, could have originated in Cilicia (indeed, in Tarsos) and then been refashioned in the preserved post-seventh-century textual renditions; these latter versions "Romanize" the account by setting its main protagonists in Rome. After all, though this has remained previously unnoticed, an earlier, non-Roman tradition did exist regarding two martyrs called "Bonifa(n)tios and Hermolaos," as attested in a bare synaxarial notice (without biographical narrative) for December 19 in the most ancient, tenth-century recension of the *Synaxarion of Constantinople*.[2]

The earliest extant textual version of the legend was written in Greek (as demonstrated by Pio Franchi de' Cavalieri) and was quickly translated into Latin and then spread in Western Europe.[3] As far as I have been able to ascertain, we may distinguish five main versions: *BHG* 279–280; *BHG* 280a (and a variation of it, *BHG* 280b); a somewhat purified version, *BHG* 281–282, which is the learned version included in Symeon Metaphrastes's *Menologion* and revises *BHG* 280b; another (late Byzantine?) version, couched in the form of a sermon pseudonymously attributed to Ephrem the Syrian;[4] and the *Synaxarion* in various recensions (*BHG* 282e), according to which (we may add) our story was set at the time

of Diocletian's persecutions (303–305 CE). Though Metaphrastes's version and the *Synaxarion* were read widely, we find no evidence of a cult, a site, or a distinct visual representation dedicated to Boniphatios in the post-1000 Byzantine world.

The text, edited critically anew and translated for this volume (*BHG* 279–280), represents what I believe to be the version closest to the (lost?) original (and thus also to the Latin translations, *BHL* 1413–1417), and is preserved mainly in a small number of Italian manuscripts. Its text is in rather plain and occasionally awkward Greek, with many Latinisms (both in vocabulary and in syntax), possibly an indication of a Greek-speaking author living and writing in an environment where the dominant language was Latin.

LIFE OF THE MAN OF GOD, ALEXIOS

The tale of the Man of God, who in most Greek versions carries the name Alexios, unfolds at the time of Emperors Honorius (393–423 CE) and Arcadius (393–408 CE). On his wedding night, the central character, who is the son of a Roman aristocrat, abandons his bride, native city, and senatorial family, and travels, unbeknown to anyone, to the Syrian city of Edessa. There, for seventeen years, he leads the life of a beggar, dwelling in extreme poverty in the narthex of a church. When his sanctity is revealed, he sets sail for Tarsos, but is brought miraculously back to Rome, where he decides to live incognito as a foreign beggar in his own family's household; and so he does, for another seventeen years. His identity and life story are made known only posthumously, facilitated by the autobiographical scroll found on his body,

which is subsequently carried triumphantly and buried at a church.

The story reproduces the same scenario—and indeed the same perspective—encountered in Boniphatios. The main character belongs to a prominent household in Rome, departs from the city in order to travel eastward, and returns, transformed, to his home city, where he achieves sainthood among Rome's citizens. The similarities do not end here, however. Alexios's mother bears the name Aglaïs, which is also that of Boniphatios's noble mistress; Alexios aims to travel to Tarsos, Boniphatios's place of martyrdom; and, moreover, according to the earliest Greek versions, Alexios's wedding and burial both take place in a church that is none other than that of Saint Boniphatios on the Aventine Hill in Rome.

The two texts are thus certainly affiliated, and it seems most plausible that the Greek version of Alexios's tale is a kind of sequel to Boniphatios's and originates in the same Greek-speaking community in Rome. Both texts are written in the same awkward, Latinizing Greek idiom; both, in their likely earliest versions, are preserved in Italian manuscripts; both were immediately translated into Latin and experienced a wide circulation among Christian communities in Europe;[5] and the two saints were celebrated jointly at the Aventine church in Rome (perhaps as early as the ninth century and definitely by the end of the tenth) before Alexios became much more popular and far superseded Boniphatios, even in Rome.[6]

When did Alexios's Greek story appear in Rome, among the devotees of Boniphatios? It is *not* in the late tenth century, as has been suggested in some earlier scholarship.[7]

Rather, I would argue, the story took shape in the congregations of refugees from the Eastern parts of the Byzantine Empire who, during the seventh century, first established the *diaconia* of Boniphatios, the charitable institution located at the Aventine Hill in Rome. A clue for the early dating of the tale in Greek, not noted in most previous discussions, is the following:[8] two Sinaite *Menaia,* gr. 609 (fols. 66v–68v) and gr. 611 (fols. 106r–8v), of the eleventh and fourteenth centuries, respectively, preserve a polystrophic hymn, a *kanôn,* in honor of our saint. Both manuscripts attribute the text to Germanos I (ca. 655–before 754 CE), patriarch of Constantinople (715–730).[9] It is impossible to know if the *kanôn* was actually written by Germanos and thus dates to the first decades of the eighth century. However, the text certainly predates another *kanôn,* which was composed during the latter part of the ninth century by Joseph the Hymnographer (ca. 812 or 818–ca. 886), a Sicilian active in Constantinople.

The antiquity of the *kanôn* attributed to Germanos is revealed by an important detail absent from Joseph's hymn. The celebrated saint is never called Alexios, but only carries the designation "the Man of God." The same anonymity is present in the Italian manuscripts, which contain the earliest, I believe, preserved Greek version of the story, the one edited for the present volume (*BHG* 51n). This feature, which has also remained unnoticed, links the hymn attributed to Germanos, probably composed in Constantinople sometime in the eighth or perhaps early ninth century, and our narrative version, probably produced in Rome in the seventh or (at the latest) eighth century, with their definite precursor, a Syriac tale about "the Man of God, from the city of Rome," attested in sixth-century manuscripts and al-

ready well known in scholarship (a few Syriacisms are evident in *BHG* 51n as well).[10] The Syriac legend essentially narrates the same story as that of Alexios, but only its first half: an anonymous son of equally anonymous noble Roman parents flees his wedding in order to spend his life as a beggar in Edessa, but dies there and his body is taken up to heaven.

What has happened, then? Greek-speaking refugees from Syro-Palestine and Asia Minor who joined others in Rome over the course of the seventh century carried with them tales from their homeland and then refashioned them for their new setting. Thus, just like Boniphatios from Tarsos, the Edessan saint becomes a Roman saint, and his parents acquire names of Greek origins. By the second half of the ninth century, the anonymous Syrian protagonist was also given the name Alexios, as attested in Joseph's hymn and the other narrative texts in honor of the saint (*BHG* 51–56h). It is possible that the name itself (which, as far as I can tell, is rarely attested before the eighth century) is a Christian response to the name of *Alex*-ander the Great; this hypothesis is perhaps strengthened by the fact that the Greek version includes in its first few lines a phrase that comes verbatim from the so-called *Alexander Romance*, the most widely circulating non-Christian popular story in the eastern Mediterranean at the time of the composition of the Greek *Man of God*, to which we shall return.[11]

LIFE OF MARKOS THE ATHENIAN

The tale of Markos (*BHG* 1039–1041) is recounted by an ascetic called Serapion, at an unspecified time, decades after Constantine the Great and the end of the persecutions of Christians. After a long and difficult journey from the "inner

Egyptian desert," via Alexandria, to the southern borders of the inhabited world, Serapion, a character mirroring Saint Anthony in the *Life of Paul of Thebes* but also other ascetics in the *Apophthegmata* tradition, meets the 130-year-old Markos on the "mountain of Thrace, which is beyond the nation of the Hittites of Ethiopia." Serapion listens to Markos's story of departure from the city of Athens and subsequent extreme asceticism on the mountain for ninety-five years, apprises him about postpersecution Christians (who "are Christian only in name, yet not in deed"), shares a wondrous meal with him, witnesses the ascension of his soul to heaven, and buries his body, before returning to his ascetic abode in Egypt.

Markos's story is one among many examples of a beneficial tale (a usually short tale that is not necessarily linked to the liturgical celebration of a saint) transformed into a saint's *Life*.[12] In this case, the transformation in genre (evident in the title) and thus in liturgical function and recital practices was never fully completed. Though furnished with a *Life* and the attribute of sainthood, Markos did not acquire a fixed liturgical date, nor did his name and story enter Greek *Synaxaria* or *Menologia.* There is one exception: Vatic. gr. 825, a thirteenth-century liturgical manuscript, where our text is the reading for March 5. That date was usually allotted, in Byzantine Greek *Synaxaria,* to the memory of Saint Markos "the monk," a supposed disciple of John Chrysostom. The association with our Markos is no surprise: the name was, after all, common in the literary tradition of Egyptian asceticism, with both stories related to (*BHG* 2246–2247 and 2254–2255) and texts attributed to (*CPG* 6090–6102) ascetics called Markos.[13]

But how ancient is the story and where does it come from? In her excellent introduction to the critical edition of the *Life of Markos* (followed closely in the new edition of the present volume), Christine Angelidi analyzed in insightful detail how the story is grafted onto a complex set of narratives of triumphant asceticism, developing further common narrative motifs, structures, and characters of the early Byzantine ascetic literature preserved in Greek, especially Jerome's *Life of Paul of Thebes,* translated into Greek by the end of the fourth century.[14] Angelidi, furthermore, hesitantly placed the time of the text's composition in the post-400 early Byzantine period, without excluding the possibility for a later dating, perhaps to the eighth century or even later.[15]

An alternative to her hypothesis is, however, possible. The story did not only exist in a Greek-speaking setting, but is attested also in Syriac, Arabic, Ethiopic, Armenian, Georgian, and later Slavic versions, while Markos is mentioned in at least one oriental church calendar.[16] Moreover, from a Coptic environment, we also have another text (dated to the tenth century?) associated with Markos the Athenian and preserved only in Syriac translation; it carries the title *By Abba Markos of the Mountain of Tarmaqa: The Revelation Which God Showed to Him Regarding Human Souls.*[17] Probably from a similar Coptic context, we also have a rather spectacular transformation of the story of Markos preserved in a *Synaxarion* entry for June 23, which survives only in Ethiopic. According to this tale, a Roman emperor (sic) named Markos, when forced to abandon virginity, travels miraculously over an imaginary sea and then spends sixty years as a hermit in a desert called Dabra Tôrmâk.[18] Last but not least, one Arabic version of Markos's *Life* is preserved in an early

tenth-century manuscript, while the earliest Syriac manuscript of the story dates to the ninth century,[19] a few centuries before any of the more than fifty-five witnesses and, by
Angelidi's estimation, three recensions of the Greek text,
which date from the twelfth or thirteenth century onward.
It is, we should note, only from this late point on, and well
into the post-Byzantine period, that the story of Markos
gained popularity, especially in monastic contexts, in Greek
and then Slavic realms.[20]

However this might be, the narrative world and original
perspective of the story are Egyptian. It is therefore quite
likely that it was first conceived (and circulated primarily
orally? in Coptic?) in early Byzantine Egypt, and was then
disseminated in various Byzantine languages, translated at
dates and contexts that we can no longer pinpoint. Translation, indeed, seems to be betrayed by a couple of somewhat confused phrases in the Greek version (see sections 12,
15, 23, and related notes) as well as by its awkward place-
names. For example, the imaginary mountain where the ascetic spends his life, Thrace, is likely a translation of the
aforementioned name Tarmaqa, as attested in the Arabic
(likely from the Coptic) and Syriac versions and reflected in
the designation Dabra *Tôrmâk* in the Ethiopic *Synaxarion* of
Markos the emperor; and Athens, the supposed city of Markos's origin, could be a misreading of Tanis, an Egyptian city
(as evident in at least one Arabic redaction).[21]

LIFE OF MAKARIOS THE ROMAN

The *Life of Makarios* is also a beneficial tale, but a rather extensive one recounted by a certain Theophilos. This narrator is said to be one of three monks from Mesopotamia who

meet Saint Makarios (almost exactly at the middle of the text) after traveling beyond the boundaries of the inhabited world, following routes and experiencing encounters known also from the aforementioned *Alexander Romance*.

Before the monks return to their monastery, Makarios tells them his story. This nested autobiography bears close resemblance to and likely reworks the first, more ancient, part of the story of Alexios the Man of God, which circulated in the East before the tale came to Rome. For, similarly to the Man of God, Makarios came from Rome (though his epithet could be also rendered as "a subject of the empire of Rome," or what we would call a "Byzantine") and, like the Man of God, Makarios fled on his wedding night after being forced to marry by his aristocrat father.[22]

Moreover, Makarios also resembles Markos the Athenian, in that he too is hairy and naked, and has led a life of extreme asceticism—though Makarios's story is enhanced by his submission to carnal sin and his subsequent struggles of repentance that recall yet another popular Byzantine story, the *Life of Mary of Egypt* (*BHG* 1042).[23] Now, unlike that of Markos the Athenian, the story of Makarios the Roman was already more or less fully integrated into the liturgical calendar by the tenth century, though the dates assigned to the reading of his story vary among the many *Menologia* and *Synaxaria* that reserve a relevant feast day (October 5, 23, and 24, and January 19). Like Markos, however—but unlike Boniphatios, Alexios, George, or Niketas—the texts pertaining to Makarios never supported any form of cult.

The origins of Makarios's story are again difficult to trace with any satisfactory precision. It is not impossible that this is a narrative that began sometime in the fifth or sixth century in a language other than Greek, a possibility accen-

tuated by the occasionally awkward syntax of what appears to be the earliest surviving Greek version, the one edited in this volume (*BHG* 1005; or 1005d, according to the *BHG*, whose identifying numbers require revision). The story, in any case, circulated in most Byzantine languages in versions and translations whose dating, origins, and interrelations have yet to be studied sufficiently.[24] In Greek, the eastward travels of the three monks and Makarios's tale as recounted by Theophilos are first attested in the fragment of one of the earliest preserved Byzantine *Menologia,* dated to the eighth century and found in the inferior layer, written in majuscule script, of a palimpsest manuscript (Mount Athos, Panteleimonos 49).[25] The rest of the fifty manuscripts, which transmit at least three separate versions of the story (*BHG* 1005, *BHG* 1004, and *BHG* 1005j), and many redactions of these, date from the eleventh century onward—this transmission trajectory also still awaits thorough investigation.[26]

The details and unfolding of the story, as preserved in Greek and other languages, demonstrate that this is a typical early Byzantine Christian low-register narrative, a mesh of textual and storytelling traditions, about exotic characters and scenarios.[27] Take the name of the main protagonist. In the famous illustrated *Menologion of Basil II* (Vatic. gr. 1613, p. 334), the hero of our story is celebrated on January 19, together with the much better-known Makarios "the Egyptian." As noted above with Markos, Makarios too is a very frequent name in the literary tradition of asceticism, with stories on (*BHG* 999g–999z), and widely circulating texts by (*CPG* 2400–2427), ascetics called Makarios.[28]

The roots of the name, which literally means "blissful" or "blessed," ran even further, however, recalling the designa-

tion *makar* as applied in Greco-Roman tradition to gods, he-
roes, and the dead, by authors from Homer to Plato and beyond. To this frame, in its Christian variety, belong stories
and texts such as the widely circulating fifth or sixth-century
Life of Zosimos, who was led to the "Land of the Blessed"
(*BHG* 1889–1890f) in a story with which Makarios's tale
shares many motifs.[29] This tradition intersected, more sig-
nificantly, with the *Alexander Romance* preserved in many
Byzantine recensions — Alexander too was said to travel to
the "Land" or "Islands of the Blessed."[30]

To the text's landscape of analogues and shared story
worlds, we should add apocalyptic literature (starting with
the relevant biblical and apocryphal texts), Paradise literature (for instance, a cycle of stories about Adam and Eve,
BHG 24–25g), and imaginary geography (for instance, the
late antique text known by its Latin title *Expositio totius
mundi et gentium*).[31] All of these provided visions of either the
end or the beginnings of human history and images of either
an exotic East or the limits of the known world. After all,
the story of the travels of Theophilos and his two fellow
monks is a kind of eschatology projected onto exotic geography.

A curious small detail in the story prompts one further
remark about the mix of early Byzantine, cross-linguistic
storytelling that lies behind our tale. As they reach the
boundaries of real and imaginary geography on their way to
and from Paradise, Theophilos's group makes a stop in the
Persian city of Ctesiphon (sections 5 and 47). They travel
there in order to venerate the tombs of the three youths
who, according to the Old Testament book of Daniel, were
martyred together with the prophet Daniel in Babylon. The

latter city would be the expected sacred site for the three youths in the Byzantine Greek tradition, while Ctesiphon is associated with them only in the context of likely fifth-century legends preserved in Coptic, Armenian, and Georgian (see the relevant Note to the Translation for section 5). Moreover, there are no Christians in Ctesiphon as imagined by the preserved Greek *Life* of Makarios (see section 47), even though around the time of the creation of the legend—likely, as noted above, during the fifth or sixth century—the Persian city was the spiritual and administrative center of those Christian populations who lived outside Byzantium and belonged to the so-called Nestorian Church, that is, the non-Chalcedonian, East Syriac Church.[32] Did elements of the original story somehow relate to these communities, beyond the borders of Byzantine orthodoxy and Greek-speaking hegemony?

Passion of Christopher

At the beginning of his tale, Christopher is called Reprebos. He is a foreigner, indeed a monstrous humanoid creature, who is captured and then conscripted into the Roman army, "in the fourth year" [sic] of the reign of Emperor Decius (249–251). Reprebos converts to Christianity, is baptized in a city called Antioch (either the capital of Pisidia, Asia Minor, or the more famous city in Syria), and takes the name *Christophoros,* "the one who carries Christ." After much resistance to the emperor's appeals and orders for harsh tortures, Christopher meets his death as a martyr, commemorated on May 9.

The story follows the process of Reprebos's gradual discovery of Christ, his parallel humanization and, one might say, his Romanization, something most evident in his acquisition of "our language." Along the way, the saint performs miracles, sees an apocalyptic vision of the battle between Good and Evil, and converts others to Christianity and martyrdom. These include the executioner who beheads him, two hundred soldiers who had come to capture him, and two "beautiful" women, sent by the emperor for Christopher's seduction—part of the story is indeed devoted to their martyrdom. At the end of the story, Christopher's relics are transferred to the city of Attaleia in Asia Minor, where he is established as the city's protector, and Decius dies a miserable death, just as the saint had requested in his final prayer.

The double designation of the protagonist of this legend as belonging to the race of the Cynocephali and Anthropophagi, the dog-headed, man-eating people,[33] suggests that he comes straight from the world of the *Alexander Romance,* itself, as already seen above, a repository of widely circulating ancient tales and images about fantastic—though, to many, presumed real—creatures. Yet, apart from or, indeed, despite his terrifying appearance and essential otherness, Christopher comes to display all the usual characteristics of a martyr in Christian passion narratives: endurance, fearlessness before the pagan tyrant (partly inspired by the *Passion of Saint George,* the next text in this volume), resistance to sexual temptation, and so on.

The origins of the tale lie in the dark, as it is quite likely that none of the surviving versions—in Greek (*BHG* 308w–

311m), Latin (*BHL* 1764–1780), Syriac (*BHO* 190–191), Armenian (*BHO* 192), Arabic, Georgian, and Slavic—preserves the first recounting of the story.[34] The possible Syriac origins of the saint's name (Reprebos, on which see the relevant Note to the Translation) could perhaps suggest that we are dealing again with a Syriac story that was then diffused through translation in environments comparable to those of the stories of Makarios the Roman or the Man of God.[35] But certainly a Greek original is also possible.

Whatever the case may be, the version (*BHG* 309) that is edited and translated here and that, in my view, preserves the earliest attested Greek version (though not the earliest in manuscript transmission) is quite rough in terms of linguistic expression as well as in its attempts to boost its historicity.[36] These features might (though not necessarily) be the result of translation activity. Moreover, the rest of the Greek versions show clear signs of revision of a version close to *BHG* 309. At the peak of this process lies the version in the *Synaxarion* (*BHG* 311m), which circulated widely, and refutes vehemently any connection of the saint with the Cynocephali and Anthropophagi. Despite such attempts to smooth it, the story, usually together with its fantastic elements, persisted in a geographically widespread cult from late antiquity to the post-Byzantine world. The earliest attestation, from a church at Chalcedon, dates exactly to the middle of the fifth century.[37]

The text edited and translated here is based on Paris. gr. 1470, a manuscript dated to the year 890, and associated, in terms of its prototype, with Rome and the early ninth century.[38] This Italian background may point us again toward the direction of stories brought to the West by refugee com-

munities from the Middle East and its melting pot of story-telling and cultic traditions.

George, The Great Martyr

PASSION

Both the place and the time in which the tale of George unfolds are conspicuously eccentric in all early versions of the story, including the one presented in this volume (*BHG* 670a). The passion takes place in the unspecified capital city of an unspecified kingdom (termed *oikoumene*), yet the inference is that we are within the Roman empire. George, a junior army officer, is said to be from Palestine (with Cappadocian family lineage) and to have sought promotion during the reign of a series of fictional "kings" who believe in the Greek pantheon and persecute Christians; their chief, who is called "Dadian the Apostate" (in some of the versions simply Dadian, or in some Latin versions Dacianus), is king of the Persians.[39]

The tale begins with Dadian releasing an edict against Christians that promises harsh tortures if they refuse to venerate the pagan gods. The twenty-two-year-old George approaches the king and requests that he abandon his impiety and his threats. George is subsequently subjected to multiple series of interrogations, followed by savage tortures described in gruesome detail. George responds aggressively to every questioning and, during his final moments, even requests from God the death of the pagan kings. He also endures bravely every kind of torment, and while he actually dies three times, he is miraculously resur-

rected by Christ on each occasion in order to return for more tortures. During the process, which lasts seven years, George performs marvels (including giving life to lifeless objects, or resurrecting "five men, nine women, and three children") and converts a host of people: a magician, a general along with his army unit (a total of 3099 souls "as well as one woman from the crowd"), the king's servants, and most notably the king's wife, Queen Alexandra. All these converts, as well as George's mother, Polychronia, undergo martyrdom themselves at the hands of the pagans.[40]

The textual, visual, and archaeological evidence regarding Saint George, the cult that evolved in his honor in Byzantium, and its cultural sphere of influence are truly immense. Archaeological evidence suggests that the cult might have originated sometime in the mid-fourth century in the Eastern Roman Empire (perhaps in Cappadocia or Palestine), while by the sixth century the saint's legend had become not only universal to Byzantium and all its Christian neighbors but had spread even further.[41] In the Greek literary tradition alone—Greek being undoubtedly the language of the original legend—there are numerous texts: different versions with multiple redactions of his martyrdom account, the earliest dating likely to the late fourth century; stories about later miracles he performed; and hymns and other poems, epigrams, and the like, composed for liturgical, devotional, or dedicatory purposes.[42] As for his cult, it may suffice to say that in Constantinople alone at least eight churches, including an imperial foundation, were dedicated to him, the earliest dating again to the fifth century.[43]

As one might expect, the most commonly transmitted Byzantine Greek versions of the legend of George's martyr-

dom date to the tenth century. The shortest of these is the relevant lemma (*BHG* 680e) in the *Synaxarion of Constantinople,* while the lengthiest, *BHG* 675z, attributed to Niketas David Paphlagon (writing in the first half of the tenth century), was included in Symeon Metaphrastes's *Menologion,* without its prologue and authorial attribution (*BHG* 676–676c), and, alternatively, further revised (*BHG* 677). With the exception of the *Synaxarion,* these texts have never been edited critically, nor are their complicated relations fully elaborated, yet they represent what we might call the "official" versions of George's story, one that followed the expectations of Byzantine rhetorical and religious orthodoxy, using learned idiom and removing what might be considered unhistorical and heretical details.[44]

However this might be, even after their appearance and swift elevation as the most frequently recited and copied versions across the Byzantine sphere due to the liturgical and imperially sponsored collections in which they belonged, these "official" texts neither obliterated nor stopped the circulation of earlier tales about George, less affected by erudition and less restrained by doctrine. This rich late antique dossier, whose Greek branch was first thoroughly surveyed and edited more than a century ago by the founder of Byzantine studies Karl Krumbacher, contains a series of texts whose earliest manuscript testimonies, in fragments and palimpsests, date to the fifth and sixth centuries.[45]

For the present volume, I have chosen to reedit and translate a version (*BHG* 670a) that, though transmitted in a single post-Byzantine liturgical manuscript (Athens gr. 422, dated to 1546), was rightly thought by Krumbacher to represent one of the earliest (late fourth-century? early fifth-

century?) preserved versions of George's story. To Krumbacher's arguments that support the antiquity of the text,
which will not be repeated here,[46] we may add only two additional pieces of evidence that were unknown to him but
that are very close to our text: first, a seventh-century fragment preserved in Oxford (Bodleian, MS Greek th. F. 6),
first discussed and edited by Albert Ehrhardt and, second,
an ancient Nubian version of the martyrdom.[47] *BHG* 670a
is a lengthy retelling of George's "apocryphal" passion,
very elaborate in imagination and distinctly lowbrow in language—some of the reasons for its selection for the present
volume.

MIRACLES

The two miracles attributed to George and included in this
volume take place in an imaginary past, during the lifetime
of George, and are set in or near Lasia, a mythical city—its
name is butchered from manuscript to manuscript, while in
a post-Byzantine version (*BHG* 687i) it is changed to "the
castle of Beirut."

The first miracle (*BHG* 687) opens in Lasia, which is ruled
by Selvios—his name also changes from manuscript to manuscript and from language to language—a wicked idolater
who shows no pity toward Christians. Near the city is a lake,
and in it a wicked dragon is born, devouring Lasia's citizens
daily. On the suggestion of the king, the citizens decide to
send their children by lot as daily sacrifice to the dragon.
When the day comes for the king's lot, he is forced to offer
his only daughter. While everyone escorts the princess and
she awaits by the lake, George happens to come by, on his

way home to Cappadocia. The two converse and, after the girl agrees to convert to Christianity, George captures the dragon and brings it, with the girl's help, into the city. When the city and its king also convert, George kills the dragon, invites the archbishop of Alexandria to baptize every Lasian ("some two hundred and forty thousand souls"), and a church is erected in the saint's honor.

In the second miracle (*BHG* 687k), George departs again for Cappadocia, but on his way he encounters a "wicked demon" and a dialogue ensues. The desperate demon is asked to introduce himself and reveals that he has come to make George submit to him. George prays and locks the demon in a rock, to be tortured by fire "until the end of time."

As already noted, in relation to his *Passion,* the progressive canonization of Saint George did not prevent unauthorized versions of his martyrdom from circulating, nor did it halt the creation of novel stories associated with this superhero. Indeed, at the very moment that the attempt to circumscribe George's original story reached its peak—through the *Synaxarion of Constantinople* and Metaphrastes's *Menologion* in the latter half of the tenth century—new accounts about George's miraculous feats appear, most of them posthumous and some more fantastic than others.[48] Such new stories are first attested in written form in the early eleventh century, though some probably circulated orally even earlier, perhaps as early as the sixth century, and quite likely first originated in a Syro-Palestinian environment and the cult of Saint George in Diospolis.[49] In any case, this new cycle of stories, which perhaps did not circulate as a comprehensive collection in Byzantine times, included the two miracles translated for this volume, which are situated dur-

ing George's lifetime. The first of these quickly became the most well-known story about George, with an international appeal that reached even beyond the confines of Christianity, as attested in late medieval and early modern art, cult, and storytelling.[50]

It would be impossible to treat here, even superficially, the mesh of tales, universal folk motifs, Greco-Roman and Near Eastern traditions, and their Christian retellings that these two miracle stories embody—especially that of the dragon.[51] Nor would it be possible to pinpoint the exact moment when the story of dragon slaying and saving the princess was projected onto George specifically: strong arguments have been put forward, for instance, that the tale originated in Christian Georgia.[52] Nevertheless, the dragon-slaying story was already, perhaps as early as the sixth century, associated in Greek with Saint Theodore the Recruit (the earliest manuscript testimony dates to the ninth century), though not in the same mythical guise and fairytale intensity as with George, and without, at least originally, the encounter with a woman, a detail we first find in tenth-century texts.[53] Similarly, the second miracle of George, though again with parallels elsewhere, is reminiscent of, and perhaps inspired from, a similar scene in the original *Passion of Saint George* (section 18).

What is clear from the manuscript evidence and the visual arts is that by the twelfth century the certainly earlier account of the two miracles was circulating widely in the Greek-speaking Byzantine world, if it did not actually originate in it, and then spread further through translations into Latin, Slavic, and other languages. What is also clear is that in the numerous transmitting Greek manuscripts (a total of

thirty-four witnesses, dating from the twelfth century into the nineteenth), the text of the two miracles is in simple language and treated as an open field, with remarkable variation in wording from manuscript to manuscript (*BHG* 687–687i; and 687k–m). Furthermore, in most cases the two miracles form a continuous story, and often follow or precede some version of the *Passion of Saint George*—though the dragon-slaying miracle is also transmitted on its own and had a much wider circulation (thirty-four witnesses, as opposed to seven).[54]

PASSION OF NIKETAS

The final tale in this volume, that of Niketas, is again set in an unnamed city (Nicomedia in some versions), just as the dead body of the saint is said to be transferred to an equally unnamed "holy" city (presumably Rome). Chronology is less vague, however. Niketas is presented as the son of none other than the emperor Maximian (Galerius), who ruled from 305 to 311 CE, and who, in the Byzantine imagination, was considered as one of the most notorious persecutors of Christians.

After converting to Christianity by divine intervention, Niketas is submitted to a series of harsh punishments by his merciless—indeed, as one of the versions suggests, cannibalistic—father. While being punished and until he dies, Niketas is assisted by an angel or, more specifically, the archangel Michael; has a vision of the future bliss that awaits him; bites off his own tongue in order to resist the sexual temptation of a beautiful virgin and then has it restored through prayer; miraculously turns a bed designed for tor-

ture into one on which he rests; receives dew from heaven; baptizes two magicians; binds and beats up a demon; resurrects the bodies of dead people; and converts "almost the entire city," including "the emperor's wife," to Christianity.

Unlike the saints celebrated in the other texts included in this volume, the figure of Niketas lay entirely outside the limits of official Christianity in Byzantium. Not only was his name excluded from *Synaxaria* (as far as I can tell)—nor have hymns in his honor been preserved as part of the Byzantine rite—but his cult was officially banned. That the saint did not invite official endorsement from the Byzantine Church is no surprise. It is not so much that the tale, partly inspired by the apocryphal *Passion of Saint George* and an episode in the *Life of Paul of Thebes,* is obviously made up.[55] Rather, Niketas's cult, in twelfth-century Constantinople and elsewhere, was associated with demonic possession and its healing, something viewed with suspicion by the authorities.[56]

Lack of endorsement, however, did not harm the appeal of Niketas, nor of his supernatural powers and extraordinary tale. His popularity is attested by the spread of his cult in Byzantium by the eleventh century (at the latest), by the sizable dossier of his Greek passion, and by his following in places like Venice and, especially, in the Slavic world, also already attested in the eleventh century.[57] Some minimal endorsement and certainly a vehicle of transmission and preservation arose from the linking of Niketas to his namesake Niketas the Goth, a popular and, by the year 1000, solidly "canonical" Christian martyr, whose relics were transferred to Constantinople and whose separate story featured prominently in *Synaxaria,* Metaphrastic *Menologia,* and then *Me-*

naia.[58] In some versions of the tale, as in the one printed in this volume (see section 20), that link becomes a complete fusion; in most of the manuscripts that preserve it, the text is assigned (when it is assigned at all) as a reading for September 15, the feast date of Niketas the Goth.

Versions of the Greek *Passion of Saint Niketas,* which of all the texts edited in this volume presents us with the highest degree of variation, are preserved in several redactions and manuscript witnesses (twenty-nine codices, according to the Pinakes database).[59] The first editor of Greek versions of the text, the great scholar Vasilij M. Istrin, worked with five of these manuscripts and did much to clarify their complicated relations, as well as their relation to the existing Slavonic translations of an unpreserved Greek original.[60] In Istrin's analysis, two redactions (*BHG* 1344 and 1345), though clearly reworkings, appear to preserve a version that is the closest to a now-lost original, itself reflected also in the Slavonic translations.[61] However, other related redactions, such as *BHG* 1346 and the unedited *BHG* 1346d, preserved in manuscripts not known to Istrin, are in my view even closer to the original, as they include an episode that is integral to the story, where Julian the Apostate (!) appears as a child and betrays Niketas (section 4).[62]

The *Passion of Saint Niketas* edited in this volume is one such previously unknown redaction, which is transmitted in a single manuscript, Munich gr. 219, dated to circa 1410–1420 CE, and has no corresponding number in the *BHG* (though it is related to *BHG* 1346d). Along with the family of redactions to which it belongs (namely, *BHG* 1344, 1345, and 1346d), all possibly linked to the original version, the redaction of the Munich manuscript also contains a rather un-

usual joint mention of the relics of the saints Boniphatios, Alexios, and his father Euphemianos, toward the end of the text (section 20). This points to likely Italian origins (and translation from Latin?) for the tale of Niketas in general. The Munich redaction, in any case, departs from other surviving versions in that it reduces the role of the archangel Michael, perhaps in an attempt to tone down any likely associations with heresy and thus reinscribe, within the limits of orthodoxy, a saintly tale that otherwise gestured toward their transgression.

This volume profited much from a series of good friends to whose support I am greatly indebted. I am very grateful, first and foremost, to the meticulous work of Alexandros Alexakis and Richard Greenfield, who reviewed the entire book; more specifically, Richard's comments substantially improved the style and readability of the English, while Alexandros's remarks saved me from errors in the Greek text. Nicole Eddy helped revise the introduction so as to fit the format of the series. Alice-Mary Talbot gave ample encouragement during the initial stages of the project, while Daria Resh, Charis Messis, and Stephanos Efthymiadis offered advice and comments throughout. Marina Detoraki and Bernard Flusin kindly read the introduction. Christine Angelidi generously provided photographs, transcriptions, and preliminary editions of manuscripts transmitting the *Life of Makarios the Roman*. André Binggeli kindly offered images of one further manuscript, related to the *Passion of Boniphatios*. Miriam Hjälm provided help with the Arabic. Maria Averkiou and Luther Karper, both supported by research funds from Brown University, produced a first typed draft

of earlier editions of the texts. Students in related seminars I conducted at Brown University, the University of Crete, the Gennadeios Library, and the Dumbarton Oaks Library also made useful remarks on the texts. Chance Bonar, a Tyler Fellow at Dumbarton Oaks, drafted the index, and Louis-Patrick St-Pierre, a research fellow at Queen's University, helped review the proofs. Finally, research for the writing of this volume has been undertaken within the frame of the research program Retracing Connections (https://retracing connections.org), financed by Riksbankens Jubileumsfond (M19–0430:1).

<h2 style="text-align:center">NOTES</h2>

1 Maya Maskarinec, *City of Saints: Rebuilding Rome in the Early Middle Ages* (Philadelphia, PA, 2018), 109–16; the most famous among the refugees, we might note, was Theodoros of Tarsos, who became archbishop of Canterbury from 668 to 690 CE.

2 *Synaxarion of Constantinople,* ed. Hippolyte Delehaye, *Synaxarium ecclesiae Constantinopolitanae e codice Sirmondiano nunc Berolinensi adiectis Synaxariis selectis,* Propylaeum ad Acta Sanctorum Novembris (Brussels, 1902), col. 325, lines 55–56. See also a similar notice, without synaxarial text, for "Athenos, Boniphatios, and Hermolaos," at col. 321, line 46 (December 18) and col. 325, line 57 (December 19). In the important liturgical calendar, compiled in Georgian by Iovane Zosime in the tenth-century, but preserving also earlier, likely early Byzantine traditions from Palestine, a "martyr Boniphatios" is commemorated on March 13; for an edition and Latin translation of the calendar, copied in manuscript Sinai, Geo. O. 34, see Gérard Garitte, *Le calendrier palestino-géorgien du Sinaiticus 34 (Xe siècle)* (Brussels, 1958) (see specifically pp. 55 and 176 for the Boniphatios entry); for Zosime, see Stig Symeon R. Frøyshov, *L'horologe 'géorgien' du Sinaiticus ibericus 34,* 2 vols. (unpublished doctoral thesis; Paris, 2004), 2, 217–30; and for the manuscript, see Daniel Galadza, *Liturgy and Byzantinization in Jerusalem* (Oxford, 2018), 370–71.

3 Pio Franchi de' Cavalieri, "Dove fu scritta la leggenda di S. Bonifazio?," *Nuovo bullettino di archeologia cristiana* 6 (1900): 205–34, where there is also

extensive comparison with other early Byzantine passions. For some of these intertexts see the Notes to the Translations.

4 Edited in Konstantinos G. Phrantzolas, Ὁσίου Ἐφραίμ τοῦ Σύρου ἔργα (Thessalonike, 1988–1998), vol. 7, pp. 187–98. For the terms "version" as well as "redaction" (used later in this Introduction), see the Note on the Texts.

5 For the several Greek redactions and their impressively numerous witnesses (*BHG* 51–56h), see "Alexius seu Homo Dei," Pinakes, https://pinakes.irht.cnrs.fr/notices/saint/43/. See also Barbara Crostini, "Mapping Miracles in Byzantine Hagiography: The Development of the Legend of St Alexios," in *Signs, Wonders, Miracles: Representation of Divine Power in the Life of the Church,* ed. Kate Cooper and Jeremy Gregory (Woodbridge and Rochester NY, 2005), 77–87. For the wide transmission of the tale in a host of medieval and early modern languages, see Christopher Storey, *An Annotated Bibliography and Guide to Alexis Studies (La Vie de saint Alexis)* (Geneva, 1987). See also Georg Graf, *Geschichte der christlichen arabischen Literatur,* vol. 1, *Die Übersetzungen* (Vatican City, 1944), 497–98, on the very interesting dissemination of the story in Arabic.

6 For the joint dedication of the Aventine church, see Riccardo Santangeli Valenzani, "L'iscrizione di Teodora da Santa Sabina: Una nuova ipotesi di interpretazione," in Για το φίλο μας: *Scritti in ricordo di Gaetano Messineo,* ed. Elisabetta Mangani and Angelo Pellegrino (Monte Compatri, 2016), 345–54. A unique joint reference in Greek to Boniphatios and Alexios (and his father Euphemianos) appears in the *Passion of Niketas* (section 20), edited in the present volume.

7 See Louis Duchesne, "Notes sur la topographie de Rome au Moyen-Âge," *Mélanges d'archéologie et d'histoire* 10 (1890): 225–50; Baudouin de Gaiffier, "Note sur la date de la légende grecque de S. Alexis," *Analecta Bollandiana* 19 (1900): 254–56. The tenth-century dating is repeated in Sergey Ivanov, *Holy Fools in Byzantium and Beyond,* trans. S. Franklin (Oxford and New York, 2006), 81–86 (with an insightful discussion of our tale), and especially 381.

8 The exception is Ἅγιος Ἀλέξιος ὁ ἄνθρωπος τοῦ Θεοῦ: Ἡ ἐμφάνεια τοῦ ἀφανοῦς ἢ ἄλλως τὸ συναξάρι τοῦ ἁγίου Ἀλεξίου τοῦ ἀνθρώπου τοῦ Θεοῦ (Athens, 2005).

9 The *kanôn* (which follows the metrical and musical pattern of another

hymn by Germanos) is edited in Elias Mpakos, Ὁ ἅγιος Ἀλέξιος ὁ ἄνθρωπος τοῦ Θεοῦ· Ἁγιολογικὰ — ὑμνογραφικὰ — ὕμνοι (Athens, 2001). For Germanos as a hymnographer, see Kosta Simic, "Liturgical Poetry in the
Middle Byzantine Period: Hymns Attributed to Germanos I, Patriarch
of Constantinople (715–730)" (PhD diss., Australian Catholic University,
2017), where, on p. 32, Simic doubts Germanos's authorship of the hymn
on Alexios; and Maria I. Sourmpa, "Το ποιητικό έργο του Γερμανού
Α', Πατριάρχη Κωνσταντινουπόλεως του Ομολογητή (+/−650–740):
Μελέτη φιλολογική" (PhD diss., National and Kapodistrian University of
Athens, 2020).

10 See *BHO* 36–42 and Arthur Amiaud, *La légende syriaque de saint Alexis,
l'homme de Dieu* (Paris, 1889). Notably, a tenth-century Arabic manuscript
contains a translation of the story of the Man of God (without the name
Alexios) from Greek; see Graf, *Geschichte,* 497. For the Syriac, see also
Hendrik Jan Willem Drijvers, "Die Legende des heiligen Alexius und der
Typus des Gottesmannes im syrischen Christentum," in *Typus, Symbol, Al-
legorie bei den östlichen Vätern und ihren Parallelen im Mittelalter,* ed. Margot
Schmidt and Carl-Friedrich Geyer (Pustet, 1982), 187–217; and especially
Aza Vladimirovna Paikova, "Легенды и сказания в памятниках сирийской
агиографии," *Palestiniskii Sbornik* 30[93] (1990): 3–143. Robert Doran,
*Stewards of the Poor: The Man of God, Rabbula, and Hiba in Fifth-Century
Edessa* (Kalamazoo, MI, 2006), carries a translation of two Syriac versions
in addition to a Greek one (*BHG* 56c), erroneously considered as the *Ur-
text* (see Crostini, "Mapping," 78–80). The oddity of *BHG* 56c in relation
to all other Greek versions requires, nevertheless, further investigation.

11 See the Note to the Translations for section 1.

12 See for example the *Lives* of Alexios and Makarios in this volume and
the *Life of Pelagia,* ed. and trans. Stratis Papaioannou, *Christian Novels from
the Menologion of Symeon Metaphrastes,* Dumbarton Oaks Medieval Library
45 (Cambridge, MA, 2017), 61–84.

13 The name Markos bore two further associations: with Mark, the evan-
gelist and founder of the Church of Alexandria; and the related name Makarios (literally, "blissful," or "blessed"), with all its heavy semantic bag-
gage (on which see the next text in this volume). See Christine Angelidi,
"Ὁ Βίος τοῦ Μάρκου τοῦ Ἀθηναίου (BHG 1039–1041)," *Σύμμεικτα* 8
(1989): 33–59, at 34–36. Though no Markos the Athenian appears in Greek

Synaxaria, it should be noted that we do encounter several bare entries, without biographical details, on a Markos the Hermit; see *Synaxarion of Constantinople,* col. 661, line 57 (May 7); col. 696, lines 59–60 (May 19); col. 697, lines 46–47, 50, and 55 (May 20); and col. 700, line 57 (May 21) and line 61 (May 22)—compare note 16, below.

14 See Angelidi, "Ὁ Βίος." For Jerome's *Life of Paul of Thebes,* see Stratis Papaioannou, "The Philosopher's Tongue: *Synaxaria* between History and Literature, with an Excursus on the Recension M of the *Synaxarion of Constantinople* and an Edition of BHG 2371n," in *L'histoire comme elle se présentait dans l'hagiographie byzantine et médiévale / Byzantine and Medieval History as Represented in Hagiography,* ed. Anna Lampadaridi, Vincent Déroche, and Christian Høgel (Uppsala, 2022), 151–97, at 160–67, with further bibliography. The association of Markos the Athenian with Paul of Thebes was noted already by the first editor of our story, the famous Bollandist Daniel Papebroch in the early eighteenth century; *AASS,* vol. 9, *Martii tomus tertius,* 775–78. See further Alison Goddard Elliott, *Roads to Paradise: Reading the Lives of the Early Saints* (Hanover, NH, 1987), 68–71; and Chrestos I. Kazilas, *Κριτικὴ ἔκδοση τοῦ Βίου τοῦ ὁσ. Μάρκου τοῦ Ἀθηναίου (Εἰσαγωγὴ—Κείμενο—Πίνακες)* (Argyroupoli, 2006), who draws parallels also to the *Life* of Saint Onouphrios (*BHG* 1378). For the edition of the Greek text included in this study, see the Note on the Texts. Moreover, Arnold Evert Look noticed the great similarity of the *Life of Markos* with a story of a dreamed journey and revelation from the *Apophthegmata Patrum;* see *BHG* 1444t and Arnold Evert Look, *The History of Abba Marcus of Mount Tharmaka* (Oxford, 1929), vii–ix.

15 Angelidi, "Ὁ Βίος," especially p. 39.

16 For the history of the story in oriental languages in general, see Joseph-Marie Sauget, "Marco di Atene," *Bibliotheca Sanctorum* 8 (1967): 701–3. For specific non-Greek versions, see the following: Syriac: *BHO* 606; see also Jeanne-Nicole Mellon Saint-Laurent and others, "Mark of Tarmaqa," The Syriac Biographical Dictionary, https://syriaca.org/person/1356, and Basile Lourié, "S. Alypius Stylite, S. Marc de Tharmaqa et l'origine des *malkə* éthiopiennes," *Scrinium* 1 (2005): 148–60, with an insistence on the Syriac origins of the story and the suggestion that its historical background was the "'monastic colonization' of the Aksumite kingdom in the 6th and 7th cent. by the Byzantine monks, including those of Syrian ori-

gin" (at p. 160). Arabic: Graf, *Geschichte,* 536 (the liturgical date assigned to Markos in these texts is April 16) and 275 (on the *Apocalypse* of pseudo-Gregorios, which cites Markos, albeit wrongly as Merkurios); see also Emile Amélineau, *Contes et romans de l'Egypte chrétienne* (Paris, 1888) vol. 2, pp. 55–73, which offers a translation of an Arabic version, likely based on a Coptic one. Armenian: *BHO* 605 and 607. Georgian: Michael Tarchnišvili, ed., *Geschichte der kirchlichen georgischen Literatur, auf Grund des ersten Bandes der georgischen Literaturgeschichte von K. Kekelidze* (Vatican, 1955), 484–85. Slavic: Oleg V. Tvorogov, *Переводные жития в русской книжности XI–XV веков: Каталог* (Saint Petersburg, 2008), 81–82; and Klimentina Ivanova, *Bibliotheca hagiographica Balcano-Slavica* (Sofia, 2008), 479–80 and 514–15. Ethiopic: see note 18 below. Finally, for the church calendar, see the late thirteenth- or early fourteenth-century Syriac *Martyrology of Rabban Sliba,* ed. Paul Peeters, "Le martyrologe de Rabban Ṣalība," *Analecta Bollandiana* 27 (1908): 129–200 (see p. 183, an entry on May 20 for Markos; compare note 13, above, on Greek *Synaxaria* for the month of May with entries on a Markos the Hermit).

17 See Arnold van Lantschoot, "Révélations de Macaire et de Marc de Tarmaqā sur le sort de l'âme après la mort," *Le Muséon* 63 (1950): 159–89; and David Frankfurter, *Christianizing Egypt: Syncretism and Local Worlds in Late Antiquity* (Princeton, 2018), 221–22.

18 See Sauget, "Marco," 703. For an English translation of this Ethiopic *synaxarion,* included in a collection (a *Sənkəssar*) dated to circa 1400 and based on a thirteenth-century Coptic *Synaxarion* written in Arabic, see Ernest Alfred Wallis Budge, *The Book of the Saints of the Ethiopian Church: A Translation of the Ethiopic Synaxarium, made from the Manuscripts Oriental 660 and 661 in the British Museum* (Cambridge, 1928), vol. 4, p. 1044. For the Ethiopic *Sənkəssar,* see further Gérard Colin and Alessandro Bausi, "Sənkəssar," in *Encylopaedia Aethiopica* 4 (2010): 621–23. Though not noted in scholarship, the *Life* of Markos of Tarmaqa is itself also preserved in Ethiopic. See the manuscript EMML (Ethiopian Manuscript Microfilm Library) 7602, a collection of (mostly Egyptian) saints' *Lives,* dated approximately between 1379 and 1413, on fols. 2r–6v (on fol. 1v, there is a portrait of Markos, and on fols. 90r–95v a *Life* of Alexios, similarly preceded by a portrait); information drawn from the Hill Museum and Manuscript Library online database, https://haf.vhmml.org/.

19 See Graf, *Geschichte*, 536 (Arabic); Look, *The History*, ix (Syriac).

20 The extant manuscript copies of this story (*BHG* 1039–1041e) are listed at "Hagiographica, Marcus Atheniensis eremita in Libya (S.), Vita," Pinakes, http://pinakes.irht.cnrs.fr/notices/oeuvre/16657/. For the late medieval reception of Markos as an exemplary ascetic father, see Johannes Koder, "Ein Dreifaltigkeitshymnus des Symeon Metaphrastes," *Jahrbuch der Österreichischen Byzantinischen Gesellschaft* 14 (1965): 133–38, at 138; and Hermann Gollancz, *The Book of Protection: Being a Collection of Charms, Now Edited for the First Time from Syriac Mss.* (London, 1912), lvi–lvii and lxv.

21 See Amélineau, *Contes*, vol. 2, p. 65. It is unclear on which manuscript Amélineau's translation was based, and if indeed Tanis is the correct rendering or a misreading of some version of the name Athens as written in Arabic, in which both names could look rather similar. As Miriam Hjälm kindly informs me, the earliest Arabic manuscript transmitting Markos's *Life*, Strasbourg, Or. 4225, dated to 901, fol. 208v, reads *Athīnūs*.

22 We may also note the similarity to the aforementioned Coptic story, preserved in Ethiopic, of the fictional emperor Markos who, before practicing extreme solitary asceticism, fled Rome when forced "by the people" to marry; see text and note 18, above.

23 Notably, the *Lives* of Makarios (*BHG* 1005) and Mary of Egypt (*BHG* 1042) are both transmitted in the oldest manuscript that preserves the entire text of our tale, Vatic. gr. 824 (eleventh century), a somewhat atypical collection of hagiographical texts; Ehr. 3, pp. 743–44.

24 See *BHL* 5104 (Latin); *BHO* 580 (Armenian); Tarchnišvili, *Geschichte*, 484 (Georgian); Ivanova, *Bibliotheca*, 263–64 and 445–46 (Slavic).

25 Ehr. 1, pp. 108–9 and Gregorios Stathis, Τὰ χειρόγραφα Βυζαντινῆς Μουσικῆς: Ἅγιον Ὄρος; Κατάλογος περιγραφικὸς τῶν χειρογράφων κωδίκων Βυζαντινῆς Μουσικῆς (Athens, 1976–), vol. 2, pp. 169–70. I was unfortunately unable to see this manuscript *in situ* and examine the two small fragments from the text on Makarios it contains.

26 For a list of surviving witnesses, see "Hagiographica, Macarius Romanus anach. (S.), Vita," Pinakes, http://pinakes.irht.cnrs.fr/notices/oeuvre /16821/. Regarding *BHG* 1005j, see Jürgen Trumpf, "Zwei Handschriften einer Kurzfassung der griechischen *Vita Macarii Romani*," *Analecta Bollandiana* 88 (1970): 23–26.

27 See the insightful discussions by Christine Angelidi, "La Vie de Macaire

le Romain: Écrire pour le plaisir?," in *La face cachée de la littérature byzantine: Le texte en tant que message immédiat,* ed. Paolo Odorico (Paris, 2012), 167–78; and by Zissis D. Ainalis, "From Hades to Hell: Christian Visions of the Underworld (2nd–5th Centuries CE)," in *Round Trip to Hades in the Eastern Mediterranean Tradition: Visits to the Underworld from Antiquity to Byzantium,* ed. Gunnel Ekroth and Ingela Nilsson (Leiden and Boston, 2018), 273–86.

28 It has been noted that in a Coptic version of a legend about Makarios the ascetic much resembles the story of Makarios the Roman (including the flight from the wedding); Alexander N. Veselovskii, *Из истории романа и повести* (Saint Petersburg, 1886), vol. 1, pp. 305–29.

29 See Jean-Claude Haelewyck, Veronique Somers, and Emmanuel Van Elverdinghe, "Diverse Perspectives on the Manuscript Tradition of the Story of Zosimus," *Oriens Christianus* 99 (2016): 1–44; Pietro D'Agostino, "Una recensione inedita della *Narratio Zosimi de vita beatorum,*" *Medioevo Greco* 15 (2015): 109–36. The motifs shared between Zosimus's *Life* and the *Life of Makarios* have been well surveyed by Daria Penskaya, "Hagiography and Fairytale Paradise and the Land of the Blessed in Byzantium," in *Byzantine Hagiography: Texts, Themes, and Projects,* ed. Antonio Rigo, Michele Trizio, and Eleftherios Despotakis (Turnhout, 2018), 141–56.

30 See Stephen Gero, "The Alexander Legend in Byzantium: Some Literary Gleanings," in *"Homo Byzantinus:* Papers in Honor of Alexander Kazhdan," ed. Anthony Cutler and Simon Franklin, special issue, *Dumbarton Oaks Papers* 46 (1992): 83–87 (here the relation of the story of Makarios to the recension L is highlighted). For the many versions and recensions of the *Alexander Romance,* see Corinne Jouanno, *Naissance et metamorphoses du Roman d'Alexandre: Domaine grec* (Paris, 2002). See further Anthony Kaldellis, "Alexander the Great in Byzantine Tradition, AD 330–1453," in *A History of Alexander the Great in World Culture,* ed. Richard Stoneman (Cambridge, 2022), 216–41. Finally, on the *Makares* in general, see, for example, Darrin M. McMahon, "From the Happiness of Virtue to the Virtue of Happiness: 400 B.C.–A.D. 1780," *Daedalus* 133, no. 2 (spring 2004): 5–17.

31 On *BHG* 24–25g, see Michael E. Stone, *A History of the Literature of Adam and Eve* (Atlanta, 1992); and, on the *Expositio totius mundi,* see Demetres P. Drakoules, "Οι Οδοιπορίες ἀπὸ Ἐδὲμ τοῦ παραδείσου ἄχρι τῶν Ῥωμαίων και οι πρώιμοι βυζαντινοί δρόμοι του μεταξιού," *Byzantiaka* 34 (2017): 11–92.

32 On the history of these Christian communities, see W. Baum and D. W. Winkler, *The Church of the East: A Concise History* (London and New York, 2003). In the *Synaxarion of Constantinople,* there is a vague memory of Ctesiphon as the center of Christianity in Persia (see entries for November 13 and April 17).

33 For the Cynocephali, see further Claude Lecouteux, "Les Cynocéphales: Étude d'une tradition tératologique de l'Antiquité au XIIe siècle," *Cahiers de civilisation médiévale* 24 (1981): 117–29; David Gordon White, *Myths of the Dog-Man* (Chicago, 1991); and Karl Steel, *How to Make a Human: Animals and Violence in the Middle Ages* (Columbus, 2011) 136–50. Christopher's tale was, of course, not the only one within early Byzantine Christian visual, storytelling, and textual culture to make reference to or appropriate such creatures (see, for example, *BHG* 109–110c).

34 See Graf, *Geschichte,* 500 (Arabic); Tarchnišvili, *Geschichte,* 482, and Garitte, *Le calendrier,* 209–10 (Georgian); and Tvorogov, *Переводные,* 128 (Slavic). For the legend, see Gian Domenico Gordini, "Cristoforo," in *Bibliotheca Sanctorum* 4 (1964): 349–53 (with a focus on the occidental versions, the earliest of which, in Latin, dates to before the eighth century), and Joseph-Marie Sauget, "Cristoforo, detto Barbaro," *Bibliotheca Sanctorum* 4 (1964): 345–46 (on the Syriac and Georgian versions); David Woods, "St. Christopher, Bishop Peter of Attalia, and the *Cohors Marmaritarum:* A Fresh Examination," *Vigiliae Christianae* 48 (1994): 170–86 (an ambitious attempt to recover a likely earlier and historically more accurate account, of Alexandrian origins, that lies behind Christopher's story); Michael Schneider, *Die Christophorus-Legende in Ost und West: Das Leben aus dem Glauben und seine bildhafte Darstellung in der frühchristlichen und abendländischen Tradition* (Cologne, 2005); Panagiotis Roilos, "*Phantasia* and the Ethics of Fictionality in Byzantium: A Cognitive Anthropological Perspective," in *Medieval Greek Storytelling: Fictionality and Narrative in Byzantium,* ed. Panagiotis Roilos (Wiesbaden, 2014), 9–30, at 16–18.

35 For some commonalities with Makarios, see the Notes to the Translations. The *surviving* Syriac versions of the tale of Christopher are thought, nevertheless, to derive from a Greek original; see Johann Popescu, *Die Erzählung oder das Martyrium des Barbaren Christophorus und seiner Genossen* (Leipzig, 1903).

36 The author tries to secure the historicity of the story by deploying

common hagiographical devices, such as chronological (Decius's reign; Babylas, bishop of Antioch) and geographical (Antioch, Attaleia, Perge) references, though almost all of these are confused in one way or another; see the relevant Notes to the Translations.

37 See Christopher Walter, *The Warrior Saints in Byzantine Art and Tradition* (Aldershot, 2003), 214–16. See further the relevant entry in the database The Cult of Saints in Late Antiquity (record s00616, http://csla.history. ox.ac.uk/record.php?recid=S00616). It should also be noted that a martyr from Lycia named Christopher is mentioned in the seventh-century(?) Latin *Martyrologium Hieronymianum* (based on earlier sources), and his memory is celebrated on July 25; Hippolyte Delehaye, *Commentarius perpetuus in Martyrologium Hieronymianum* (Brussels, 1931), 396.

38 See Paul Canart, "Le patriarche Méthode de Constantinople copiste à Rome," in *Palaeographica, diplomatica et archivistica: Studi in onore di Giulio Battelli* (Rome, 1979), 343–53; and Irmgard Hutter, "Patmos 33 im Kontext," *Rivista di Studi Bizantini e Neoellenici* 46 (2009): 73–126, at 82–94.

39 In the later but widely circulating versions of the *Passion* (*BHG* 680e and *BHG* 676–676c), Dadian's name is replaced by that of an historical person, the arch-evil ruler in Christian passions, the Roman emperor Diocletian (243–311 CE); in yet other versions, such as for instance *BHG* 677, Diocletian is joined by the other arch-evil ruler in Christian imagination, Diocletian's Caesar in the East, Maximian (known otherwise as Galerius; ca. 260–311 CE). On Maximian, see the Notes to the Translations for the *Passion of Saint Niketas.*

40 The location of George's martyrdom, commemorated on April 23, remains unspecified in many Greek versions. The Palestinian city of Lydda (Diospolis, or modern-day Lod, Israel), a city with a well-attested ancient cult devoted to George, appears in some of them (for instance, *BHG* 670g, 675, and 679). The dedication of a church of Saint George supposedly built by Constantine the Great in Lydda is celebrated on November 3 or 10 in church calendars preserved in Georgian and Syriac, reflecting Palestinian traditions that go back to as early as the fifth century—see Galadza, *Liturgy,* 291–93; the same dedication is also cited on November 3 in Greek *Synaxaria* of the so-called M recension—for this recension, see Papaioannou, "Philosopher's Tongue," 169–79.

41 See Hippolyte Delehaye, *Les légendes grecques des saints militaires* (Paris,

1909), 45–76; Temily Mark-Weiner, *Narrative Cycles of the Life of St. George in Byzantine Art* (PhD diss., New York University, 1977); Wolfgang Haubrichs, *Georgslied und Georgslegende im frühen Mittelalter: Text und Rekonstruktion* (Königstein, 1979), 225–33; Wolfgang Haubrichs, "Georg, Heiliger," *Theologische Realenzyklopädie* 12 (1984): 380–85; Walter, *Warrior Saints,* 109–44; Samantha Riches, *St George: A Saint for All* (Stroud, UK, 2015); Simone Cristoforetti, *San Giorgio in Levante: Il culto del santo cavaliere nella regione di Antiochia* (Reggio Calabria, 2020); and the relevant lemmas (such as s00259) in the Cult of Saints in Late Antiquity (CSLA) database (http://csla.history.ox.ac.uk/).

42 Pinakes ("Georgius m. Diospoli in Palaestina," https://pinakes.irht.cnrs.fr/notices/saint/353/), following the *BHG,* records sixty-two narrative and encomiastic texts (including poetry) dedicated to Saint George. This number would be greatly expanded if we added hymnography or inscriptions on various types of surfaces. For a survey of George-related texts in late antique and medieval languages (Latin, Coptic, Syriac, Ethiopic, Armenian, Georgian, etc., with an emphasis on the Latin versions and their later translations), see Haubrichs, *Georgslied,* 203–77.

43 Raymond Janin, *La géographie ecclésiastique de l'Empire byzantin,* part 1, *Le siège de Constantinople et le patriarcat oecuménique,* vol. 3, *Les églises et les monastères,* 2nd ed. (Paris, 1969), 69–78.

44 The first attested official attempt to ban the "apocryphal" George narratives dates to the sixth century, as part of the so-called *Decretum Gelasianum;* see Ernst von Dobschütz, *Das "Decretum Gelasianum de libris recipiendis et non recipiendis" in kritischem Text* (Leipzig, 1912). After that point, the *Passion* of Saint George was consistently included in various lists of "apocryphal," that is, "prohibited" texts; see Marina Detoraki, "Livres censurés: Le cas de l' hagiographie byzantine," *Bulgaria Medievalis* 3 (2012): 45–58; and, also, Bernard Flusin, "Entre innovation et tradition: Hagiographie nouvelle et saints anciens (VIIIe–Xe s.)," in *Proceedings of the 23rd International Congress of Byzantine Studies, Belgrade, 22–27 August 2016: Plenary Papers,* ed. Smilja Marjanovic-Dušanic (Belgrade, 2016), 13–33, at 22–24. Compare also note 56, below.

45 Karl Krumbacher, *Der heilige Georg in der griechischen Überlieferung,* ed. Albert Ehrhard (Munich, 1911). Krumbacher's magisterial study was published posthumously. See further Haubrichs, *Georgslied,* especially pp. 244–

46; Alexander N. Veselovskii, "Св. Георгий в легенде, песне и обряде," *Sbornik Otdeleniia russkago iazyka i slovesnosti Imp. akademii nauk* 21, no. 2 (1881): 1–228; Paul Canart, "La collection hagiographique palimpseste du Palatinus graecus 205 et la Passion de S. Georges *BHG* 670g," *Analecta Bollandiana* 100 (1982): 95–109; and W. C. H. Frend, "Fragments of a Version of the *Acta S. Georgii* from Qasr Ibrim," *Jarhbuch für Antike und Christentum* 32 (1989): 89–104.

46 Krumbacher, *Der heilige,* 117–26.

47 See, respectively, Ehr. 1, pp. 72–74, and G. M. Browne, *The Old Nubian Martyrdom of Saint George* (Leuven, 1998).

48 The miracles, a total of nineteen, were edited in Joannes B. Aufhauser, *Miracula S. Georgii* (Leipzig, 1913), and discussed in Johannes B. Aufhauser, *Das Drachenwunder des Heiligen Georg in der griechischen und lateinischen Überlieferung* (Leipzig, 1911), 1–29. See also André-Jean Festugière, *Sainte Thècle, saints Côme et Damien, saints Cyr et Jean (extraits), saint Georges: Traduits et annotés* (Paris, 1971), 259–347 (with French translation and introduction; at 321–27, the translation of the two *Miracles* also included in the present volume).

49 Compare Aufhauser, *Das Drachenwunder,* 28, with Festugière, *Sainte,* 261–67. The earliest Greek manuscript witness with four miracles (yet not *BHG* 687 and 687k) is Moscow, State Historical Museum, Synod. gr. 15 (formerly Vladimir 381), dated to 1023, a manuscript from the Georgian monastery of Iviron on Mount Athos and a significant volume, for which see the edition of the *Life of Theodoros of Edessa* by Euthymios "the Iberian," now in preparation by Stratis Papaioannou (in collaboration with Charis Messis, and others) to be published in the series *Studia Byzantina Upsaliensia.*

50 See Walter, *Warrior Saints,* 109–44; see also the earlier Aleksandr V. Rystenko, *Легенда о св. Георгии и драконе в византийской и славянорусской литературах* (Odessa, 1909); and, for the wider Christian tradition, Michèle Ballez, Jean-Luc Depotte, and Benoît Kanabus, *Saint Georges et le dragon: Genèse et génération de récits* (Louvain-la-Neuve, 2018).

51 See Daniel Ogden, *Dragons, Serpents and Slayers in the Classical and Early Christian Worlds: A Sourcebook* (Oxford, 2013), especially pp. 249–52, where Ogden offers a translation and discussion of *BHG* 687. See further William Hansen, *Ariadne's Thread: A Guide to International Tales Found in Classical*

Literature (Ithaca, NY, 2002), 119–30. For the Byzantine tradition, see Titos Papamastorakis, "Ιστορίες και ιστορήσεις Βυζαντινών παλληκαριών," *Δελτίον της Χριστιανικής Αρχαιολογικής Εταιρείας* 20 (1998): 375–92; Oya Pancaroğlu, "The Itinerant Dragon-Slayer: Forging Paths of Image and Identity in Medieval Anatolia," *Gesta* 43 (2004): 151–64; and Monica White, "The Rise of the Dragon in Middle Byzantine Hagiography," *Byzantine and Modern Greek Studies* 32 (2008): 149–67.

52 Most recently (and including earlier bibliography) in Kevin Tuite, "The Old Georgian Version of the Miracle of St George, the Princess and the Dragon, I: Text, Commentary and Translation" (unpublished manuscript, Jul 19, 2020); and "The Old Georgian Version of the Miracle of St George, the Princess and the Dragon, II: Representations of George and His Female Counterpart in Vernacular Religion and Folklore" (unpublished manuscript, Aug 31, 2020), accessed February 13, 2022, https://uni-jena .academia.edu/KevinTuite/Drafts.

53 Willy Hengstenberg, "Der Drachenkampf des Heiligen Theodor," *Oriens Christianus,* n.s., 2 (1912): 78–106 and 241–80; Willy Hengstenberg, "Nachtrag zu dem Aufsatz 'Der Drachenkampf des Heiligen Theodor,'" *Oriens Christianus,* n.s., 3 (1913): 135–37. See also John Haldon, *A Tale of Two Saints: The Martyrdoms and Miracles of Saints Theodore "the Recruit" and "the General"* (Liverpool, 2016) 3–5, 28–32, and 40.

54 The manuscript that contains the Georgian text of the two miracles (Jerusalem, Greek Patriarchate, Geo. 2) dates to the eleventh century, and thus antedates all Greek witnesses; furthermore, according to Tuite, "The Old Georgian Version I," this Georgian version is closer to two Greek witnesses that date to the early fourteenth and sixteenth centuries (Messina, Biblioteca Universitaria, S. Salv. gr 29, and Athens, National Library of Greece, gr. 838). Nevertheless, all this does not automatically make their version the earliest one; my impression is that all three manuscripts present a text that shows signs of elaboration and smoothing out of the rough edges—both in linguistic form and narrative content—that are evident in other versions and, certainly, in *BHG* 687, the version of the present volume. The matter, of course, cannot be resolved here.

55 See Papaioannou, "Philosopher's Tongue," 167–69.

56 See a scholion by Theodoros Balsamon on the sixtieth canon of the council in Trullo, where we read about the condemnation of "many who sit

INTRODUCTION

with chains in the church of the great martyr Saint Niketas and others who walk around the streets and pretend to be possessed by demons"; here the "chains" are likely inspired by an episode in the *Passion of Niketas* (see section 14), while our Niketas was confused with Niketas the Goth, to whom the church in question was dedicated; see further below. For Balsamon's text, see Charis Messis, *Le corpus nomocanonique oriental et ses scholiastes du XIIe siècle: Les commentaires sur le concile in Trullo (691–692)* (Paris 2020), 335–36. Prayers of exorcism addressed to Niketas exist in Slavonic; Vasilij M. Istrin, *Апокрифическое мучение Никиты* (Odessa, 1899), 35–36. Meanwhile, Niketas's passion was considered "apocryphal" by lists of "prohibited books" also preserved in Slavonic and dating from the eleventh century onward; Istrin, *Апокрифическое*, 3–6, and Aleksandr I. Iatsimirskii, *Библиографический обзор апокрифов в южнославянской и русской письменности (Списки памятников) Выпуск 1. Апокрифы ветхозаветные* (Saint Petersburg, 1921), 52–53.

57 For Niketas's cult, see Angeliki Katsioti, "Χάλκινος λιτανικός σταυρός από τη Νίσυρο με παράσταση του αρχαγγέλου Μιχαήλ: Η πιθανή προέλευσή του," in *Χάρις Χαίρε, Μελέτες στη μνήμη της Χάρης Κάντζια*, vol. 1 (Athens 2004), 471–85. For the Venetian tradition, see *BHL* 6087 and Paolo Chiesa, "Recuperi agiografici veneziani dai codici Milano, Braidense, Gerli ms. 26 e Firenze, Nazionale, Conv. Soppr. G.5.1212," *Hagiographica* 5 (1998): 219–71, at 226–27. For the Slavic world, see Miodrag Marković, "St. Niketas the Goth and St. Niketas of Nikomedeia: Apropos Depictions of St. Niketas the Martyr on Medieval Crosses," *Zbornik za likovne umetnosti Matice srpske* 36 (2008): 19–42. The Slavonic translations of Niketas's *Passion* date to the twelfth century, according to Istrin, *Апокрифическое*, 38; see further Tvorogov, *Переводные*, 128, and Ivanova, *Bibliotheca*, 214.

58 See Marković, "St. Niketas" (with further bibliography).

59 See "Nicetas filius Maximiani imp.," Pinakes, https://pinakes.irht.cnrs.fr/notices/saint/662/. To these we may add the seventeenth-century manuscript Meteora, Μεταμορφώσεως, MS 447, fols. 80r–86v, which preserves an unedited Modern Greek *metaphrasis* of Niketas's passion; see Nikos A. Bees, *Τὰ χειρόγραφα τῶν Μετεώρων* (Athens, 1967–1993), vol. 1, p. 454.

60 Istrin, *Апокрифическое;* see also the review by Eduard Kurtz in *Byzantinische Zeitschrift* 10, no. 1 (1901): 242–44.

61 For *BHG* 1344, see Istrin, *Апокрифическое,* pp. 50–63, and for *BHG* 1345, see pp. 49–50 and the apparatus on pp. 50–63.

62 This episode is otherwise preserved in the somewhat "cleaner" version of the text (*BHG* 1343) that Istrin considered a later one and edited based only on a thirteenth-century manuscript; Istrin, *Апокрифическое,* 42–49. *BHG* 1343 is also transmitted, we might add, by the *earliest* manuscript in Niketas's dossier (Milan, Ambrosiana D 092 sup.), dated to the second half of the tenth century, made in southern Italy. See further the Note on the Texts, for the manuscripts and the different redactions.

PASSION OF
BONIPHATIOS

Μαρτύριον τοῦ Ἁγίου Βονιφατίου, ἐν Ταρσῷ μαρτυρήσαντος

Ὁ Θεὸς ὁ φιλάνθρωπος, ὁ χρήζων τῆς τῶν ἀνθρώπων σωτηρίας, ὁ εἰπὼν διὰ τοῦ προφήτου "Οὐ βούλομαι τὸν θάνατον τοῦ ἁμαρτωλοῦ, ἀλλὰ τὴν ἐπιστροφὴν καὶ τὴν ζωήν," ὁ εἰπὼν "Οὐκ ἦλθον καλέσαι δικαίους, ἀλλὰ ἁμαρτωλοὺς εἰς μετάνοιαν," ὁ ταχὺς ἐν ἐλέει, καὶ πλούσιος ἐν οἰκτιρμοῖς, ὁ εἰπὼν "Ὅταν ἐπιστραφεὶς στενάξῃς, τότε σωθήσῃ," ὁ δοὺς ἡμῖν ὑποδείγματα σωτηρίας πρὸς τὸ ἐπιστρέφειν εἰς αὐτόν, τῇ οἰκείᾳ αὐτοῦ ἀγαθότητι προνοούμενος, ὑπογραμμοὺς δίδωσιν σωτηρίας, πρὸς τὸ μὴ ἀπαγορεύειν ἑαυτῶν (εἴ ποτε ἐν ἁμαρτίαις ὑπὸ τοῦ ἐχθροῦ παγιδευθῶμεν), ἀλλ᾽ ἐλπίζειν ἐπὶ τὴν ἄφατον αὐτοῦ ἀγαθότητα, καὶ ἐπὶ τὸ ἄμετρον πέλαγος τῆς αὐτοῦ εὐσπλαγχνίας.

Πολλοὶ γὰρ συναρπασθέντες καὶ περιπλακέντες ἁμαρτήμασι χαλεποῖς, ἐπὶ τέλει ἀνανήψαντες, τοὺς στεφάνους τῆς νίκης ἀπηνέγκαντο. Ὧν εἷς ὑπάρχει καὶ ὁ ἡμέτερος στεφανίτης, ὁ μακάριος Βονιφάτιος, σὺν τῇ αὐτοῦ κυρίᾳ, περὶ ὧν νυνὶ διηγήσομαι τῇ ὑμετέρᾳ ἀγάπῃ.

2 Ἦν τις ἐν τῇ Ῥώμῃ γυνὴ μεγάλη ὀνόματι Ἀγλαΐς, θυγάτηρ Ἀκακίου, γένους κλάρου, ἀνθυπάτου γενομένου. Αὕτη δὲ τρίτον κάνδιδα ἔπραξεν ἐν τῇ Ῥώμῃ καὶ

Passion of Saint Boniphatios,
who was martyred in Tarsos

God, who loves humankind, who desires the salvation of human beings, who said through his prophet "*I do not wish the death of the sinner,* but rather his turning back and living," who said "I did *not* come *to call the righteous, but sinners to repentance,*" who is swift in compassion, and rich in mercies, who said "*When* you turn back *and groan, then you shall be saved,*" who gives us models of salvation to turn us back to him, providing them in his characteristic goodness, this God gives us examples of salvation, so that we do not despair of ourselves (if we are ever ensnared in sins by the enemy), but rather may place our hopes upon his ineffable goodness, and upon the immeasurable sea of his compassion.

Many indeed were snatched away, entwined by severe sins, yet in the end, when they came to their senses, secured the crowns of victory. One among them is also our very own crown bearer, the blessed Boniphatios, together with his own mistress. It is their story that I shall now recount to you, my beloved friends.

There was a *great woman* in Rome by the name of Aglaïs. 2
She was the daughter of Akakios, a man from a noble family, who had been a proconsul. Three times she sponsored

3

ἐπαρχότητα, ἔχουσα ὑφ' ἑαυτὴν ἑβδομήκοντα τρεῖς φρον-
τιστὰς εἰς τὴν κτῆσιν αὐτῆς, καὶ ἕνα μειζότερον ἐπάνω
πάντων, ὀνόματι Βονιφάτιον, ὃς καὶ συνεκοινώνει αὐτῇ
εἰς ἁμαρτίαν.

Ἦν δὲ οὗτος μεθυστής, καὶ πόρνος, καὶ πάντων φίλος
ὢν μισεῖ Κύριος ὁ Θεός. Τρία δὲ εἶχεν κατορθώματα· φιλόξενος, εὐμετάδοτος, καὶ ἐλεήμων· εἴ ποτε γὰρ ἴδεν ξένον
ἢ ὁδοιπόρον, μετὰ πάσης σπουδῆς καὶ προθυμίας προτρε-
πόμενος, διηκόνει αὐτῷ· καὶ νυκτὸς περιάγων τὰς πλατείας
καὶ ῥύμας, διεδίδου τοῖς δεομένοις τὰ δέοντα πρὸς τὴν
χρείαν.

3   Μετὰ οὖν χρόνους ἱκανούς, τῆς χάριτος τοῦ Θεοῦ
κατανυξάσης ταύτην, προσκαλεῖται τὸν παῖδα αὐτῆς τὸν
καὶ μειζότερον, καὶ λέγει αὐτῷ, "Ἀδελφὲ Βονιφάτιε, οἶδας
εἰς πόσας ἁμαρτίας ἐμπεφυρμένοι ἐσμέν, μὴ λογιζόμενοι
ὅτι τῷ Θεῷ παραστῆναι ἔχομεν, καὶ ἀποδοῦναι λόγον περὶ
ὧν διεπραξάμεθα κακῶν ἐν τῷ κόσμῳ τούτῳ. Καὶ νῦν
ἀκήκοα Χριστιανῶν λεγόντων ὅτι, ὅστις ἐξυπηρετήσεται
τοῖς ἁγίοις, τοῖς διὰ Χριστὸν ἀγωνισαμένοις καὶ ἀθλήσασιν
ὑπὲρ αὐτοῦ, συμμέτοχος αὐτῶν γίνεται ἐν τῇ φοβερᾷ
ἡμέρᾳ τῆς δικαιοκρισίας τοῦ Θεοῦ. Καὶ νῦν ἰδοὺ μεμάθηκα,
ὅτι οἱ δοῦλοι τοῦ Χριστοῦ ἀγωνίζονται κατὰ τοῦ διαβόλου
ἐν τῇ Ἀνατολῇ, παραδιδόντες τὰ ἑαυτῶν σώματα, ἵνα μὴ
ἀρνήσωνται τὸν Χριστόν. Πορευθεὶς οὖν φέρε ἡμῖν λείψανα ἁγίων μαρτύρων, εἴ πως ἐξυπηρετησάμενοι τούτοις,
καὶ εὐκτηρίους οἴκους οἰκοδομήσαντες, ἀξίους τῆς ἀθλήσεως αὐτῶν, σωθῶμεν δι' αὐτῶν—καὶ ἡμεῖς, καὶ ἄλλοι
πολλοί."

gladiatorial games in Rome and served as prefect. In her retinue, she had seventy-three stewards for her estates and there was one, the foreman of all others, called Boniphatios who was joined with her in sin.

Boniphatios was addicted to drinking and sex, and he liked everything that the Lord God despises. But he had three good qualities: hospitality, generosity, and charity. If he ever saw a foreigner or a traveler, he would immediately and most eagerly welcome him, and look after him; and at night, he would go around the squares and the streets, and give away what was needed to those in need.

After many years had passed, Aglaïs was moved to compunction by the grace of God. She thus summoned her slave, the foreman, and she said to him, "Brother Boniphatios, you know well how many sins we're mixed up in, without thinking that we shall have to stand before God and give an account for all the wicked things we have done in this world. Now I have heard the Christians saying that whoever aids the saints, those who fought and were martyred on behalf of Christ, will be on their side on that awesome day of God's judgment. And just now I learned that the servants of Christ are fighting against the devil in the East, sacrificing their bodies so as not to deny Christ. You should therefore go and bring us relics of the holy martyrs, so that perhaps by aiding them and by building houses of worship worthy of their martyrdom, we may be saved through them—we and many others." 3

4 Ἔλαβε δὲ ὁ παῖς χρυσίον ἱκανὸν ὥστε ἀγοράσαι λείψανα ἁγίων μαρτύρων, καὶ εἰς διάδοσιν τῶν πτωχῶν, καὶ δώδεκα ἱππεῖς, καὶ τρία λεκτίκια, καὶ μῦρα διάφορα, εἰς τιμὴν τῶν ἁγίων μαρτύρων. Καὶ ἐν τῷ μέλλειν ἐξιέναι αὐτόν, λέγει τῇ κυρίᾳ αὐτοῦ χαριέντως, "Δέσποινά μου, ἐὰν εὕρω λείψανα ἁγίων μαρτύρων, φέρω· ἐπεὶ τὸ ἐμὸν λείψανον ἐὰν ἔλθῃ, εἰς ὄνομα μάρτυρος δέχῃ αὐτό."

Εἶπεν δὲ αὐτῷ ἡ κυρία αὐτοῦ, "Ἀπὸ σοῦ ποίησον τὴν μέθην, καὶ τὴν μωρολογίαν, καὶ οὕτως ἄπελθε, ὡς εἰδὼς ὅτι λείψανα ἁγίων μαρτύρων βαστάσαι ἔχεις. Ἐγὼ δὲ ἡ ἁμαρτωλός, προσδέχομαί σε ἐν τάχει. Ὁ δὲ Κύριος καὶ Θεὸς τῶν ὅλων, ὁ δι' ἡμᾶς μορφὴν δούλου λαβών, ὁ τὸ ἑαυτοῦ αἷμα ἐκχέας διὰ τὴν σωτηρίαν τοῦ γένους τῶν ἀνθρώπων, αὐτὸς ἐξαποστείλαι τὸν ἄγγελον αὐτοῦ πρὸ προσώπου σου, καὶ κατευθύναι τὰ διαβήματά σου ἐν τῇ αὐτοῦ εὐσπλαγχνίᾳ, καὶ πληρώσει τὴν ἐπιθυμίαν μου, παρ- ιδὼν τὰ παραπτώματά μου."

5 Ἐξελθὼν δὲ ὁ Βονιφάτιος κατὰ τὴν ὁδόν, ἐν ἑαυτῷ ἐνεθυμεῖτο λέγων, "Δίκαιόν ἐστιν, μήτε κρεῶν ἅψασθαί με, μήτε οἴνου μεταλαβεῖν, διότι εἰ καὶ ἀνάξιός εἰμι καὶ ἁμαρτωλός, λείψανα ἁγίων μαρτύρων βαστάσαι ἔχω."

Καὶ ἀνατείνας τὸ ὄμμα εἰς τὸν οὐρανὸν εἶπεν, "Δέσποτα Παντοκράτορ, ὁ Θεός, ὁ τοῦ μονογενοῦς σου παιδὸς πατήρ, ἐλθὲ εἰς τὴν βοήθειάν μου τοῦ δούλου σου, καὶ εὐόδωσον τὴν ὁδόν μου, δι' ἧς ἐγὼ πορεύομαι ἐν αὐτῇ, ὅπως δοξασθῇ τὸ ὄνομά σου τὸ ἅγιον εἰς τοὺς αἰῶνας, ἀμήν." Καὶ τελέσαντος αὐτοῦ τὴν εὐχήν, εἴχετο τῆς ὁδοῦ.

6 Ἐλθὼν οὖν δι' ἡμερῶν τινων ἐν Ταρσῷ τῇ πόλει, καὶ

The slave took with him sufficient money to purchase   4
relics of holy martyrs and also give to the poor; he also took
twelve horsemen, three litters, and various kinds of perfumed unguents for the veneration of the holy martyrs.
When he was about to depart, he said to his mistress jokingly, "My mistress, if I find relics of holy martyrs, I will
bring them; but if my own relic is what comes back, then
take that instead of a martyr's."

And his mistress said to him, "Stop your drunkenness and
foolish talk, and set off in the knowledge that you are going
to carry the relics of holy martyrs. As for me, sinner that I
am, I shall wait for your swift return. And may the Lord and
God of all, who *took the form of a slave* for our sake, who shed
his own blood for the salvation of the human race, send his
angel in front of you, and direct your *steps* in his compassion,
and thus *satisfy* my *desire,* overlooking my iniquities."

As he went out on his way, Boniphatios began to think to   5
himself and say, "It's right that I should neither touch meat,
nor have wine, since, even though I'm unworthy and a sinner, I'm going to carry the relics of holy martyrs."

Then he raised his eyes to heaven, and said, "Lord God
Almighty, the father of your only begotten son, come to the
aid of me, your servant, and help me on my way, as I make
my journey, so that your holy name may be glorified unto the
ages, amen." When he finished his prayer, he began his journey.

In a few days, he arrived at the city of Tarsos. When he   6

γνοὺς ὅτι οἱ ἅγιοι τοῦ Χριστοῦ ἀθληταὶ ἀγωνίζονται ἐν τῷ μαρτυρίῳ, λέγει τοῖς σὺν αὐτῷ, "Ἀδελφοί, πορευθέντες ἐπιζητήσατε ξενοδοχεῖον, κἀκεῖ διαναπαύσατε τὰ ζῶα. Ἐγὼ δὲ ἀπέρχομαι θεάσασθαι οὓς πάνυ ἐπιποθῶ."

Ἀπελθὼν οὖν ἐν τῷ σταδίῳ πρὸς τοὺς ἁγίους μάρτυρας, ἴδεν αὐτοὺς ἐν ταῖς βασάνοις· καὶ τὸν μὲν αὐτῶν κρεμάμενον κατὰ κεφαλῆς, καὶ πυρὰν ὑποκάτω αὐτοῦ ἐστρωμένην· ἄλλον ἠκρωτηριασμένον τὰς ὄψεις· ἄλλον διατεταμένον εἰς τέσσαρα ξύλα· ἄλλον πριζόμενον ὑπὸ δημίων· ἄλλον ξεόμενον· ἄλλον χειροκοπηθέντα· ἄλλον πάλον εἰς τὸν τράχηλον αὐτοῦ ἐμπαγέντα καὶ διηλαμένον ἐν τῇ γῇ· ἄλλον ἀνακλασθέντα χερσὶν καὶ ποσὶν εἰς τὰ ὀπίσω, καὶ οὕτω βάκλοις ὑπὸ δημίων τυπτόμενον. Καὶ ἦν ἁπλῶς σκότος δεινὸν τοῖς ὁρῶσιν τὰ τοιαῦτα βασανιστήρια· μᾶλλον δὲ ἦν ἰδεῖν τὸν διάβολον ἡττώμενον, τοὺς δὲ δούλους τοῦ Χριστοῦ ἀγωνιζομένους.

7   Προσελθὼν οὖν ὁ Βονιφάτιος, κατεφίλει τοὺς ἁγίους μάρτυρας ὄντας ἐν κολάσει τῶν δεινῶν (ἦσαν γὰρ τὸν ἀριθμὸν ἄνδρες εἴκοσι)· καὶ ἀναβοήσας εἶπεν, "Μέγας ὁ Θεὸς τῶν Χριστιανῶν! Μέγας ὁ Θεὸς τῶν ἁγίων μαρτύρων! Δέομαι ὑμῶν, δοῦλοι τοῦ Χριστοῦ, πρεσβεύσατε περὶ ἐμοῦ, ἵνα κἀγὼ συμμέτοχος ὑμῶν εὑρεθῶ, ἀγωνισάμενος κατὰ τοῦ διαβόλου."

Καὶ παρακαθίσας τοῖς ποσὶ τῶν ἁγίων μαρτύρων, περιεπτύσσετο τὰ δεσμὰ αὐτῶν καταφιλῶν καὶ λέγων, "Ἀγωνίσασθε, ἀθλοφόροι μάρτυρες, πατῆσαι τὸν διάβολον! Ὀλίγον ὑπομείνατε· ὀλίγος γὰρ ὁ κόπος, πολλὴ δὲ ἡ ἀνάπαυσις· μικρὰ ἡ στρέβλη, καὶ ἄφατος ἡ δορυφορία· ἐπὶ γῆς

learned that the holy athletes of Christ were fighting in martyrdom, he said to his companions, "Brothers, go and find an inn, and stable the animals there. I'm going to go and watch those whom I greatly desire."

So he went off to the stadium, to the holy martyrs, and he saw them being tortured. One was hanging head down, with fire spread out below him; another had his eyes cut out; another was stretched on four wooden pillars; another was being sawn apart by executioners; another was being scraped; another was having his hands cut off; another had a stake driven through his neck and into the ground; another's hands and feet were tied behind his back, and he was being beaten by the executioners with rods. Such tortures were simply *a terrible darkness* for the onlookers; or, rather, it was possible to see the devil being defeated, and Christ's servants triumphing.

Then Boniphatios approached and *began to kiss* the holy 7
martyrs (there were twenty men in number) while they were tortured in this terrible fashion. And he shouted out and said, "Great is the God of the Christians! Great is the God of the holy martyrs! I beseech you, servants of Christ, intercede on my behalf, so that I too may be found by your side, fighting against the devil."

And he sat down by the feet of the holy martyrs, embraced and kissed their fetters, and said, "Keep fighting, victorious martyrs, so as to trample upon the devil! Hang on a little longer! The toil is small, while the repose is great; the torment is trivial, but the honor indescribable; on earth

στρεβλοῦται τὸ σῶμα ὑπὸ δημίων, ἐν δὲ τῷ μέλλοντι αἰῶνι, ὑπὸ ἀγγέλων δορυφορεῖται."

8 Ἀτενίσας δὲ ὁ ἄρχων εἰς τὸν ὄχλον, καὶ ἰδὼν αὐτόν, εἶπεν, "Τίς ἐστιν ἐκεῖνος, ὁ ἐπὶ καταφρονήσει μου καὶ τῶν θεῶν ταῦτα δρῶν; Ἀχθήτω τοίνυν ἐπὶ τοῦ βήματός μου!"

Καί φησιν ὁ ἄρχων, "Λέγε σύ, τίς εἶ, ὅτι κατεφρόνησας τοῦ καθαρωτάτου δικαστηρίου μου."

Βονιφάτιος εἶπεν, "Ἐγὼ Χριστιανός εἰμι, καὶ τὸν Δεσπότην μου Χριστὸν ἔχων, καταφρονῶ καὶ σοῦ, καὶ τοῦ βήματός σου."

Ὁ ἄρχων εἶπεν, "Τί τὸ ὄνομά σου κέκληται;"

Βονιφάτιος εἶπεν, "Ἤδη εἶπόν σοι ὅτι Χριστιανός εἰμι. Εἰ δὲ τὸ κοινὸν ὄνομα θέλεις μαθεῖν, Βονιφάτιος καλοῦμαι."

Ὁ ἄρχων εἶπεν, "Πρὶν ἢ ἅψομαί σου τῶν πλευρῶν, προσελθὼν θῦσον τοῖς θεοῖς."

Βονιφάτιος εἶπεν, "Εἶπόν σοι πλειστάκις, ὅτι Χριστιανός εἰμι, καὶ οὐ θύω δαιμονίοις. Εἴ τι οὖν θέλεις ποιεῖν, ποίει. Ἰδοὺ πρόκειταί σοι τὸ σῶμά μου."

9 Καὶ θυμωθεὶς ὁ ἄρχων, ἐκέλευσεν κρεμασθῆναι αὐτὸν κατακέφαλα, καὶ εὐτόνως ξέεσθαι· καὶ ἐπὶ τοσοῦτον ἔξεσαν αὐτὸν οἱ δήμιοι, ὥστε τὰ ὀστᾶ αὐτοῦ φαίνεσθαι. Ὁ δὲ μακάριος οὐδὲν ἀπεκρίνατο, ἀλλ᾽ εἶχεν τοὺς ὀφθαλμοὺς αὐτοῦ εἰς τοὺς ἁγίους μάρτυρας. Καὶ ἐκέλευσεν ὁ ἄρχων ἀνεθῆναι αὐτόν.

Διαστάσης δὲ ὡσεὶ ὥρας μιᾶς, λέγει πρὸς αὐτὸν ὁ ἄρχων, "Θῦσον, ἄθλιε, καὶ ἐλέησον σεαυτόν."

Ὁ δὲ μακάριος ἀπεκρίνατο αὐτῷ, "Οὐκ αἰσχύνῃ,

your body is tormented by executioners, but in the age to come it will be given an honor guard by angels."

The ruler gazed at the crowd, and when he saw Boniphatios, he said, "Who is that man who is acting in this way in contempt of me and the gods? He must be brought to my tribunal!" 8

And the ruler said, "You there, speak! Who are you to show contempt against my fairest court of law?"

Boniphatios responded, "I am a Christian. And since Christ is my Lord, I am contemptuous of both you and your tribunal."

The ruler said, "What is your name?"

Boniphatios said, "I already told you that I am a Christian. But if you want to learn my common name, I am called Boniphatios."

The ruler said, "Before I lay my hands upon your sides, come and sacrifice to the gods."

Boniphatios said, "I've told you multiple times that I am a Christian, and I'm not sacrificing to demons. Do whatever you wish to do with me. Here is *my body,* take it."

The ruler became very angry, and ordered that Boniphatios should be hung head down, and be fiercely scraped; and the executioners scraped his body so much that his bones could be seen. The blessed man, however, gave no response, but had his eyes fixed on the holy martyrs. So the ruler ordered that he should be given a break. 9

After about an hour had passed, the ruler said to him, "Sacrifice, you miserable man, and take pity on yourself."

But the blessed man responded to him, "Are you not

τρισάθλιε, πάντοτε λέγων 'θῦσον,' ἐμοῦ μὴ ἀνεχομένου ἀκοῦσαι περὶ ἀπολλυμένων εἰδώλων;"

Καὶ θυμωθεὶς ὁ ἄρχων, ἐκέλευσε καλάμους ὀξυνθῆναι, καὶ ἐμπαγῆναι εἰς τοὺς ὄνυχας τῶν χειρῶν αὐτοῦ. Καὶ ἀναβλέψας ὁ ἅγιος εἰς οὐρανόν, ῥᾷον τοὺς πόνους ὑπέφερεν.

10 Θεωρήσας δὲ ὁ ἄρχων, ὅτι οὐκ ᾔσθετο τῶν βασάνων, ἐκέλευσεν ἀνοιγῆναι αὐτοῦ τὸ στόμα, καὶ μόλιβδον κοχλάζοντα ἐκχέαι αὐτῷ. Ὁ δὲ μακάριος ἀθλητὴς τοῦ Χριστοῦ, ἀναβλέψας εἰς τὸν οὐρανόν, προσηύξατο λέγων, "Εὐχαριστῶ σοι, Δέσποτα Ἰησοῦ Χριστέ, υἱὲ τοῦ Θεοῦ· ἐλθὲ εἰς τὴν βοήθειάν μου τοῦ δούλου σου, καὶ κούφισόν με τῶν πόνων τούτων, καὶ μὴ συγχωρήσῃς με ἡττηθῆναι ὑπὸ τοῦ μιαροῦ ἄρχοντος τούτου· οἶδας γὰρ ὅτι διὰ τὸ ὄνομά σου ταῦτα πάσχω."

Καὶ τελέσαντος αὐτοῦ τὴν εὐχήν, ἔκραξεν τοῖς ἁγίοις λέγων, "Δέομαι ὑμῶν, δοῦλοι τοῦ Χριστοῦ, εὔξασθε ὑπὲρ τοῦ δούλου ὑμῶν."

Καὶ οἱ ἅγιοι, ὡς ἐξ ἑνὸς στόματος, εἶπον, "Ὁ Κύριος ἡμῶν Ἰησοῦς Χριστὸς αὐτὸς ἀποστείλῃ τὸν ἄγγελον αὐτοῦ, καὶ ῥύσεταί σε ἐκ τοῦ μιαρωτάτου ἄρχοντος τούτου, καὶ τελειώσει τὸν δρόμον σου ἐν τάχει, καὶ τάξει τὸ ὄνομά σου μετὰ τῶν πρωτοτόκων."

Καὶ πληρώσαντες τὴν εὐχήν, καὶ εἰπόντες τὸ "Ἀμήν," ἐγένετο κλαυθμὸς τοῦ πλήθους, καὶ κραυγὴ μεγάλη λεγόντων, "Μέγας ὁ Θεὸς τῶν Χριστιανῶν, μέγας ὁ Θεὸς τῶν μαρτύρων. Χριστέ, υἱὲ τοῦ Θεοῦ, σῶσον ἡμᾶς· πάντες γὰρ σοὶ πιστεύομεν, καὶ πρός σε καταφεύγομεν. Ἀνάθεμα

ashamed, you thrice miserable man, always telling me to sacrifice, while I cannot bear to hear about perishable idols?"

And then the ruler became angry, and ordered that reeds be sharpened, and stuck under the nails of Boniphatios's hands. But the saint gazed upward toward heaven, and easily endured the pain.

When the ruler realized that Boniphatios did not feel the tortures, he ordered that his mouth be opened and boiling lead be poured into it. The blessed athlete of Christ gazed upward toward heaven, and prayed with the following words: "I thank you, Lord Jesus Christ, son of God; come to the aid of me your servant, and lighten these pains for me, and do not let me be defeated by this abominable ruler; for you know that I am suffering these things on behalf of your name."

And when he finished his prayer, he cried out to the saints, saying, "I beg you, servants of Christ, pray for your servant."

And the saints *as though from one mouth* responded, "Our Lord Jesus Christ will himself send his angel, and he will save you from this abominable ruler, and he will bring your course swiftly to completion, and he will place your name among the firstborn."

And when they finished their prayer and said "Amen," the crowd began to wail, and gave a great shout, saying, "Great is the God of the Christians, great is the God of the martyrs. Christ, son of God, save us; for we all believe in you, and seek refuge with you. Anathema to the idols of the nations!"

τὰ εἴδωλα τῶν ἐθνῶν!" Καὶ ὥρμησεν πᾶς ὁ λαός· καὶ κατέστρεψεν τὸν βωμόν· καὶ τὸν ἄρχοντα ἐλίθασαν. Καὶ ἀναστὰς ὁ ἄρχων, ὑπεχώρησε διὰ τὴν ταραχήν, φοβηθεὶς τὸν ὄχλον.

11 Καὶ τῇ ἕωθεν καθίσας ἐπὶ τοῦ βήματος, ἐκέλευσε παραστῆναι αὐτῷ τὸν ἅγιον· καὶ λέγει αὐτῷ ὁ ἄρχων, "Διὰ τί, ἄθλιε, οὕτως μαίνῃ, εἰς ἄνθρωπον ἔχων τὰς ἐλπίδας, καὶ αὐτὸν σταυρωθέντα ὡς κακοῦργον;"

Λέγει αὐτῷ ὁ μάρτυς, "Φιμώθητι, καὶ μὴ ἀνοίξῃς τὰ μιαρά σου χείλη περὶ τοῦ Κυρίου Ἰησοῦ Χριστοῦ, ἐσκοτισμένε τῇ διανοίᾳ, ὄφι *πεπαλαιωμένε ἡμερῶν κακῶν,* ἀνάθεμά σοι! ὁ γὰρ Δεσπότης μου Χριστὸς ταῦτα ὑπέμεινεν, θέλων σῶσαι τὸ γένος τῶν ἀνθρώπων."

Καὶ θυμωθεὶς ὁ ἄρχων, ἐκέλευσε λέβητα πίσσης γεμισθῆναι, καὶ κοχλαζούσης τῆς πίσσης, ἐμβληθῆναι τὸν ἅγιον κατὰ κεφαλῆς. Ὁ δὲ ἅγιος τοῦ Χριστοῦ μάρτυς ποιήσας τὴν ἐν Χριστῷ σφραγῖδα, ἐβλήθη εἰς τὸν λέβητα. Ἄγγελος δὲ Κυρίου καταβὰς ἐξ οὐρανοῦ, ἥψατο τοῦ λέβητος, καὶ εὐθέως διελύθη *ὡς κηρὸς ὅταν ὀσφρανθῇ πυρός.* Καὶ τὸν μὲν ἅγιον οὐ παρενώχλησεν· κατέκαυσε δὲ τῶν παρεστηκότων ἄνδρας πολλούς.

12 Φοβηθεὶς δὲ ὁ ἄρχων τὴν δύναμιν τοῦ Χριστοῦ, καὶ θαυμάσας τὴν ὑπομονὴν τοῦ ἁγίου μάρτυρος, ἐκέλευσεν ξίφει τὴν κεφαλὴν αὐτοῦ ἀποτμηθῆναι, εἰπών, "Τὸν τοῖς νόμοις τῶν βασιλέων μὴ πειθαρχήσαντα, τοῦτον κελεύει ἡ ἡμετέρα ἐξουσία κεφαλικὴν τιμωρίαν ὑπομεῖναι." Οἱ δὲ δορυφόροι ἦραν αὐτὸν μετὰ σπουδῆς ἐκ τοῦ βήματος.

Ὁ δὲ ἅγιος τοῦ Χριστοῦ μάρτυς, ποιήσας τὴν ἐν Χριστῷ

And all the people rushed, and destroyed the altar, and they threw stones at the ruler. And the ruler got up and retreated because of the commotion since he was scared of the crowd.

And early the next day, he sat on his tribunal and ordered 11 that the saint be presented before him. And the ruler said to Boniphatios, "Why, you miserable man, are you crazy enough to invest your hopes in someone who is human and, at that, crucified as a criminal?"

The martyr said to him, "Shut your mouth, and never open your abominable lips about the Lord Jesus Christ! You pervert! You snake, *who has grown old in wicked days!* Anathema to you! My Lord Christ suffered these things wishing to save the human race."

The ruler became enraged and ordered that a cauldron be filled with pitch, and when the pitch was simmering, that the saint be thrown headfirst into it. The holy martyr of Christ made the sign of Christ, and was thrown into the cauldron. But an angel of the Lord came down from heaven, touched the cauldron, and it immediately dissolved *as wax melts* when it smells *fire;* and the boiler did not harm the saint at all, but it burned many of the bystanders.

Scared of Christ's power, and amazed at the patience of 12 the holy martyr, the ruler ordered that Boniphatios's head be cut off with a sword, saying, "My sovereignty orders that this man who did not abide by the laws of the emperors should be liable to capital punishment." The bodyguards then quickly took him away from the tribunal.

Then, the holy martyr of Christ made the sign of Christ,

σφραγῖδα, παρεκάλεσε τοὺς δημίους ἐνδοῦναι αὐτῷ μι-
κρὰν ὥραν, ὅπως προσεύξηται. Καὶ στὰς κατ' ἀνατολάς,
προσηύξατο λέγων, "Κύριε, Κύριε Παντοκράτορ, ὁ πατὴρ
τοῦ Κυρίου ἡμῶν Ἰησοῦ Χριστοῦ, ἐλθὲ εἰς τὴν βοήθειάν
μου τοῦ σοῦ δούλου, καὶ ἐξαπόστειλον τὸν ἄγγελόν σου·
καὶ πρόσδεξαι ἐν εἰρήνῃ τὴν ψυχήν μου, ἵνα μὴ ἐμποδίσῃ
με ὁ μιαρὸς καὶ φονιώδης δράκων, καὶ παρεμποδίσῃ αὐτὴν
ἐν τῇ πονηρίᾳ αὐτοῦ, καὶ μὴ ἀπατήσῃ ἐν τῇ ἀπάτῃ αὐτοῦ,
ἀλλὰ συνανάπαυσον αὐτὴν τῷ χορῷ τῶν ἁγίων σου
μαρτύρων· καὶ ῥῦσαι, Κύριε, τὸν λαόν σου ἐκ τῆς θλίψεως
ταύτης τῶν ἀθέων, ὅτι σοι πρέπει τιμὴ καὶ κράτος σὺν τῷ
μονογενεῖ σου Υἱῷ, ἅμα τῷ Ἁγίῳ Πνεύματι, εἰς τοὺς
αἰῶνας τῶν αἰώνων, ἀμήν."

Καὶ πληρώσαντος αὐτοῦ τὴν εὐχήν, ἐκρούσθη ὑπὸ τοῦ
σπεκουλάτωρος· καὶ ἐγένετο σεισμὸς μέγας, ὥστε πάντας
ἀναβοῆσαι καὶ εἰπεῖν, "Μέγας ὁ Θεὸς τῶν Χριστιανῶν,"
καὶ πιστεῦσαι πολλοὺς ἐπὶ τὸν Κύριον Ἰησοῦν Χριστόν.

13 Οἱ δὲ σύνδουλοι αὐτοῦ περιῆγον πανταχοῦ ζητοῦντες
αὐτόν· καὶ μὴ εὑρόντες, ἤρξαντο λέγειν πρὸς ἀλλήλους,
"Ἐκεῖνος ἄρτι ἐν πορνείῳ ἢ ἐν καπηλείῳ κατακείμενος,
εὐφραίνεται· καὶ ἡμεῖς περιάγομεν, ζητοῦντες αὐτόν." Ἐν
δὲ τῷ διαλογίζεσθαι αὐτοὺς ταῦτα, συνέβη ἀπαντῆσαι αὐτοῖς τὸν ἀδελφὸν τοῦ κο<μ>μενταρησίου, καὶ λέγουσιν
αὐτῷ, "Μὴ ἑώρακάς τινα ἐνταῦθα ξένον Ῥωμαῖον;"

Ὁ δὲ λέγει αὐτοῖς, "Τῇ χθὲς ἡμέρᾳ, ἀνὴρ ξένος ἐμαρτύρησεν ὑπὲρ Χριστοῦ, καὶ ἀπετμήθη τὴν κεφαλήν."

Οἱ δὲ λέγουσιν αὐτῷ, "Καὶ ποῦ ἐστιν οὗτος;"

and asked his executioners to allow him a moment to pray. He thus stood facing east, and prayed, saying, "Lord, Lord Almighty, the father of our Lord Jesus Christ, come to the aid of me, your servant, and send your angel; and receive my soul in peace, so that the abominable and murderous serpent may not hinder me, and obstruct my soul in his wickedness, and deceive it in his deceit; rather, let it rest with the chorus of your holy martyrs; and also, Lord, save your people from this affliction by the godless ones, because the honor and the power belong to you, together with your only begotten Son, and along with your Holy Spirit, unto the ages of ages, amen."

And when he had completed his prayer, he was struck by the executioner, *and there was a great earthquake,* so that everyone shouted and said, "Great is the God of the Christians!" and many believed in the Lord Jesus Christ.

In the meantime, Boniphatios's fellow slaves were going 13 around searching everywhere for him. And when they were unable to find him, they began saying to each other, "He must be lying down right now in some whorehouse or some tavern and having a good time; and we're walking around looking for him." As they were discussing these things, they happened to meet the brother of the *kommentaresios,* and they said to him, "You haven't seen a foreigner from Rome here, have you?"

He said to them, "Yesterday, a foreigner was martyred for Christ, and his head was cut off."

They said to him, "And where is he?"

Ὁ δὲ εἶπεν, "Ἐν τῷ σταδίῳ·" καὶ λέγει αὐτοῖς, "Ποίας ἰδέας ἐστίν;"

Οἱ δὲ εἶπον αὐτῷ, "Ἀνὴρ τετραγωναῖος, παχύς, ξανθός, ῥούσιον ἀρμελαύσιον φορῶν."

Καὶ εἶπεν αὐτοῖς, "Ὃν ζητεῖτε, παρ' ἡμῖν χθὲς ἐμαρτύρησεν."

Οἱ δὲ εἶπον αὐτῷ, "Ὁ ἄνθρωπος ὃν ζητοῦμεν, πόρνος ἐστὶ καὶ μεθυστής."

Εἶπεν δὲ αὐτοῖς ἐκεῖνος, "Τί γὰρ ὑμᾶς ἀδικήσει ἐλθεῖν ἕως τοῦ σταδίου, καὶ θεάσασθαι αὐτόν;"

Οἱ δὲ ἠκολούθησαν αὐτῷ ἕως τοῦ σταδίου· καὶ ἔδειξεν αὐτοῖς τὸ σκήνωμα κείμενον.

Λέγουσιν αὐτῷ, "Δεόμεθά σου, δεῖξον ἡμῖν τὴν κεφαλὴν αὐτοῦ."

Ὁ δὲ ἀπελθών, ἤνεγκεν αὐτοῖς τὴν κεφαλὴν αὐτοῦ. Ἰδοῦσα δὲ ἡ ὄψις τοῦ μάρτυρος τοὺς συντρόφους αὐτοῦ, ἐγέλασεν ἐν Πνεύματι Ἁγίῳ· καὶ ἐπιγνόντες οἱ παῖδες, ἔκλαυσαν πικρῶς λέγοντες, "Μὴ μνησθῇς ἡμῶν εἰς ἁμαρτίαν, ὅσα κατελαλήσαμέν σου, δοῦλε τοῦ Χριστοῦ."

Καὶ λέγουσι τῷ ταξεώτῃ, "Οὗτός ἐστιν ὃν ζητοῦμεν· δεόμεθά σου, δώρησαι ἡμῖν αὐτόν."

Λέγει αὐτοῖς ὁ ταξεώτης, "Ἐγὼ δωρεὰν τὸ λείψανον ἀπολῦσαι ὑμῖν οὐ δύναμαι."

Οἱ δὲ δεδωκότες αὐτῷ νομίσματα πεντακόσια, ἔλαβον τὸ λείψανον τοῦ ἁγίου μάρτυρος· καὶ μυρίσαντες μύροις ἱκανοῖς, καὶ περιβαλόντες ὀθόνην πολυτίμητον, ἐνέβαλον ἐν ἑνὶ τῶν λεκτικίων· καὶ ὥδευσαν τὴν ὁδὸν αὐτῶν,

He said, "In the stadium." And he added, "What does he look like?"

They said to him, "He's square built, fat, blond, wearing a red sleeveless tunic."

And he said to them, "The man you're looking for was martyred by us yesterday."

And they said to him, "The man we're looking for is addicted to sex and drinking."

That man said to them, "What harm would there be for you to come to the stadium and have a look at him?"

They followed him to the stadium, and he showed them Boniphatios's corpse lying there.

They said to him, "Please, show us his head."

He went off and brought them Boniphatios's head. When the face of the martyr saw his companions, he laughed in the Holy Spirit. Recognizing him, his fellow slaves *wept bitterly,* saying, "Do not remember as a sin whatever we said against you, servant of Christ."

And they said to the officer, "That's the man we're looking for; please, give him to us."

And the officer said to them, "I can't release the relic to you for free."

So they gave him five hundred coins, and obtained the relic of the holy martyr; and they anointed it with many perfumed unguents, and wrapped it with a most precious cloth, and placed it in one of the litters; and they went on their

χαίροντες καὶ δοξάζοντες τὸν Θεὸν ἐπὶ τῇ τελειώσει τοῦ
ἁγίου μάρτυρος.

14 Ἄγγελος δὲ Κυρίου ὤφθη τῇ κυρίᾳ αὐτοῦ, λέγων, "Τόν
ποτε δοῦλόν σου, νῦν δὲ ἡμέτερον ἀδελφὸν δέξαι ὡς
δεσπότην, καὶ ἀνάπαυσον καλῶς· δι' αὐτοῦ γὰρ πᾶσαι αἱ
ἁμαρτίαι σου συγχωρηθήσονταί σοι." Καὶ ἀναστᾶσα ἡ
Ἀγλαΐς συντόμως, καὶ παραλαβοῦσα κληρικοὺς <καὶ ἄν-
δρας> εὐλαβεῖς, μετὰ λιτῆς καὶ κηρῶν καὶ θυμιαμάτων,
ὑπήντησε τῷ ἁγίῳ λειψάνῳ· καὶ ἀπέθετο ὡς ἀπὸ σταδίων
πέντε τῆς πόλεως Ῥώμης, οἰκοδομήσασα οἶκον ἄξιον τῆς
ἀθλήσεως τοῦ καλλινίκου μάρτυρος, ἐν ᾧ μέχρι τῆς σήμερον δαίμονες ἀπελαύνονται, καὶ πᾶσα νόσος φυγαδεύεται,
τῇ ἐνεργείᾳ τοῦ μάρτυρος καὶ προστασίᾳ.

15 Ἡ δὲ μακαρία Ἀγλαΐς ἀπετάξατο τῷ κόσμῳ· καὶ πάντα
τὰ ὑπάρχοντα αὐτῆς διαδώσασα πτωχοῖς, καὶ εἰς μοναστήρια καὶ ξενεῶνας, ἐλευθερώσασα καὶ τὴν οἰκετίαν, μετ'
ὀλίγων κορασίων σὺν αὐτῇ ἀποταξαμένων, ἐδούλευσεν τῷ
Χριστῷ. Καὶ οὕτως ἐγένετο τιμία, ὥστε καὶ χάριν παρὰ
Θεοῦ λαβοῦσα, δαίμονας ἀπελαύνειν, καὶ παντοῖα πάθη
διὰ προσευχῆς θεραπεύειν. Ἐπιζήσασα δὲ ἡ μακαρία ἐν τῇ
ἀσκήσει ἔτη δεκατρία, ἐκοιμήθη ἐν εἰρήνῃ.

16 Οὕτως ἀγωνισάμενος ὁ καλλίνικος μάρτυς, τὸν τῆς
νίκης στέφανον ἀνεδήσατο, εἰς δόξαν τοῦ Πατρός, καὶ τοῦ
Υἱοῦ καὶ τοῦ Ἁγίου Πνεύματος, εἰς τοὺς αἰῶνας τῶν
αἰώνων, ἀμήν.

way, rejoicing and glorifying God for the death of the holy martyr.

An angel of the Lord appeared to Boniphatios's mistress, 14 saying, "Welcome as your master the man who used to be your slave, but is now our brother, and lay him well to rest; for through him, all your sins will be forgiven." Aglaïs got up quickly, took clerics and *devout men* with her with candles and censers, and went to meet the holy relic. She buried it about five stades outside the city of Rome, where she built a church worthy of the contest of the all-victorious martyr; there, down to this very day, demons are driven away and every illness is banished by the power and protection of the martyr.

As for the blessed Aglaïs, she renounced the world. After 15 giving away all her possessions to the poor, to monasteries and hostels, and after freeing her servants, she served Christ together with a few of her maidens. And she became so saintly, that she even received from God the gift of driving away demons, and curing all sorts of illnesses, through prayer. The blessed woman lived on in ascetic discipline another thirteen years, and died in peace.

Having fought in this way, the all-victorious martyr Bo- 16 niphatios was crowned with the crown of victory to the glory of the Father and the Son and the Holy Spirit, unto the ages of ages, amen.

LIFE OF THE MAN OF GOD, ALEXIOS

Βίος καὶ πολιτεία τοῦ Ἀνθρώπου τοῦ Θεοῦ {Ἀλεξίου}

Ἐγένετο ἀνὴρ εὐσεβὴς ἐν τῇ Ῥώμῃ, ὀνόματι Εὐφημιανός, ἐπὶ Ὀνορίου καὶ Ἀρκαδίου τῶν θειοτάτων βασιλέων Ῥώμης, μέγας γενάμενος τῆς συγκλήτου· ὑπῆρχον δὲ αὐτῷ, τρισχίλιοι παῖδες, χρυσόζωνοι καὶ σηρικοφόροι. Οὐκ ἦν δὲ αὐτοῖς τέκνον, καθ᾽ ὅτι ἡ γυνὴ αὐτοῦ ἄτεκνος ἦν.

2   Οὗτος εὐσεβὴς ὑπάρχων, καὶ τὰς ἐντολὰς ποιούμενος τοῦ Θεοῦ, ὁ τοιοῦτος ἄνθρωπος, νηστεύων καθ᾽ ἑκάστην ἡμέραν, ἕως ὥρας ἐννάτης. Καὶ τρεῖς τράπεζαι ἐτίθεντο εἰς τὸν οἶκον αὐτοῦ, ὑπὲρ ὀρφανῶν καὶ χηρῶν, ξένων καὶ παροδιτῶν, νοσούντων καὶ πτωχῶν. Αὐτὸς δέ, τὴν ἐννάτην ὥραν, μετὰ ξένων καὶ μοναχῶν, ἤσθιεν τὸν ἄρτον αὐτοῦ. Καὶ καθ᾽ ὅτι προήρχετο τὴν ἐντολὴν αὐτοῦ, προέπεμπεν ἔμπροσθεν αὐτοῦ λέγων, ὅτι: "Οὐκ εἰμὶ ἄξιος περιπατεῖν ἐν τῇ γῇ τοῦ Θεοῦ."

3   Ἡ δὲ σύμβιος αὐτοῦ, ὀνόματι Ἀγλαΐς, γυνὴ φοβουμένη τὸν Θεόν, καθ᾽ ἑκάστην ἡμέραν τὰς ἐντολὰς ἐποίει, παρακαλοῦσα καὶ λέγουσα, "Μνήσθητί μου, Κύριε, τῆς ἀναξίας δούλης σου καὶ δώρησαί μοι σπέρμα ἀνδρός, ὅπως γένηταί μοι εἰς γηροβόσκην καὶ εἰς παραμύθιον τῆς ψυχῆς μου." Καὶ ἐμνήσθη αὐτῆς ὁ Θεός, κατὰ τὰς ἐντολὰς αὐτῆς· καὶ

Life and conduct of the Man of God, Alexios

At the time of the most divine emperors of Rome Honorius and Arcadius, there was a pious man in Rome by the name of Euphemianos, who had become an important member of the senate; he possessed three thousand slaves, gold girdled and silk wearing. But he and his wife had no children, since she was childless.

This great man was pious, following God's command- 2 ments, fasting each day until the ninth hour. And he would have three tables set in his house, one for the orphans and the widows, one for the foreigners and the travelers, and another for the sick and the poor. At the ninth hour, he himself would sit with the foreigners and the monks and eat his bread. And as he began his almsgiving, he would precede it by first saying, "I am unworthy to walk on God's land."

His spouse, a God-fearing woman who was named Aglaïs, 3 would give alms every day, beseeching and saying, "Remember *me, Lord, your* unworthy *servant,* and grant me a man's *offspring* so that he may take care of me in my old age and be my soul's consolation." And God remembered her, because

συνέλαβεν κατὰ τὸν καιρὸν ἐκεῖνον, καὶ ἔτεκεν υἱόν, καὶ ηὐφράνθη ὁ ἄνθρωπος καὶ ἡ σύμβιος αὐτοῦ ἐπὶ τῷ Θεῷ.

4 Ὅτε οὖν ἐγένετο τὸ νήπιον ἐν καιρῷ διδαχῆς, δέδωκαν αὐτὸν εἰς τὴν προπαιδείαν τῆς γραμματικῆς ἐπιστήμης, καὶ τῆς ἐκκλησιαστικῆς ἱστορίας, καὶ τῆς ῥητορικῆς ἁψάμενον, ὥστε πάνσοφον ἐγένετο τὸ παιδίον.

5 Καὶ ὡς ἐγένετο τῆς ἐννόμου ἡλικίας, εἶπεν Εὐφημιανὸς πρὸς τὴν σύμβιον αὐτοῦ, "Ποιήσωμεν γάμους τῷ υἱῷ ἡμῶν." Καὶ ηὐφράνθη ἡ γυνὴ ἐπὶ τῷ ῥήματι τοῦ ἀνδρός· καὶ δραμοῦσα ἔπεσεν ἐπὶ τοὺς πόδας αὐτοῦ καὶ εἶπεν, "Στήσῃ ὁ Θεὸς τὸν λόγον ὃν ἐλάλησας, κύριέ μου· καὶ ποιήσωμεν γάμους τῷ φιλτοτάτῳ ἡμῶν τέκνῳ, ἵνα ἴδω καὶ χαρῶ, καὶ εὐφρανθῇ ἡ ψυχή μου, καὶ ἐπικυρώσω πτωχῶν καὶ πενήτων ἐντολάς."

6 Καὶ ὡρμάσαντο αὐτῷ ἀπὸ αἵματος καὶ γένους βασιλικοῦ κόρην. Καὶ δύσαντες θάλαμον, ἐστεφάνωσαν αὐτοὺς ἐν τῷ ναῷ τοῦ Ἁγίου Βονιφατίου ὑπὸ τιμίων ἱερέων. Καὶ ἤγαγον αὐτοὺς εἰς τὸν θάλαμον· καὶ ἐποίησαν πᾶσαν τὴν ἡμέραν, εὐφραινόμενοι ἕως ἑσπέρας. Καὶ εἶπεν Εὐφημιανὸς πρὸς τὸν υἱὸν αὐτοῦ, "Εἴσελθε, τέκνον, καὶ ἰδὲ τὴν νύμφην σου, καὶ γνώρισον τὴν σύμβιόν σου." Καὶ εἰσελθὼν εἰς τὸν θάλαμον, ηὗρεν τὴν νύμφην καθεζομένην ἐπὶ τοῦ δίφρου· καὶ ἐπάρας τὸ δακτυλίδιον τὸ χρυσοῦν καὶ τὴν ῥένδαν ἐνετύλιξεν εἰς πράνδιον καὶ πορφυροῦν πασμάνην· καὶ εἶπεν αὐτῇ, "Προσλαβοῦσα ταῦτα φύλαξον, καὶ ἔσται ὁ Θεὸς ἀναμέσον ἐμοῦ καὶ σοῦ· καὶ τὰ μυστήρια ἡμῶν τινα μὴ φθέγξῃ."

7 Καὶ ἐξῆλθεν ἐκ τοῦ θαλάμου, καὶ ἀπῆλθεν εἰς τὸν

of her almsgiving; and she conceived a child at that time, and she bore a son, and the man and his wife rejoiced in God.

When the infant reached school age, they sent him for 4 his primary instruction in the knowledge of grammar and ecclesiastical education; the child also engaged with rhetoric, so that he became very wise.

And when the boy reached the legal marital age, Euphe- 5 mianos said to his wife, "Let us arrange our son's marriage." And his wife rejoiced because of her husband's words; and she ran and fell at his feet, and said, "May God make the words you've spoken come true, my lord; and let us arrange the marriage of our dearest child, so that I may see this and be happy, and my soul may rejoice, and I shall endorse it with alms to the poor and the needy."

They thus betrothed him to a girl of royal blood and lin- 6 eage. And they prepared a wedding chamber, and had them crowned by holy priests in the church of Saint Boniphatios. And they led them into the chamber, and spent all day rejoicing until the evening. Then Euphemianos said to his son, "Go inside, my child, and see your bride, and come to know your consort." So he went inside the chamber and found his bride sitting on the couch; and he took off the golden ring and his belt and wrapped them in a band and a purple headscarf; and he said to her, "Take these and keep them, and *God* will be *between me and you;* and do not tell anyone about our secret."

And he left the chamber and went to his own bedroom, 7

κοιτῶνα αὐτοῦ· καὶ λαβὼν ἐκ τοῦ ἰδίου πλούτου, κατέλιπεν τὴν Ῥώμην. Καὶ κατελθὼν εἰς τὸ Καπετόλιον, ηὗρεν σκάφος, καὶ κατέλαβεν μαγνίαν πόλιν Λαοδικείας Συρίας. Καὶ ἐξελθόντος αὐτοῦ ἐκ τοῦ πλοίου, ὑπήντησεν αὐτῷ ὀνηλάτης καὶ συνοδοιπόρος γέγονεν μετ᾽ αὐτοῦ, μέχρις ἂν κατέλαβεν Ἔδεσσαν τὴν Μεσοποταμίαν, ἔνθα ἡ ἀχειροποίητος κεῖται τοῦ Δεσποτικοῦ χαρακτῆρος τοῦ Κυρίου ἡμῶν Ἰησοῦ Χριστοῦ ἣν δέδωκεν Ἀβάρῳ ἐν τῇ ζωῇ αὐτοῦ.

8 Καὶ εἰσελθὼν ἐν τῇ πόλει, ἐπώλησεν πάντα τὰ ὑπάρχοντα αὐτοῦ, καὶ ἔδωκεν πτωχοῖς· καὶ ἐνεδύσατο ἱμάτια πενιχρά, καὶ ὡς προσαίτης, ἐκαθίζετο εἰς τὸν νάρθηκα τοῦ ναοῦ τῆς Δεσποίνης ἡμῶν τῆς ἁγίας Θεοτόκου. Καὶ ἡρετίσατο ἀπὸ Κυριακῆς εἰς Κυριακήν, μεταλαμβάνων τῶν θείων καὶ ἀχράντων μυστηρίων. Καὶ τὸ πρόσωπον αὐτοῦ, μέσον τῶν βραχιόνων αὐτοῦ· ἡ δὲ καρδία αὐτοῦ ἦν πρὸς τὸν Θεόν. Καὶ εἴ τι ἐὰν ἐλάμβανεν ἐντολήν, ἐδίδει εἰς τὰ γηροκομία.

9 Ἐγένετο δὲ πολλὴ ζήτησις ἐν τῇ Ῥώμῃ, καὶ οὐχ ηὕρισκον αὐτόν. Καὶ ἀπέστειλεν ὁ πατὴρ αὐτοῦ τοὺς τρισχιλίους παῖδας, καὶ οὐχ εὕρισκον αὐτόν· ὥστε καταλαβόντες Ἔδεσσαν τὴν Μεσοποταμίαν, ἔδωκαν αὐτῷ ἐντολήν, μὴ γνωρίσαντες αὐτὸν τίς ἐστιν. Καὶ θεωρήσας αὐτοὺς καὶ γνωρίσας, ἐδόξαζεν τὸν Θεὸν λέγων, "Εὐχαριστῶ σοι, Κύριε, ὅτι κατηξίωσάς με λαβεῖν ἐντολὴν ἐκ τῶν οἰκιακῶν μου παίδων, διὰ τὸ ὄνομά σου, Κύριε." Καὶ ἐπανελθόντες οἱ παῖδες ἐν τῇ Ῥώμῃ, ἀπήγγειλαν τῷ κυρίῳ αὐτῶν, ὅτι· "Οὐχ ηὕραμεν αὐτόν."

10 Ἡ δὲ μήτηρ αὐτοῦ ἀπὸ τῆς ἡμέρας τοῦ γάμου, ὅτε ἐζήτουν αὐτὸν καὶ οὐχ εὗρον, ἀπελθοῦσα εἰς τὸν οἶκον

and taking some money from his own fortune, left Rome. And he went down to the Capitolium, found a vessel, and arrived at the great city of Laodicea in Syria. And when he disembarked from the boat, a donkey driver met him and traveled with him until he reached Edessa in Mesopotamia, where the *acheiropoietos* icon of the face of our Master and Lord Jesus Christ is kept, the one he gave to Abgar during his lifetime.

And when he entered the city, he sold all his belongings, 8 and gave them to the poor; and he put on some cheap clothes, and sat as a beggar in the narthex of the church of our Lady the holy Mother of God. He chose to partake only in the divine and holy mysteries from one Sunday to the next. And his face was hidden between his arms, but his heart was turned to God. And whatever alms he received he gave to the almshouses.

There was a great search in Rome, but they could not find 9 him. His father sent his three thousand slaves to look for him, and they could not find him. They even reached Edessa in Mesopotamia, and gave him alms without recognizing who he was. And looking at them and recognizing them, he glorified God, saying, "Thank you, Lord, that you made me worthy to receive alms from my own household slaves on account of your name, Lord." And the slaves returned to Rome and announced to their master, "We didn't find him."

From the day of the wedding, when they looked for her 10 son but could not find him, his mother went to her own

29

αὐτῆς, ἤνοιξεν θυρίδα πρὸς ταφὴν αὐτῆς. Καὶ προσέπεσεν πρὸς τὴν θυρίδα, καὶ προσέθετο *σάκκον καὶ σποδὸν* ἐπὶ τῆς γῆς· καὶ ἦν ἐκεῖ ῥιγμένη ἐπὶ πρόσωπον δεομένη καὶ προσ-ευχομένη τῷ Θεῷ λέγουσα, ὅτι: "Οὐ μὴ ἀναστῶ ἐκ τοῦ ἐδάφους τούτου, ἕως ἂν μάθω περὶ τοῦ υἱοῦ μου τοῦ μονογενοῦς τὸ τί γέγονεν." Ὁ δὲ πατὴρ αὐτοῦ ἀπὸ τῆς ἡμέρας ἧς ἐγεννήθη ὁ υἱὸς αὐτοῦ, εἰς κοίτην μετὰ τῆς ἰδίας γυναικὸς οὐκ ἐκοιμήθη, παρακαλῶν αὐτὴν καὶ λέ-γων, ὅτι: "Ἐσόμεθα ἰδιάζοντες καὶ ἐγκρατευόμενοι, ὅπως ὁ Θεὸς χαρίσεται ἡμῖν ὃν δέδωκεν παῖδα."

11 Τοῦ δὲ παιδὸς ποιήσαντος ἔτη ιζ´ εἰς τὸν νάρθηκα τῆς Δεσποίνης ἡμῶν τῆς ἁγίας Θεοτόκου, *εὐηρέστησεν Κυρίῳ τῷ Θεῷ.* Καὶ ἰδοὺ ἡ εἰκὼν τῆς Θεοτόκου εἶπεν πρὸς τὸν προσμονάριον, "Εἰσάγαγε τὸν Ἄνθρωπον τοῦ Θεοῦ ὅτι ἄξιός ἐστιν τῆς βασιλείας τῶν οὐρανῶν· καὶ *ὀσμὴ εὐωδίας* ἡ προσευχὴ αὐτοῦ· καὶ ὡς διάδημα βασιλέως, οὕτως ἀναπέπαυται τὸ Πνεῦμα τὸ Ἅγιον ἐπ᾽ αὐτόν· καὶ *ὡς ἥλιος διεκλάμπων τῷ κόσμῳ,* οὕτως διέλαμψεν ἡ πολιτεία αὐτοῦ ἐνώπιον τῶν ἀγγέλων." Καὶ ἐξέρχεται ὁ προσμονάριος ζητῶν τὸν τοιοῦτον ἅγιον, καὶ οὐχ εὕρισκεν αὐτόν. Καὶ εἰσέρχεται παρακαλῶν καὶ δεόμενος τῇ Θεοτόκῳ, ὅπως ἀποκαλύψῃ αὐτῷ τὸν τοιοῦτον Ἄνθρωπον τοῦ Θεοῦ. Καὶ ἀπεκάλυψεν αὐτῷ, ὅτι ὁ πτωχὸς ὁ καθήμενος πρὸς τὴν θύραν ἐκεῖνός ἐστιν ὁ Ἄνθρωπος τοῦ Θεοῦ. Καὶ ἐπελάβετο τῆς χειρὸς αὐτοῦ, καὶ εἰσήγαγεν αὐτὸν <εἰς τὸν ναόν>.

12 Ὅτε οὖν ἐγνωρίσθη τοῖς ἀνθρώποις, ἀπέδρασεν ἀπὸ τῆς Ἐδεσσέων πόλεως. Καὶ κατελθὼν εἰς Λαοδίκειαν,

room and made an opening for her burial. And she prostrated herself in that opening and in addition she put *sackcloth and ashes* on the ground; and she flung herself face down there, beseeching and praying to God with these words: "I shall not get up from this ground, until I find out what happened to my only begotten son." The father who had not slept with his own wife since the day his son was born, would ask her and say, "Let us keep separate quarters and remain chaste, so that God will return to us the child he has given us."

Meanwhile, their son spent seventeen years in the narthex of the church of our Lady the holy Mother of God, and *pleased the Lord* God. And, lo and behold, the icon of the Mother of God said to the sacristan, "Bring inside the Man of God, since he is worthy of the kingdom of heaven; and his prayer is *an odor of fragrance;* and the Holy Spirit rests on him like a crown on a king; and just *like the sun shining on* the world, his life has shone in front of the angels." So the sacristan went out looking for this great saint, but did not find him. And he thus went back inside asking and begging the Mother of God to reveal this great Man of God to him. And she did reveal to him that it was the beggar sitting by the gate who was the Man of God. And the sacristan took him by the hand and brought him into the church. 11

Since, then, he became known to people, he fled from the city of Edessa. And he went down to Laodicea, boarded a 12

εἰσῆλθεν εἰς πλοῖον, καὶ ἠβουλήθη περᾶσαι ἐν Ταρσῷ τῆς Κιλικίας λέγων, ὅτι· "Ἀπέρχομαι εἰς τὸν οἶκον τοῦ Ἁγίου Παύλου εἰς Ταρσόν, καθ᾽ ὅτι ἀγνώριστός εἰμι τῶν ἐκεῖ." Καὶ ἡρπάγη τὸ πλοῖον βιαίου ἀνέμου, καὶ ἔπλευσεν ἐν Ῥώμῃ.

13   Καὶ ἐξελθόντος αὐτοῦ ἐκ τοῦ πλοίου εἶπεν, "Ζῇ Κύριος ὁ Θεός μου! ὅτι οὐ μὴ ἐπιβαρὴς γένωμαι οὐδενὸς ἑτέρου, ἀλλ᾽ εἰς τὸν οἶκον τοῦ πατρός μου εἰσέρχομαι, καθ᾽ ὅτι ἀγνώριστός εἰμι τῶν ἐκεῖ." Καὶ ὑπήντησεν αὐτῷ ὁ πατὴρ αὐτοῦ, μίσσας ἔχων ἐκ τοῦ θείου παλατίου, ἐπανήκοντα μετὰ τοῦ ὀψικίου αὐτοῦ. Καὶ προσεκύνησεν αὐτὸν λέγων, "Δοῦλε Κυρίου, ποίησον ἐντολὴν εἰς ἐμὲ τὸν πτωχὸν καὶ πένητα, καὶ δέξαι με εἰς τὸν οἶκόν σου, καὶ ἐκ τῶν ψιχίων τῶν πιπτόντων ἐκ τῆς τραπέζης σου μετὰ τῶν οἰκιακῶν σου παίδων ἐμπλησθήσομαι. Καὶ ὁ Θεὸς ὁ ἅγιος εὐλογήσει τοὺς χρόνους σου, καὶ δῴη σοι τὴν βασιλείαν τῶν οὐρανῶν· καὶ οὓς ἔχεις ἐπὶ ξένης, ὁ Θεὸς εὐλογήσει, καὶ ἐμπλήσει τῆς ἐλπίδος αὐτοῦ."

14   Μᾶλλον ἀκούσας ὁ πατὴρ αὐτοῦ περὶ τῶν ξένων, θερμότερος ἐγένετο τοῦ ὑποδέξασθαι αὐτὸν μνημονεύσας τοῦ μονογενοῦς αὐτοῦ υἱοῦ· καὶ λαβὼν αὐτὸν εἰς τὸν οἶκον αὐτοῦ, εἶπεν πρὸς τοὺς οἰκιακοὺς αὐτοῦ παῖδας, "Τίς ἐξ ὑμῶν θέλει δουλεῦσαι αὐτῷ; Καὶ (ζῇ Κύριος ὁ Θεός!) ἐλεύθερός ἐστιν, καὶ ἐκ τοῦ οἴκου μου λήψεται κληρονομίαν. Ἀλλ᾽ εἰς τὸν νάρθηκα τῆς εἰσόδου μου, ποιήσατε αὐτῷ χαλάδριον, ἵνα εἰσερχομένου μου καὶ ἐξερχομένου μου θεωρῶ αὐτόν. Μὴ θλίψετε αὐτὸν ἔν τινι, <καὶ> ἐκ τῆς τραπέζης μου ἐσθιέτω." Καὶ ἦν οὕτως διὰ παντός.

boat, and wanted to cross to Tarsos in Cilicia, saying, "I shall go to the temple of Saint Paul in Tarsos, since no one knows me there." But the ship was snatched by a violent wind, and sailed to Rome.

He disembarked from the ship and said, "*As the Lord my God lives!* I shall not become a burden to anyone else; rather, I shall go into my father's home, since no one will recognize me there." And his own father, who had been dismissed from the sacred palace and was thus returning home with his entourage, met him. He bowed before his father and said, "Servant of the Lord, give alms to me, the poor beggar, and receive me in your home, and I shall receive my fill with your household slaves from *the crumbs that fall* from your *table*. And God the holy one will bless your years, and grant you the kingdom of heaven; as for those from your family who are abroad, God will bless them too, and fill them with his hope." 13

His father, especially when he heard about persons abroad, became more eager to receive him, being reminded of his own only begotten son; so he took him into his own home, and said to his household slaves, "Who among you wants to serve him? And *(as the Lord my God lives!)* he is to be a free man, and he will receive an inheritance from my household. Place a pallet for him in the entrance hall, so that I may see him whenever I come in and out. Don't hurt him in any way, and give him food to eat from my table." And so it was for a long time. 14

15   Ἡ δὲ μήτηρ αὐτοῦ ἔχουσα τὴν θλίψιν καὶ τὸ πένθος, εἰς τὸν κοιτῶνα αὐτῆς προσεκαρτέρει. Ἡ δὲ νύμφη ἑστῶσα πρὸς τὴν πενθερὰν ἔλεγεν, ὅτι: "Οὐ μὴ ἀναχωρήσω ἔνθεν ἐν τῇ ζωῇ μου, ἀλλὰ τὴν τρυγόνα μιμοῦμαι τὴν φιλέρημον καὶ μόνανδρον, καθ' ὅτι ἐὰν κυνηγηθῇ ὁ ὁμόζυγος αὐτῆς, μένει κελαδοῦσα καὶ δονοῦσα τὰς κοιλάδας, καὶ ζητοῦσα τὸν ἑαυτῆς ἄνδρα. Κἀγὼ προσκαρτερήσω καὶ ἐκδέξομαι, ἕως ἂν μάθω περὶ τοῦ ὁμοζύγου μου τὸ τί γέγονεν, καθ' ὅτι τὴν τιμίαν καὶ ἐνάρετον πολιτείαν κέκτηται."

16   Οἱ δὲ παῖδες ἡνίκα ἑσπέρας σιγὴ ἐγένετο, ἔθλιβον αὐτὸν καὶ ἐπείραζον· ἕτεροι δὲ τὸν πίνακα πλύνοντες, εἰς τὴν κεφαλὴν αὐτοῦ ἐξέχυνον. Καὶ ἰδὼν ὁ Ἄνθρωπος τοῦ Θεοῦ ὅτι ἐκ διαβολικῆς ἐνεργείας καὶ πόλεμος τοῦ μισοκάλου ἐστίν, μετὰ χαρᾶς καὶ προθυμίας καὶ ὑπομονῆς ἐδέχετο. Καὶ ἐποίησεν ἔτη ιζ΄ εἰς τὸν οἶκον τὸν γονικὸν αὐτοῦ, μὴ γνωριζόμενος τὸ τίς ἐστιν.

17   Καὶ ὅτε ἔφθασεν ὁ καιρὸς τοῦ ἐξελθεῖν αὐτὸν ἐκ τοῦ σώματος, ἡνίκα ηὐδόκησεν ὁ Κύριος παραλαβεῖν τὴν παρακαταθήκην αὐτοῦ ἐξ αὐτοῦ, εἶπεν πρὸς τὸν παῖδα τὸν ὑπηρετοῦντα αὐτῷ, "Ἀδελφέ, φέρε μοι χάρτην, καὶ μέλαν, καὶ κάλαμον." Καὶ ἔγραψεν πάντα τὸν βίον αὐτοῦ, καὶ τὰ μυστήρια ἃ εἶχεν μεταξὺ τοῦ πατρὸς καὶ τῆς μητρός, καὶ ἃ ἐλάλησεν τῇ νύμφῃ ἐν τῷ γάμῳ, καὶ ὡς ἀπέδωκεν αὐτοῦ τὸ δακτυλίδιον τὸ χρυσοῦν, καὶ τὴν ῥένδαν ἐντετυλιγμένην εἰς πράνδιον καὶ πορφυροῦν πασμάνην· καὶ πάντα τὸν βίον αὐτοῦ ἔγραψεν, ὅπως γνωρίσωσιν ὅτι οὗτός ἐστιν ὁ υἱὸς αὐτῶν.

Meanwhile, his mother, afflicted with sorrow and be- 15
reavement, waited patiently in her own bedroom. As for his
bride, she stood near her mother-in-law and would say, "I
shall never, ever leave this spot while I am alive, but rather I
will imitate the turtledove who is fond of solitude and has
only a single mate; and if ever her life partner is captured,
she remains singing, with her voice reverberating in the valleys, seeking her spouse. So too I shall remain patient and
keep waiting, until I find out what happened to my bride-
groom, since he has acquired the venerable and virtuous
life."

Some slaves, however, when it was quiet at night, would 16
abuse and provoke him; others, while washing a dish, would
pour it out on his head. And the Man of God, realizing that
all this derived from the devil's activity and was war waged
by the one who hates the good, accepted the abuse with joy
and eagerness and patience. He thus spent seventeen years
in the household of his parents, without anyone recognizing
who he was.

And when the time came for him to depart his body, 17
when the Lord decided to take back from him that with
which he had entrusted him, he said to the slave who was
serving him, "Brother, bring me paper, ink, and a pen." And
he wrote down everything about his life, and the secrets
from his father and mother, and the words he said to his
bride at the wedding, and how he gave her back his golden
ring and his belt, wrapped in a band and a purple headscarf;
and he wrote down everything about his life, so that they
would recognize that he was their son.

18   Καὶ ἐγένετο ἐν μιᾷ τῶν ἡμερῶν Κυριακῆς οὔσης, μετὰ τὴν θείαν καὶ ἄχραντον λειτουργίαν καὶ μετὰ τὸ μεταλαβεῖν τὸν λαόν, ἔτι ὄντος τοῦ ἀρχιεπισκόπου Μαρκιανοῦ καὶ τῶν θειοτάτων βασιλέων Ῥώμης, φωνὴ ἠκούσθη ἀόρατος, ἐκ τοῦ ἁγίου θυσιαστηρίου λέγουσα, "*Δεῦτε πάντες πρὸς μὲ οἱ κεκοπιακότες καὶ πεφορτισμένοι, κἀγὼ ἀναπαύσω ὑμᾶς.*" Ἔκστασις δὲ καὶ φόβος ἔλαβεν πάντας· *καὶ πεσόντες ἐπὶ πρόσωπον,* τὸ "Κύριε ἐλέησον" ἔλεγον. Δεύτερον δὲ φωνὴ ἐπὶ τὸ αὐτὸ λέγουσα, "Ζητήσατε τὸν Ἄνθρωπον τοῦ Θεοῦ, καὶ εὔξηται τῇ Ῥώμῃ. Καὶ διαφαυσάσης Παρασκευῆς, *ἐξῆλθεν ἐκ τοῦ σώματος* καὶ παρέλαβεν Κύριος, *τὴν παρα-καταθήκην αὐτοῦ ἐξ αὐτοῦ.*"

19   Τῇ δὲ Πέμπτῃ ἑσπέρας, ἐπορεύθησαν ἅπαντες εἰς τὴν ἐκκλησίαν τοῦ ἀποκαλυφθῆναι αὐτοῖς τὸν τοιοῦτον ἅγιον. Καὶ ἐγένετο φωνὴ λέγουσα, "Εἰς τὸν οἶκον Εὐφημιανοῦ ἐστιν τὸ λείψανον." Καὶ στραφέντες πρὸς Εὐφημιανὸν λέγουσιν αὐτῷ, "Εἰς τὸν οἶκόν σου τοιαύτην χάριν ἔχεις, καὶ ἡμῖν οὐκ ἀπεκάλυψας αὐτήν;" Ὁ δὲ Εὐφημιανὸς εἶπεν πρὸς τοὺς θειοτάτους βασιλεῖς, "*Ζῇ Κύριος ὁ Θεός μου,* οὐ γιγνώσκω." Καὶ ταχέως προσκαλεσάμενος τὸν πρόοικον τῶν παίδων αὐτοῦ, εἶπεν πρὸς αὐτόν, "Γινώσκεις τινὰ ἐκ τῶν συντρόφων σου τοιαύτην χάριν ἔχοντα;" Ἔφη ὁ παῖς, "*Ζῇ Κύριος ὁ Θεός μου,* οὐ γινώσκω· πάντες γὰρ ἀκαμπεῖς καὶ ἐξοδιάριοι εἰσίν." Τότε κελεύουσιν οἱ θειότατοι βασιλεῖς εἰς τὸν οἶκον Εὐφημιανοῦ ἀπελθεῖν καὶ ἐπιζητῆσαι τὸν Ἄν-θρωπον τοῦ Θεοῦ.

20   Καὶ κελεύει λοιπὸν Εὐφημιανὸς πρὸς τοὺς οἰκιακοὺς αὐτοῦ παῖδας, σκάμνα καὶ θρόνους ποιήσασθαι πρὸς

And one day, on a Sunday, after the divine and immacu-   18
late liturgy, and after the people had received holy communion, while the archbishop Markianos and the most divine
emperors of Rome were present, it happened that a voice
from an invisible source, from the direction of the altar, was
heard saying, "*Come to me, all who* have labored *and are heavy
laden, and I will give you rest.*" Astonishment and fear overtook everyone; and they *fell face down* and were saying,
"Lord, have mercy." A second time a voice was heard in the
same way, saying, "Look for the Man of God, and he may
pray for Rome. By Friday at dawn, he will have departed
from his body and the Lord will have received back from
him that with which he had entrusted him."

On Thursday evening, everyone went to the church for   19
this saint to be revealed to them. And a voice came, saying,
"The relic is in the house of Euphemianos." And they turned
to Euphemianos and said to him, "You have such a blessing
in your house, and you have not revealed this to us?" Euphemianos said to the most divine emperors, "*As the Lord my
God lives,* I don't know." Straightaway he summoned the
foreman of his slaves and said to him, "Do you know anyone
in your cohort who possesses such grace?" The slave said,
"*As the Lord my God lives,* I don't think so; all of them are ob-
stinate and useless." Then, the most divine emperors gave
orders to go to Euphemianos's house and look for the Man
of God.

And so Euphemianos ordered his house slaves to prepare   20
benches and chairs for the presentation, and to welcome

κατάστασιν, καὶ μετὰ λαμπάδων φαινουσῶν καὶ εὐωδίας θυμιαμάτων δέξασθαι αὐτούς. Καὶ ἀνελθόντων ἁπάντων, σιγὴ πολλὴ ἐγένετο. Ἡ δὲ μήτηρ αὐτοῦ ἁπλώσασα βαμβάκινα σάβανα ἐπὶ τῇ θυρίδι αὐτῆς, εἶπεν, "Τίς ἡ ταραχὴ καὶ ὁ θόρυβος καὶ τὰ λεγόμενα;" Ἡ δὲ νύμφη ἑστῶσα ἐν τῷ σολαρίῳ, ἐθεώρει πάντας, τὸ τίς ἐστιν ἡ κίνησις ἡ λεγομένη. Ὁ δὲ ὑπηρέτης τοῦ Ἀνθρώπου τοῦ Θεοῦ εἶπεν πρὸς τὸν δεσπότην αὐτοῦ, "Κύριέ μου, μὴ οὗτός ἐστιν ὁ Ἄνθρωπος τοῦ Θεοῦ ὁ πτωχὸς ὃν δέδωκάς μοι; Μεγάλα γὰρ καὶ πανάριστα αὐτοῦ ἔργα ἐθεώρησα. Ἀπὸ Κυριακῆς εἰς Κυριακὴν μεταλαμβάνων τῶν θείων καὶ ἀχράντων τοῦ Θεοῦ μυστηρίων, καὶ δύο οὑγκίαι ἄρτου ἤσθιεν, καὶ δύο οὑγκίαι ὕδατος ἦν ὁ πότος αὐτοῦ, ἦν δὲ ἐγκρατευόμενος τὴν ἑβδομάδα. Καὶ πάντα τὸν χρόνον αὐτοῦ, ἄϋπνος ἐποίει τὰς νύκτας. Ἀλλὰ καί τινες τῶν παίδων ἔθλιβον καὶ ἐπείραζον αὐτόν· αὐτὸς δὲ μετὰ χαρᾶς καὶ προθυμίας καὶ ὑπομονῆς ἐδέχετο πάντα."

21 Καὶ εὐθέως ὁ Εὐφημιανὸς σπεύσας, ἔδραμεν πρὸς αὐτόν· καὶ συνετύγχανεν παρεστὼς αὐτῷ. Ἐν αὐτῷ δὲ οὐκ ἦν φωνὴ οὔτε ἀκρόασις· καὶ ἀπεκάλυψεν αὐτοῦ τὸ πρόσωπον, καὶ εἶδεν αὐτὸ λάμπον ὡς ἀγγέλου, καὶ ὅτι χαρτίον ἐκράτει ἐν τῇ χειρὶ αὐτοῦ, καὶ οὐκ ἐπεδίδει αὐτῷ. Ὁ δὲ Εὐφημιανὸς εἰσελθὼν πρὸς τοὺς θειοτάτους βασιλεῖς, εἶπεν πρὸς αὐτούς, "Ὃν ζητοῦμεν εὕραμεν." Καὶ λοιπὸν ἀφηγεῖτο τὰ πρὸ ἐτῶν ιζ´, καὶ τὰ ἑξῆς γινόμενα, καὶ ὅτι "Ἐτελειώθη, καὶ χαρτίον κατέχει ἐν τῇ χειρὶ αὐτοῦ, καὶ οὐκ ἐπιδίδει ἡμῖν τὸ χαρτίον."

22 Τότε κελεύουσιν οἱ θειότατοι βασιλεῖς, <κλίνην στρω-

them with lit candles and the fragrance of incense. And everyone went up to the house, and it became very quiet. The mother, who had spread linen cloths on the opening she had made, said, "What's all this commotion and noise and what is being said?" The bride, who was standing on the balcony, looked at everyone to see what the commotion was that she had mentioned. As for the servant of the Man of God, he said to his master, "My lord, isn't the Man of God the beggar whom you entrusted to me? For I witnessed him performing great and perfect deeds. From one Sunday to the next, he would partake in the divine and holy mysteries, eat two ounces of bread, and drink two ounces of water, and then he would fast during the week. And all the time he stayed awake during the night. And on top of that, some of the slaves would abuse and provoke him; yet he accepted everything with joy and eagerness and patience."

Immediately, Euphemianos rushed to the Man of God; 21 and, standing beside him, he began to talk to him. But there was *neither sound* nor *hearing* in the man; and Euphemianos uncovered *his face* and saw it shining *like that of an angel,* and he saw that he was holding a paper in his hand, but would not give it to him. Euphemianos went to the most divine emperors and said to them, "We have found the man for whom we were looking." And then he recounted what had happened seventeen years ago, as well as what had happened since; and he said, "He has died and is holding a paper in his hand, and he will not give the paper to me."

Then the most divine emperors gave orders that a bier 22

θῆναι καὶ τεθῆναι τὸ τίμιον λείψανον ἐπ᾽ αὐτῆς. Καὶ ἀνέστησαν οἱ θειότατοι βασιλεῖς>, καὶ ὁ ἀρχιεπίσκοπος, καὶ ὁ Εὐφημιανὸς καὶ πᾶσα ἡ σύγκλητος· καὶ λέγουσιν οἱ βασιλεῖς πρὸς τὸν Ἄνθρωπον τοῦ Θεοῦ, "Κἂν ἁμαρτωλοί ἐσμεν, βασιλεῖς ἐσμεν, καὶ αὐτὸς πατὴρ τῆς οἰκουμένης ὑπάρχεις. Ἐπίδος ἡμῖν τὸ χαρτίον! Ἴδωμεν τί ἐστι ἐν σοὶ γεγραμμένον!" Τότε ἐπέδωκεν αὐτοῖς τὸ χαρτίον· καὶ λαβόντες δέδωκαν αὐτὸ Ἀετίῳ τῷ χαρτουλαρίῳ τῆς ἁγιωτάτης ἐκκλησίας. Καὶ ἐκάθισαν ἅπαντες—οἵ τε βασιλεῖς καὶ ὁ ἀρχιεπίσκοπος καὶ ὁ Εὐφημιανός, καὶ πᾶσα ἡ σύγκλητος· καὶ ἦν πολλὴ σιωπὴ ἐν τῷ οἴκῳ· καὶ ἀνεγινώσκετο τὸ χαρτίον.

23 Καὶ ὅτε ἤκουσεν ὁ πατὴρ αὐτοῦ τῆς ἀναγνώσεως τοῦ χαρτίου, ἀνέστη ταχέως ἐκ τοῦ δίφρου, καὶ διέρρηξεν τὸν χιτῶνα αὐτοῦ, καὶ ἔκοπτεν τὰς τρίχας τῆς κεφαλῆς αὐτοῦ τὰς πολιάς, καὶ ὅλος διερρήγνυτο τρέχων καὶ σπεύδων εἰς τὸ τίμιον λείψανον λέγων, "Οἴμοι, κύριέ μου, τί μοι οὕτως ἐποίησας καὶ ἔθλιψας τὴν ψυχήν μου, καὶ στεναγμὸν ἀπέστειλας τῇ καρδίᾳ μου; Τοσαῦτα ἔτη ἔρημος ἐγενόμην, προσδοκῶν που ἀκοῦσαι τῆς φωνῆς σου, ἢ τῆς ἀκοῆς τὸ τί ἐγένου. Οἴμοι, τῷ ταπεινῷ καὶ πενιχρῷ, ὅτι τὸν μονογενῆν μου υἱὸν θεωρῶ ἐν κλίνῃ ὄντα νεκρόν, καὶ μὴ λαλοῦντα πρὸς μέ! Οἴμοι, τὴν γηροβόσκην μου! Τί λαλήσω, ἢ πῶς δώσω πένθος τῇ καρδίᾳ μου;"

24 Ἡ δὲ μήτηρ αὐτοῦ ὥσπερ λέαινα ἀπὸ ζώγρου διαρρήξασα τὴν θυρίδα, διέρρηξεν τὰ ἱμάτια αὐτῆς, καὶ λυσίκομος τὸν οὐρανὸν λοξῶς ἐβλέπετο· τοὺς ἀνθρώπους παρεκάλει (ἐπειδὴ πολυοχλία ἦν ἐν τῷ οἴκῳ), λέγουσα, "Δότε

should be set down and the holy relic placed on it. And the most divine emperors, and the archbishop, and Euphemianos, and all the senators stood up; and the emperors said to the Man of God, "Even if we are sinners, we are still emperors, and you are a saintly father of the whole inhabited world. Give us the paper! Let us see what it is that you wrote!" So he gave them the paper; and they took it and gave it to Aetios, the *chartoularios* of the most holy church. And everyone sat down—the emperors, and the archbishop, and Euphemianos, and all the senators; and it was very quiet in the house; and the paper was read aloud.

And when the father heard the recital of the text, he 23 leaped up from his seat, ripped his cloak, and began tearing the gray hair of his head; breaking down completely, he ran and rushed to the holy relic, saying, "Alas, my lord, why have you done this to me, and troubled my soul, and brought grievous distress to my heart? For so many years I was bereft, expecting to somehow hear your voice or at least a rumor about what happened to you. Alas for me, the lowly, the nobody, that I should see my only begotten son lying dead on a bier and saying nothing to me! Alas, for the care of my old age! What shall I say? How shall I express the grief in my heart?"

Like a lioness breaking down the door and escaping a 24 cage, the mother tore apart her clothes, and with her hair loose looked askance at the heavens; she asked the people there (because there was a large crowd in the house), saying,

μοι, ἄνδρες, τὸ πῶς τύχω τοῦ ποθητοῦ μου! Δότε μοι, ἄνδρες, θεωρῆσαι καὶ σπεῦσαι πρὸς τὸ τέκνον μου! Οἴμοι, δότε μοι τὸν μονογενῆν μου υἱόν! Οἴμοι, δότε μοι τὸ ἀρνίον τῆς ψυχῆς μου, τὸ ὄρνεον τῆς νοσσιᾶς μου, τὸν θήλακα τῶν μασθῶν μου!" Καὶ τὸ στῆθος τύπτουσα, ἐβόα λέγουσα φωνῇ μεγάλῃ, "Δεῦτε, σὺν ἐμοὶ θρηνήσατε, ὅτι ιζ΄ ἔτη ὢν ἐν τῇ οἰκίᾳ μου, οὐδεὶς ἐπέγνωσεν, ὅτι ὁ μονογενής μου υἱὸς ἦν, ἀλλὰ ῥαπίσματα καὶ ὕβρεις καὶ πτύσματα <ἦν> λαμβάνων ἐκ τῶν δούλων αὐτοῦ. Οἴμοι, τέκνον μου ποθητόν, φῶς τῶν ἐμῶν ὀφθαλμῶν, πῶς οὐκ ἐγνώρισά σε τοσαῦτα ἔτη ὢν ἐν τῇ οἰκίᾳ μου;" Ἐτίθη δὲ τὰς χεῖρας ἐπὶ τὸ πρόσωπον αὐτῆς, καὶ δεινῶς ἀνεστέναζεν· καὶ οἱ ὀφθαλμοὶ αὐτῆς τῶν δακρύων ἀεννάως πηγάζειν οὐκ ἐπαύοντο· καὶ ἥπλωσεν τὰς χεῖρας αὐτῆς ὡς ὄρνεον ἐκπετάζον τὰς πτέρυγας αὐτοῦ ζητοῦσα τὸ φιλτότατον αὐτῆς τέκνον: "Οἴμοι, δότε μοι τῆς καρδίας μου τὸν πόνον, τὴν ἐλπίδα τῶν βραχιόνων μου!" Καὶ καταφιλοῦσα τὸ τίμιον λείψανον, ἐβόα λέγουσα, "Οἴμοι, κύριέ μου, τί μοι οὕτως ἐποίησας, θεωρῶν με κατοδυρομένην εἰς τὸν οἶκον τὸν δουλικόν σου καὶ πατρικόν σου, καὶ οὐκ ἀπεκάλυψάς μοι σεαυτόν;" Ἡ δὲ νύμφη δραμοῦσα ἐν μελανοῖς ἐστολισμένη, ἔκλαιεν λέγουσα, "Οἴμοι, φιλέρημέ μου τρυγών, ἔρημος ἐγενάμην, σήμερον ἐφάνην χήρα, καὶ οὐκ ἔχω ποῦ θεωρεῖν ἢ τί ἐκδέξασθαι! Καὶ ἀπὸ τοῦ νῦν κλαύσομαι τὴν τετραυματισμένην μου καρδίαν." Ὁ δὲ λαὸς ἔκθαμβος γενόμενος, ἀεννάως τῶν δακρύων οὐκ ἐπαύοντο.

25   Τότε κελεύουσιν οἱ θειότατοι βασιλεῖς, προτεθῆναι τὴν κλίνην ἐν μέσῳ τῆς πόλεως, καὶ ἔλεγον τοῖς ὄχλοις, "Ἴδε,

"Gentlemen, let me have him whom I desire! Let me see my child, gentlemen, and hurry to him! Alas, give me my only begotten son! Alas, give me the lamb of my soul, the bird of my nest, the suckling of my breasts!" Beating her chest, she cried out and said with a loud voice, "Come, mourn with me, because for seventeen years he was in my house and no one recognized that he was my only begotten son; instead, he was receiving blows and curses, and was spat on by his own slaves. Alas, my beloved child, light of my eyes, how did I not recognize you all these years that you were in my house?" She put her hands to her face and gave out a terrible groan; and her eyes shed tears, ceaselessly, without pause; and she spread her hands like a bird spreading out its wings, seeking her dearest child: "Alas, give me my heart's labor, the hope of my arms!" And while she was kissing the holy relic, she cried out these words: "Alas, my lord, how could you do this to me, and when you saw me mourning in the house of your slaves and your father, why did you not reveal yourself to me?" Then the bride ran to the bier dressed in black, and wept and said, "Alas, my solitary turtledove, I have become bereft, today I have become a widow, and I have nowhere to look and nothing to expect! From now on I shall weep for my wounded heart." And the people in utter amazement, cried ceaselessly, without pause.

Then the most divine emperors gave orders that the bier 25 should be put on public display in the middle of the city, and

εὑρέθη ὃν ἐζήτει ἡ πίστις ἡμῶν." Καὶ πάντες ἔδραμον ὑπαντῆσαι τῷ τιμίῳ λειψάνῳ· ὅσοι γὰρ ἐθεώρησαν αὐτόν, ἐλυτρώθησαν ἀπὸ πάσης ἀσθενείας, ἄλαλοι ἐλάλησαν, τυφλοὶ ἀνέβλεψαν, λεπροὶ ἐκαθαρίζοντο, δαίμονες ἀπελαύνοντο καὶ πᾶσα ἀσθένεια. Θεωρήσαντες δὲ οἱ βασιλεῖς τὸ θαῦμα, ἐβάστασαν τὴν κλίνην, καὶ ὁ ἀρχιεπίσκοπος, ὅπως ἁγιασθῶσιν ἐκ τοῦ τιμίου λειψάνου. Ἡ δὲ μήτηρ αὐτοῦ ἔνθεν ὁμοίως τῆς κλίνης, ἐκράτει τὴν χεῖρα τοῦ τιμίου λειψάνου, καὶ ἐν τοῖς πλοκάμοις τῶν τριχῶν αὐτῆς κατέσειεν ἐπάνω τοῦ τιμίου λειψάνου. Ἡ δὲ νύμφη ἔχουσα τὴν λύπην καὶ τὸ πένθος, ὀπίσω τῆς κλίνης ἠκολούθει κατοδυρομένη. Ὁ δὲ λαὸς ἐκώλυεν τὴν κλίνην, καὶ οὐκ ἠδύναντο περιπατεῖν.

26 Τότε κελεύουσιν οἱ θειότατοι βασιλεῖς, χρυσίον καὶ ἄργυρον ὑπὸ τὰς ὁδοὺς ῥιφῆναι, ὅπως ὁ λαὸς ἐγκλίνῃ εἰς τὸ χρῆμα. Οὐδεὶς δὲ προσεῖχεν τῷ χρήματι, ἀλλὰ τὸν πόθον ἔχοντες εἰς τὸ τίμιον λείψανον· μόλις ἠδυνήθησαν ἀγάγαι τὴν κλίνην εἰς τὸν οἶκον τοῦ Ἁγίου Βονιφατίου. Κἀκεῖσε ἐπανηγύρισαν ζ´ ἡμέρας· τοῦ πατρὸς καὶ τῆς μητρός, καὶ τῆς νύμφης παρισταμένης, ἐπένθησαν.

27 Καὶ ἐποίησαν οἱ βασιλεῖς λάρνακα χρυσῆν διὰ λίθου καὶ σμαράγδου, καὶ ἔθηκαν αὐτοῦ τὸ τίμιον λείψανον ἐν τῇ λάρνακι, μηνὶ ἰουνίῳ ιζ´, ἐπὶ Ὁνορίου καὶ Ἀρκαδίου τῶν θειοτάτων βασιλέων Ῥώμης. Καὶ ἔβρυσεν μύρον εὐωδίας ὁ λάρναξ· καὶ εἴ τις ἐὰν ἠτήσατο, ἔδωκεν αὐτῷ ὁ Θεὸς τὴν ἀντιμισθίαν εἰς ἔργον ἀγαθόν, ἐπὶ πάντας τοὺς ἐλπίζοντας ἐπὶ Κύριον, ὅτι αὐτῷ ἡ δόξα καὶ τὸ κράτος, εἰς τοὺς αἰῶνας τῶν αἰώνων, ἀμήν.

they said to the crowds, "Look, the man whom our faith was seeking has been found." And everyone ran to meet the holy relic; for whoever looked at him was liberated from every kind of illness: mute people talked, *the blind received their sight, lepers were cleansed,* demons and every sort of ailment were driven away. When the emperors saw the miracles, they and the archbishop took up the bier, so as to partake in the holiness of the sacred relic. Likewise, standing beside the bier, the mother held the hand of the holy relic and brushed over the holy relic with the locks of her hair. The bride in her grief and mourning followed the bier, deep in sorrow. But the people were blocking the bier, and they could not walk forward.

Then the most divine emperors gave orders that gold and silver should be thrown down on the streets, so that the people would turn to the money. Yet no one paid attention to the money, but kept their desire fixed upon the holy relic; so only with great difficulty did they manage to bring the bier to the church of Saint Boniphatios. There, they celebrated for seven days; in the presence of the father, the mother, and the bride, they grieved. 26

The emperors had a golden sarcophagus made, decorated with precious stones and emeralds, and they placed his holy relic in the sarcophagus, on the seventeenth of the month of June, during the reign of Honorius and Arcadius, the most divine emperors of Rome. And the sarcophagus gushed with fragrant myrrh; and if anyone asked, God gave the reward for their good deeds to everyone who placed their hopes in the Lord, since glory and power belong to him, unto the ages of ages, amen. 27

Βίος τοῦ ὁσίου πατρὸς ἡμῶν Μάρκου τοῦ Ἀθηναίου, ἀσκήσαντος ἐν τῷ ὄρει τῆς Θράκης, τῆς οὔσης ἐπέκεινα τοῦ ἔθνους τῶν Χετταίων Αἰθιοπίας

Διηγήσατο ἡμῖν ὁ Ἀββᾶς Σεραπίων, ὁ ὑπάρχων ἐν τῇ ἐσωτέρᾳ ἐρήμῳ τῆς Αἰγύπτου, λέγων οὕτως, ὅτι:

Ὄντος μού ποτε πρὸς τὸν Ἀββᾶν Ἰωάννην τὸν μέγαν γέροντα, μιᾷ τῶν νυκτῶν καθεύδοντός μου, ὁρῶ κατ᾽ ὄναρ, ὅτι παρεγένοντο πρὸς αὐτὸν δύο ἀσκηταί. Καὶ εὐλογηθέντες ὑπ᾽ αὐτοῦ εἶπον αὐτῷ, δείξαντες ἐμέ, "Ὁ Ἀββᾶς Σεραπίων ἐστὶν οὗτος;" Λέγει ὁ εἷς τῷ ἑτέρῳ, "Ναί, ἀλλ᾽ ἀναστάντες εὐλογηθῶμεν ὑπ᾽ αὐτοῦ." Λέγει αὐτοῖς ὁ Ἀββᾶς Ἰωάννης, "Ἐάσατε αὐτὸν ἀναπαύσασθαι ὀλίγον· ἀρτίως γὰρ παρεγένετο ἐκ τῆς ἐρήμου καὶ πάνυ ἐστὶ κατάκοπος." Λέγουσιν αὐτῷ ἐκεῖνοι, "Πόσος καιρός ἐστι ἀφ᾽ οὗ κοπιᾷς ἐν τῇ ἐρήμῳ ταύτῃ, καὶ πρὸς τὸν Ἀββᾶν Μάρκον τὸν ἐν τῷ ὄρει ὄντα τῆς Θράκης Αἰθιοπίας οὐκ εἰσῆλθες; Ἐν πᾶσι γὰρ τοῖς ἀσκηταῖς ἁπάσης τῆς ἐρήμου, οὐκ ἔστιν κατ᾽ αὐτὸν ἕτερος· ὑπάρχει γὰρ ὁ γέρων, ἑκατὸν τριάκοντα ἐτῶν, καὶ ἐνενήκοντα πέντε χρόνους ἔχει ἐξ ὅτου ἄνθρωπον οὐκ ἐθεάσατο· καὶ διὰ τεσσαράκοντα ἡμερῶν, παραγίνονται οἱ ἅγιοι πατέρες οἱ ὄντες ἐν χώρᾳ τῶν ζώντων, καὶ παραλαμβάνουσιν αὐτὸν μεθ᾽ ἑαυτῶν."

Life of our holy father Markos the Athenian, who practiced his ascetic discipline on the mountain of Thrace, which is beyond the nation of the Hittites of Ethiopia

Abba Serapion, the one living in the inner desert of Egypt, told us the following story:

Once, when I was with Abba John, the great elder, while I was asleep one night, I saw in a dream two ascetics come to him. After they received his blessing, they pointed at me and said to him, "Is that Abba Serapion?" Then the one said to the other, "Yes, let's go and get his blessing." Abba John said to them, "Let him rest a little; he's just arrived from the desert and is totally exhausted." They said to him, "How long have you been toiling away in this desert yet you haven't visited Abba Markos, who's on the mountain of Thrace in Ethiopia? There's no one like him among all the ascetics in the whole desert; that elder is a hundred and thirty years old, and it's been ninety-five years since he saw anyone. In forty days' time the holy fathers, those who are *in the land of the living,* will come and take him away with them."

2   Καὶ ταῦτα εἰπόντων αὐτῶν, ἔξυπνος ἐγενόμην. Καὶ ἰδοὺ οὐδεὶς λοιπὸν ἦν πρὸς τὸν Ἀββᾶν Ἰωάννην. Ὧι καὶ προσεγγίσας, εἶπον ἅπερ κατ᾽ ὄναρ ἑώρακα. Αὐτὸς δὲ λέγει μοι, "Θεϊκόν ἐστι τὸ ὅραμα. Ἀλλὰ ποῦ ἐστι τὸ ὄρος τῆς Θράκης, ἵνα ἀπέλθῃς;" Λέγω αὐτῷ, "Εὔξαι ὑπὲρ ἐμοῦ, πάτερ." Καὶ ποιησαμένων ἡμῶν εὐχήν, ἠσπασάμην αὐτόν.

3   Καὶ ὁδεύσας ἐπὶ Ἀλεξάνδρειαν, ἔχουσαν πορείαν ἡμερῶν δώδεκα, αὐτὸς μετὰ σπουδῆς πολλῆς κατέλαβον αὐτὴν δι᾽ ἡμερῶν πέντε, πεζεύσας ἐν τῇ τραχυτέρᾳ ἐρήμῳ ἐκείνῃ ἡμέρας καὶ νύκτας ἐν τῷ καύματι τοῦ ἡλίου, ὃ καὶ τὸν χοῦν τῆς γῆς κατακαίει. Εἰσελθόντος δέ μου ἐν αὐτῇ, ἠρώτησά τινα τῶν ἐμπόρων τῶν τὰς ὁδοὺς ἐκείνας ἀκριβῶς ἐπισταμένων, εἰπών, "Τὸ ὄρος τῆς Θράκης τῆς ἐπὶ Αἰθιοπίαν, μακράν ἐστι;" Ὁ δὲ λέγει μοι, "Ὄντως, ἀββᾶ, πολὺ μῆκός ἐστι." Εἶτα πάλιν εἶπον αὐτῷ, "Ἆρα πόσον ἐστὶ τὸ διάστημα τούτου;" Καὶ εἶπέ μοι, "Ὡς εἰκάζω, πάτερ, ἐστὶν εἴκοσιν ἡμερῶν, εἰς τὰ μέρη τῆς Αἰθιοπίας, ἐν τῇ μεγάλῃ θαλάσσῃ τοῦ ἔθνους τῶν Χετταίων." Καὶ λέγω αὐτῷ, "Πῶς μοι γενήσεται ἁρμόδιον; Θέλω γὰρ πορευθῆναι ἐκεῖσε." Καὶ λέγει μοι ὁ ἔμπορος, "Πάτερ, εἰ μὲν διὰ θαλάσσης γένηται ἡ ὁδοιπορία σου, οὐ πολὺ ἀπέχει ἔνθεν· εἰ δὲ διὰ τῆς ἠπείρου, ἐν ἡμέραις τριάκοντα."

4   Ἐγὼ δὲ λαβὼν εἰς φλασκίον κολοκύνθινον ὕδωρ, καὶ ὀλίγους φοίνικας, ἀνεθέμην ἑαυτὸν τῷ Θεῷ, ὁδεύσας ἐν τῇ ἐρήμῳ ἐκείνῃ τῇ φοβερᾷ, ἡμέρας εἴκοσι. Καὶ οὔτε θηρίον ἑώρακα, οὔτε ὄρνεον, οὔτε ἄλλο τι, διὰ τὸ μὴ εὑρίσκειν ταῦτα βρῶσιν τὴν οἱανοῦν, ἢ πόσιν· οὐ γὰρ κατέρχεται ποσῶς ἐν αὐτῇ ὑετός, ἢ δρόσος.

After they had said these things, I woke up. And, lo and behold, there was no one with Abba John anymore. So I approached him and told him what I had seen in the dream. And he said to me, "This vision is from God. But where is the mountain of Thrace so you can go there?" I said to him, "Pray for me, father." And after we had prayed, I gave him a farewell embrace. 2

I traveled toward Alexandria and, although it is a journey of twelve days, in my great haste I reached it in five, walking through that harshest desert, day and night, under the blazing sun, which scorches even *the dust of the earth*. When I entered the city, I asked one of the merchants who know those routes well; I said, "Is it far to the mountain of Thrace, the one in Ethiopia?" And he said to me, "Truly, abba, it's a very long way." Then, I asked him again, "How far away is it?" And he said to me, "In my estimation, father, it's twenty days into the land of Ethiopia in the great sea of the nation of the Hittites." And I said to him, "What's the best way for me to do this? For I want to go there." And the merchant said to me, "Father, if you travel by sea, it's not far from here; but if you go by land, it's thirty days." 3

So taking some water with me in a gourd flask and a few dates, I entrusted myself to God and walked through that terrible desert for twenty days. And I saw no beast, no bird, nor any other creature, since they can find no food or drink of any sort in that desert, as no rain or dew whatsoever falls there. 4

5 Μετὰ γοῦν τὰς εἴκοσι ἡμέρας, ἐξέλιπεν τὸ ὕδωρ, καὶ ἐκ τῆς δίψης ἐκινδύνευον· οὐ γὰρ ἴσχυον ὁδεῦσαι ἔτι. Καὶ πεσών, ἐκείμην ὡσεὶ νεκρός. Καὶ ἰδοὺ ἐκεῖνοι οἱ δύο ἀδελφοὶ οὓς εἶδον ἐν ὁράματι τὸ πρότερον, στάντες ἔμπροσθέν μου, εἶπον, "Ἀνάστα καὶ πορεύου σὺν ἡμῖν." Καὶ ἀναστάς, εἶδον ἕνα τούτων ἀτενίσαντα εἰς τὴν γῆν· ὃς καὶ στραφεὶς πρός με, λέγει μοι, "Θέλεις μεταλαβεῖν μικρὸν ὕδατος;" Καὶ λέγω αὐτῷ, "Ὡς κελεύεις, πάτερ." Καὶ ἔδειξέ μοι ῥίζαν κόμμεως ἐρημικοῦ, καὶ εἶπέ μοι, "Λαβὼν φάγε ἐκ ταύτης, καὶ ὅδευσον ἐπὶ τῇ τοῦ Κυρίου δυνάμει." Ἐξ ἧς φαγὼν ὀλίγον ἵδρωσα ὥσπερ ἐν ὕδατι κυλινδούμενος, καὶ ἐλιπάνθη μου ἡ ψυχή, καὶ ἐγενόμην ὡς μηδέποτε ὀλιγωρῶν. Καὶ λοιπὸν ὑποδείξαντές μοι τὴν τρίβον ἐν ᾗ πρὸς τὸν ἅγιον ἐκεῖνον πορεύσωμαι, καὶ εἰπόντες μοι "Μὴ χρονίσῃς," εὐθέως ἀφανεῖς ἐγένοντο.

6 Ἔγωγε οὖν ὁδεύσας ἄλλας ἑπτὰ ἡμέρας, κατέλαβον ἐκεῖνο τὸ ὄρος, καὶ ἀνῆλθον μέχρι τῆς ἀκρωρείας αὐτοῦ. Καὶ οὐκ ἦν ἐν αὐτῷ τὸ σύνολον, ἢ δένδρον, ἢ φρύγανον. Ἀλλ᾽ οὕτως ἦν ὑψηλόν, ὡς δοκεῖν ἐπαίρεσθαι *εἰς τὸ ὕψος τοῦ οὐρανοῦ*. Καταλαβὼν οὖν τὴν ἀκρώρειαν αὐτοῦ (ὡς εἴρηται), *εἶδον καὶ ἰδοὺ θάλασσα μεγάλη* ἦν κεκολλημένη ἐν ταῖς ἀκρωρείαις αὐτοῦ. Καὶ διῆλθον ἐν τῷ ὄρει ἔνθεν καὶ ἔνθεν ἡμέρας ἑπτά.

7 Καὶ ἐν αὐτῇ τῇ ἐπελθούσῃ νυκτί, εἶδον τοὺς ἀγγέλους τοῦ Θεοῦ καταβαίνοντας πρὸς τὸν ἅγιον ἐκεῖνον, καὶ δοξολογοῦντας καὶ λέγοντας, "Μακάριος εἶ καὶ *καλῶς ἔσται τῇ ψυχῇ σου*, Ἀββᾶ Μάρκε. Ἰδοὺ ἀνηνέγκαμεν τὸν Ἀββᾶν Σεραπίωνα, ὃν ἐπόθησεν ἡ ψυχή σου θεάσασθαι, ἐπειδὴ

After those twenty days, I ran out of water and was in 5
danger of dying from thirst for I didn't have the strength to
walk any more. I fell down and lay like a corpse. And, lo and
behold, those two brothers, whom I had seen in the earlier
vision, stood in front of me and said, "Get up and come with
us." When I got up, I saw one of them looking intently at
the ground; then he turned to me and said to me, "Would
you like some water?" And I said to him, "As you order, father." And he showed me a root of a desert gum and said to
me, "Take, eat from this root, and keep on going, fortified by
the Lord." After I ate a small piece of it, I broke out in a
sweat as though I had dipped myself in water, and my soul
was invigorated, and it was as if I had never lost heart. Then,
they showed me the way to get to that holy man and, saying
"Don't linger!" they immediately disappeared.

After traveling for another seven days, I reached that 6
mountain, and I went up to the top. There wasn't a tree nor
a shrub anywhere there. But it was so high that it seemed to
be raised up to *the height of heaven.* When I reached the top
(as I said), *I looked and, lo and behold,* a great sea was joined to
its upper ridges. And I walked about on the mountain, here
and there, for seven days.

And on the following night, I saw the angels of God de- 7
scending upon that holy man, and praising him and saying,
"Blessed are you and *it shall be well* with your soul, Abba
Markos. Look, we have brought Abba Serapion, whom your

ἕτερόν τινα τοῦ γένους τῶν ἀνθρώπων, οὐκ ἐπόθησεν ἡ ψυχή σου θεάσασθαι." Ἃ καὶ ἀκούσας καὶ ἄφοβος γενόμενος, ᾤδευσα ἐπὶ τῇ ὀπτασίᾳ, ἕως οὗ κατέλαβον ἐκεῖνο τὸ ἅγιον ἄντρον ἐν ᾧ ὑπῆρχεν ὁ ἅγιος Μάρκος.

8   Πλησιάσας δὲ τῇ θύρᾳ τοῦ σπηλαίου, ἀκήκοα αὐτοῦ στιχολογοῦντος ἐκ τῶν ἁγίων γραφῶν οὕτως, ὅτι: "*Χίλια ἔτη ἐν ὀφθαλμοῖς σου, Κύριε, ὡς ἡ ἡμέρα ἡ ἐχθές.*" Καὶ τὰ λοιπὰ τοῦ Ψαλμοῦ.

Καὶ πάλιν ἔλεγεν, "Μακαρία ἡ ψυχή σου, Μάρκε, ὅτι οὐκ ἐβορβόρωται, οὐδὲ μεμόλυνται ἐν τῷ κόσμῳ τούτῳ. Μακάριον τὸ σῶμά σου, ὅτι οὐκ ἐκραιπάλησεν ἐν ταῖς ἐπιθυμίαις τῶν ματαίων λογισμῶν. Μακάριοι οἱ ὀφθαλμοί σου, οὓς οὐκ ἴσχυσεν ὁ διάβολος ἀποπλανῆσαι τοῦ θεάσασθαι ἀλλοτρίας μορφάς. Μακάριον τὸ οὖς σου, ὅτι οὐκ εἰσήκουσε τὴν κραυγὴν τῶν σειρήνων γυναικῶν τοῦ ματαίου κόσμου. Μακάριαι αἱ χεῖρές σου, ὅτι οὐκ ἐκράτησαν ἢ ἐψηλάφησάν τι τῶν ἀνθρωπίνων πραγμάτων. Οὔτε τοὺς μυκτῆράς μου ἔφραξεν ἡ ὀσμὴ τοῦ διαβόλου, οὔτε οἱ πόδες μου ἐβάδισαν τὰς ὁδοὺς τὰς ἀπαγούσας εἰς θάνατον, οὔτε *ὑπεσκελίσθησαν τὰ διαβήματά μου.* Ἡ ψυχή μου ἐπλήσθη τῆς Πνευματικῆς ζωῆς, καὶ τὸ σῶμά μου ἡγιάσθη τῇ αἴγλῃ τῶν ἀγγέλων.

"*Εὐλόγει ἡ ψυχή μου τὸν Κύριον, καὶ πάντα τὰ ἐντός μου, τὸ ὄνομα τὸ ἅγιον αὐτοῦ. Εὐλόγει ἡ ψυχή μου τὸν Κύριον, καὶ μὴ ἐπιλανθάνου πάσας τὰς ἀνταποδόσεις αὐτοῦ. Τί λυπῇ, ψυχή μου; Μὴ φοβοῦ!* οὐ μὴ γὰρ κρατηθῇς ἐν ταῖς φυλακαῖς τοῦ Ἅιδου καὶ τῶν δαιμόνων, οὐδ' οὐ μὴν δυνηθῶσιν

soul longed to see, since your soul longed to see no one else from the human race." When I heard these words, I became fearless and walked toward the vision, until I reached that holy cavern where the holy Markos was.

As I approached the entrance of the cave, I heard him 8 reciting verses from the holy scriptures as follows: "*Because a thousand years in your sight,* Lord, *are like the day of yesterday that passed,*" and the rest of the Psalm.

And then again he said, "Blessed is your soul, Markos, because it has not been sullied nor stained in this world. Blessed is your body, because it did not get drunk on the desires which come from vain thoughts. Blessed are your eyes, which the devil was unable to lead astray by staring at the outward appearance of others. Blessed is your ear, because it did not hear the cry of the siren women of this vain world. Blessed are your hands, because they did not hold or fondle any human things. Nor did the devil's scent clog my nostrils, nor did my feet walk the roads that lead to death, nor *have* my *steps been tripped up.* My soul has been filled with the life of the Spirit, and my body has been sanctified with the radiance of the angels.

"*Bless the Lord, O my soul, and all that is within me, his holy name. Bless the Lord, O my soul, and do not forget all his rewards.* Why are you vexed, my soul? Do not be afraid! for you shall not be held in the prisons of Hades and of the demons, nor

κατηγορῆσαί σου· οὐκ ἔστιν γὰρ ἐν σοὶ λύθρον ἁμαρτη-
μάτων αὐτῶν.

"Ἄκουε δὲ τοῦ Δαβὶδ λέγοντος, 'Παρεμβαλεῖ ἄγγελος
Κυρίου κύκλῳ τῶν φοβουμένων καὶ ῥύσεται αὐτούς.' Καὶ ὁ
Κύριός φησι, 'Μακάριος ὁ δοῦλος ἐκεῖνος ὁ ποιήσας τὸ θέλημα τοῦ Κυρίου αὐτοῦ.'" Καὶ ἄλλα πολλὰ εἰπὼν ἐκ τῶν
θείων γραφῶν, ἐξῆλθε πρὸς τὴν θύραν τοῦ σπηλαίου.

9   Καὶ κλαίων ἐλεεινά, ἐκάλεσέ με λέγων, "Ἐν εἰρήνῃ τοῦ
Θεοῦ γέγονας, Ἀββᾶ Σεραπίων. Ἔγγισόν μοι, τέκνον." Καὶ
ἐγγίσας αὐτῷ, κατεφίλησέ με λέγων, "Ὀσμὴ τοῦ υἱοῦ μου
Σεραπίωνος, ὡς ὀσμὴ πνευματικοῦ τέκνου! Ἀποδῴη σοι
Κύριος τὸν μισθὸν τοῦ κόπου σου οὗ κεκοπίακας τοῦ θεάσασθαι τὴν πολιὰν ταύτην. Ἐνενήκοντα πέντε ἔτη ἔχω,
τέκνον, ὅτι οὐκ ἐθεασάμην ἄνθρωπον, εἰμὴ σήμερον τὴν
σὴν ἁγιωσύνην, ἧς ὠρεγόμην ἐκ πολλῶν χρόνων. Καὶ
εὐχαριστῶ σοι ὅτι τοσούτων κόπων οὐκ ὤκνησας ἀνα-
δέξασθαι ἰδεῖν ἐλεεινὸν γέροντα. Ἀλλὰ δώσοι σοι Κύριος
καθ' ἃ εἴρηκα τὸν μισθὸν ἐν ἡμέρᾳ ᾗ μέλλει κρῖναι τὰ
κρυπτὰ τῶν ἀνθρώπων."

10 Καὶ ταῦτα εἰπών, κελεύσας ἐκαθέσθημεν. Καὶ ἠρξάμην
ἐρωτᾶν αὐτὸν περὶ τῆς ἀμέμπτου πολιτείας αὐτοῦ. Ὑπο-
λαβὼν δὲ λέγει μοι, "Ἰδού, τέκνον, ἐνενήκοντα πέντε ἔτη
ἔχω ἐν τῷ μικρῷ φωλεῷ τούτῳ, καὶ οὐχ ἑώρακα οὔτε θηρίον, οὔτε ὄρνεον, οὔτε ἄρτον ἀνθρώπινον ἔφαγον, οὔτε
ἔνδυμα κοσμικὸν περιεβαλόμην. Τριάκοντα χρόνους ἐποίησα ἐν μεγάλῃ ἀνάγκῃ καὶ πολλῇ στενοχωρίᾳ ὑπὸ πείνης
καὶ δίψης καὶ γυμνότητος—ἃ οὐκ ἤρκει μοι· εἶχον δὲ καὶ
τοὺς δαίμονας ἐνοχλοῦντάς μοι, καὶ παγίδας ἱστῶντας καὶ

will they be able to accuse you; for the filth of their sins is not in you.

"Listen to David, who says, '*An angel of the Lord will encamp around those who fear him, and will rescue them.*' And the Lord says, '*Blessed is that servant* who does the will of his Lord.'" After saying many more words from the holy scriptures, he came out to the entrance of the cave.

Weeping pitifully, he addressed me by my name, and said, 9 "In *the peace of God* you have arrived, Abba Serapion. *Come near to me, child.*" When I came close to him, *he covered me with kisses,* saying, "*The scent of my son* Serapion *is like the scent* of a spiritual child! May the Lord repay you for the toil with which you toiled to see this old man. It was ninety-five years, child, since I last saw anyone, until your holiness today, for whom I have longed for many years. And I thank you for not having shied away from such toils in order to visit a pitiful old man. May the Lord give you your reward, as I said, on *that day* when he is going to judge *the secrets of men.*"

When he had said these words, he suggested that we 10 should sit down, and I began to ask him about his blameless way of life. In response, he said to me, "Look, child, I have spent ninety-five years in this little lair, and I have seen neither beast nor bird, nor have I eaten human bread, nor put on a worldly garment. For thirty years, I was in great need and much distress because of hunger and thirst and nakedness—and all this was not enough for me. I also had the demons pestering me, setting up snares, and lying in ambush—

ἐνεδρεύοντας—ἃ ἀδύνατον καταλέγειν σοι. Καὶ ἔφαγον χοῦν, τέκνον, ἀπὸ πείνης, καὶ ἔπιον ὕδωρ ἐκ τῆς θαλάσσης. Εἴκοσι ἐνιαυτοὺς διῆγον γυμνός, καὶ ἤμην ἐν μεγάλῃ στενώσει. Ὤμωσαν καθ᾽ ἑαυτῶν οἱ δαίμονες μυριάκις τοῦ πνίξαι με ἐν τῇ θαλάσσῃ· ἔσυράν με πλειστάκις μέχρι τῶν κατωτάτων μερῶν τοῦ ὄρους, ἕως ὅτου οὐχ ὑπελείφθη ἐν ἐμοὶ οὔτε δέρμα οὔτε σάρξ, κράζοντες καὶ λέγοντες, ῾Ἔξελθε ἐκ τῆς γῆς ἡμῶν! Ἀπ᾽ ἀρχῆς κόσμου οὐκ εἰσῆλθεν ἐνταῦθα ἕτερός τις, καὶ σὺ πῶς ἐτόλμησας εἰσελθεῖν;᾽

"Καρτερήσας δὲ ἐν ὑπομονῇ πολλῇ τριάκοντα ἔτη, πεινῶν καὶ διψῶν καὶ γυμνητεύων (ὡς εἴρηται), καὶ πολέμῳ δαιμόνων ἀφορήτῳ, ἔκτοτε ἐπεφοίτησεν ἡ τοῦ Θεοῦ χάρις καὶ πολλὴ εὐσπλαγχνία ἐπ᾽ ἐμέ. Καὶ τῇ αὐτοῦ προστάξει, μετετράπησαν τὰ σωματικὰ ἰδιώματα, καὶ ἐφύησαν τρίχες ἐν τῷ σώματί μου, ἕως οὗ ἐβαρύνθη ἐξ αὐτῶν. Καὶ βρῶσις πνευματικὴ ἀδιαλείπτως ἐφέρετό μοι, καὶ ἄγγελοι κατέβαινον πρός με. Καὶ ἐθεασάμην, τέκνον, τὰς χώρας τῆς βασιλείας τῶν οὐρανῶν, καὶ τὰς μονὰς τῶν ἁγίων ψυχῶν. Εἶδον ἐπαγγελίας μακαριότητος ἑτοιμασθείσας τοῖς ποιοῦσιν τὰ ἀγαθά· εἶδον τὸν Παράδεισον τοῦ Θεοῦ· καὶ ἐδείχθη μοι τὸ τῆς γνώσεως ξύλον ἀφ᾽ οὗ ἔφαγον οἱ προπάτορες. Εἶδον τὸν Ἐνὼχ καὶ τὸν Ἠλίαν ἐν γῇ ζώντων. Οὐκ ἔστι, τέκνον, τὶ ὅπερ ᾐτησάμην παρὰ Θεοῦ, καὶ οὐκ ἔδειξέ μοι."

11 Ταῦτα εἰπόντος τοῦ ἁγίου, λέγω αὐτῷ, "Εἰπέ μοι, πάτερ: πόθεν εἶ, καὶ πῶς ἐνταῦθα γέγονεν ἡ ἔλευσίς σου;" Ὁ

it would be impossible to describe it all in detail to you. I ate earth, child, out of hunger, and I drank sea water. For twenty years I lived naked and was in dire straits. The demons swore among themselves countless times to drown me in the sea. On many occasions they dragged me to the very bottom of the mountain, until neither skin nor flesh was left on me, and they would shout and say, 'Get out of our land! Since the beginning of the world no one else has set foot here; so how did you dare to come here?'

"But after I had endured thirty years of hunger and thirst and nakedness with great patience (as I already mentioned), as well as an unbearable war from the demons, then God's grace and great mercy came upon me. And by his command, my bodily features were transformed, and hair grew on my body, until it became heavy with it. And spiritual food was brought to me ceaselessly, and angels have been descending upon me. And I saw, child, the lands of the kingdom of heaven, and the dwellings of the holy souls. I beheld the promised bliss that has been prepared for those who are good; I beheld God's Paradise; and the tree of knowledge, from which our forefathers ate, was shown to me. I saw Enoch and Elijah in the land of the living. There is nothing, child, which I requested from God that he did not show to me."

After the holy man said this, I said to him, "Tell me, fa- 11
ther, where are you from and how did you get here?" The

δὲ ὅσιος ἀπεκρίνατο, "Ἐγώ, τέκνον, ἀπὸ Ἀθήνας ἐγενόμην. Ἀποθανόντων δὲ τῶν γονέων μου, εἶπον ἐν ἑαυτῷ, ὅτι ʽΚἀγὼ θνητός εἰμι ὥσπερ οἱ πατέρες μου, ἀλλ᾽ ἀναστὰς ὑποχωρήσω τοῦ κόσμου, πρὸ τοῦ ἐλθεῖν καὶ ἁρπάσαι με τοὺς ἀγγέλους τοῦ Θεοῦ.᾽ Καὶ εὐθέως ἀπεδυσάμην τὰ ἱμάτιά μου, καὶ ἔρριψα ἐμαυτὸν ἐπὶ σανίδος ἐν τῇ θαλάσσῃ, καὶ κατέλαβον τὸ ὄρος τοῦτο."

12   Καὶ ταῦτα εἰπόντος τοῦ ἁγίου, ἔφθασεν ἡμέρα. Καὶ θεασάμενος τὸ σῶμα αὐτοῦ δι᾽ ὅλου κεκαλυμμένον ταῖς θριξὶν ὡς θηρός, ἐδειλίασα. Καὶ ἔμφοβος γενόμενος, ἐτρόμαξα, διὰ τὸ μὴ ὁρᾶν τὸ σύνολον ἐν αὐτῷ μορφὴν ἀνθρώπου· ἄλλοθεν γὰρ ἐπιγινώσκεσθαι ἀδύνατον ἦν, εἰμὴ διὰ λαλιᾶς τῆς ἐξερχομένης ἐκ τοῦ στόματος αὐτοῦ.

Ὡς οὖν εἶδέ με οὕτω φοβηθέντα, λέγει μοι, "Τέκνον μου, τί ἐφοβήθης ἐκ τῆς θέας τοῦ σώματος τοῦ δυστήνου τούτου; Οὐδὲν ἄλλο ἐστί, εἰμὴ σῶμα φθαρτὸν ἀπαρτισθὲν ἀπὸ σώματος φθαρτοῦ εἰς τὸ σχῆμα τοῦτο."

13   Καὶ πάλιν, ἐπυνθάνετο λέγων, "Ἵσταται ὁ κόσμος καὶ θάλλει κατὰ τὸ ἀρχαῖον ἔθος;" Καὶ λέγω αὐτῷ, "Ναί, πάτερ, χάριτι Χριστοῦ, καὶ ὑπὲρ τοὺς πρώτους καιροὺς πλεῖον θάλλει ὁ κόσμος ἕως τὴν σήμερον." Καὶ πάλιν λέγει μοι, "Ἔστιν ἑλληνισμὸς ἢ διωγμὸς τῶν Χριστιανῶν ἕως τοῦ νῦν;" Λέγω αὐτῷ, "Τῇ τῶν σῶν ἁγίων εὐχῶν βοηθείᾳ, πέπαυται ὁ διωγμὸς τῶν Χριστιανῶν ἕως ἄρτι, καὶ οὐκ ἔστιν εἰδωλολατρεία, φανερῶς πολιτευομένη."

14   Ὁ καὶ ἀκούσας ὁ γέρων, ἐχάρη χαρὰν μεγάλην. Καὶ αὖθις λέγει μοι, "Εἰσί τινες ἅγιοι ἐν τῷ κόσμῳ σήμερον ἐνεργοῦντες δυνάμεις καὶ θαυματουργίας, καθὼς εἶπεν ὁ

holy man responded, "I, child, came from Athens. When my parents died, I told myself, 'I too am mortal, like my parents; let me get up and withdraw from this world before the angels of God come and snatch me away.' And immediately I took off my clothes and threw myself onto a plank in the sea and reached this mountain."

After the holy man had said this, daybreak came. And 12 when I saw his body covered, like a beast, entirely by hair, I was frightened. And when I became fearful I trembled, since there was nothing human whatsoever to be seen about him; it was impossible to recognize him as such except by the speech that came out of his mouth.

When he saw that I was so scared, he said to me, "My child, why were you scared by the sight of this miserable body of mine? It is still just a corruptible body which has been completely changed into this appearance from a corruptible body."

And then again he started making inquiries of me: "Is the 13 world still there and thriving in the same old way?" And I said to him, "Yes, father, and by the grace of Christ the world thrives even more today than in earlier times." And then again he said to me, "Does paganism or the persecution of the Christians still continue now?" I said to him, "By the help of your holy prayers the persecution of the Christians has now ceased, and idolatry is no longer practiced openly."

When the elder heard this he was overjoyed. And again 14 he said to me, "Are there any holy men in the world today who perform mighty works and miracles, just as the Lord

Κύριος ἐν τοῖς θείοις Εὐαγγελίοις, ὅτι ἐὰν ἔχητε πίστιν ὡς κόκκον σινάπεως ἐρεῖτε τῷ ὄρει τούτῳ, Ἄρθητι καὶ ἐμβλήθητι εἰς τὴν θάλασσαν,' καὶ γενήσεται;" Καὶ τοῦτο εἰπόντος τοῦ ἁγίου, ἐπήρθη παραυτίκα τὸ ὄρος ὡσεὶ πήχεις πέντε, καὶ ἐβλήθη εἰς τὴν θάλασσαν. Ἀναβλέψας δὲ καὶ ἰδὼν αὐτὸ περιπατοῦν τύψας τῇ χειρὶ τὴν ὄψιν εἶπε, "Τί σοι γέγονεν, ὄρος; Οὐχί σοι εἶπον ἀρθῆναι. Στῆθι ἐν τῷ τόπῳ σου." Καὶ αὐτίκα ἀπεκατέστη οὗ ἀπεσχίσθη. Ὁ καὶ ἰδὼν ἐγώ, ἐκ τοῦ φόβου ἔπεσον χαμαί. Ὁ δὲ ἅγιος κρατήσας μου τῆς χειρός, ἤγειρέ με εἰπών, "Οὐκ ἐθεάσω τοιαῦτα θαύματα ἐν ταῖς ἡμέραις σου;" Κἀγὼ εἶπον, "Οὐχί." Καὶ στενάξας ἔκλαυσε καὶ εἶπεν, "Οὐαὶ τῇ γῇ, ὅτι Χριστιανοὶ μόνῳ ὀνόματί εἰσιν, οὐ μὴν δὲ ἔργοις. Εὐλογητὸς ὁ Θεός, ὁ ἀγαγών με εἰς τὸν ἅγιον τόπον τοῦτον, ἵνα μὴ ἀποθάνω ἐν τῇ ἰδίᾳ πατρίδι, καὶ ταφῶ ἐν γῇ μεμιασμένῃ ἐν ἁμαρτίαις πολλαῖς."

15 Ὀψίας δὲ γενομένης, εἶπέ μοι, "Ἀδελφὲ Σεραπίων, οὐκ ἔστιν καιρὸς τοῦ ποιῆσαι ἡμᾶς εὐχαριστίαν καὶ ἀγάπην;" Ἐγὼ δὲ <οὐκ> ἀπεκρίθην αὐτῷ ῥῆμα. Καὶ εὐθέως ἀναστάς, καὶ τὰς χεῖρας εἰς τὸν οὐρανὸν ἐκτείνας, εἶπε τὸν ψαλμὸν τοῦτον: Κύριος ποιμαίνει με καὶ οὐδέν με ὑστερήσει, καὶ τὰ λοιπὰ τοῦ ψαλμοῦ. Τότε στραφεὶς ἐπὶ τὸ ἄντρον, φωνῇ μεγάλῃ εἶπε, "Σκεύασον, τέκνον, τράπεζαν." Καὶ λέγει μοι, "Εἰσέλθωμεν, τέκνον, καὶ μεταλάβωμεν τροφῆς, ἣν ὁ Θεὸς ἀπέστειλεν ἡμῖν." Κἀγὼ θαυμάσας, διηπόρουν κατ' ἐμαυτὸν καὶ ἔκθαμβος ἐγενόμην, ὅτι μηδὲν πρὸ τούτου ἑωρακὼς ἐν τῷ σπηλαίῳ, εἰμὴ μόνον τὸν ἅγιον, νῦν τράπεζαν ἐσκευασμένην παντοίοις ἐδωδίμοις ἑώρων,

said in the divine Gospels that *if you have faith as a grain of mustard seed, you shall say to this mountain, 'Lift yourself up, and cast yourself into the sea,' and it will be done?"* And as soon as the holy man said this, the mountain was instantly lifted up about five cubits, and was cast into the sea. When he looked up and saw the mountain walking, he struck its face with his hand and said, "What happened to you, mountain? I did not tell *you* to lift yourself up. Get back in your place." And it immediately returned to where it had split off. When I saw this, I fell on the ground out of fear. But the holy man took my hand and raised me up, saying, "Have you not witnessed such miracles in your time?" And I said, "No." Sighing, he wept and said, "Woe to the earth, because Christians are Christians only in name, yet not in deed. Blessed be God who brought me to this holy place so as not to die in my fatherland and be buried in a land defiled by many sins."

When the evening came, he said to me, "Brother Serapion, is it not time for us to give thanks and have a meal?" I didn't say a word. Immediately he got up, raised his hands toward the heaven and recited this psalm: *The Lord is my shepherd, and I shall not want,* and the rest of the psalm. Then he turned toward the cavern and said in a loud voice, "Set the table, child." And he said to me, "Let's go inside, child, and have some of the food that God has sent to us." I was amazed and wondered to myself and was astounded because until then I had seen nothing in the cave except the holy man alone, and now I could see a table prepared with all

15

63

καὶ δίφρους δύο κειμένους, καὶ ἄρτον πρόσφατον ἁπαλὸν
καὶ λαμπρὸν ὡσεὶ χιόνα, καὶ ἄνθη εὐπρεπῆ, καὶ δύο ἰχθύας
ὀπτούς, καὶ λάχανα κάλλιστα, καὶ ἐλαίας καὶ φοίνικας, καὶ
ἅλας, καὶ βαυκάλιον πλῆρες ὕδατος γλυκαίου ὑπὲρ μέλι.

16   Καὶ καθησάντων ἡμῶν, εἶπέ μοι, "Εὐλόγησον, Ἀδελφὲ
Σεραπίων." Κἀγὼ εἶπον, "Συγχώρησόν μοι, πάτερ." Καὶ
αὐτὸς εὐθέως εἶπε, "Κύριε, εὐλόγησον." Καὶ ἰδοὺ ἐθεασάμην καθάπερ δεξιὰν ἁπλωθεῖσαν ἐκ τοῦ οὐρανοῦ, καὶ
τὸν σταυρὸν ἐπὶ τῆς τραπέζης τυπώσασαν. Καὶ φαγόντων
ἡμῶν, εἶπεν, "Ἆρον, τέκνον, ἔνθεν." Καὶ εὐθέως ἤρθη ἡ
τράπεζα ἀφανῶς. Ἐγὼ δὲ πάσας τῆς ζωῆς μου ἡμέρας, οὐκ
ἐγευσάμην τροφῆς τοιαύτης οὔτε ὕδατος κατ᾽ ἐκεῖνο τὸ
ὕδωρ.

17   Τότε ὁ ἅγιος ἀποκριθείς, εἶπέ μοι, "Εἶδες, ἀδελφέ,
πόσον ἀγαπᾷ ὁ Θεὸς τοὺς δούλους αὐτοῦ; Καθ᾽ ἡμέραν
γὰρ εἷς ἰχθὺς ἐπέμπετό μοι, καὶ σήμερον διὰ σὲ ὁ Θεὸς
ἀπέστειλε δύο. Οὕτως ὁ Θεὸς ἀποστέλλει μοι τροφὴν
πνευματικὴν καὶ πόμα πνευματικόν. Τριάκοντα χρόνους
ἐγενόμην ἐν τῷ τόπῳ τούτῳ, καὶ οὐχ εὗρον οὐδὲ μίαν ῥίζαν βοτάνης. Πεῖναν καὶ δίψαν ὑπέμεινεν ἡ ψυχή μου·
ἔφαγον χοῦν ἀπὸ πείνης, καὶ ἔπιον πικρὸν ὕδωρ ἀπὸ θα-
λάσσης· καὶ διῆλθον γυμνὸς καὶ ἀνυπόδετος, ἕως διελύθη
μου τὰ μέλη ἐκ τοῦ δέρματος αὐτῶν ἀπὸ τοῦ ψύχους, καὶ
ἔκαυσεν ὁ ἥλιος τὰς σάρκας μου, καὶ ἤμην κείμενος ὡσεὶ
νεκρός. Καὶ οἱ δαίμονες ἐπολέμουν με ἀενάως νυκτὸς καὶ
ἡμέρας, ἔνθεν κἀκεῖθέν με ἐν τῷ ἀέρι σύροντες. Καὶ ἐγκα-
τέλιπέ με ὁ Θεός, τριάκοντα ἐνιαυτοὺς ὑπὸ πείνης καὶ
δίψης καὶ γυμνότητος χειμαζόμενον, καὶ τῆς βίας τοῦ

sorts of things to eat, and two seats set, and fresh bread, soft and white as snow, and beautiful flowers, and two grilled fish, and the finest vegetables, and olives and dates, and salt, and a jar full of water sweeter *than honey.*

And when we sat down, he said to me, "Give the blessing, 16 Brother Serapion." And I said, "Excuse me, father." And immediately he said, "Lord, give the blessing." And lo and behold, I saw something like a right hand stretch out from heaven and make the sign of the cross over the table. And after we ate, he said, "Take yourself off from here, child." And the table immediately disappeared. All the days of my life, I have never tasted such food or water like that water.

Then the holy man responded and said to me, "Did you 17 see, brother, how much God loves his servants? For every single day only one fish was dispatched to me; and today, on your account, God sent two. This is how God sends me spiritual food and spiritual drink. For thirty years I have been in this place and have not found even a single plant root. My soul endured hunger and thirst; I ate earth out of hunger and drank bitter water from the sea; and I walked naked and barefoot until the skin of my limbs was worn off by the cold, and the sun scorched my flesh, and I was lying on the ground as dead. And the demons waged a ceaseless war against me, day and night, dragging me here and there in the air. And God abandoned me for thirty years while I was battered by hunger and thirst and nakedness as well as by the violence of

ψύχους καὶ τοῦ καύσωνος. Καὶ οὔτε θηρίον οὔτε ὄρνεον τεθέαμαι ἐν τούτῳ τῷ ὄρει. Καὶ ἰδοὺ ἐνενήκοντα πέντε ἔτη ἔχω, ἀφ᾽ οὗ ἦλθον ἐνταῦθα, καὶ οὐχ ἑώρακαν οἱ ὀφθαλμοί μού τι τῶν κτισθέντων ζῴων ὑπὸ τοῦ Θεοῦ τοὺς τριάκοντα χρόνους, εἰμὴ δαίμονας καὶ μόνον.

"Τελεσθέντων δὲ τῶν τριάκοντα χρόνων ἐν οἷς ἤμην κινδύνοις, ἐκέλευσεν ὁ Θεὸς τῷ σώματί μου καὶ ἐφύησάν μοι τρίχες ὡς ὁρᾷς, αἳ καὶ ἐκάλυψάν μου πάντα τὰ μέλη. Ἔκτοτε δὲ ἕως τοῦ νῦν, οὔτε οἱ δαίμονες ἴσχυσαν πλησιάσαι μοι, οὔτε λιμός, οὔτε δίψα, οὔτε ψῦχος οὔτε καύσων κατεκυρίευσάν μου, ἀλλ᾽ οὔτε τὸ παράπαν ἠσθένησα. Σήμερον δὲ τετέλεσται τὸ μέτρον τῆς ζωῆς μου, καὶ ἀπέστειλέ σε ὁ Θεὸς τοῦ ταῖς ἁγίαις χερσίν σου κηδευθῆναί μου τὸ ταπεινὸν τοῦτο σῶμα."

18 Ταῦτα δὲ εἶπε μετὰ τὸ μεταλαβεῖν τῆς τροφῆς. Εἶτα αὖθις, λέγει μοι, "Ἀδελφὲ Σεραπίων, σύγγνωθί μοι ἐπ᾽ ὀλίγον· ἐν τῇ ὥρᾳ τῇδε τοῦ χωρισμοῦ μου, ποίησον ἀγρυπνίαν." Καὶ ποιήσαντες τὴν πρώτην εὐχήν, ἐτελέσαμεν ὅλους τοὺς τοῦ Δαβὶδ ψαλμούς. Καὶ μετὰ τοῦτο λέγει μοι, "Ἀδελφὲ Σεραπίων, ἐπὰν κηδεύσῃς τὸ σῶμά μου, θὲς αὐτὸ ἐν τούτῳ τῷ σπηλαίῳ ἐν εἰρήνῃ Χριστοῦ· καὶ φράξας λίθοις τὸ στόμα τοῦ σπηλαίου, πορεύου ἐν εἰρήνῃ καὶ μὴ μείνῃς ἐνταῦθα." Ἐμοῦ δὲ ἀρξαμένου κλαίειν καὶ ἀποδύρεσθαι, συγκεχυμένῃ φωνῇ λέγω αὐτῷ, "Πάτερ, αἴτησαι τοῦ λαβεῖν με σύν σοι ὅπου δ᾽ ἂν πορεύῃ."

19 Ἀπεκρίθη ἐκεῖνος καὶ εἶπεν, "Ἐν ἡμέρᾳ τῆς εὐφροσύνης μου μὴ κλαῖε, τέκνον. Ὁ δὲ Θεὸς ὁ ὁδηγήσας σε καὶ ἐνέγκας σε ἐνταῦθα, αὐτὸς διασώσει σε ἐν εὐφροσύνῃ—

the cold and the heat. And I saw neither beast nor bird on this mountain. Look, it is ninety-five years since I came here, and my eyes did not see a single one of God's creatures for thirty years except only demons.

"When the thirty years of my perils were over, however, God gave a command to my body and, as you see, hair grew, which covered all my limbs. From then till now, the demons have been unable to approach me, nor have famine, thirst, cold or heat had any power over me, and I have never been ill at all. But today the measure of my life has reached its end and God has sent you so that this humble body of mine may be buried by your holy hands."

This is what he said after the meal. Then again he said to me, "Brother Serapion, forgive me a little, and at this hour of my departure perform the night office." We said the initial prayer and completed all the psalms of David. After this, he said to me, "Brother Serapion, when you do bury my body, place it in this cave in the peace of Christ; then, after sealing the mouth of the cave with rocks, go in peace and don't stay here." I started weeping and bitterly lamenting, and with a shaking voice I said to him, "Father, ask God to take me with you to wherever you are going." 18

He replied and said, "Don't weep on the day of my joy, child. God, who guided you and brought you here, will also keep you safe in joy—though your return journey will not 19

67

πλήν, οὐκ ἐν τῇ τρίβῳ τῆς ἐλεύσεώς σου ἔσται ἡ ἀπο-
στροφή σου. Ἀδελφὲ Σεραπίων, μεγάλη μοί ἐστιν ἡ ἡμέρα
αὕτη ὑπὲρ πάσας τὰς ἡμέρας τῆς ζωῆς μου· σήμερον γὰρ
καταλιμπάνει ἡ ψυχὴ τὸ παθητὸν τοῦτο σῶμα, καὶ ἀπ-
έρχεται τοῦ καταπαῦσαι ἐν μοναῖς ζωῆς. Σήμερον ἀναπαύ-
σεται τὸ σῶμά μου τῶν πολλῶν κόπων καὶ πόνων. Σήμερον παρεμβαλοῦμαι ἐν τῇ χώρᾳ τῆς ἀναπαύσεώς μου."

20   Ὧδε δὲ τελέσαντος τὸν λόγον αὐτοῦ, αἴφνης ἐπλήσθη
τὸ σπήλαιον φωτὸς τηλαυγέστερον ἡλίου, καὶ εὐωδίας
ἀρωμάτων ἐπληρώθη τὸ ὄρος ἐκεῖνο. Ὁ δὲ κρατήσας τῆς
χειρός μου, πάλιν ἤρξατο λέγειν οὕτω: "Σώζου ἄντρον, ἐν
ᾧ τῷ Θεῷ εὐηρέστησα μετὰ τοῦ σώματος τοῦ ἐν σοὶ κατα-
σκηνώσαντος ἐν τῇ ζωῇ μου, καὶ πάλιν ἐνταῦθα μένοντος
μέχρι τῆς κοινῆς ἀναστάσεως. Σώζου δὲ καὶ σὺ σῶμα, ὁ
οἶκος τῶν πόνων καὶ τῶν ἀναγκῶν καὶ κόπων, ὃ τῷ Κυρίῳ
ἀνατίθημι, δι᾽ ὃν ὑπέμεινα πεῖναν καὶ δίψαν, ψῦχος καὶ
καύσωνα, γυμνότητα καὶ στενοχωρίαν. Αὐτὸς ἔνδυσον
τοῦτο ἔνδυμα δόξης ἐν τῇ φρικτῇ ἡμέρᾳ τῆς παρουσίας
Σου. Σώζοισθε οἱ ὀφθαλμοί μου οὓς ἐμάραναν αἱ πάννυχοι
ἀγρυπνίαι, καὶ λοιπὸν ἀναπαύεσθε. Σώζοισθε οἱ πόδες
μου, οὓς κατέθλασα ὁλονύκτοις στάσεσιν προσευχῆς. Σώζοισθε ἀσκηταί, οἱ ἐν φάραγξι τῶν ὀρέων κεκοιμημένοι.
Σώζοισθε δέσμιοι, οἱ διὰ τὴν τῶν οὐρανῶν βασιλείαν
καταπονούμενοι. Σώζοισθε οἱ ἐζωγρημένοι καὶ παρηγό-
ρους μὴ ἔχοντες. Σώζοισθε λαῦραι, σώζου πιστὴ ἐκκλησία
ὁ ἱλασμὸς τῶν ἁμαρτιῶν. Σώζοισθε ἱερεῖς Κυρίου, μεσῖται
Θεοῦ καὶ ἀνθρώπων. Σώζοισθε τέκνα, τὰ τῷ Χριστῷ
ἁρμοσθέντα διὰ τοῦ θείου βαπτίσματος. Σώζοισθε οἱ τοὺς

follow the same course as that of your journey here. Brother Serapion, this is a great day for me, greater than all the other days of my life; for today my soul is leaving this pathetic body behind and is departing to rest in the dwellings of life. Today my body will be at rest from its many toils and labors. Today I shall take my place in the land of my repose."

After he had completed his speech in this way, the cave 20 was suddenly flooded with light brighter than the sun and that mountain was filled with the fragrance of perfumes. He took my hand and started speaking again: "Farewell, cavern in which I pleased God with this body that dwelled in you during my lifetime and that will again remain here until our common resurrection. Farewell to you too, body, the home of my labors and distresses and toils, the body which I dedicate to the Lord, for whom I endured hunger and thirst, cold and heat, nakedness and distress. May You dress it in a garment of glory on the awesome day of Your second coming. Farewell to you, my eyes which the all-night vigils wasted away; rest now! Farewell to you, my feet, which I wore out by standing in prayer through entire nights. Farewell to you, ascetics, who have reposed in the ravines of the mountains. Farewell to you, prisoners, who toil for the kingdom of heaven. Farewell to you, *captives,* who have no one to console you. Farewell to you, lavras. Farewell to you, faithful church, the *expiation for sins.* Farewell to you, *priests of the Lord,* mediators between God and humans. Farewell to you, children, who were joined with Christ through the holy baptism. Farewell to you who welcome strangers as Christ,

ξένους ὡς τὸν Χριστὸν ὑποδεχόμενοι, φίλοι Θεοῦ καὶ ξενοδόχοι. Σώζοισθε οἱ ἐλεήμονες, σώζοισθε οἱ πλούσιοι, σώζοισθε βασιλεῖς καὶ ἄρχοντες, οἱ ὄντες συμπαθεῖς πρὸς τοὺς πένητας καὶ τοὺς πλησίον. Σώζοισθε οἱ ταπεινόφρονες νηστευταὶ καὶ ἀγωνισταὶ οἱ τοῖς πόνοις *μὴ ἐκλυόμενοι.* Σώζοισθε οἱ σπουδαῖοι ἐν ταῖς προσευχαῖς καὶ ἐν ταῖς ἁγίαις ἐκκλησίαις ἐπαγρυπνοῦντες. Σώζοισθε πάντες· σώζου τὸ ὅρος τοῦτο· σώζου γῆ καὶ πάντες οἱ κατοικοῦντες ἐν αὐτῇ, ἐν ἀγάπῃ καὶ εἰρήνῃ Χριστοῦ."

21   Στραφεὶς δὲ καὶ πρός με ἠσπάσατό με εἰπών, "Σώζου, Ἀδελφὲ Σεραπίων. Χριστός, οὗ ἐλπίδι τῆς ἀνταποδόσεως τὸν δι' ἐμὲ κόπον ὑπέμεινας, αὐτὸς παράσχοι σοι τὸν μισθὸν τοῦ κόπου σου ἐν τῇ ἡμέρᾳ τῆς παρουσίας αὐτοῦ." Καὶ πάλιν λέγει μοι, "Ἀδελφὲ Σεραπίων, ὁρκίζω σε κατὰ τοῦ Χριστοῦ τοῦ υἱοῦ τοῦ Θεοῦ τοῦ ζῶντος μὴ λάβῃς τι ἐκ τοῦ ταπεινοῦ μου σώματος ἕως μιᾶς τριχός, μηδὲ προσάψῃς αὐτῷ ἔνδυμα ἱματίου, ἀλλὰ αἱ τρίχες αἷς ἐνέδυσεν αὐτὸ ὁ Θεός, ἔστωσαν αὐτῷ ἐντάφια. Καὶ μὴ μείνῃς ἐνταῦθα σήμερον."

22   Καὶ ταῦτα εἰπόντος αὐτοῦ καὶ ἐμοῦ θρηνοῦντος, *φωνὴ γέγονεν ἐκ τοῦ οὐρανοῦ λέγουσα, "Ἀγάγετέ μοι τὸ σκεῦος τῆς ἐκλογῆς τῆς ἐρήμου. Ἀγάγετέ μοι τὸν ἐργάτην τῆς δικαιοσύνης καὶ τέλειον Χριστιανὸν καὶ δοῦλον πιστόν. Δεῦρο, Μάρκε, δεῦρο ἀναπαύου ἐν τῇ χώρᾳ τῆς χαρᾶς καὶ τῆς πνευματικῆς ζωῆς."* Καὶ εὐθέως ὁ ἅγιος λέγει μοι, "Κλίνωμεν γόνυ, ἀδελφέ." Καὶ κλινάντων ἡμῶν τὰ γόνατα, εἰσήκουσα τῆς φωνῆς ἀγγέλου λεγούσης πρὸς τὸν ἕτερον, "Ἔκτεινον τὰς ἀγκάλας καὶ δέξαι." Ἃ καὶ ἀκούσας ἐγὼ

you friends of God and his hosts. Farewell to you, merciful ones, farewell to you, who are wealthy, farewell to you, *kings and governors,* all of you who show compassion to the poor and to your neighbors. Farewell to you, the humble, the fasters and contenders who are *not fainthearted* in their labors. Farewell to you, who are diligent in your prayers and who keep vigil in the holy churches. Farewell to everyone, farewell to this mountain, farewell to the earth and all who dwell on it in the love and peace of Christ."

Then he also turned to me and embraced me, saying, 21 "Farewell, Brother Serapion. May Christ, in the hope of whose reward you endured those toils on my behalf, repay you for your trouble on the day of his second coming." And again he said to me, "Brother Serapion, I bind you by oath before Christ the son of the living God not to take anything from my wretched body, not even a single hair, and not to put any clothing on my body, but to let the hair with which God clothed it be its burial shroud. And do not linger here today."

When he had said these words and I was mourning, *a* 22 *voice* came *from heaven,* saying, "Bring me *the chosen instrument* of the desert. Bring me the worker of righteousness, the perfect Christian and faithful servant. Come, Markos, come; take your repose in the land of joy and spiritual life." And immediately the holy man said to me, "Let us kneel, brother." And when we were kneeling, I heard an angel's voice say to another, "Stretch out your arms and take him."

ἐξέστην. Καὶ ἀτενίσας, εἶδον τὴν ψυχὴν τοῦ ἁγίου βαστα-
ζομένην ὑπὸ ἀγγέλων, καὶ ἐνδεδυμένην στολὴν λευκήν,
καὶ ἀναφερομένην εἰς τοὺς οὐρανούς. Καὶ ἀνεκαλύφθη ἡ
στέγη τοῦ οὐρανοῦ, καὶ εἶδον τὰς φυλὰς τῶν δαιμόνων
ἱσταμένας ἑτοίμως· καὶ ἤκουσα φωνῆς λεγούσης, "Φύγετε,
υἱοὶ τοῦ σκότους! Φύγετε ἀπὸ προσώπου τοῦ φωτὸς τῆς
δικαιοσύνης." Καὶ ἐνεποδίσθη ἡ ψυχὴ τοῦ ἁγίου ὡσεὶ ὥραν
μίαν. Καὶ ἤκουσα φωνῆς λεγούσης καὶ προτρεπομένης
τοὺς ἀγγέλους, "Ἄρατε, πορεύεσθε, τὸν καταισχύναντα
τοὺς δαίμονας." Παρελθούσης δὲ τῆς ψυχῆς αὐτοῦ τὰς
φυλὰς τῶν δαιμόνων, εὐθέως ἐθεασάμην ὡς ὁμοίωμα δε-
ξιᾶς χειρός, ἐκταθείσης ἐκ τοῦ οὐρανοῦ καὶ δεξαμένης τὴν
ψυχὴν αὐτοῦ. Καὶ οὐκέτι οὐδὲν ἑώρακα. Ἦν δὲ ὥρα ἕκτη
τῆς νυκτός.

23   Καὶ ποιήσας πᾶσαν τὴν νύκτα προσευχόμενος ἕως
πρωί, καὶ τὴν ὑμνῳδίαν τελέσας ἐπάνω τοῦ σώματος, βα-
στάσας ἐθέμην ἐν τῷ σπηλαίῳ· οὗ τὸ στόμιον φράξας
λίθοις, κατῆλθον τοῦ ὄρους, ἱκετεύων καὶ δεόμενος τὸν
Θεὸν γενέσθαι μοι βοηθόν, τοῦ ὑπεξελθεῖν τὴν φοβερὰν
ἐκείνην ἔρημον. Καὶ περὶ δυσμὰς ἡλίου, ἰδοὺ οἱ δύο ἡσυ-
χασταὶ ἐκεῖνοι οἱ ὀφθέντες μοι καθημένῳ πρὸς τὸν Ἀββᾶν
Ἰωάννην, καὶ αὖθις ὀφθέντες μοι ἐν τῇ ἐρήμῳ, παρεγένοντο λέγοντές μοι, "Ἀληθῶς, ἀδελφέ, ἐκήδευσας σήμερον σῶμα, οὗ οὐκ ἔστιν ὁ κόσμος ἀντάξιος. Ἀναστὰς οὖν
ὁδοιπόρησον νύκτωρ μεθ᾿ ἡμῶν· ἀὴρ γάρ ἐστιν καταψύ-
χων· τὴν γὰρ ἡμέραν οὐ δυνήσει περιπατεῖν διὰ τὴν τοῦ
ἡλίου θερμότητα." Καὶ ἀναστὰς συνεπορεύθην αὐτοῖς ἕως

And when I heard these words, I was astounded. And I turned my gaze and saw the soul of the holy man being held by angels and clothed in a white garment and borne up to the heavens. And the roof of the heaven was opened up and I saw the tribes of the demons standing ready; and I heard a voice saying, "Get away, you sons of darkness! Get away from the face of *the light of righteousness!*" And the holy man's soul was held back for about an hour. And then I heard a voice speak, urging the angels, "Go, get the one who put the demons to shame." As his soul passed through the tribes of the demons, I saw immediately something resembling a right hand stretching out from heaven and receiving his soul. And then, I no longer saw anything. It was the sixth hour of the night.

I spent the entire night praying until dawn, and when I had completed the service over his body, I picked it up and placed it in the cave. After I had sealed the entrance with rocks, I came down from the mountain beseeching and praying to God to give me a helper so that I might get out of that terrible desert. And, about sunset, lo and behold, those two hesychasts, who had appeared to me while I was seated by Abba John and whom I had seen again in the desert, came to me, saying, "Truly, brother, today you have buried a body *of whom the world is not worthy.* So get up and walk during the night with us; for the air is cooling and you will not be able to walk during the day because of the heat of the sun." I got

πρωί. Εἶτα, λέγει μοι, "Πορεύου ἐν εἰρήνῃ καὶ εὔχου ὑπὲρ ἡμῶν."

24   Οὐ μακρὰν δὲ γενόμενος αὐτῶν, ἀτενίσας εἶδον, καὶ ἰδοὺ ἱστάμην εἰς τὴν θύραν τῆς ἐκκλησίας τοῦ Ἀββᾶ Ἰωάννη. Καὶ ἔκθαμβος γεγονώς, ἐδόξαζον τὸν Θεὸν φωνῇ μεγάλῃ, ἀναμνησθεὶς τῶν λόγων τοῦ Ἁγίου Μάρκου εἰπόντος μοι, ὅτι "Οὐκ ἐν τῇ τρίβῳ τῆς ἐνταῦθα ἐλεύσεώς σου ἔσται ἡ ὑποστροφή σου." Καὶ πεπίστευκα ὡς ἀοράτῳ βασταγμῷ διὰ τῶν εὐχῶν αὐτοῦ ἀπενεχθῆναι ἔνθα ἤμην τὸ πρότερον. Καὶ ἐμεγάλυνον τὰ ἐλέη τοῦ ἀγαθοῦ καὶ φιλανθρώπου Θεοῦ ἡμῶν, ἃ ἐποίησέ μοι, τῷ ἀναξίῳ, διὰ τῶν πρεσβειῶν καὶ εὐχῶν τοῦ Ἁγίου Μάρκου καὶ πιστοῦ δούλου αὐτοῦ.

25   Τούτων τῶν φωνῶν ἀκούσας ὁ Ἀββᾶς Ἰωάννης, ἐξῆλθε καὶ λέγει μοι, "Ἐν εἰρήνῃ μετὰ Θεὸν παρεγένου, Ἀββᾶ Σεραπίων." Καὶ εἰσελθὼν σὺν αὐτῷ ἐν τῇ ἐκκλησίᾳ, διηγησάμην αὐτῷ καὶ τοῖς συνελθοῦσιν ἅπαντα κατὰ μέρος τὰ γεγονότα. Καὶ πάντες ἐδόξαζον τὸν Θεόν, τὸν ποιοῦντα μεγάλα τε καὶ ἐξαίσια ὧν οὐκ ἔστιν ἀριθμός. Ὁ δὲ Ἀββᾶς Ἰωάννης ἀναστὰς μέσον, εἶπεν, "Ἀληθῶς, ἀδελφοί, ἐκεῖνος ἦν τέλειος Χριστιανός, ἐπεὶ ἡμεῖς ὀνόματι μόνῳ, ἔργῳ δὲ οὐδαμῶς." Ὁ δὲ φιλάνθρωπος καὶ ἐλεήμων Θεός, ὁ παραλαβὼν τὸν Ἅγιον Μάρκον καὶ δοῦλον αὐτοῦ, εἰς τὰς αἰωνίους αὐτοῦ αὐλὰς τῆς βασιλείας τῶν οὐρανῶν, αὐτὸς σκεπάσαι ἡμᾶς ὑπὸ τὰς πτέρυγας τῆς χάριτος αὐτοῦ καὶ ὁδηγήσαι ἡμᾶς εἰς τὸ θέλημα αὐτοῦ, εὐχαῖς καὶ πρεσβείαις τοῦ ὁσίου πατρὸς ἡμῶν Μάρκου, καὶ πάντων τῶν ἁγίων, ἀμήν.

up and I walked with them until dawn. Then, he said to me, "Walk in peace and pray for us."

I had not gone too far away from them when I looked up 24 and I saw, lo and behold, I was standing at the door of the church of Abba John. And I was astounded and began to glorify God with a loud voice, remembering the words of Saint Markos who told me that "Your return journey will not follow the same course as that of your journey here." And I believe that I was brought back to where I was before through his prayers, as if by invisible transportation. And I extolled the mercies that our good and philanthropic God bestowed upon me, the unworthy one, through the intercessions and prayers of Saint Markos, his loyal servant.

When Abba John heard these cries, he came out; and he 25 said to me, "You've come here in peace with God's help, Abba Serapion." And I went with him into the church, and I told him and those who gathered there everything in detail that had happened. And everyone began to glorify God, *who works great and extraordinary things without number.* Abba John stood up in the center and said, "Truly, brothers, that man was a perfect Christian, while we are Christians in name only and not at all in deed." May the compassionate and merciful God, who received Saint Markos, his servant, into his eternal courts of the kingdom of heaven, shelter us under the wings of his grace, and lead us into his will, by the prayers and the intercessions of our holy father Markos, and of all the saints, amen.

LIFE OF MAKARIOS
THE ROMAN

Βίος καὶ πολιτεία τοῦ ὁσίου πατρὸς ἡμῶν Μακαρίου τοῦ Ῥωμαίου, τοῦ εὑρεθέντος ἀπὸ εἴκοσι μιλίων τοῦ Παραδείσου

Παρακαλοῦμεν ἡμεῖς οἱ ταπεινοὶ καὶ ἐλάχιστοι μοναχοί, Θεόφιλος, καὶ Σέργιος, καὶ Ὑγιεῖνος, πάντας τοὺς ὁσίους πατέρας καὶ ἀδελφούς, ἀκούσατε νουνεχῶς τὴν πολιτείαν τοῦ Ἁγίου Μακαρίου τοῦ Ῥωμαίου.

2   Ἀποταξάμενοι οὖν ἡμεῖς τὸν βίον τοῦ κόσμου τούτου, εἰσήλθομεν ἐν τῷ μοναστηρίῳ τοῦ μεγάλου ἀνδρός, Ἀσκληπιοῦ τοῦ ἡγουμένου, ἐν τῇ Μεσοποταμίᾳ Συρίας, μεταξὺ τῶν δύο ποταμῶν, τοῦ τ᾽ Εὐφράτου καὶ τοῦ Τίγρη. Καὶ ποιησάντων ἡμῶν τὴν ἐννάτην ὥραν τῆς εὐχῆς, ἀπήλθομεν οἱ τρεῖς ἐν ἰδιάζοντι τόπῳ, καὶ ἐκαθέσθημεν ὁμοῦ, καὶ ἠρξάμεθα ὁμιλεῖν εἰς ἀλλήλους, περὶ ἐγκρατείας καὶ ἀσκήσεως.

3   Καὶ ἐν τῷ ὁμιλεῖν ἡμᾶς ταῦτα, εἰσῆλθεν ἐν τῷ νοΐ μου τοῦ ταπεινοῦ Θεοφίλου λογισμὸς τοιοῦτος· καὶ εἶπον τοῖς μετ᾽ ἐμὲ ἀδελφοῖς, Σεργίῳ καὶ Ὑγιείνῳ λέγων, "Ἤθελον, ἀγαπητοί, πάντα τὰ ἔτη τῆς ζωῆς μου, περιπατεῖν ἕως οὗ ἴδω, ποῦ ἀναπέπαυται ὁ οὐρανός, ἐπειδὴ λέγουσιν αἱ γραφαί, ὅτι ἐπὶ στύλου σιδηροῦ ἀναπέπαυται." Καὶ εἶπον οἱ ἀδελφοί, "Ἀδελφὲ Θεόφιλε, ἀντὶ τοῦ μεγάλου ἀνδρὸς

Life and conduct of our
holy father Makarios the Roman,
who was discovered
twenty miles from Paradise

We, the humble and least among monks, Theophilos, Sergios, and Hygienos, ask all of you, holy fathers and brothers, to please listen carefully to the life of Saint Makarios the Roman.

After we renounced the life of this world, we joined the 2 monastery of the great man Asklepios the abbot; this was in Mesopotamia in Syria, between the two rivers, Euphrates and Tigris. When we had completed the prayers of the ninth hour, the three of us went to a private place on our own, sat together, and began talking to each other about chastity and ascetic discipline.

And as we were talking about these matters, the follow- · 3 ing thought came into my mind, me, humble Theophilos; and I said these words to Sergios and Hygienos, the brothers who were with me: "Dear friends, all the years of my life I have wanted to walk until I could see where the heaven rests, because the scriptures say that it rests on an iron pillar." And the brothers said, "Brother Theophilos, we

καὶ ἡγουμένου ἔχομέν σε ὡς πρῶτον ἀδελφὸν καὶ πατέρα πνευματικόν, καὶ ἀπὸ τοῦ νῦν ὅπου δ' ἂν πορεύῃ ἀχώριστοί σου ἐσόμεθα· καὶ γὰρ καὶ ἡμῖν ἤρεσεν ὁ λόγος οὗτος."

4   Καὶ γενομένης ἑσπέρας βαθείας, ἐξήλθομεν ἐκ τοῦ μοναστηρίου ἀμφότεροι, λαθραίως τοῦ ἡγουμένου καὶ τῶν ἀδελφῶν. Καὶ ὁδεύσαντες, ἤλθομεν ἐν Ἱεροσολύμοις δι' ἡμερῶν δεκαοκτώ, προσκυνήσαντες τὴν ἁγίαν Ἀνάστασιν καὶ τὸν τίμιον καὶ ζωοποιὸν σταυρόν. Ἀπήλθομεν δὲ καὶ εἰς τὴν ἁγίαν Βηθλεέμ, καὶ προσκυνήσαντες τὸ τίμιον καὶ ἅγιον σπήλαιον ἔνθα ἐγεννήθη ὁ Χριστός, εἴδομεν καὶ τὸν ἀστέρα Χριστοῦ καὶ τὸ φρέαρ τοῦ ὕδατος. Ὡς ἀπὸ μιλίων δύο ἀπήλθομεν καὶ εἰς τὸν τόπον ὅπου οἱ ἄγγελοι μετὰ τῶν ποιμένων ἔψαλλον τὸ "Δόξα ἐν ὑψίστοις Θεῷ καὶ ἐπὶ γῆς εἰρήνη ἐν ἀνθρώποις εὐδοκία!" Καὶ ὑποστρέψαντες ἀνήλθομεν εἰς τὸ Ὄρος τῶν Ἐλαιῶν, ἔνθα ὁ Κύριος ἀνελήφθη. Μετὰ δὲ ταῦτα ὑποστρέψαντες πάλιν εἰσήλθομεν εἰς Ἱερουσαλήμ, καὶ ἐποιήσαμεν ἐκεῖ ἡμέρας εἴκοσι, περιερχόμενοι εἰς τὰ ἁγιάσματα, καὶ εἰς τὰ ἐκεῖσε μοναστήρια, εὐχόμενοι καὶ εὐλογούμενοι. Καὶ δοξάζοντες τὸν Θεὸν ἐσφραγίσαμεν ἑαυτούς, ὡς μὴ προσδοκῶντες ἔτι ἰδεῖν τὸν κόσμον τοῦτον.

5   Διοδεύσαντες οὖν ἐπὶ ἡμέρας πεντήκοντα πέντε, καὶ περάσαντες τὸν Τίγρην ποταμόν, εἰσήλθομεν εἰς τὴν χώραν τῶν Περσῶν. Καὶ ἤλθομεν εἰς κάμπον ὁμαλὸν καλούμενον Ἀσίαν, ὅπου ὁ Ἅγιος Μερκούριος, ἀνεῖλεν Ἰουλιανὸν τὸν Παραβάτην. Ἤλθομεν δὲ καὶ εἰς τὰ μέρη τῆς Περσίδος, εἰς πόλιν καλουμένην Κτησιφῶν, ἐν ᾗ

consider you our superior brother and spiritual father, instead of the great man, the abbot; and from now on, wherever you go, we shall be inseparable from you; for we like your plan."

And when it became late in the evening, all three of us 4 left the monastery secretly from the abbot and the brothers. And after journeying for eighteen days, we arrived in Jerusalem and paid our respects at the holy church of the Anastasis and at the precious and life-giving cross. We also went to holy Bethlehem, and paid our respects at the precious and holy cave where Christ was born, and saw Christ's star and the well of water. About two miles from there, we came also to the place where the angels, together with the shepherds, sang *"Glory to God in the highest, and on earth peace among men with whom he is pleased!"* And when we returned, we went up to the Mount of Olives, the place of Christ's assumption. After all this, we went back into Jerusalem and spent twenty days there, visiting the holy sites and the monasteries there, praying, being blessed. And glorifying God, we made the sign of the cross upon ourselves like people who did not expect to see this world again.

After we had journeyed for another fifty-five days and 5 crossed the river Tigris, we came into the land of the Persians. And we arrived at a level plain called Asia, where Saint Merkourios killed Julian the Apostate. We also went to the region of Persis, into the city which is called Ctesiphon,

κατάκεινται οἱ ἅγιοι τρεῖς παῖδες, Ἀνανίας Ἀζαρίας καὶ Μισαήλ· καὶ προσκυνήσαντες αὐτούς, ἐδοξάσαμεν τὸν Κύριον, τὸν καταξιώσαντα ἡμᾶς προσκυνῆσαι αὐτούς.

6   Καὶ ἐξελθόντες ἐκ τῆς πόλεως Κτησιφῶν, διωδεύσαμεν καὶ διὰ τεσσάρων μηνῶν περάσαντες τὴν χώραν τῶν Περσῶν ἤλθομεν εἰς τὴν χώραν τῆς Ἰνδίας. Καὶ εἰσελθόντες εἰς μίαν σκηνὴν τῶν Ἰνδῶν, τὴν παρακειμένην ἐπὶ δυσμάς, ἐδίωξαν ἡμᾶς οἱ ἄνδρες τῆς Ἰνδίας (οὐ γὰρ ἔχουσι πόλιν, ἀλλὰ σκηνὰς κατὰ τόπον).

7   Καὶ πάλιν ἀπήλθομεν εἰς ἄλλην σκηνήν, μὴ ἔχουσαν ἄνθρωπον. Καὶ μείναντες ἐν αὐτῇ ἡμέρας δύο, ἦλθεν ἀνδρόγυνον, φοροῦντα ἐν τῇ κεφαλῇ αὐτῶν ἐν τάξει στεφάνων, ἔχοντα ὀξεῖα βέλη. Καὶ ἰδόντες ἡμᾶς σφόδρα ἐφοβήθησαν· νομίζοντες γὰρ ὅτι κατάσκοποί ἐσμεν τῆς χώρας αὐτῶν, ἀπελθόντες πρὸς αὐτῶν ὁμοφύλους, συνήχθησαν ὡς δισχίλιοι ἄνδρες· καὶ κυκλώσαντες τὴν σκηνήν, εὗρον ἡμᾶς προσευχομένους καὶ δυσωποῦντας τὸν Θεόν. Εἶτα πάραυτα βαλόντες πῦρ γύρωθεν, ἐβούλοντο ἡμᾶς κατακαῦσαι. Ἡμεῖς δὲ φοβηθέντες, ἐξήλθομεν ἀπὸ τῆς σκηνῆς, καὶ εὑρέθημεν ἱστάμενοι μέσον αὐτῶν, μὴ δυνάμενοι φυγεῖν. Κἀκεῖνοι ἐλάλουν ἡμῖν τῇ ἰδίᾳ διαλέκτῳ· ἡμεῖς δὲ τί ἔλεγον οὐκ οἴδαμεν· καὶ μὴ γνωρίζοντες τὴν φωνὴν αὐτῶν, οὐδὲν ἀπεκρινάμεθα.

8   Κρατήσαντες οὖν ἡμᾶς, ἐνέκλεισαν ἐν οἴκῳ στενωτάτῳ, παραγγείλαντες ἕως ἡμερῶν δέκα, μήτε φαγεῖν, μήτε πιεῖν δοθῆναι ἡμῖν. Ἡμεῖς δὲ ἐν εὐχαῖς καὶ δάκρυσιν καὶ ὑπομονῇ τῷ Θεῷ εὐχαριστοῦμεν, ἡμέρας τε καὶ νυκτός. Καὶ μετὰ τὰς δέκα ἡμέρας, νομίζοντες ὅτι τεθνήκαμεν,

where the three holy youths, Ananias, Azarias, and Misael, are buried; we paid our respects to them, and glorified the Lord who deemed us worthy to pay our respects to them.

And when we left the city of Ctesiphon, we journeyed for 6 four months as we crossed the land of the Persians, and we arrived in the land of India. And when we entered one of the tents of the Indians which lay toward the west (for they do not have a city but live in tents set up here and there), the men of India threw us out.

And again we went to another tent, where there was no 7 one. And, after we had stayed there for two days, an androgyne came, wearing on their head sharp arrows instead of crowns. And when they saw us, they became very scared; thinking that we were spies in their land, they went off to their kinsmen, and gathered about two thousand men; and when they surrounded our tent, they found us praying and beseeching God. They then immediately began to throw fire at us from all directions, wishing to burn us up. As we were frightened, we came out of the tent, and found ourselves in the middle of them and unable to flee. And they started talking to us in their own language, but we could not understand what they were saying, and since we did not know their tongue, we didn't respond a word.

After they captured us, they shut us up in a very con- 8 stricted tent, with orders that we should be given neither food nor drink for ten days. Day and night we gave thanks to God in prayers and tears and with perseverance. And after the ten days, thinking that we were dead, they gathered a

συλλαβόντες μεθ᾽ ἑαυτῶν ὄχλον πολύν, καὶ ἀνοίξαντες τὴν σκηνήν, εὗρον ἡμᾶς κεκλικότας τὰ γόνατα, καὶ τῷ Κυρίῳ προσευχομένους. Καὶ βουλευσάμενοι εἰς ἑαυτούς, ἀπήλασαν ἡμᾶς ἀπ᾽ αὐτῶν, τύπτοντες μετὰ ξύλων ἀγρίων. Εἴχομεν δὲ ἡμέρας πολλάς, μὴ γευσάμενοι βρώσεώς τινος. Τότε σφραγίσαντες ἑαυτούς, ἐν ὀνόματι τοῦ Πατρὸς καὶ τοῦ Υἱοῦ καὶ τοῦ Ἁγίου Πνεύματος, τῇ φερομένῃ ὡδεύσαμεν ὁδῷ ἐπὶ ἡμέρας πολλὰς κατὰ ἀνατολάς.

9 Καὶ περιπατούντων ἡμῶν ἐπὶ ἡμέρας τεσσαράκοντα, ἐφθάσαμεν εἰς τόπον ἔνδοξον καὶ εὔκαρπον, οὗ ἦσαν δένδρα πολλὰ καρποφόρα, ὡραῖα τῷ εἴδει καὶ τῇ βρώσει ὑπέρκαλα, πλῆθος πολὺ γέμοντα καρπῶν. Καὶ δοξάσαντες τὸν Κύριον ἡμῶν Ἰησοῦν Χριστόν, ἐφάγομεν τοῦ καρποῦ αὐτῶν, καὶ ἐνεπλήσθημεν εἰς κόρον. Κἀκεῖθεν ἤλθομεν εἰς τὴν χώραν τῶν Κυνοκεφάλων. Καὶ διοδεύσαντες ἐν μέσῳ αὐτῶν, ἐθαύμαζον τρανίζοντες καὶ μηδὲν ἀδικοῦντες, μόνον δὲ προσεῖχον ἡμῖν. Κατὰ τόπον δὲ ἐκάθηντο σὺν γυναιξὶ καὶ τέκνοις γυμνοί, ἕκαστος ἔχων φωλεὰν ὑποκάτω πέτρας, ἄγριοι ὥσπερ θηρία. Ἡμεῖς δὲ τῇ φερομένῃ περιπατοῦντες κατὰ ἀνατολὰς δι᾽ ἡμερῶν ἑκατὸν ἢ καὶ πλείω, ἤλθομεν εἰς τὴν χώραν τῶν πιθήκων. Καὶ θεωροῦντες ἡμᾶς, ἔφυγον ἀφ᾽ ἡμῶν. Καὶ ἐδοξάσαμεν τὸν Κύριον, τὸν ῥυσάμενον ἡμᾶς ἐκ τοῦ στόματος αὐτῶν.

10 Καὶ πάλιν ἤλθομεν εἰς ὄρος ὑψηλὸν λίαν, ὅπου οὔτε ἥλιος ἔλαμπεν, οὔτε δένδρον ὥρατο, οὔτε βοτάνη ἐφύη ποτέ· εἰ μὴ μόνον ἑρπετὰ ἰοβόλα κατῴκουν ἐν αὐτῷ, ἀσπίδες, καὶ ἔχιδνες, καὶ δράκοντες, πρὸς ἀλλήλους συρίζοντες, καὶ τρισμὸν ὀδόντων ἀποτελοῦντες. Εἴδομεν δὲ καὶ

great crowd with them, opened the tent, and found us kneeling and praying to the Lord. And, after deliberating among themselves, they expelled us from there, striking us with cruel clubs. We had not eaten anything for many days. Then we made the sign of the cross upon ourselves, in the name of the Father and the Son and the Holy Spirit, and went on our way, traveling eastward for many days.

And after we had walked for forty days, we reached a glorious and fertile place, where there were many fruit-bearing trees, beautiful to look at and beyond beauty as food, filled with a great multitude of fruits. And after we had glorified our Lord Jesus Christ, we ate from their fruits, and were filled to satisfaction. And from there we came to the land of the Cynocephali. We passed among them, and they were in awe, staring at us, and not doing us any harm but only with their eyes fixed on us. They were sitting naked here and there, with their wives and children, each with a lair under rocks, wild like beasts. We went on our way eastward for a hundred or even more days, and came into the land of the apes. And when they saw us, they fled away from us. And we glorified the Lord, who saved us from their mouths. 9

And again we came to a very high mountain, where neither the sun shone, nor a tree could be seen, nor a plant ever grew; only poisonous reptiles lived there, asps, and vipers, and serpents, hissing at each other, and producing a gnashing of teeth. We also saw many other beasts, whose names 10

θηρία ἕτερα πολλά, ὧν τὰ ὀνόματα οὐκ οἴδαμεν καλέσαι·
ἐγνωρίσαμεν δὲ βουβάλους καὶ βασιλίσκους καὶ μονο-
κέρους καὶ ὀνοκενταύρους καὶ λεοπάρδους, καὶ τὰ ἄλλα
πάντα ὅσα εἰσὶν ἐπὶ τῆς γῆς· καὶ ἐδοξάσαμεν τὸν Κύριον,
τὸν ῥυσάμενον ἡμᾶς ἐκ τοῦ στόματος αὐτῶν, καὶ ἐνισχύ-
οντα ἡμᾶς ἐν πάσῃ ὁδῷ. Καὶ περιπατούντων ἡμῶν ἐπὶ
ἡμέρας εἴκοσι, ἀκούοντες τὴν φωνὴν τῶν δρακόντων
ἐφράζομεν τὰ ὦτα ἡμῶν ἐκ κηροῦ, ὡς μὴ δυναμένων ἡμῶν
ὑπομεῖναι τὴν φωνὴν τοῦ συριγμοῦ αὐτῶν· καὶ τοῦ Θεοῦ
κελεύοντος οὐδὲν ἠδικήθημεν παρ' αὐτῶν, ἀλλὰ διήλθομεν τὸ ὄρος ἐκεῖνο ἀβλαβεῖς.

11 Ὅθεν πάλιν ἤλθομεν εἰς κρημνὸν μέγαν, καὶ βαθύν,
ἔνθα οὐδὲ ἴχνος ἐφαίνετο, ὅτι οὐδέπω ἀνθρωπίνη φύσις
ἐκεῖ γέγονεν. Καὶ παραμείναντες ἐκεῖ ἡμέρας ἑπτά, ἐδεήθημεν τοῦ Κυρίου τοῦ σωθῆναι ἡμᾶς ἀπὸ τοῦ μεγάλου καὶ
φοβεροῦ ἐκείνου κρημνοῦ. Καὶ ἰδοὺ ἦλθεν ἔλαφος μέγας,
καὶ ἐμυκήσατο ἀπέναντι ἡμῶν. Καὶ ἀκολουθήσαντες τὴν
φωνὴν αὐτοῦ, εὑρέθημεν καὶ εἰς ἑτέρους κρημνοὺς φοβε-
ρούς· ὅθεν κατελθόντες μετὰ φόβου πολλοῦ καὶ μεγάλου,
μόλις ἤλθομεν εἰς πεδινὸν τόπον. Ἦσαν δὲ ἐκεῖ βοσκόμε-
νοι ἐλέφαντες πολλοί, καὶ εἰς μέσον αὐτῶν διελθόντες
οὐδὲν ἠδικήθημεν παρ' αὐτῶν. Καὶ λοιπὸν οὐκέτι εὑρίσκο-
μεν ὁδὸν εὐθεῖαν. Τότε δεηθέντες τοῦ φιλανθρώπου Θεοῦ,
τῇ φερομένῃ ὁδῷ ὡδεύσαμεν, μηδενὸς γευσάμενοι.

12 Περιπατησάντων δὲ ἡμῶν ἐπὶ ἡμέρας ο', ἤλθομεν εἰς
τόπον ὁμαλόν, καὶ πάνυ πολύδενδρον, ἔχοντα καρπὸν
ἡδύτατον, καὶ οὐκέτι λοιπὸν τὸ φῶς ἐπέλαμψεν ἡμῖν· οὔτε
γὰρ φῶς ἐφαίνετο ἐν τῷ τόπῳ ἐκείνῳ, εἰ μὴ μόνον ὁμίχλη

we did not know; but we did recognize antelopes, and basilisks, and unicorns, donkey-centaurs, and leopards, and all the other beasts living on earth; and we glorified the Lord who saved us from their mouths, and strengthened us in every way. After we had walked for twenty days, hearing the sound of the serpents, we blocked our ears with wax, as we couldn't stand the sound of their hissing. And at God's command, we suffered no harm from them but passed by that mountain safe and sound.

From there, we came again to a huge, high cliff, where no 11 track could be seen, since no human being had ever been there before. And we stayed there for seven days, praying to the Lord that he might save us from that huge and terrifying cliff. And lo and behold, a large deer came and bellowed in front of us. And we followed its voice, and found ourselves at other terrifying cliffs; coming down from there, with much great fear, we just made it to a plain. There, many elephants were grazing, and passing between them, we suffered no harm from them. And from that point on, we could no longer find a straight path. Then we prayed to God who loves mankind, and went on our way, having eaten nothing.

After we had walked for seventy days, we came to a flat 12 place, full of trees which bore the sweetest fruit, but the light no longer shone upon us; for no light could be seen in that place, only a dark fog. And after we had sat down for a

σκοτεινή. Καὶ καθεσθέντες μικρόν, ἐποιήσαμεν ἐκεῖ θρῆνον, καὶ κλαυθμὸν μέγαν, διότι ἐκλείσθη ἡμῶν ἡ ὁδοιπορία καὶ τὸ φῶς τῆς ἡμέρας. Κλαιόντων δὲ ἡμῶν ἐπὶ
ἡμέρας ἑπτὰ καὶ εὐχομένων πρὸς Κύριον, ἀπέστειλεν ἡμῖν
περιστεράν· καὶ καθίσασα εἰς τόπον ὑψηλόν, πάλιν ἀνέστη
περιπετομένη ἔμπροσθεν ἡμῶν. Ἡμεῖς δὲ λαβόντες χαρὰν
μεγάλην, ἐδοξάσαμεν τὸν Κύριον· καὶ ἀκολουθήσαντες
τὴν περιστεράν, εὕρομεν ἀψίδα καμαρωτὴν μεγάλην, ἐπι-
γράφουσαν εἰς τὸν κύκλον τῆς ἀψίδος οὕτως:

"Ταύτην τὴν ἀψίδα ἀνήγειρεν Ἀλέξανδρος, ὁ βασιλεὺς
τῶν Μακεδόνων, ὅταν κατεδίωκεν ἀπὸ Καλχηδόνος Δά-
ριον τὸν Πέρσην ἕως ἐνταῦθα. Ταῦτα δέ εἰσιν τὰ σκοτεινὰ
ἃ διῆλθεν.

"Ὁ θέλων οὖν παρέσω εἰσελθεῖν εἰς τὰ ἀριστερὰ μέρη
περιπατείτω· πάντα γὰρ τὰ ὕδατα τοῦ κόσμου ἐκ τοῦ
ἀριστεροῦ μέρους ἐκπορεύονται. Ὁ γοῦν διερχόμενος τῇ
φωνῇ τῶν ὑδάτων ἀκολουθείτω, καὶ ἐξελεύσεται εἰς τὸ
φῶς. Τὰ δὲ δεξιά, ὄρη εἰσὶ πάντα καὶ κρημνοί, καὶ λίμνη
παμμεγέθης, ὄφεων καὶ σκορπίων μεμεστωμένη."

Ὡς οὖν ἀνέγνωμεν ταῦτα εἰς τὴν ἀψίδα τοῦ Ἀλεξάνδρου, ἐλάβομεν θάρρος καὶ προθυμίαν, καὶ ἐδοξάσαμεν
τὸν Κύριον, τὸν πανταχοῦ διασώζοντα ἡμᾶς. Καὶ ἠρξάμεθα διοδεύειν ἐπὶ τὰ ἀριστερὰ μέρη τῆς ἀψίδος.

13 Καὶ περιπατησάντων ἡμῶν ἐπὶ ἡμέρας τεσσαράκοντα,
ἀπήντησεν ἡμῖν ὀσμὴ δυσωδίας δριμυτάτης· καὶ μὴ φέρον-
τες τὴν τοιαύτην ὀσμὴν τῆς δυσωδίας γεγόναμεν ὡσεὶ
νεκροί. Παρεκαλοῦμεν δὲ καθ᾽ ἑκάστην τῷ Κυρίῳ, τοῦ

little, we began to mourn and lament greatly, because both
our journey and the daylight had been cut off from us. When
we had cried for seven days and prayed to the Lord, he sent
us a dove. And after she had sat on a high place, she then got
up and began flying in front of us. We were overjoyed and
glorified the Lord; and when we followed the dove, we found
a large, vaulted arch. The following was inscribed on the
rounded part of the arch:

"Alexander, the king of the Macedonians, erected this
arch when he was pursuing Darios the Persian all the way
here from Kalchedon. These are the dark lands which he
went through.

"Anyone who wishes to go any further should walk to the
left; for all the waters of the world come from the left. Thus,
anyone traveling through here should follow the sound of
the waters, and he will come out into the light. But to the
right are all mountains, cliffs, and an enormous lake, full of
snakes and scorpions."

When we read these words on the arch of Alexander, we
took courage and inspiration, and we glorified God who
protected us everywhere. So we started walking to the left
of the arch.

After we had walked for forty days, we encountered the 13
stench of a most pungent odor; and as we were unable to
bear such a pungent odor, we became like corpses. Every
day we asked the Lord to let us give up our souls, and we

ἀποδοῦναι τὰς ψυχάς, καὶ ἦμεν ἐν θλίψει ἀνεικάστῳ· ἀνήρχετο δὲ καὶ ὀλολυγμὸς μέγας ὥσπερ χρεμετιζόντων ἵππων.

14 Ὡς οὖν προεκόψαμεν τὴν ὁδόν, εἴδομεν ἀπέναντι ἡμῶν,
καὶ ἰδοὺ λίμνη παμμεγέθης, γέμουσα πλῆθος ὄφεων, ὡς
μὴ φαίνεσθαι τὸ ὕδωρ αὐτῆς ἐξ αὐτῶν· καὶ ἰδοὺ θρῆνος
καὶ ὀλολυγμός, καὶ ὀδυρμὸς πολύς, ὡς ἀπὸ πλήθους
ἀνθρώπων, ἀνήρχετο ἐκ τῆς λίμνης τοῦ ὕδατος. Καὶ ἡκού-
σαμεν φωνὴν ἐκ τῶν οὐρανῶν λέγουσαν, "Οὗτός ἐστιν
ὁ Λάκκος τῆς Κρίσεως· καὶ οὗτοί εἰσιν οἱ ἀρνησάμενοι
τὸν Κύριον." Καὶ μετὰ φόβου μεγάλου παρήλθομεν τὴν
Λίμνην ἐκείνην τῆς Κρίσεως.

15 Ἔτι δὲ πάλιν περιπατησάντων ἡμῶν, οὐκ ὀλίγων ἡμερῶν διάστημα, ἠνέχθημεν ἔν τινι τόπῳ, καὶ εὕρομεν ἐκεῖ
ὄρη δύο ὑψηλά. Καὶ ἦν ἀναμέσον τῶν δύο ὀρέων ἄνθρωπος μακρὸς καὶ ὑψηλός. Καὶ ἦν δεδεμένος ἐν ὅλῳ τῷ σώματι αὐτοῦ ἁλύσεσι χαλκαῖς ὀκτώ· καὶ αἱ μὲν τέσσαρες
ἁλύσεις ἦσαν δεδεμέναι εἰς τὸ δεξιὸν ὄρος, αἱ δὲ ἄλλαι
τέσσαρες εἰς τὸ ἀριστερόν. Ἦν δὲ καὶ πῦρ μέγα καιόμενον
γύρωθεν τοῦ σώματος τοῦ ἀνδρὸς ἐκείνου· καὶ ἀπήρχετο
ἡ φωνὴ αὐτοῦ ὡς ἀπὸ μιλίων τριάκοντα. Καὶ ἰδὼν ἡμᾶς ὁ
ἄνθρωπος ἐκεῖνος, ἤρξατο κλαίειν καὶ θρηνεῖν, καὶ ῥήσ-
σειν τὴν κεφαλὴν αὐτοῦ ἐπὶ τὴν γῆν. Ἦν δὲ ὅλος πεφλο-
γισμένος ὑπὸ τῆς πυρᾶς, ὡς μὴ φαίνεσθαι αὐτοῦ τρίχα
μίαν. Ἡμεῖς δὲ ἐκ τοῦ φόβου καὶ τοῦ τρόμου σκεπάσαντες
τὰς ὄψεις ἡμῶν, διήλθομεν τὰ δύο ὄρη ἐκεῖνα (εἶχεν δὲ
ἡμᾶς φόβος καὶ τρόμος πολύς)· καὶ ἐπὶ ἡμέρας πέντε περιπατούντων ἡμῶν, ἡκούομεν τὴν φωνὴν τοῦ στεναγμοῦ
αὐτοῦ.

were in unimaginable distress; on top of this, there was a great shrieking like horses neighing.

As we went forward on our way, we saw opposite us, lo and behold, an enormous lake, filled with such a mass of snakes, that its water was no longer visible because of the snakes; and, lo and behold, lamentation and shrieks and a great wailing, as from a mass of people, was coming from the water of the lake. And we heard a voice from heaven saying, "This is the Pit of Judgment; and these people are those who rejected Lord." And, with great fear, we passed by that Lake of Judgment. 14

After we had walked on again for the space of many days, we reached some place and we found two high mountains there. And in between these two mountains, there was a man, large and tall. And his whole body was bound by eight brazen chains; and four of the chains were bound to the mountain on the right, and the other four to that on the left. A great fire was also burning all around the body of that man; and his voice reached almost thirty miles. When that man saw us, he began crying and lamenting and throwing his head toward the ground. He was all in flames by the fire, so that not a single hair of his could be seen. Out of fear and terror, we covered our faces, and we passed by these two mountains (for great fear and terror had overcome us); and for five days, as we walked on, we could hear the sound of his groaning. 15

16   Καὶ πάλιν ἤλθομεν ἐν τόπῳ κρημνώδει· καὶ ἦν ἐκεῖ βό-
θυνος παμμεγέθης. Καὶ γυνή τις λυσίτριχος ἔστηκεν ἐπὶ
τοῦ χείλους τοῦ βοθύνου· καὶ ἦν δράκων μέγας, ἐνειλημ-
μένος ἐπ’ αὐτήν, ἀπὸ τῶν ποδῶν ἕως τοῦ τραχήλου αὐτῆς.
Καὶ ὅτε ἤθελεν ἀνοῖξαι τὸ στόμα αὐτῆς τοῦ λαλῆσαι, ἐκό-
λαπτεν ὁ δράκων τὰ χείλη αὐτῆς—ἦσαν δὲ αἱ τρίχες αὐτῆς,
λελυμέναι ἕως τῆς γῆς. Καὶ ἄλλη δὲ φωνὴ ἀνήρχετο ἐκ
τοῦ βοθύνου ἐκείνου, ὥσπερ ἀπὸ ὄχλου πολλοῦ, λέγουσα
ταῦτα: “Ἐλέησον ἡμᾶς, Κύριε, Υἱὲ τοῦ Θεοῦ τοῦ ὑψίστου.”
Ἡμεῖς δὲ ἐκ τοῦ φόβου εἴπομεν, “Κύριε Ἰησοῦ Χριστέ,
πλήρωσον ἡμῶν τὴν ζωὴν ἐν τῷ τόπῳ τούτῳ, ὅτι εἶδον οἱ
ὀφθαλμοὶ ἡμῶν ξένα καὶ παράδοξα μυστήρια καὶ κρίσεις
μεγάλας.”

17   Καὶ πάλιν κλαίοντες καὶ θρηνοῦντες ἤλθομεν εἰς τόπον
τινά, καὶ ἦν ἐκεῖ δένδρον παμμεγέθη, οὗ ἡ ἰδέα ὑπῆρχεν
ὡς ἰδέα συκῆς· καὶ ἦσαν ἐκεῖ ὄρνεα, μυριάδες μυριάδων,
ἅτινα ἦσαν τῇ ἰδέᾳ ὡς στρουθία μικρά, καὶ ἡ λαλιὰ αὐτῶν
πλήρης ἀνθρωπίνης λαλιᾶς. Καὶ ὅλα μιᾷ φωνῇ ἔκραζον
λέγοντα, “Ἄνες ἡμῖν, Κύριε, ἄνες ἡμῖν ὡς ἐλεήμων Θεός,
ὅτι ἡμεῖς ἡμάρτομεν παρὰ πᾶσαν τὴν κτίσιν ἐνώπιόν σου.”
Ἡμεῖς δὲ οἱ ταπεινοὶ θεωροῦντες ταῦτα τὰ φοβερὰ καὶ
ξένα σημεῖα, φόβῳ πολλῷ περιεσχέθημεν· καὶ τῷ Θεῷ
ἐδεήθημεν, ὅπως γνωρίσῃ ἡμῖν τῶν πραγμάτων ἐκείνων
τὴν ἔκβασιν. Καὶ εὐθέως ἐσχίσθη ἡ γῆ ἔμπροσθεν ἡμῶν,
καὶ ἀνέβη φωνὴ λέγουσα, “Οὐκ ἔστιν ὑμῖν δοτὸν μαθεῖν
τὰ μυστήρια ταῦτα· ἀλλὰ πορεύεσθε τὴν ὁδὸν ὑμῶν.”

18   Καὶ διήλθομεν τὸν τόπον ἐκεῖνον μετὰ φόβου. Καὶ πάλιν ἤλθομεν εἰς τόπον ὁμαλόν, φοβερὸν καὶ ἔνδοξον. Καὶ

And again we came to a precipitous place, and there was 16
an enormous pit there. And a woman, with her hair loose,
stood on the edge of the pit; and a large serpent was wrapped
around her, from her feet to her neck. Whenever she wanted
to open her mouth to speak, the serpent would strike her
lips—her hair was let down all the way to the ground. And
another sound came from that pit, as if from a large crowd,
saying this: "Have mercy on us, Lord, *Son of the most high
God*." Out of fear, we said, "Lord Jesus Christ, bring our life
to an end right here, because our eyes have seen strange and
extraordinary secrets and great trials."

And again with tears and lamentation we came to a place 17
where there was an enormous tree, whose appearance re-
sembled the appearance of a fig tree; and there were myriads
upon myriads of birds there, which had the appearance of
small sparrows, and their voices were human voices. All of
them, in unison, were crying out loud, saying, "Forgive us,
Lord, forgive us as a merciful God, because we have sinned
before you above all creation." We, abject men, witnessing
all these terrifying and strange signs, were overcome by
great fear; and we implored God to let us know the outcome
of these matters. Immediately, the earth was split in front of
us, and a voice came up, saying, "It is not for you to learn
these secrets; just go on your way."

And we went through that place full of fear. And again we 18
came to a level place that was terrifying and glorious. And

ἵσταντο ἐκεῖ τέσσαρες ἄνδρες μετὰ τιμῆς μεγάλης, ἔχοντες ἰδέαν ἀνεκδιήγητον· καὶ ἦσαν ἔμπροσθεν τούτων τῶν ἁγίων ἀνδρῶν, ξίφη ἠκονισμένα καὶ ἀποστίλβοντα, εἴδη πολλὰ καὶ διάφορα, ἄσφαλτον καὶ θεῖον, δράκοντες καὶ ἔχιδνες γύρωθεν ταῦτα πάντα, ἔμπροσθεν δὲ αὐτῶν πῦρ μέγα. Καὶ οἱ τέσσαρες ἅγιοι ἄνδρες ἐκεῖνοι ἦσαν φοροῦντες ἐν ταῖς κεφαλαῖς αὐτῶν στεφάνους βασιλικοὺς διαχρύσους· καὶ ἐν ταῖς χερσὶν αὐτῶν ἐκράτουν βραβεῖα χρυσᾶ. Καὶ ταῦτα ἰδόντες ἡμεῖς ἐφοβήθημεν· καὶ ἐρρίψαμεν ἑαυτοὺς ἐπὶ τὴν γῆν εἰς τὸ ἔδαφος, κράζοντες καὶ λέγοντες, "Ἐλεήσατε ἡμᾶς, ἄνδρες οὐράνιοι, καὶ μὴ ἅψωνται ἡμῶν τὰ θηρία καὶ τὰ ξίφη καὶ τὸ πῦρ." Καὶ ἀπεκρίθησαν οἱ ἅγιοι λέγοντες ἡμῖν: "Μὴ φοβεῖσθε, ἀλλὰ ἀναστάντες πορεύεσθε τὴν ὁδὸν ὑμῶν ἐν εἰρήνῃ, ἣν ὁ Κύριος ἐφανέρωσεν ὑμῖν βαδίζειν ἐν αὐτῇ, μηδὲν φοβούμενοι· οὐκ ἔχουσιν γὰρ ἐξουσίαν εἰς ὑμᾶς, διότι ἡμεῖς ἐκελεύσθημεν ταῦτα φυλάττειν ἕως τῆς ἡμέρας ἐκείνης, ὅταν ἔρχεται ὁ Θεὸς ἐν τούτῳ τῷ κόσμῳ." Ταῦτα ἀκούσαντες ἡμεῖς παρ' αὐτῶν, ἀπὸ μακρόθεν προσκυνήσαντες αὐτούς, ἐδοξάσαμεν τὸν Κύριον, καὶ διήλθομεν ἐκεῖθεν ὡς ψυχὴν μὴ ἔχοντες ἐκ τοῦ φόβου, ὁδηγοῦντος ἡμᾶς τοῦ Κυρίου.

19   Καὶ πάλιν περιπατούντων ἡμῶν ἐπὶ ἡμέρας τεσσαράκοντα, μὴ γευσάμενοί τινος εἰ μὴ μόνου ὕδατος, ἐξαίφνης ἦλθεν ἡμῖν φωνὴ ὥσπερ ὄχλων πολλῶν ψαλλόντων, καὶ ὀσμὴ θυμιαμάτων ἀνεικάστων, καὶ ὠσφράνθημεν εὐωδίαν μύρου πολυτίμου. Καὶ ἐκ τῆς φωνῆς τῶν ψαλλόντων καὶ τῆς εὐωδίας τῶν θυμιαμάτων εἰς ὕπνον ἐτράπημεν, ὥστε καὶ ἐκοιμήθημεν, ἐν οἷς καὶ τὰ χείλη ἡμῶν ἐγλυκάνθησαν

four men stood there, with great dignity, with an indescribable appearance; and in front of these holy men there were sharpened and glittering swords, of many different kinds, and there was tar and sulfur, and serpents and vipers all around, and in front of them a great fire. And these four holy men were wearing royal crowns made of gold on their heads; and in their hands they were holding golden wands. When we saw these things, we were scared; and we threw ourselves to the ground on the earth, crying out loud and saying, "Have mercy on us, heavenly men, and do not let those beasts and those swords and this fire touch us." The saints replied to us with these words: "Do not be afraid; but get up and go in peace on your way, which the Lord revealed for you to take fearlessly; for these have no power over you, because we have been ordered to guard them until that day when God shall come to this world." When we heard this from them, we paid our respects to them from afar, glorified the Lord, and passed by there like people dead from fear, but with the Lord guiding us.

And again we went on walking for forty days, without 19 tasting anything except water. All of a sudden, a sound, like a large crowd chanting, reached us, along with the fragrance of unimaginable incense; and we smelled the sweet scent of precious perfumed oil. And because of the sound of those chanting and the sweet scent of the incense we became sleepy and indeed fell asleep, as our lips indulged in sweet-

ὑπὲρ μέλι καὶ κηρίον. Καὶ διυπνισθέντες προσεβλέψαμεν, καὶ ἰδοὺ ναὸς μέγας κρυστάλλινος, καὶ ἔσω τοῦ ναοῦ ὡς θυσιαστηρίου τύπος· καὶ ἀνήρχετο ἐκ τοῦ θυσιαστηρίου ἐκείνου πηγὴ ὕδατος· καὶ ἦν τὸ ὕδωρ λευκὸν ὡς ἰδέα γάλακτος, ὥστε νομίζειν ἡμᾶς ὅτι ἀληθῶς γάλα ἐστί. Καὶ κύκλῳ τῆς πηγῆς, εἱστήκεσαν ἅγιοι ἄνδρες, φοβεροὶ καὶ θαυμαστοί, ψάλλοντες φωνὰς χερουβικὰς καὶ μελῳδίας ἀγγελικάς. Καὶ ἰδόντες αὐτοὺς ἔντρομοι γεγόναμεν· καὶ ἐμείναμεν ἐν τῷ τόπῳ στήκοντες ὡσεὶ νεκροί.

Καὶ ἰδοὺ εἷς ἐξ αὐτῶν, ἀνὴρ ἅγιος, ὡραῖος τῇ ὄψει σφόδρα, ἐκ τῶν ἑστώτων εἰς τὸ ὕδωρ ἐκείνης τῆς πηγῆς, εἶπε πρὸς ἡμᾶς, "Αὕτη ἐστὶν ἡ ἀθάνατος πηγή, ἡ τετηρημένη τοῖς δικαίοις εἰς ἀπόλαυσιν αὐτῶν καὶ ἀνάπαυσιν." Ἡμεῖς δὲ οἱ ἀκούσαντες ταῦτα, πεσόντες ἐπὶ τῆς γῆς, ἐδοξάσαμεν τὸν Θεὸν καὶ τὸν ἅγιον ἄνδρα ἐκεῖνον μετὰ τοὺς συνόντας αὐτῷ. Καὶ λοιπὸν μετὰ πολλοῦ φόβου καὶ χαρᾶς, διήλθομεν τὸν τόπον ἐκεῖνον μηδενὸς γευσάμενοι, ἀλλὰ τὰ χείλη ἡμῶν, ἐκ τῆς γλυκασίας τῆς ἀτμίδος τοῦ ὕδατος ἐκείνου, ἐκολλῶντο ἐπὶ ἡμέρας τρεῖς ὡς ἀπὸ μέλιτος Ἀττικοῦ.

20   Καὶ πάλιν ἤλθομεν ἔγγιστα ποταμοῦ μεγάλου, καὶ πιόντες ἐξ αὐτοῦ ἐκορέσθημεν, καὶ ἐδοξάσαμεν τὸν Κύριον· ἦν δὲ ὥρα ἕκτη μεσημβρίας, καύματος μεγάλου. Καὶ καθίσαντες παρὰ τὸ χεῖλος αὐτοῦ, διενοούμεθα πρὸς ἀλλήλους τί ποιήσωμεν.

Ἦν δὲ λοιπὸν ἀπὸ τοῦ ποταμοῦ ἐκείνου φῶς διπλάσιον τοῦ φωτὸς τούτου. Καὶ ἀναβλέψαντες εἰς τὰς τέσσαρας γωνίας τοῦ οὐρανοῦ καὶ τῆς γῆς, οὐκ ἔπνεον ἐκεῖ οἱ ἄνεμοι

ness surpassing *honey and honeycomb*. And when we woke up, we opened our eyes and lo and behold, a large crystal church was there, and within the church what looked like some kind of altar; and a fountain of water came forth from that altar; and the water was white like the appearance of milk so much so that we thought that it truly was milk. And in a circle around the fountain, stood holy men, fearsome and marvelous, chanting with the voices of cherubim and the melodies of angels. And when we saw them, we started trembling; and we remained standing at that place like dead men.

And, lo and behold, one of those standing near the water of that fountain, a holy man, extremely beautiful in his appearance, said to us, "This is the fountain of immortality, preserved for the righteous, for their pleasure and rest." When we heard these words, we fell to the ground, and we glorified God and that holy man and his companions. And then, with great fear and joy, we passed by that place without tasting anything, but our lips, because of the sweetness of that water's vapor, were glued together for three days as if by Attic honey.

And again we came near a large river, and when we drank 20 from its water we were satisfied, and we glorified the Lord; it was the sixth hour, midday; the heat was great. And we sat by the river's bank and deliberated with each other what we should do.

So the light of that river was double this light. And as we raised our eyes toward the four corners of the heaven and the earth, the winds there did not blow like the winds here;

καθὰ πνέουσιν οἱ ἄνεμοι τῶν ἐνταῦθα· καὶ γὰρ οἱ ἄνεμοι τῶν ἐκεῖ ἄλλην πνοὴν εἶχον· ἡ γὰρ γωνία τῆς ἀνατολῆς ἔχει χροιὰν ὅμοιαν βαλάνου, ἡ δὲ γωνία τῆς δύσεως ἔχει χροιὰν πράσινον, ἡ δὲ γωνία τῆς ἄρκτου χροιὰν αἵματος καθαροῦ, καὶ ἡ γωνία τῆς μεσημβρίας λευκὴν ὡσεὶ χιών. Οἱ δὲ ἀστέρες τοῦ οὐρανοῦ λαμπροτέραν ἔχουσιν ἀκτῖνα λαμπηδόνος· καὶ ὁ ἥλιος ἐκεῖνος θερμότερός ἐστιν ἑπταπλάσιον τούτου· καὶ τὰ δένδρα ἐκεῖνα παμμεγεθέστερα καὶ εὐθαλῆ καὶ δασύκομά εἰσιν, εἴτε εὔκαρπα εἴτε ἄκαρπα· καὶ τὰ ὄρη ἐκεῖνα ὑψηλότερα καὶ εὐειδέστερά εἰσι· καὶ ἡ γῆ πᾶσα ἐκείνη διπρόσωπός ἐστιν, πυροειδὴς καὶ γαλακτίζουσα· ὁμοίως καὶ τὰ ὄρνεα ἐκεῖνα, ἕκαστον κατὰ γένος ἄλλην ἰδέαν ἔχει, καὶ ἄλλως κελαδοῦσιν.

Εἴχομεν δὲ ἡμέρας πολλὰς μηδενὸς γευσάμενοι, εἰ μὴ μόνον τὸ ὕδωρ ἐκεῖνο. Καὶ ἐξαίφνης ἦλθεν πρὸς ἡμᾶς ὄχλος πολύς, ἀνδρῶν τε καὶ γυναικῶν καὶ παίδων—οὐκ οἶδα πόθεν· εἶχον δὲ τὸ μῆκος αὐτῶν ὡσεὶ πῆχυν ἕνα, οἱ δὲ ἄλλοι ἐξ αὐτῶν κονδότεροι. Καὶ ἰδόντες αὐτοὺς ἡμεῖς σφόδρα ἐφοβήθημεν, μήπως καταφάγωσιν ἡμᾶς, καὶ ἐσκεπτόμεθα τί ποιήσωμεν. Ἐγὼ δὲ ὁ ἐλάχιστος Θεόφιλος, εἶπον τοῖς μετ' ἐμέ, "Δεῦτε, ἀδελφοί, ἀναστάντες διαλύσωμεν ἡμῶν τὰς τρίχας τῆς κεφαλῆς, ὡς κατάκομοι ὄντες, καὶ ἐπιδράμωμεν ἐπ' αὐτοὺς καὶ ἢ φεύγουσιν ἡμᾶς, ἢ καταφάγωνται." Καὶ ἀναστάντες ἐποιήσαμεν οὕτως. Οἱ δὲ ἰδόντες ἡμᾶς ἐφοβήθησαν καὶ ἔφυγον τρίζοντες τοὺς ὀδόντας αὐτῶν καὶ ἁρπάζοντες αὐτῶν τὰ τέκνα.

21 Ἡμεῖς δὲ περάσαντες τὸν ποταμὸν ἐκεῖνον, ἀπήλθομεν ἐκεῖθεν· καὶ εὕρομεν ἐκεῖ εἶδος βοτάνης λευκὸν ὥσπερ

for winds there had a different way of blowing: the corner of the east had a hue similar to that of the acorn; the corner of the west had a green hue; the corner of the north had the hue of pure blood; and the corner of the south was white like that of snow. The stars of the heaven there have rays that are brighter than lightning; and that sun is seven times hotter than ours; and those trees are colossal and blooming and with thick foliage, whether they are fruit bearing or not; and those mountains are higher and more beautiful; and that entire earth has a double character, fiery as well as milky; similarly also those birds, each kind has a different appearance and they sing differently.

We were there for many days, tasting nothing, except that water. And suddenly a great crowd of men, women, and children came to us—I don't know from where; their height was about one cubit, and some of them were even shorter. When we saw them, we were very afraid that they would eat us, and we began to think what to do. I, the least Theophilos, said to those with me, "Come on, brothers, let's get up, loosen the hair on our heads, since we have long hair, and run at them, and they'll either flee from us, or they'll devour us." And so we got up and did that. When they saw us, they became afraid and fled, gnashing their teeth and grabbing their children.

After we had crossed that river, we left there; and we 21 found a type of plant there, white like milk, whose taste was

γάλα, οὗ ἡ βρῶσις ἦν ὥσπερ *μέλι καὶ κηρίον,* ἵσταται δὲ ἐπάνω τῆς γῆς ὡς ἐπὶ πῆχυν μίαν· καὶ φαγόντες ἐξ αὐτῆς τῆς βοτάνης ἐκορέσθημεν, καὶ ἠλλάγη ἡμῶν ἡ ὄψις, καὶ ἡ ἰσχὺς ἐνεδυναμώθη, καὶ ἐδοξάσαμεν τὸν Θεὸν τὸν καθ᾽ ἑκάστην ἡμέραν τρέφοντα καὶ ὁδηγοῦντα ἡμᾶς.

22   Καὶ πάλιν ὡδεύσαμεν τῇ φερομένῃ ὁδῷ, ἐπὶ ἡμέρας δεκαοκτώ, μὴ ἐπιστάμενοι τὴν ὁδόν· κατ᾽ οἰκονομίαν δὲ τοῦ Σωτῆρος Θεοῦ, εὕρομεν τὴν ὁδὸν εὐθεῖαν καὶ τρίβον ἀσφαλῆ, ἣν ἐβάδισεν ὁ ἅγιος καὶ ὅσιος Μακάριος, καὶ ἐδοξάσαμεν τὸν Θεὸν μετὰ χαρᾶς μεγάλης. Καὶ ἀκολουθήσαντες τὴν εὐθεῖαν ὁδὸν ἐπὶ ἡμέρας πολλάς, εὕρομεν τὸ σπήλαιον τοῦ Ἁγίου Μακαρίου κεκοσμημένον ὡς ναὸν ἅγιον. Τότε εὐξάμενοι ἐσφραγίσαμεν ἑαυτούς, καὶ λαβόντες προθυμίαν εἰσήλθομεν εἰς τὸ σπήλαιον, καὶ μὴ εὑρόντες τινά, εἴπομεν πρὸς ἀλλήλους, "Αὕτη ἡ φιλοκαλία ἀνθρωπίνης φύσεως ὑπάρχει, ἀλλ᾽ ἐκδεξώμεθα ἕως ἑσπέρας, καὶ ἴδωμεν τὸν κατοικοῦντα ἐν αὐτῷ." Ὡς οὖν ἐκαθέσθημεν μικρόν, ἰδοὺ εὐωδία μεγάλη γέγονεν μύρου ἐν τῷ σπηλαίῳ, καὶ ἤρχετο εἰς τὰς ῥῖνας ἡμῶν, ὥστε νυστάξαι ἡμᾶς καὶ ὑπνῶσαι πεποίηκεν. Καὶ ἐξυπνήσαντες ἐξήλθομεν τοῦ σπηλαίου ἐκείνου, καὶ βλέψαντες ἐπὶ ἀνατολάς, εἴδομεν ὁμοίωμα *στολισμοῦ ἀνδρὸς φοβεροῦ,* ἐνδεδυμένον ἀπὸ λευκῶν τριχῶν. Ἦν δὲ οὗτος ὁ ὄντως μέγας καὶ ὅσιος Μακάριος· καὶ αὐξήσασαι ἐκ τοῦ χρόνου, αἱ τρίχες τῆς κεφαλῆς αὐτοῦ ἔσκεπον ὅλον τὸ σῶμα αὐτοῦ.

23   Ἐρχομένου δὲ αὐτοῦ ἐπὶ τὸ σπήλαιον, ὠσφράνθη ἀπὸ μακρόθεν τὴν ὀσμὴν τοῦ σώματος ἡμῶν· καὶ ἔρριψεν ἑαυτὸν ἐπὶ τὴν γῆν, κατακρίνων ἡμᾶς μεθ᾽ ὅρκου καὶ λέγων,

like *honey and honeycomb,* and which stood about one cubit above the earth; when we had eaten from that plant we were satisfied, and our countenance was altered, and our strength was increased, and we glorified God who fed and guided us each day.

And again, we went on our way, for eighteen days, without knowing our way. By the Savior God's divine plan, we found the straight way and safe path, which saint and holy Makarios had walked, and we glorified God in great joy. And after we had followed that straight way for many days, we found the cave of Saint Makarios, adorned like a holy church. Then, after we had prayed, we signed ourselves with the cross and, taking courage, we entered the cave; and when we found no one, we said to each other, "This beauty is the work of a human, so let's wait until the evening and we may see the man who is living in it." So we sat for a little while and, lo and behold, a great fragrance of perfumed oil pervaded the cave and reached our noses, making us dose off and fall asleep. And when we woke up, we went out of that cave, and when we turned our gaze toward the east, we saw what looked like terrifying *man's clothing,* someone dressed in white hair. This was the truly great and holy Makarios; and the hair of his head covered his entire body, having grown over time.

As he approached the cave, he sensed from afar the smell of our bodies; and he threw himself to the ground, commanding us to swear by oath and saying, "If you are from

22

23

"Εἰ ἀπὸ Θεοῦ ἐστε, ἐμφανίσατέ μοι καὶ ἐγγίσατε· εἰ δὲ ἀπὸ τοῦ διαβόλου, ἀναχωρεῖτε ἀπ᾽ ἐμοῦ τοῦ ταπεινοῦ καὶ ἁμαρτωλοῦ." Ἡμεῖς δὲ ἐβοήσαμεν λέγοντες, "᾽Ελέησον ἡμᾶς καὶ εὐλόγησον, ὅσιε πάτερ· καὶ ἡμεῖς γὰρ δοῦλοί ἐσμεν τοῦ Κυρίου Ἰησοῦ Χριστοῦ, καὶ τῷ διαβόλῳ ἀπεταξάμεθα." Τότε ἀκούσας ἔρχεται πρὸς ἡμᾶς· καὶ ὡς ἤγγισεν ἡμῖν, εὐθέως ἐκτείνας τὰς χεῖρας εἰς τὸν οὐρανὸν καὶ εὐξάμενος πρὸς Κύριον τὸν Θεὸν ηὐλόγησεν ἡμᾶς καὶ ὡμίλησεν.

24 Ἦσαν δὲ αἱ τρίχες τῆς κεφαλῆς αὐτοῦ καὶ τοῦ πώγωνος λευκαὶ ὡσεὶ χιών, ἐκ δὲ τοῦ πολλοῦ γήρους οὐκ ἐφαίνοντο οἱ ὀφθαλμοὶ αὐτοῦ· οἱ γὰρ ὀφρύες αὐτοῦ χαλασθέντες ἐσκέπασαν τοὺς ὀφθαλμοὺς αὐτοῦ. Οἱ δὲ ὄνυχες τῶν χειρῶν αὐτοῦ καὶ τῶν ποδῶν ἐγένοντο μεγάλοι ὡσεὶ παρδάλεως. Καὶ αἱ τρίχες τοῦ μύστακος αὐτοῦ ἐσκέπασαν αὐτοῦ τὸ στόμα, καὶ ἐμίγνυντο σὺν τῷ πώγωνι αὐτοῦ· ὅθεν ὡς ὡμίλει ἡμῖν ἐνομίζομεν, ὅτι ἀπὸ βάθους τινὸς φθέγγεται πρὸς ἡμᾶς. Καὶ εἴδομεν τὸ σῶμα αὐτοῦ, καὶ οὕτως ἦν ἄγριον πλῆρες, ὥσπερ δέρμα χελώνης.

25 Καὶ ἤρξατο ἐπερωτᾶν ἡμᾶς λέγων, "Πόθεν ἐστέ, καὶ διὰ τί ἐληλύθατε ἐνταῦθα;" Καὶ ἀπηγγείλαμεν αὐτῷ πάντα τὰ συμβεβηκότα ἡμῖν ἐν τῇ ὁδῷ, καὶ ὅτι ἐβουλευσάμεθα ἀπελθεῖν ὅπου ὁ οὐρανὸς ἀναπέπαυται. Καὶ ἀποκριθεὶς ὁ ἅγιος Μακάριος εἶπεν ἡμῖν, "Ἀκούσατέ μου, τέκνα· ἀπὸ τοῦ τόπου τούτου οὐκ ἔστι δυνατὸν ἄνθρωπον ἐν σώματι ὄντα, παρέσω εἰσελθεῖν καὶ καταμαθεῖν ἢ κατανοῆσαι τὰ θαυμάσια καὶ τὴν δύναμιν τοῦ Κυρίου. Κἀγὼ γὰρ ὁ ἁμαρτωλὸς πολλὰ ἠγωνισάμην, τοῦ ἀπελθεῖν ἔνθα ὁ οὐρανὸς

God, show yourselves to me and come near; but if you are from the devil, go away from me, humble and sinful man that I am." We called out and said, "Have mercy on us and give us your blessing, holy father; we too are servants of the Lord Jesus Christ, and we have renounced the devil." Then, when he heard this, he came toward us; and when he was near us, he immediately stretched out his hands toward heaven and after praying to the Lord our God, he gave us his blessing, and talked with us.

The hair of his head and his beard were white like snow, 24 and because of his great age his eyes were no longer visible, since his long eyebrows covered his eyes. The nails of his hand and feet were long like those of a leopard. And the hair of his mustache covered his mouth and joined his beard; thus when he talked to us, we thought that he was speaking from some kind of depth. And we saw his body, and it was extremely rough, like the skin of a turtle.

And he began asking us questions, saying, "Where are 25 you from, and why did you come here?" And we recounted to him everything that had happened to us on our way, and that we wanted to go where the heavens rest. Saint Makarios replied and said to us, "Listen to me, my children; it is not possible for a human who still has a body to go further on from this place and learn or comprehend the Lord's wonders and power. For I too, sinner that I am, struggled hard

ἀναπέπαυται, καὶ διὰ νυκτὸς ἐφάνη μοι ἄγγελος Κυρίου λέγων, ʻΜὴ θελήσῃς, Μακάριε, πειράζειν τόν σε κτίσαντα· οὐ δυνήσῃ γὰρ ἔτι διελθεῖν τὸν τόπον τοῦτον.ʼ Κἀγὼ εἶπον, ʻΔιὰ τί, κύριέ μου;ʼ Καὶ λέγει μοι ὁ ἄγγελος, ʻʼΕπειδὴ ὡς ἀπὸ μιλίων εἴκοσι τῶν ὧδε ἔστιν ὁ Παράδεισος, ὅπου ἦν ποτε ὁ Ἀδὰμ καὶ ἡ Εὔα· καὶ ἄνωθεν τοῦ Παραδείσου κατὰ ἀνατολάς, ὁ οὐρανὸς ἀναπέπαυται. Ἔξωθεν δὲ τοῦ Παραδείσου ἔταξεν ὁ Θεὸς τὰ χερουβὶμ καὶ τὴν φλογίνην ῥομφαίαν τὴν στρεφομένην φυλάττειν τὴν ὁδὸν τοῦ ξύλου τῆς ζωῆς. Εἰσὶ δὲ τὰ χερουβὶμ τῇ ἰδέᾳ, ἀπὸ μὲν τῶν ποδῶν ἕως τοῦ ὀμφαλοῦ ἄνθρωποι, τὸ δὲ στῆθος λέοντος, ἡ δὲ κεφαλὴ σχῆμα ἄλλο, καὶ αἱ χεῖρες κρυστάλλιναι, ξίφη πύρινα κατέχοντες ἐν ταῖς ἑαυτῶν χερσί, τοῦ μὴ τολμῆσαί τινα εἰσελθεῖν εἰς τὸν Παράδεισον· πᾶσαι γὰρ αἱ δυνάμεις αἱ φοβεραί, καὶ οἱ ἄγγελοι οἱ ἰσχυροί, καὶ αἱ ζῶναι τοῦ οὐρανοῦ ἐκεῖ ἵστανται, ὅπου ὁ οὐρανὸς ἀναπέπαυται.ʼʼʼ

26   Ταῦτα ἀκούσαντες ἡμεῖς παρὰ τοῦ Ἁγίου Μακαρίου ὃς διηγήσατο ἡμῖν εἰπόντος αὐτῷ τοῦ θείου ἀγγέλου ἐφοβήθημεν φόβῳ μεγάλῳ. Καὶ πεσόντες χαμαὶ ἐδοξάσαμεν τὸν Κύριον, καὶ τὸν Ἅγιον Μακάριον ἐμεγαλύναμεν, ὅτι ἀνήγγειλεν ἡμῖν πάντα τὰ θαυμάσια τοῦ Θεοῦ.

Καὶ γενομένης ἑσπέρας, ὁ Ἅγιος Μακάριος ἦλθεν πρὸς ἡμᾶς καὶ λέγει ἡμῖν, ʻʼΑπέλθατε, ἀδελφοί, κατ᾽ ἰδίαν μικρόν· ἔχω γὰρ δύο παιδία, ἐνταῦθα κατοικοῦντα μετ᾽ ἐμοῦ· καὶ πᾶσαν τὴν ἡμέραν εἰς τὰ ὄρη διάγουσιν, μόνον δὲ ἀπὸ ἑσπέρας εἰς ἑσπέραν ἔρχονται πρός με· καὶ φοβοῦμαι μὴ ξενιζόμενοι ἀδικήσωσιν ὑμᾶς.ʼʼ

to go where the heavens rest, and an angel of the Lord appeared to me at night, saying, 'Do not wish, Makarios, to tempt your creator; for you will not be able to pass this place.' And I said, 'Why, my lord?' And the angel said to me, 'Because about twenty miles from here is Paradise, where Adam and Eve once were; and above Paradise, toward the East, is where the heavens rest. Outside Paradise God *has placed the cherubim and the flaming sword that turns every way, to guard the way to the tree of life.* In their appearance the cherubim are as follows: from their feet to their belly's navel they are human, their chest is that of a lion, their heads are of another shape, and their hands are crystal, and they hold fiery swords in their hands, so that no one might dare to enter Paradise; for all the terrifying powers, and the powerful angels, and the zones of heaven stand there, where the heavens rest.'"

When we heard Saint Makarios relate what the divine angel had said to him, we became very afraid. And we fell to the ground and glorified the Lord, and exalted Saint Makarios who had recounted to us all the wonders of God. 26

When the evening came, Saint Makarios came to us and said, "Go away, brothers, in private for a short while; for I have two children who live here with me; and they spend all day on the mountains, and only come to me from one evening to the next; and I'm afraid that they might be surprised and harm you."

27 Ἡμεῖς οὖν ἐνομίζομεν ὅτι περὶ ἀνθρώπων λέγει, καὶ ἰδι-
άσαμεν ἀπ᾽ αὐτοῦ. Καὶ ἰδοὺ λέοντες δύο, ἦλθον δρομαῖοι
ἀπὸ τῆς ἐρήμου, καὶ πεσόντες εἰς τοὺς πόδας αὐτοῦ ὠρυ-
όμενοι, προσεκύνουν αὐτόν. Ἡμεῖς δὲ ἐκ τοῦ φόβου ἐπέ-
σαμεν χαμαί, μὴ δυνάμενοί τι λαλῆσαι. Καὶ ἐπιθεὶς τὰς
χεῖρας αὐτοῦ ἐπ᾽ αὐτούς, λέγει αὐτοῖς, "Τεκνία μου καλά,
τρεῖς ἀδελφοὶ ἐκ τῆς τῶν ἀνθρώπων φύσεως ἐληλύθασιν
πρὸς ἡμᾶς. Μηδὲν οὖν αὐτοὺς ἀδικήσητε· δοῦλοι γάρ
εἰσιν τοῦ Θεοῦ." Καὶ φωνήσας πρὸς ἡμᾶς ὁ Ἅγιος Μακάριος εἶπεν, "Δεῦτε, ἀδελφοί, ἐγγίσατε ἡμῖν, μηδὲν φοβούμενοι, καὶ ποιήσωμεν τὴν ἑσπερινὴν εὐχήν." Καὶ ὡς ἐξήλθομεν φοβούμενοι τοῦ ἀπελθεῖν πρὸς αὐτόν, ἔδραμον οἱ
δύο λέοντες εἰς ἀπάντησιν ἡμῶν, καὶ ὡς ἄνθρωποι λογικοὶ
κάμπτοντες τοὺς πόδας, ἐκυλινδοῦντο ἔμπροσθεν ἡμῶν.
Τότε καὶ ἡμεῖς ἐδοξάσαμεν τὸν Θεὸν τὸν ἡμερώσαντα
αὐτοὺς πρὸς ἡμᾶς· καὶ ποιήσαντες τὸν ἑσπερινὸν ὕμνον,
ἡσυχάσαμεν πᾶσαν τὴν νύκτα ἐκείνην.

28 Καὶ τῇ ἐπαύριον ἀναστάντες τοῦ ὕπνου καὶ τὸν Θεὸν
δοξάσαντες, εἴπομεν πρὸς τὸν Ἅγιον Μακάριον, "Δεόμεθά σου, τίμιε πάτερ, αὐτὸς πῶς ἐλήλυθας ἐνταῦθα;" Καὶ
ἀποκριθεὶς λέγει ἡμῖν, "Ἀδελφοὶ καὶ πατέρες, κλίνατε τὸ
οὖς ὑμῶν εἰς τὰ ῥήματά μου, καὶ ἀκούσατε πῶς ὧδε ἐγὼ
ἐλήλυθα. Ὁ ταπεινὸς ἐγώ, ὁ ταλαίπωρος καὶ ἁμαρτωλός,
ἐγενόμην υἱός τινος Ἰωάννου, Ῥωμαίου συγκλητικοῦ· καὶ
μὴ θέλοντός μου ὁ πατήρ μου ἔζευξέ με γυναικί. Καὶ ποιήσας κατὰ βίαν τοὺς γάμους, τῇ ἑσπέρᾳ ὅτε ἔμελλεν ὁ
πατήρ μου κοιμίζειν ἡμᾶς εἰς μίαν κλίνην συνάφειας
τρόπῳ, χρείαν γαστρὸς πρόφασιν χρησάμενος, ἐξῆλθον

So we thought that he was talking about humans, and   27
went away from him in private. And lo and behold, two lions
came running from the desert, fell roaring at his feet, and
showed him respect. Out of fear, we fell to the ground unable to speak a word. And he laid his hands on them, and
said to them, "My good children, three brothers from the
human species have come to visit us. So please do not harm
them; for they are servants of God." And then Saint Makarios called us and said, "Come, brothers, come closer to
us, for there's nothing to fear, and let us perform the evening
prayer." And as we came out, afraid of approaching him, the
two lions ran to meet us, and like rational humans, they bent
their knees and rolled on the ground in front of us. Then we
too glorified God who made them tame toward us; and after
we had performed the vesper hymn, we rested for that entire night.

And when we woke up from our sleep on the next day and   28
had glorified God, we said to Saint Makarios, "Please, honorable father, how did you come here yourself?" And in response, he said to us, "Brothers and fathers, *incline your ears
to my words,* and listen to how I came here. I, a humble man,
a wretch and a sinner, was the son of a certain John, a Roman consul; and my father, against my will, joined me in
marriage with a woman. After he had coerced our wedding,
in the evening when my father was going to have us sleep
together in one bed and have intercourse, I used the needs
of the belly as my excuse, and went out on my own, secretly

μόνος, ἐν κρυφῇ καθ᾽ ἑαυτόν. Καὶ ἀπελθὼν ἐκρύβην ἐν
οἰκήματι μιᾶς χήρας καὶ πενιχρᾶς ἡμέρας ἑπτά· ἐν οἷς ἡ
ἀείμνηστος γραῦς ἐκείνη ἦν φέρουσα τὰς ἀποκρίσεις ἐμοί,
γνωρίζουσά μοι καθ᾽ ἑκάστην τοὺς λόγους αὐτῶν, καὶ τὸν
κλαυθμόν, καὶ τὴν ἐξαίφνης ἀπροσδόκητον αὐτῶν θλίψιν.
Ὅμως, ἐπὶ πολὺ ζητήσαντές με καὶ μὴ εὑρόντες, ἐποίησαν
θρῆνον μέγαν καὶ κοπετὸν πολύν· ἐγὼ δὲ μετὰ τὰς ἑπτὰ
ἡμέρας, ἀναστὰς μέσῃ νυκτός, ἐδόξασα τὸν Θεόν, καὶ
εὐχαριστήσας τῇ πενιχρᾷ γυναικί, ἐξῆλθον ἐκ τῆς κέλλης
αὐτῆς ἐπὶ τὴν δημοσίαν ὁδόν.

29   Ὁ δὲ φιλάνθρωπος Κύριος, ὁ μὴ καταλιμπάνων τινί,
ἀλλὰ χεῖρα διδοὺς πᾶσι τοῖς ἐπικαλουμένοις τὸ ὄνομα αὐτοῦ,
ἀπέστειλέν μοι τὸν ἄγγελον αὐτοῦ Ῥαφαήλ, ἐν σχήματι
ἀνδρὸς γέροντος, ὁδεύοντος καὶ συνοδοιποροῦντός μοι.
Ἐν οἷς καὶ ἠρώτησα αὐτόν, ᾽Ποῦ πορεύῃ, τίμιε πάτερ;᾽ Ὁ
δὲ εἶπέν μοι, ῞Ὅπου αὐτὸς ἔχεις τὸν νοῦν σου, ἐκεῖ κἀγὼ
πορεύομαι.᾽ Ἐγὼ δὲ εἶπον αὐτῷ, ῞Ὁδήγησόν με εἰς τὴν
ὁδὸν τῆς ζωῆς.᾽ Καὶ κατηκολούθουν αὐτῷ πᾶσαν τὴν ὁδόν.
Ζητοῦντες δὲ εἰς τὰς κώμας ἄρτον καὶ ὕδωρ, ἐλαμβάνομεν
εἰς διατροφὴν ἡμῶν. Καὶ βαδίσαντες πᾶσαν τὴν ὁδόν, ἣν
καὶ ὑμεῖς ἐθεάσασθε, ἔδειξέν μοι ὁ ἄγγελος Κυρίου, ὁ
ἐν σχήματι γέροντος συμπεριπατῶν μοι καὶ ὁδηγῶν με,
πάντα ταῦτα. Ἡ δὲ ὁδοιπορία ἡμῶν καὶ ὁ χρόνος ἐγένετο
ἔτη τρία, ἕως τῆς προκειμένης ὁδοῦ, οὗ ἐμέλλομεν ἀνα-
παύεσθαι. Καὶ ἀποκαταστήσας με ὁ ἄγγελος Κυρίου εἰς
τὸ σπήλαιον τοῦτο, εἰσελθόντες ἔνδον ἐκοιμήθημεν οἱ δύο
ἅμα ἐν τούτῳ τῷ τόπῳ.

30   Ἐγὼ δὲ διυπνήσας οὐκέτι εἶδον αὐτόν. Καὶ ἀρξάμενος

by myself. And I went off and hid in the house of a poor widow for seven days; during this time, that old woman of everlasting memory would bring me the news, reporting to me every day their words, their mourning, and their sudden, unexpected sorrow. Nevertheless, after they had searched for me for a long time and could not find me, they made a great dirge and much lamentation; as for me, after the seven days had passed, I got up in the middle of the night, glorified God and, after thanking the poor woman, left her cell for the public road.

"The Lord, who loves mankind, who abandons no one, 29 but gives a hand *to all those who call on* his *name,* sent me his angel Raphael, in the form of an old man, walking and traveling as my companion. When I asked him, 'Where are you going, honorable father?' he said to me, 'Wherever you yourself have decided, that's where I too am going.' I said to him, 'Lead me on *the way of life.*' And I followed him all the way. In villages, we would ask for and receive food and water for our sustenance. And as we walked the entire way which you too have witnessed, the angel of the Lord, who had the form of an old man walking as my companion and guide, showed me everything. The duration of our journey was three years, until the end of the road, where we were to rest. And once the angel of the Lord brought me to this cave, we went inside and the two of us slept side by side in this place.

"When I woke up, I could no longer see him. And as I 30

ῥαθυμεῖν καὶ λυπεῖσθαι καὶ κλαίειν, εὐθέως ἐμφανίζει μοι ὁ ἄγγελος Κυρίου ἑαυτὸν λέγων, Ἐγώ εἰμι Ῥαφαὴλ ὁ ἀρχάγγελος Κυρίου, ὁ ἀγαγών σε ἐνταῦθα ἐν σχήματι γέροντος, ὡς ὁ Κύριος ἐκέλευσεν. Ἀποθέμενος οὖν τὴν λύπην σου μηδὲν δειλιάσῃς, ἀλλὰ δὸς δόξαν τῷ Θεῷ σου καθ᾽ ἑκάστην ἡμέραν. Ἰδοὺ διῆλθες τὰ σκοτεινὰ καὶ εἶδες πάντα τὰ θαυμάσια τοῦ Θεοῦ, καὶ τὰς κρίσεις τῶν ἁμαρτωλῶν, καὶ τοὺς τόπους τῶν ἁγίων καὶ δικαίων, καὶ τὴν ἀθάνατον πηγήν, καὶ ἐλήλυθας εἰς τὸ φῶς τῆς ζωῆς. Μηκέτι οὖν λυποῦ, μηδὲ σκυθρώπαζε, ἀλλὰ μᾶλλον χαίρων δόξαζε καθ᾽ ἑκάστην Κύριον τὸν Θεὸν τὸν ῥυσάμενόν σε ἐκ τῆς ματαίας πλάνης καὶ ἀπάτης τῶν ἀνθρώπων τοῦ κόσμου. Καὶ ταῦτα εἰπὼν Ῥαφαὴλ ὁ ἀρχάγγελος Κυρίου, ἤρθη ἐξ ὀφθαλμῶν μου καὶ γέγονεν ἄφαντος ἀπ᾽ ἐμοῦ.

31 Ἐγὼ δὲ ἠρξάμην ὁδεύειν, καὶ εὐθέως ὑπήντησέν μοι ὄναγρος βοσκομένη, καὶ ὥρκισα αὐτὴν λέγων, Τὸν Θεὸν τὸν κτίσαντά σε, δεῖξόν μοι ἀνθρώπινον οἰκητήριον. Καὶ εὐθέως ἔστη, καὶ ὠγκήσατο ἔμπροσθέν μου, καὶ ἠκολούθουν αὐτῇ ἡμέρας δύο. Καὶ πάλιν ἀπαντᾷ μοι ἔλαφος μέγας, καὶ ἰδὼν ὁ ὄναγρος τὸν ἔλαφον ἀνεχώρησεν καὶ ὑπέστρεψεν εἰς τόπον τὸν ἴδιον· καὶ ὡδήγησέν με ὁ ἔλαφος ἡμέρας τρεῖς. Καὶ ἰδοὺ πάλιν ἀπαντᾷ μοι δράκων μέγας συρόμενος, καὶ ἰδὼν ὁ ἔλαφος τὸν δράκοντα ἀνεχώρησεν καὶ ὑπέστρεψεν εἰς τὸν ἴδιον τόπον.

32 Ἐγὼ δὲ φοβηθεὶς τὸν δράκοντα ἠρξάμην ὁρκίζειν αὐτὸν κατὰ τοῦ Θεοῦ τοῦ ζῶντος, τοῦ μὴ ἀδικῆσαί με. Καὶ ἀνορθώσας ἑαυτὸν ὁ δράκων καὶ σταθεὶς ἐπὶ τὴν οὐρὰν αὐτοῦ ἀνοίξας τε τὸ στόμα αὐτοῦ, παραχρῆμα ἐλάλει μοι

began to lose heart, and be sad, and cry, immediately the angel of the Lord showed himself to me, saying, 'I am Raphael, the archangel of the Lord, who led you here in the form of an old man, as the Lord commanded. So, set aside your sorrow and do not be afraid, but give glory to your God every day. Look, you passed through the dark places and saw all the wonders of God, the trials of the sinners and the places of the saints and the righteous, and the fountain of immortality, and you arrived at *the light of life*. So, don't be sad or downcast, but rather glorify the Lord your God every day with joy, who saved you from the vain errors and deception of the men of this world.' And when Raphael, the archangel of the Lord had said these words, he was taken from my sight and could no longer be seen by me.

"I started out on my way, and straightaway I encountered 31 a grazing onager, and I commanded her, saying, 'By God your creator, show me a dwelling for humans.' And instantly, she stood up and brayed in front me, and I followed her for two days. And then again, I encountered a great stag; and when the onager saw the stag she left and returned to her own place; and the stag led me for three days. And lo and behold, once more I encountered a large serpent crawling along; and, when the deer saw the serpent, he left and returned to his own place.

"As I was afraid of the serpent, I started commanding 32 him by the living God not to hurt me. The serpent raised himself up, stood on his tail, opened his mouth, and at once

ἀνθρωπίνως λέγων, Καλῶς ἐλήλυθας ἐνταῦθα, δοῦλε τοῦ
Θεοῦ Μακάριε· ἔτη γάρ εἰσι δώδεκα ἀφ' οὗ ἐκδέχεταί σε
τὸ ὄρος τοῦτο. Ἰδοὺ γὰρ καὶ οἶκον κατοικητήριον ἡτοί-
μασά σοι, κελευσθεὶς παρὰ Ῥαφαὴλ τοῦ ἀρχαγγέλου. Σὺ
γὰρ εἶ Μακάριος, ὃν καὶ προεμήνυσέ μοι ὁ ἀρχάγγελος
Ῥαφαήλ, ἀλλὰ καὶ ἱστόρησέν μοι τὴν ἰδέαν σου, καὶ προ-
ϋπέδειξέν μοι τοῦ προσώπου σου τὴν θέαν καὶ τὴν λαλιάν.
Καὶ ἰδοὺ ἠξιώθην ἰδεῖν σε σήμερον· εἰσὶ γὰρ ἡμέραι δέκα
ἀφ' οὗ προσεδεχόμην σε, μήτε ἐπὶ βρώσεως μήτε ἐπὶ πό-
σεως ἀνελθὼν ἐντεῦθεν. Καὶ τὴν ἑσπέραν ταύτην εἶδόν σε
καθήμενον ἐπὶ νεφέλης φωτεινῆς· καὶ ἦλθεν πρός με φωνὴ
λέγουσα, "Ἀνάστα λοιπόν, δέξαι τὸν δοῦλον τοῦ Θεοῦ
Μακάριον." Καὶ νῦν δεῦρο ἀκολούθει μοι, καὶ ὑποδείξω σοι
τὸν ἴδιόν σου τόπον, τοῦ δοξάζειν ἀπαύστως τὸν Θεὸν ἐν
αὐτῷ.'

33 "Ταῦτα τοίνυν λαλήσας ὁ δράκων, θεωροῦντός μου
αὐτόν, οὕτως περιεπάτει ἔμπροσθέν μου ὡς ἀνὴρ νεανί-
σκος· καὶ ἐλθόντων ἡμῶν ἐπὶ τὴν θύραν τοῦ σπηλαίου, καὶ
στήσας με ἐπ' αὐτῷ, ἄφαντος ἐγένετο ἐξ ὀφθαλμῶν μου.
Ἐγὼ δὲ ὁ ἁμαρτωλὸς εἰσελθὼν ἐν τῷ σπηλαίῳ, εὗρον
λέαιναν νεκράν, κειμένην ἐπὶ τοῦ ἐδάφους, καὶ τὰ δύο
αὐτῆς σκύμνα ἐπικείμενα ἐπ' αὐτῇ καὶ κλαίοντα καὶ μὴ
εὑρίσκοντα γάλα θηλάσαι. Καὶ λαβὼν ἐγὼ τὰ δύο σκυμνά-
ρια, ἀνέθρεψα αὐτὰ ἐκ τῶν ἀκροδρύων ὡς τέκνα μου γνή-
σια· τὴν δὲ μητέρα αὐτῶν ἐκβαλὼν ἔξω ἔθαψα εἰς τὴν γῆν·
καὶ ἠρξάμην δοξάζειν τὸν φιλάνθρωπον Θεόν."

34 Καὶ ἔτι ἡμῖν ὁμιλοῦντος ταῦτα τοῦ Ἁγίου Μακαρίου,
ἰδοὺ κόραξ ἐπέστη, καὶ ἐκάθισεν ἐν τῷ μέσῳ ἡμῶν, ἔχων

spoke to me like a human, saying, 'You are welcome here, servant of God Makarios; for this mountain has been expecting you for twelve years. Look, I have even prepared a place for you to live, as I was ordered by Raphael the archangel. You are the Makarios, about whom the archangel Raphael has already notified me, and he even described your appearance, and showed me in advance what your face looked like and your voice. And lo and behold, I have been deemed worthy to see you today; for I have been waiting for you for ten days, without going out from here, for either food or drink. And this very evening I saw you seated upon a *bright cloud;* and a voice came to me, saying, "Get up now and receive the servant of God Makarios." And now, *come, follow me,* and I shall show you your place where you can glorify God unceasingly.'

"That's what the serpent said, and as I was looking at 33 him, he walked in front of me like a young man; and when we came to the entrance of the cave, he stopped me there and disappeared from my sight. I, the sinner, entered the cave and found a dead lioness, lying on the ground, and her two cubs lying on her, and crying, and unable to find milk to suck. And I took the two cubs, and I raised them on fruits as my own children; as for their mother, I took her out and buried her in the earth; and I began glorifying God who loves humankind."

While Saint Makarios was saying these things to us, lo 34 and behold, a raven arrived and settled in the middle of us,

ἐπὶ τοῦ στόματος αὐτοῦ ἄρτους δύο· καὶ ἔθηκεν αὐτοὺς ἐνώπιον ἡμῶν καὶ ἀπῆλθεν. Καὶ ἀπεκρίθη ἡμῖν ὁ γέρων, "Νῦν ἔγνων, ἀδελφοί, ὅτι οὐκ ἐγκατέλιπεν ἡμῖν ὁ Κύριος, ἀλλὰ καὶ ὑμῶν καὶ ἡμῶν ἀπέστειλεν τὴν τροφήν· ἰδοὺ γὰρ ἕως σήμερόν εἰσιν ἔτη ἱκανὰ ἀφ' οὗ δέχομαι τὴν τροφὴν παρὰ τοῦ κόρακος τούτου καθ' ἡμέραν ἥμισυ ἄρτου, ἀπὸ τοῦ παντοδυνάμου Θεοῦ ἀπὸ τοῦ πετεινοῦ τούτου· ἐδεξά-μεθα οὖν σήμερον ἀνὰ ἕκαστος ἥμισυ ἄρτου. Φάγωμεν οὖν, καὶ ἀναγγελῶ ὑμῖν τὰς ἁμαρτίας μου· τούτου γὰρ ἕνεκεν ἀπεστάλητε πρός με τὸν ταπεινὸν καὶ ἁμαρτωλόν, παρὰ τοῦ φιλανθρώπου Θεοῦ." Καὶ ποιησάντων ἡμῶν εὐχήν, καὶ καθεσθέντων, ἐκορέσθημεν τῆς τροφῆς, καὶ ἐδοξάσαμεν τὸν Κύριον.

35   Καὶ μετὰ ταῦτα ἤρξατο ἡμῖν πάλιν διηγεῖσθαι, λέγων οὕτως, ὅτι· "Μετὰ τὸ οἰκῆσαί με ἐνταῦθα καὶ ποιῆσαι ἔτη δώδεκα, ἐξῆλθον ἔξω τοῦ σπηλαίου περὶ ὥραν ἑβδόμην, καὶ ἐκαθέσθην εἰς τὸν ἥλιον μετὰ τῶν δύο λεόντων. Καὶ ἰδοὺ ὁ Σατανᾶς ἤρξατο πειράζειν. Καὶ ποιήσας ἑαυτὸν ὁ πονηρὸς ὡς σουδάριον γυναικὸς πάνυ ἔντιμον καὶ ψιλόν, ἔκειτο ἀπέναντί μου χαμαί. Ἐγὼ δὲ ὁ ταλαίπωρος πωρω-θεὶς τὸν λογισμὸν καὶ μὴ νοήσας, ἐπάρας αὐτὸ ἀπέθηκα ἔνδον τοῦ σπηλαίου, καὶ διελογιζόμην ἐν ἑαυτῷ τὸ τί ἐστι τοῦτο καὶ πόθεν; καὶ περιφρονήσας οὐκ ἐσφράγισα ἐμαυτόν· ὁ γὰρ ἅγιος σταυρὸς φυγαδευτήριον δαιμόνων ἐστί. Καὶ πάλιν τῇ ἐπαύριον ἐξῆλθον καὶ εὑρίσκω ὑπό-δημα ἀληθινὸν γυναικός· περιφρονήσας δὲ τοῦ μὴ κατασφραγισθῆναι, ἀλλὰ μᾶλλον ἐπάρας καὶ αὐτό, ἔθηκα

with two loaves of bread in his mouth; and he placed these in front of us and left. The elder turned to us and said, "Now I know, brothers, that the Lord has not forsaken us, since he has sent food both for you and for me; for see, I've been receiving food through this raven for many years until today, half a loaf every day, from the almighty God through this bird; so today each of us has received half a loaf. So let's eat and I shall confess my sins to you; for that's the reason why you were sent to me, humble and sinful man that I am, by God who loves humankind." After we had prayed, we sat and had our fill of the food, and we glorified the Lord.

And after that he began again to tell us his story with the following words: "After I had lived here for twelve years, I came out of the cave around the seventh hour, and I sat under the sun with my two lions. And lo and behold, Satan began to tempt me. The wicked one had turned himself into what looked like a very expensive and fine woman's head scarf, lying on the ground in front of me. I, wretch that I am, being blinded in my mind and not understanding, picked it up and placed it inside the cave, wondering to myself what it was and where it had come from; thinking nothing of it, I did not sign myself with the cross; for the holy cross drives demons away. And again, the next day, I came out and found a woman's shoe made of silk; thinking nothing of it, I did not make the sign of the cross, but rather picked up this

35

πρὸς τὸ σουδάριον· καὶ πάλιν πωρωθεὶς τὴν καρδίαν ἀσφράγιστος ἔμεινα.

36 Τῇ δὲ τρίτῃ ἡμέρᾳ ἐξῆλθον τοῦ σπηλαίου προσκυνῆσαι τὸν φιλάνθρωπον Θεόν. Καὶ πωρωθεὶς ὑπὸ τοῦ Σατανᾶ, οὐ κατεσφράγισα ἐμαυτόν, εἴ πως διὰ τοῦ τιμίου σταυροῦ ἐκφύγω τὴν ἀνομίαν μου· καὶ πάλιν θεωρῶ ἄλλην φαντασίαν τοῦ ἐχθροῦ. Ἰδοὺ γὰρ ἐκάθητο ὁ διάβολος ἐπάνω λίθου, ὥσπερ γυνὴ κεκοσμημένη, ἐν ἱματισμῷ καὶ χρυσίῳ πολυτελεῖ, τοῦ δὲ κάλλους αὐτῆς οὐκ ἦν κόρος· καὶ ἔκλαιεν πικρῶς, ὥστε κἀμοὶ ἤνεγκεν εἰς τὸ κλαῦσαι. Καὶ εἶπον πρὸς αὐτήν, Πόθεν ὧδε παραγέγονας; Ἡ δὲ εἶπεν πρός με, Ἐγὼ ἡ ταλαίπωρος, γυνή εἰμι ὀνόματι Μαρία, θυγάτηρ πέλουσα Ῥωμαίου τινός. Καὶ ἠνάγκασάν με οἱ γονεῖς μου συναφθῆναι ἀνδρί· κἀγὼ μὴ βουλομένη τοῦτο ποιῆσαι, προφάσει γαστρὸς λαθοῦσα τοὺς χορεύοντας καὶ τὸν ἄνδρα, ἀπὸ τοῦ παστοῦ ἔφυγον, μηδενὸς γινώσκοντος· καὶ μὴ γνωρίζουσα τὴν εὐθεῖαν ὁδὸν πλανωμένη διὰ τῶν ὀρέων καὶ τῶν κρημνῶν, μόλις πάρειμι ὧδε, μὴ γνωρίζουσα ποῦ ἔρχομαι.

37 Ἐγὼ δὲ ὁ ταπεινὸς ἔτι ὑπάρχων πεπωρωμένος, ἐπίστευον αὐτῇ ὅσα ἐλάλει μοι· τῇ δὲ τέχνῃ τῆς ἀπατηλῆς μεθόδου, ἐδέλεαζε τὴν ταπεινήν μου ψυχήν. Καὶ ἐπιλαβόμενος αὐτῆς τῆς χειρὸς εἰσήγαγον αὐτὴν ἐν τῷ σπηλαίῳ τούτῳ· τὰ δὲ δάκρυα αὐτῆς οὐδ᾽ ὅλως ἐπαύοντο. Καὶ συμπαθήσας αὐτῇ διὰ τὴν τῆς ἀνθρωπίνης σαρκὸς πεῖναν, ἐπιδέδωκα αὐτὴν φαγεῖν ἐκ τῶν ἀκροδρύων τούτων, μήπως λιμῷ ἀποθάνῃ καὶ κηλιδώσῃ μου τὴν ψυχήν. Ὅμως ἔτι ὑπῆρχεν ἡ ψυχή μου πεπωρωμένη καὶ ἀσφράγιστος.

item too and put it next to the head scarf; and again blinded in my heart, I remained without the seal of the cross.

"On the third day, I came out of the cave to make my devotions to God who loves humankind. And blinded by Satan, I did not seal myself with the cross, for perhaps through the venerable cross I might have avoided my iniquity; and again I saw another false apparition of the enemy. For lo and behold, the devil was sitting on a rock as a woman adorned with expensive clothes and gold, and I couldn't have enough of her beauty; and she was crying so bitterly that it moved me as well to tears. And I said to her, 'Where did you come here from?' She said to me, 'I, wretch that I am, am a woman called Maria, and I'm the daughter of a certain Roman. And my parents forced me to marry a man; and as I did not want to do that, I used my belly as an excuse for escaping the notice of the wedding party and my husband, and I fled from the bridal chamber without anyone knowing; and being ignorant of the straight path, I've wandered through mountains and cliffs, and barely managed to make it here, without knowing where I'm going.' 36

"I, humble man that I am, still blind to the truth, believed whatever she said to me; with her art of deceptive manners she seduced my humble soul. So I *took* her *by the hand* and led her into this cave; but her tears would not stop at all. And feeling sorry for her, thinking of her hunger due to the human flesh, I gave her to eat from these fruits, so that she would not die of hunger and thus defile my soul. Yet still my soul was blinded and was without the seal of the cross. 37

38 "Καὶ γενομένης ἑσπέρας, ἐποίησα παρὰ προαίρεσιν τὸν ἑσπερινὸν ὕμνον· καὶ εἶθ' οὕτως ἔθηκα ἐμαυτὸν ἐπὶ τὴν γῆν ὀλίγον ἐφυπνῶσαι. Ἐμοῦ δὲ τοῦ ἀθλίου καθεύδοντος, ἐκείνη εὐθὺς ἔρχεται ἔγγιστά μου· καὶ ἐπαροῦσα μικρὸν τὸν ἐπενδύτην μου, βαλοῦσα ἔσωθεν τὴν χεῖρα αὐτῆς, ἐψηλάφισέ μου ὅλον τὸ σῶμα, καὶ ἤμην ἐν τῷ ὕπνῳ μου ὅλος βεβαρημένος. Ἐγὼ δὲ ὁ ἄθλιος καὶ ταλαίπωρος, ὁ μήποτε ἐνθυμηθεὶς κακὴν πρᾶξιν, ἢ κινηθεὶς εἰς ἐπιθυμίαν πορνείας, ἢ πωρωθεὶς εἰς κρίσιν ψυχῆς, τὴν αὐτὴν ὥραν ἠρξάμην ταράσσεσθαι εἰς ἁμαρτίαν, καὶ προσλαβόμενος αὐτὴν πρὸς ἐμαυτὸν ἠβουλήθην συγγενέσθαι αὐτῇ εἰς ἁμαρτίαν ὡς ἐρασθεὶς αὐτῆς. Ἐκείνη δὲ ἄφνω ἀφανὴς ἐγένετο ἀπ' ἐμοῦ.

39 "Ἐγὼ δὲ ὁ ἄθλιος ὡς πωρωθεὶς τῷ νοήματι, εὑρέθην κείμενος ὕπτιος ἐπὶ τὴν γῆν, ὥσπερ ἀπὸ ὕπνου βαθυτάτου. Καὶ ὅτε ἀνένηψα ἐκ τῆς πλάνης τοῦ διαβόλου, ἦλθον εἰς ἐμαυτόν· καὶ ἐπιγνοὺς τὴν αἰσχύνην μου, καὶ τὴν δεινὴν καὶ ἀφόρητον ἁμαρτίαν καὶ ἀνομίαν, ὅτι μεγάλη καὶ ἀνείκαστός ἐστιν, ἐξελθὼν ἐκ τοῦ σπηλαίου ἔκλαυσα πικρῶς σφόδρα.

40 "Καὶ νοήσαντες οὗτοι οἱ λέοντες τὴν ἀνομίαν μου καὶ τὴν ἁμαρτίαν, ἐπὶ δέκα ἡμέρας οὐχ ὑπετάσσοντό μοι, οὐδὲ ἤρχοντο πρός με. Ἐγὼ δὲ ὁ ἄθλιος καὶ ταλαίπωρος θεωρήσας ἀπὸ μακρόθεν τὰ δύο λεοντάρια ἔκλαυσα πικρῶς, καὶ παρεκάλεσα τὸν φιλάνθρωπον Θεόν, τοῦ συγχωρῆσαί μου τὴν ἀνομίαν ταύτην. Ὁ δὲ εὔσπλαγχνος καὶ ἐλεήμων Θεός, ἀπέστειλεν τὰ δύο λεοντάρια πρός με μετὰ τὰς δέκα ἡμέρας· καὶ συνελθόντα σὺν ἐμοὶ εἰς τὸ

"And when evening came, I prayed unwillingly the vesper 38
hymn; and then in this way I laid myself on the ground to
sleep a little. When I, wretch that I am, had fallen asleep,
she immediately came very close to me; lifting my cloak a
little, she put her hand inside, and fondled my entire body;
meanwhile I was totally *heavy with sleep.* I, wretched and
miserable man that I am, who had never conceived a wicked
deed, or ever been moved to sexual desire, or blinded to an
ordeal of my soul, at that very moment began to be stirred
to sin and, drawing her toward me, I wanted to consort with
her in sin, as I craved her. But she suddenly disappeared
from my sight.

"I, wretch that I am, blinded in my mind, found myself 39
lying on my back on the ground, as if emerging from the
deepest sleep. And when I came to my senses from the devil's deception, I became myself again; and when I realized
my shame and how great and unimaginable my terrible and
unbearable sin and iniquity were, I left the cave and *wept in*
utter *bitterness.*

"And when these lions realized my iniquity and my sin, 40
for ten days they would neither obey me nor come to me.
Wretched and miserable man that I am, while I was gazing
at the two lions from afar, I *wept bitterly,* and I asked God
who loves humankind to forgive me this iniquity. The compassionate and merciful God sent the two lions back to me
after the ten days; and when they joined me in the cave, I

σπήλαιον, παρεκάλεσα αὐτὰ τοῦ ὀρύξαι μοι λάκκον βα-
θύν· καὶ ὤρυξαν τοῖς ὄνυξιν ἑαυτῶν. Τότε ἔρριψα ἐμαυτὸν
ἐν τῷ λάκκῳ· καὶ ἐπὶ ἡμέρας πέντε κείμενος ἐκεῖ, ἔκλαιον
πικρῶς, παρακαλῶν αὐτοὺς καὶ δεόμενος, ὅπως χώσωσι
καὶ σκεπάσωσίν με· καὶ μόλις δάκρυα βάλλοντες ἀνθρώ-
πινα κἀκεῖνοι, ἔχωσάν με. Καὶ ἔμεινα κεχωσμένος ἐπὶ τῆς
γῆς, διὰ τὴν δεινὴν ἀνομίαν, ἔτη τρία, καὶ ἐγενόμην γῆ καὶ
σποδός, καὶ οὐκ ἀπέθνησκα, ὅτι ὁ Κύριος ἀντιλήπτωρ μου
ἦν.

41   "Μετὰ δὲ τοὺς τρεῖς χρόνους κατὰ πρόνοιαν Θεοῦ, γίνεται χειμὼν μέγας· καὶ κατὰ βούλησιν Θεοῦ τρυπᾶται τὸ
σπήλαιον ἄνωθεν τῆς κεφαλῆς μου καὶ κατὰ τῆς ὄψεώς
μου. Καὶ τοῦ σταλαγμοῦ κατερχομένου, ἐπλάτυνε τὴν
τρύπην τοῦ σπηλαίου· καὶ εἶδον τὸ φῶς τῆς ἡμέρας, καὶ
ἐδόξασα τὸν Θεόν, τὸν ἐξαλείψαντά μου τὴν δεινὴν ἀνομίαν καὶ εἰπόντα, 'Οὐκ ἦλθον καλέσαι δικαίους, ἀλλὰ ἁμαρτωλοὺς εἰς μετάνοιαν.' Τότε ἐκτείνας τὴν χεῖρά μου διὰ τῆς
τρύπης ἔξω τοῦ σπηλαίου, ἐθέρισα τὴν βοτάνην καὶ ἔφαγον ἐξ αὐτῆς καὶ ἐνεπλήσθην εἰς κόρον. Θελήσει δὲ τοῦ
Θεοῦ εἰσῆλθον καὶ οἱ δύο λέοντες εἰς τὸ σπήλαιον, καὶ
ἰδόντες τὴν κεφαλήν μου καὶ τὴν ὄψιν, ἐπένθησάν μου τὸ
σῶμα. Καὶ ἀνορύξαντες τοῖς ποσὶν αὐτῶν, ἀνῆλθον κἀγὼ
τοῦ ὀρύγματος, ὅλος ὑγιής, προστάξει καὶ φιλανθρωπίᾳ
τοῦ Κυρίου. Καὶ εἶχον τὴν ἰσχύν μου διπλασίονα τῆς πρώ-
της. Καὶ εὐξάμενος, ἐδόξασα τὸν εὔσπλαγχνον Θεόν, καὶ
ἐξῆλθον τοῦ σπηλαίου.

42   "Καὶ κλίνας τὰ γόνατα ἐπὶ τὴν γῆν ἡμέρας τεσσαράκοντα, ἀναστὰς ἀπὸ τῆς γῆς παρέκυψα εἰς τὸ σπήλαιον.

asked them to dig a deep pit for me; and they did so with their claws. I then threw myself into the pit; and for five days I lay there, and *I wept bitterly,* asking and begging them to bury me and cover me; and they, almost shedding human tears, did bury me. And I remained buried in the ground, for my terrible iniquity, for three years, and I became *earth and ashes,* but I would not die, because *the Lord* was *my supporter.*

"After three years, by God's providence, there was a great 41 storm; and by God's will, the cave was breached right above my head and toward my face. And as the drops fell down, they widened the opening in the cave; and I saw daylight, and I glorified God, who had absolved me from my terrible iniquity, and who has said, '*I did not come to call the righteous, but sinners to repentance.*' Then I stretched out my hand outside the cave through the hole, and I reaped from a plant, and ate from it, and was filled to satisfaction. By God's will, the two lions also came into the cave and, upon seeing my head and my face, they lamented over my body. And they dug it out with their claws, and thus I too came out of the hole, entirely healthy, by the Lord's command and love of humankind. And my strength was double what it was before. And I prayed, and I glorified the merciful God, and I came out of the cave.

"After kneeling on the ground for forty days, when I 42 stood up from the ground, I stooped to look into the cave.

Καὶ εἶδον τὰς τέσσαρας γωνίας τοῦ σπηλαίου, ἐχούσας φωταγωγίαν μεγάλην, ἐν δὲ τῷ μέσῳ τοῦ σπηλαίου ὑπῆρχε λαμπρότερον φῶς τῶν ἡλιακῶν ἀκτίνων, καὶ μέσον τοῦ φωτὸς ἐκείνου, ἐν σχήματι ἀνθρώπου, τὸν Σωτῆρα Χριστόν. Καὶ ἦν φορῶν ἐπάνω τῆς κεφαλῆς αὐτοῦ στέφανον χρυσοῦν ἀπὸ λίθων τιμίων· καὶ ἔψαλλεν ᾠδὴν θαυμαστὴν καὶ οὐράνιον· ἦν δὲ ἡ φωνὴ αὐτοῦ μεγάλη καὶ ἰσχυρά.

43   "Καὶ ὡς ἐπλήρωσεν τὴν ᾠδήν, ἦλθεν ἄλλη φωνὴ ἐκ τοῦ οὐρανοῦ λέγουσα τρίτον, 'Ἀμήν, ἀμήν, ἀμήν, εἰς αἰῶνα αἰῶνος.' Καὶ πάλιν εἰσελθοῦσα νεφέλη πυρὸς εἰς τὸ σπήλαιον, ἀνιμήσατο ἐκ μέσου τοῦ σπηλαίου τὸ φοβερὸν ἐκεῖνο καὶ ὑπέρλαμπρον φῶς. Καὶ ἀνερχομένης τῆς νεφέλης εἰς τὸν οὐρανόν, ἐγένοντο μεγάλοι σεισμοί, καὶ ἀστραπαὶ καὶ βρονταί, καὶ τὰ πετεινὰ τοῦ οὐρανοῦ ἕκαστον τὴν ἰδίαν φωνὴν ἔκραζον λέγοντα, 'Ἅγιος, ἅγιος, ἅγιος Κύριος.' Ἐξέστην δὲ ἐγὼ καὶ ἄφωνος ἐγενόμην ἐπὶ ἡμέρας πολλάς, τὰ δὲ δύο λεοντάρια οὐκ ἀνεχώρησαν ἀπ' ἐμοῦ. Καὶ τότε ἐπείσθην ὅτι ἀληθῶς ὁ Σωτὴρ τοῦ κόσμου Χριστὸς μετὰ νεφέλης καὶ πυρὸς ἦλθεν εἰς τὸ σπήλαιον καὶ ἡγίασεν αὐτό. Ἐγὼ δὲ ὁ ταλαίπωρος καὶ ἁμαρτωλὸς θαυμάζω, πῶς εὐτελὴς καὶ ἀνάξιος ὢν ἠξιώθην ταῦτα θεάσασθαι. Καὶ ἀπὸ τότε εἰσὶν ἔτη ἑβδομήκοντα ἢ καὶ πλεῖον· ἤμην δὲ τότε ἐτῶν τεσσαράκοντα ὀκτώ.

44   "Καὶ ἰδού, πατέρες τίμιοι, ὡς καλοὺς καὶ γνησίους ἀδελφούς, πάντα ὅσα ἔπραξα ἀνήγγειλα ὑμῖν. Καὶ εἰ μὲν δύνασθε βαστάζειν καὶ ὑπομένειν τοὺς πειρασμοὺς τοῦ διαβόλου, καρτερήσατε ἐνταῦθα· εἰ δὲ μὴ δύνασθε, ὁ Κύριος ἐν εἰρήνῃ διαφυλάξοι ὑμᾶς."

And I saw that the four corners of the cave were brilliantly illuminated, and in the middle of the cave there was a light brighter than the rays of the sun, and in the middle of this light I saw Christ the Savior in the form of a man. And, on his head, he was wearing a golden crown with precious gems; and he was chanting a marvelous and heavenly song; and his voice was loud and powerful.

"And when he completed the song, another voice came 43 from heaven, saying three times, 'Amen, amen, amen, to the ages of ages.' And again a cloud of fire came into the cave and drew that awesome and most brilliant light up from the middle of the cave. And as the cloud was ascending to the heaven, there were great earthquakes, and lightning, and thunder, and the birds of the sky, each in their own voice, called out, '*Holy, holy, holy, Lord.*' I was astounded and became speechless for many days, and the two lions did not leave me. And then I became convinced that Christ the Savior of the world truly did come in cloud and fire into my cave and sanctified it. And I, miserable and sinful man that I am, am amazed at how I was deemed worthy to witness these things, even though I am abject and worthless. And since then, it's been seventy years or more; and I was forty-eight years old then.

"And there it is, honorable fathers! I have confessed to 44 you, as good and genuine brothers, everything I have done. And if you are able to bear and endure the temptations of the devil, persevere here; if not, may the Lord keep you safe in peace."

45 Ἡμεῖς δὲ οἱ ταπεινοὶ ταῦτα ἀκούσαντες παρὰ τοῦ ἁγίου ἀνδρὸς ἐκείνου, ἐξέστημεν καὶ ἐδοξάσαμεν τὸν Θεόν. Καὶ ἰδοὺ ἐξαίφνης ἔρχονται οἱ δύο λέοντες ἐκ τῆς ἐρήμου, καὶ ἐπιθεὶς τὰς χεῖρας ηὐλόγει αὐτούς· καὶ πεσόντες χαμαὶ προσεκύνησαν ἡμᾶς. Ἡμεῖς δὲ φοβηθέντες προσεκυνήσαμεν τὸν Ἅγιον Μακάριον ἐπὶ τὴν γῆν. Ὁ δὲ ὄντως Μακάριος λέγει ἡμῖν, "Ἐπίθετε, ἀδελφοί, τὰς χεῖρας ὑμῶν ἐπ᾽ αὐτά." Καὶ ἐπεθήκαμεν τὰς χεῖρας ἡμῶν μετὰ πολλοῦ φόβου· ὁ δὲ Κύριος ἡμέρωσεν αὐτοὺς τοῦ μὴ ἀδικηθῆναι ἡμᾶς ὑπ᾽ αὐτῶν.

46 Τότε εἴπομεν πρὸς τὸν Ἅγιον Μακάριον, "Δὸς ἡμῖν εὐλογίαν καὶ εὐχήν, ὅσιε καὶ ἅγιε πάτερ, ἵνα ὑποστρέψαντες εἰς τὸν κόσμον, ἀπαγγείλωμεν τὰ περὶ σοῦ, καὶ τὴν ἁγίαν σου πολιτείαν κηρύξωμεν πανταχοῦ." Ὁ δὲ ποιήσας εὐχὴν μεγάλην ὑπὲρ ἡμῶν, καὶ ἀσπασάμενος, παρέθετο ἡμᾶς τῷ Θεῷ, τοῦ διασῶσαι καὶ ὁδηγῆσαι ἡμᾶς ἐν πάσῃ τῇ ὁδῷ· παρέδωκεν δὲ ἡμῖν τοῦ ἀποσῶσαι ἡμᾶς κατὰ τὴν ὁδὸν τοὺς λέοντας. Καὶ τοῦ Κυρίου συνεργοῦντος, ὡδήγησαν ἡμᾶς καὶ ἀπέσωσαν πᾶσαν τὴν ὁδόν, καὶ ἤγαγον ἡμᾶς ἕως τῆς σκοτεινῆς. Ἰδόντες δὲ ἡμεῖς πάλιν τὴν ἀψίδα τοῦ Ἀλεξάνδρου, καὶ γνωρίσαντες τὸν τόπον, κλίναντες τὰς κεφαλὰς αὐτῶν οἱ λέοντες, προσεκύνησαν ἡμᾶς, καὶ ὑπέστρεψαν πρὸς τὸν ὅσιον ἐν τῷ σπηλαίῳ.

47 Ὁ δὲ ἐλεήμων καὶ φιλάνθρωπος Θεὸς διεφύλαξεν ἡμᾶς ἀκινδύνους καὶ ἀθλίπτους ἀπὸ πάντων τῶν ἐθνῶν. Ἐν οἷς καὶ φθάσαντες εἰς τὴν χώραν τῶν Περσῶν, εἰσήλθομεν εἰς πόλιν καλουμένην Κτησιφῶν, καὶ προσκυνήσαντες τοὺς ἁγίους τρεῖς παῖδας, καὶ περάσαντες τὸν Τίγρην ποταμὸν

When we, humble as we are, heard these words from that 45
holy man, we were astounded and glorified God. And, lo and
behold, the two lions suddenly came from the desert and,
placing his hands on them, he blessed them; and they fell
down and paid their respects before us. We were frightened
and made our devotions on the ground before Saint Makarios. And the truly blessed Makarios said to us, "Brothers,
place your hands on them." And we did place our hands on
them in great fear; and the Lord kept them tame so that we
were not harmed by them.

Then we said to Saint Makarios, "Give us your blessing 46
and prayer, holy and saintly father, so that we may return to
the world, and tell your story, and make your holy life known
everywhere." He then made a long prayer on our behalf, embraced us, and committed us to God, to keep us safe and
guide us the whole way; he also gave us the lions to escort us
on our way. And with the Lord's assistance, they guided us
and escorted us all the way, and brought us to the darkness.
When we saw the arch of Alexander again, and recognized
the place, the lions bowed their heads, paid their respects to
us, and returned back to the cave to the holy man.

The merciful God who loves humankind preserved us 47
from danger and trouble from all the peoples. So we reached
the land of the Persians, and entered the city called Ctesiphon, paid our respects to the three holy youths, and
crossed the river Tigris, where we encountered Christians.

ἐνετύχομεν Χριστιανοῖς. Ἐν οἷς καὶ ἐρωτηθέντες παρ' αὐτῶν, ἀπεκαλύψαμεν αὐτοῖς τὰ τῆς ὁδοιπορίας ἡμῶν μυστήρια καὶ τοῦ ἁγίου ἐκείνου ἀνθρώπου τὴν πολιτείαν.

48   Καὶ περιπατήσαντες ἐπὶ ἡμέρας πεντήκοντα πέντε,
εἰσήλθομεν εἰς τὴν ἁγίαν πόλιν Ἰερουσαλήμ. Καὶ προσκυνήσαντες τὴν ἁγίαν Ἀνάστασιν τοῦ Χριστοῦ καὶ τοὺς
ἁγίους καὶ σεβασμίους τόπους, ἤλθομεν εἰς τὸ Ὄρος τῶν
Ἐλαιῶν. Καὶ ἐξηγησάμενοι τὴν μεγάλην καὶ ἀκατάληπτον
δύναμιν τοῦ Σωτῆρος ἡμῶν Θεοῦ καὶ τὴν πολιτείαν τοῦ
Ἁγίου Μακαρίου, πάντες οἱ ἀκούσαντες ἐδόξασαν τὸν φιλάνθρωπον Θεόν, καὶ συνέταξαν εἰς βίβλους πᾶσαν τὴν
πολιτείαν τοῦ Ἁγίου Μακαρίου, διὰ τὸν πόθον τῶν φιλο-
θέων ἀκροατῶν.

49   Καὶ ἐξελθόντες τῶν Ἰεροσολύμων ἀπήλθομεν εἰς τὴν
Μεσοποταμίαν Συρίας εἰς τὸ μοναστήριον ἡμῶν. Καὶ
εἰσελθόντες ἐν τῇ μονῇ, προσεκυνήσαμεν τὸν ὅσιον καὶ
ἅγιον Ἀσκληπιόν, τὸν ἡγούμενον ἡμῶν, καὶ τοὺς ἀδελ-
φοὺς ἅπαντας. Εἶθ' οὕτως ἀπηγγείλαμεν αὐτοῖς καθ' ἑξῆς
πάντα τὰ θαυμάσια τοῦ Θεοῦ καὶ τὴν πολιτείαν τοῦ Ἁγίου
Μακαρίου. Ὅθεν οἱ ἀκούσαντες ἅπαντες καὶ οἱ μετὰ
ταῦτα μέλλοντες ἀκούειν δόξαν ἀναπέμπουσιν τῷ Πατρὶ
καὶ τῷ Υἱῷ, καὶ τῷ Ἁγίῳ Πνεύματι, νῦν καὶ ἀεὶ καὶ εἰς τοὺς
αἰῶνας τῶν αἰώνων, ἀμήν.

When we were asked by them, we revealed to them the secrets of our journey as well as the life of that holy man.

And after we had walked for fifty-five days, we entered 48 the holy city of Jerusalem. We paid our respects at the holy Anastasis of Christ, and at the holy and sacred places, and we came to the Mount of Olives. And when we spoke about the great and incomprehensible power of God our Savior and the life of Saint Makarios, all those who heard glorified God who loves humankind, and recorded in books the whole life of Saint Makarios, in order to satisfy the desire of God-loving listeners.

And when we had left Jerusalem for Mesopotamia in 49 Syria, we entered our monastery. And after we entered the monastery, we paid our respects to the holy and saintly Asklepios our abbot and to all the brothers. Then we told them in detail all about the wonders of God and the life of Saint Makarios. All the listeners then as well as all the future ones give glory to the Father and the Son and the Holy Spirit, now and forever and unto the ages, amen.

PASSION OF
CHRISTOPHER

Μαρτύριον τοῦ Ἁγίου Χριστοφόρου

Ἔτους τετάρτου τῆς βασιλείας Δεκίου, ἦν πολλὴ μανία τῶν τὰ εἴδωλα σεβομένων. Ταύτης κατισχυούσης τῆς πίστεως τῶν Χριστιανῶν, <ὁ> ἀπαίδευτος σάκραν διὰ τῶν ἀρχόντων κατήνεγκεν ἐπὶ τὸ πάντα τὸν θρησκεύοντα τὴν εὐσεβῆ τοῦ Θεοῦ θρησκείαν, μιαρῶν ἐδεσμάτων ἀπογευσαμένους σώζεσθαι. Εἶτα δὴ τῶν ἀρχόντων δεξαμένων τὸ πρόσταγμα ὑπὸ τῶν ἀνόμων αὐτοῦ χειρῶν, ἐλυμήναντο τὰς ἐκκλησίας τοῦ Θεοῦ ἐπιδεικνύντες τὰ τοῦ βασιλέως γράμματα.

2   Καὶ πάντων τὴν ὑπακοὴν πληρούντων, ἦν τις ἐν ταῖς ἡμέραις ἐκείναις τῶν ποτε κομήτων πολέμῳ συλλαβόμενος τὸν μακάριον Ῥέπρεβον, καὶ στρατεύσας ἐν τῷ νουμέρῳ τῶν Μαρμαριτῶν. Ἦν δὲ ὁ ἀνὴρ οὗτος φρόνιμος σφόδρα—ἵνα δὴ εἰδῆτε πάντες, ὅτι οὐ μόνον Χριστιανοῖς βοηθεῖ ὁ Θεὸς ἡμῶν, ἀλλὰ καὶ τοῖς ἐξ ἐθνῶν πιστεύουσι μισθαποδότης γίνεται, καὶ δοκίμους καθιστᾷ πρὸς τὴν ἑαυτοῦ γνῶσιν. Ἦν οὖν ὁ ἀνὴρ ἀπὸ τοῦ γένους τῶν Κυνοκεφάλων, γῆς τῶν Ἀνθρωποφάγων· ἦν δὲ πιστὸς τῷ φρονήματι, μελετῶν τὰ λόγια τοῦ Θεοῦ ἐν τῇ συνειδήσει αὐτοῦ· οὐ γὰρ ἠδύνατο λαλεῖν ἐν τῇ ἡμετέρᾳ διαλέκτῳ.

3   Ἰδὼν οὖν ὁ μακάριος οὗτος τὴν γινομένην κατατομὴν τῶν Χριστιανῶν, ἐλυπεῖτο σφόδρα. Ἐλθόντος δὲ αὐτοῦ

Passion of Saint Christopher

In the fourth year of Decius's reign, the folly of those who venerated the idols was widespread. As it overpowered the faith of the Christians, that thug issued an edict to the governors, that all those who followed the true religion of God could save their lives if they partook of the abominable sacrificial food. Then, once they had received this dictate from the emperor's lawless hands, the governors were maltreating God's churches while publicly displaying the emperor's letters.

Everyone complied in full obedience, but there was in those days one of the counts who had captured the blessed Reprebos during a war, and then enlisted him in the army unit of the Marmaritai. This man Reprebos was very smart— so that all of you may understand that our God does not only help Christians, but also *rewards* heathens, and makes them worthy to know him. Indeed, this man belonged to the race of the Cynocephali, from the land of the Anthropophagi, yet he was a man of faith in his understanding, meditating upon God's words in his mind as he could not speak our language.

When this blessed man saw the ongoing slaughter of Christians, he was greatly saddened. So he went out of the

ἔξω τῆς πόλεως, ἔρριψεν ἑαυτὸν κατὰ πρόσωπον, καὶ
προσηύξατο λέγων, "Κύριε ὁ Θεὸς ὁ Παντοκράτωρ, ἐπάκουσον τῆς ταπεινώσεώς μου, καὶ δεῖξον τὴν εὐσπλαγ-
χνίαν σου ἐν ἐμοὶ τῷ ταπεινῷ, καὶ ἄνοιξον τὰ χείλη μου καὶ
δός μοι λαλεῖν, ὅπως ἀπελθὼν ἐλέγξω τὸν τύραννον."

Καὶ ἰδοὺ ἀνὴρ παρέστη αὐτῷ ἐν ἐσθῆτι λαμπρᾷ καὶ
λέγει αὐτῷ, "Ῥέπρεβε, ἡ προσευχή σου εἰσηκούσθη· ἀνάστηθι!" Καὶ ἁψάμενος τῶν χειλέων αὐτοῦ, ἐνεφύσησεν
αὐτῷ, καὶ ἐδόθη αὐτῷ ὁμιλία καθὼς ἠθέλησεν.

4   Ἀναστὰς δὲ εἰσῆλθεν εἰς τὴν πόλιν λέγων πᾶσιν, "Ὦ
πάσης ῥᾳδιουργίας πεπληρωμένοι, ἔστω, ὑμεῖς τὰς ὑμετέρας ψυχὰς τοῦ Σατανᾶ πεποιήκατε· τί καὶ ἡμᾶς σπου-
δάζετε σὺν ὑμῖν ἀπολέσθαι; Ἐγὼ Χριστιανός εἰμι καὶ οὐ
προστέταγμαι θύειν ματαίοις <θεοῖς>."

Ἀνὴρ δέ τις ὀνόματι Βαχθιοῦς ἐγγίσας, ἐρράπισεν
αὐτόν. Εἶπεν δὲ πρὸς αὐτὸν ὁ Ῥέπρεβος, "Κατέχομαι ὑπὸ
τοῦ Χριστοῦ, δέδεμαι ὑπὸ τοῦ Σωτῆρος, καὶ οὐ δύναμαί
σοί τι ποιῆσαι· ἐὰν δὲ ἡ καρδία μου πικρανθῇ, ὑμεῖς παρ᾽
ἐμοὶ οὐχ ὑπάρξετε, οὐδὲ τὸ βασίλειον ὑμῶν τὸ διεφθαρ-
μένον."

5   Ἀναχωρήσας δὲ ἀπ᾽ αὐτοῦ ὁ Βαχθιοῦς, ἦλθεν πρὸς τὸν
βασιλέα καὶ λέγει αὐτῷ, "Βασιλεῦ, εἰς τοὺς αἰῶνας ζῆθι!
Κατὰ τὸ θεῖον θέσπισμα τοῦ προστάγματός σου, ἐπιδει-
κνύντος τοῦ ἄρχοντος καὶ πάντων τὴν ὑπακοὴν πληρούντων, ἐφάνη ἐνώπιον τοῦ λαοῦ ἀνὴρ φοβερὸς τῷ εἴδει καὶ
ὑπερμεγέθης. Ὃ εἶδον ἀναγγελῶ τῷ κυρίῳ μου· ἡ κεφαλὴ
αὐτοῦ ὃν τρόπον κυνὸς οὕτως ἐστί· ἡ δὲ θρὶξ αὐτοῦ ὑπερμεγέθης ἡπλωμένη· καὶ οἱ ὀφθαλμοί, ὡς ὁ ἀστὴρ ὁ πρωὶ

city, threw himself face down, and prayed with the following words: "Lord, God Almighty, hearken to my lowliness, and show your mercy to lowly me, and open my lips and give me speech, so that I may go and rebuke the tyrant."

And lo and behold, a man in shining clothing appeared to of him, and said to him, "Reprebos, your prayer has been heard. Stand up!" And the man touched Reprebos's lips and breathed into him, and speech was given to him according to his wish.

So he got up and went into the city, saying to everyone, 4 "Alright, you people who are full of every sort of deceit, you may have given your own souls to Satan, but why are you so keen for us to be ruined along with you? I am a Christian and cannot be ordered to sacrifice to fake gods."

A man by the name of Bachthious approached him and slapped him. Reprebos said to him, "I am held back by Christ, I am bound by the Savior, and I cannot do anything to you; but if my heart is irritated, both you and your corrupt emperor shall cease to exist because of me."

Bachthious left him and went to the emperor, and said to 5 him, "Emperor, may you live forever! Concerning the divine decree of your edict, while the governor has published it and everyone has complied in full obedience, a man, who's terrifying to look at and enormous, has appeared in public. Allow me to report to you, my master, what I saw: his head is like that of a dog; and his hair, which is loose, is extremely long; and his eyes are like the star that shines in the morning; and

ἀνατέλλων· καὶ οἱ ὀδόντες αὐτοῦ ἐξέχουσιν ὡς συάγρου. Οὗτος ἐλθών, ἐλάλει ῥήματα βλάσφημα κατὰ τῶν θεῶν καὶ κατὰ τῆς θειότητός σου· ἐγὼ δὲ ἀκούσας ἐρράπισα αὐτόν. Εἶπεν δέ μοι ὅτι· 'Κατέχομαι ὑπό' τινος 'Χριστοῦ· ἐὰν δὲ ἡ καρδία μου πικρανθῇ, ἔτι ὑμεῖς παρ' ἐμοὶ οὐχ ὑπάρξετε.' Ἐγὼ οὖν ἐμήνυσα τῷ κυρίῳ μου, ἵνα εἰδῇς τὰ περὶ τοῦ ἀνδρός, μή ποτε ὑπήκουσεν ὁ θεὸς τῶν Χριστιανῶν τῆς δεήσεως αὐτῶν."

Δέκιος εἶπεν, "Δαιμόνιον ἔχεις καὶ οὕτως σοι ἐφάνη." Ἐκέλευσεν οὖν παρ' αὐτὰ διακοσίους στρατιώτας ἀπελθόντας πιάσαι αὐτὸν λέγων αὐτοῖς· "Ἐὰν ἀντιστῇ ὑμῖν, κρεοκοπήσατε αὐτόν." Καὶ τούτους ἀποστείλας εἰς βοήθειαν αὐτοῦ εἶπεν πρὸς αὐτούς, "Μόνον τὴν κεφαλὴν αὐτοῦ ἐνέγκατέ μοι, ἵνα ἴδω αὐτὴν ὁποία ἐστίν, ἐπειδὴ πολὺ θαυμάζει εἶναι αὐτὸν δυνατόν."

6   Αὐτῶν δὲ ταῦτα σκεπτομένων, ὁ μακάριος Ῥέπρεβος ἀπελθὼν ἔμπροσθεν τῆς ἐκκλησίας ἐξ ἐναντίας τῆς θύρας, ἐκάθισεν πήξας τὴν ῥάβδον αὐτοῦ. Καὶ τὴν τρίχαν αὐτοῦ διαρρίψας ἔνθεν καὶ ἔνθεν, τὴν δὲ ὄψιν ἐπὶ τὰ γόνατα θέμενος, προσηύχετο λέγων·

"Κύριε ὁ Θεὸς ὁ Παντοκράτωρ, ἐπάκουσόν μου, ὁ ἐπακούσας τῶν τριῶν δούλων σου ἐν πυρί· ὁ ἐν οὐρανοῖς ὑπὸ τῶν εἴκοσι τεσσάρων πρεσβυτέρων δοξαζόμενος καὶ ὑπὸ τῶν τεσσάρων ζῴων ὑμνούμενος, καὶ ἐπὶ τῇ κινήσει αὐτῶν τερπόμενος, τὴν ἐκείνων σοι πάντων δέησιν, ἐπάκουσόν μου σήμερον εἰς ἀγαθόν, ἵνα γνωσθῇ σου ἡ πολλὴ ἀγαθότης ἐπ' ἐμοὶ τῷ ἀλόγῳ. Καὶ δὸς βλαστῆσαι, Κύριε, τὸ

his teeth protrude like those of a wild boar. This man came and uttered blasphemies against the gods and against your godliness; when I heard him, I slapped him. And he said to me, 'I am held back by' some 'Christ; but if my heart is irritated, you shall cease to exist because of me.' So I have reported this to you, my master, so that you might know about this man, lest the god of the Christians has listened to their requests."

Decius said, "You're possessed by a demon if he looked like that to you." So he at once ordered two hundred soldiers to go and catch Reprebos, saying to them: "If he resists you, cut him to pieces." And, as he sent them off, in order to help Bachthious he said to them, "Just bring me his head so that I can see what it looks like, since this one is so amazed by that man's strength."

While these men were considering these things, the 6 blessed Reprebos went in front of the church opposite the gate, and, after he had sat down, stuck his staff into the ground; he then threw back his hair on either side of his head, placed his face between his knees, and began to pray with these words:

"Lord, God Almighty, answer me, you who answered your three servants in the fire; you whom the *twenty-four elders* glorify in the heavens and to whom the *four living creatures* sing hymns, and who are pleased by their motion; by the intercession of all of them with you, answer me today for the sake of the good, so that your great goodness may be made known through me, I who am without speech. And grant,

ξύλον τοῦτο, ὅπως κἀγὼ προθυμότερον εἰς τὴν δόξαν σου εἰσέλθω."

Καὶ εὐθέως ἡ ῥάβδος ἐβλάστησε καὶ τὸν ἄνδρα ἰσχυροποίησεν.

7   Ταῦτα δὲ αὐτοῦ προσευχομένου, ἰδοὺ εἰσῆλθεν γυνὴ συλλέξαι ῥόδα· καὶ τοῦτον ἰδοῦσα καθήμενον καὶ κλαίοντα, ὄπισθεν ἑαυτὴν δέδωκεν, καὶ ἐλθοῦσα διηγεῖτό τισιν· "Ὅτι μὲν ναὸς Θεοῦ ἐστιν, δῆλον· ὃ δὲ εἶδον δράκων ἐστὶν καὶ διὰ τοῦτο κλαίει." Καὶ ταῦτα λέγουσα ἦλθον οἱ στρατιῶται ζητοῦντες αὐτόν.

Ὡς δὲ ἤκουσαν τὰ ῥήματα τῆς γυναικός, ἠρώτων αὐτὴν λέγοντες, "Ποῦ εἶδες τὸν ἄνθρωπον;" Ἡ δὲ ὑπέδειξεν αὐτόν. Κατὰ δὲ τὴν φήμην τοῦ ἀνδρός, οὐκ ἐτόλμων προσκολλᾶσθαι αὐτῷ· ἐκ δὲ τοῦ ὄρους καταδραμόντες, ἐσκόπουν τὸν ἄνδρα.

Ὁ δὲ ἀθλητὴς τοῦ Χριστοῦ ἀναστὰς καὶ τὰς χεῖρας ἐκτείνας, ἐδέετο τοῦ Κυρίου. Οἱ δὲ στρατιῶται λέγουσιν αὐτῷ, "Τίς εἶ σὺ καὶ τί σοί ἐστιν ὅτι κλαίεις ἰσχυρῶς;"

Καὶ ἀποκριθεὶς Ῥέπρεβος εἶπεν, "Κλαῦσαί με δεῖ παρὰ πάντα ἄνθρωπον ὅτι μὴ γνοὺς Θεὸν οὐκ ἐνεκλήθην, νῦν δὲ ἐπιγνοὺς αὐτὸν τυραννοῦμαι."

Εἶπαν δὲ πρὸς αὐτόν, "Ἡμεῖς πρὸς σὲ ἀπεστάλημεν ἀπάξαι σε δέσμιον πρὸς τὸν ἡμῶν βασιλέα, ἵνα θεοὺς ὁμολογῇς καὶ μὴ θεόν."

Εἶπεν δὲ πρὸς αὐτοὺς ὁ ἀθλητὴς τοῦ Χριστοῦ, "Ἐὰν μὲν ἰδίῳ θελήματι θελήσω ἐλθεῖν πρὸς αὐτόν, ἔλθω μεθ' ὑμῶν, ἐπεὶ δέσμιόν με οὐκ ἀπάξετε· ὁ γὰρ Χριστός μου

Lord, that this staff may produce living shoots, so that I too may enter into your glory more eagerly."

And the rod immediately put forth living shoots and fortified the man.

While he was praying in this way, lo and behold a woman 7 came to gather roses; and when she saw him sitting there crying, she backed off, and went and recounted this to some people: "That it's a temple of God is clear. Yet what I saw was a monster and he was crying for that reason." And as she was saying these things, the soldiers came looking for him.

When they heard the woman's words, they asked her, saying, "Where did you see the man?" And she showed him to them. Because of his reputation, they did not dare come near him; rather, they came down from the hill and observed him.

Meanwhile, the athlete of Christ who had stood up and stretched out his hands, was praying to the Lord. The soldiers then said to him, "Who are you, and what's wrong with you to make you cry so intensely?"

Reprebos responded and said to them, "I must cry more than any other person, because when I did not know God, I was never accused, but now that I've come to know him, I'm being subjected to violence."

They said to him, "We've been sent to take you in chains to our emperor, so that you may confess your faith in the gods, and not in a single god."

The athlete of Christ said to them, "If I want to come to him of my own free will, I'll come with you, since you're not going to take me there in chains; for my Christ came

ἐλθών, τὰ δεσμὰ τῶν ἁμαρτιῶν ἔλυσεν καὶ ἐρρύσατο ἡμᾶς ἐκ τοῦ πατρὸς ὑμῶν τοῦ Σατανᾶ."

8   Λέγουσιν αὐτῷ οἱ στρατιῶται, "Ἐὰν βούλῃ ἐλθεῖν μεθ' ἡμῶν, ἐλθέ· εἰ δὲ μή, ἡμεῖς ἀπελθόντες λέγομεν τῷ βασιλεῖ ὅτι 'οὐχ εὕρομεν αὐτόν,' καὶ σὺ ἀναχωρήσας πορεύου ὅπου βούλει."

Εἶπεν δὲ ὁ ἅγιος τοῦ Χριστοῦ μάρτυς, "Οὐχί, ἀλλὰ κἀγὼ ἐλθὼν μεθ' ὑμῶν, ὑποδείξω ὑμῖν τοῦ Χριστοῦ τὴν χάριν. Μόνον ἐκδέξασθέ με μικρόν."

Εἶπον δὲ πρὸς αὐτὸν οἱ στρατιῶται, "Αἱ δαπάναι ἡμῶν ἀνηλώθησαν καὶ οὐ δυνάμεθά σε περιμένειν."

Εἶπεν δὲ πρὸς αὐτούς, "*Εἰσακούσατέ μου τῆς φωνῆς, καὶ φάγεσθε ἀγαθὰ* καὶ ὄψεσθε τὴν δύναμιν τοῦ Κυρίου μου· θέτε τὰ καταλειφθέντα ὑμῖν." Οἱ δὲ ὑπήκουσαν προθύμως καὶ ἔρριψαν τὰ παρ' αὐτοῖς ὀλίγα βρώματα.

Αὐτὸς δὲ κλίνας τὰ γόνατα, προσηύξατο λέγων, "Κύριε Ἰησοῦ Χριστέ, ὁ τοὺς πέντε ἄρτους εὐλογήσας καὶ πλήθη ἱκανὰ χορτάσας, καὶ νῦν ὁ αὐτὸς εἶ, Κύριε Ἰησοῦ Χριστέ· ἐπάκουσόν μου ἐν τῇ ὥρᾳ ταύτῃ, ἵνα οὗτοι πάντες, βλέποντες τὰ θαυμάσιά σου, δοξάσωσίν σε τὸν ἀληθινὸν Θεόν."

Καὶ εὐθέως ἐγένετο εὐλογία Θεοῦ, καὶ ἐπληθύνθησαν οἱ ἄρτοι αὐτῶν, καὶ ἐπληρώθησαν πάντες ὅσον χρείαν εἶχεν ἕκαστος αὐτῶν. Ἰδόντες δὲ τὰ θαυμάσια τοῦ Θεοῦ, ἐπίστευσαν εἰς τὸν Θεὸν καὶ ἐπηκολούθησαν τῷ ἁγίῳ μάρτυρι. Λαβὼν δὲ αὐτοὺς ὁ ἀθλητὴς τοῦ Χριστοῦ, ἦλθεν ἐν πόλει Ἀντιοχείᾳ τῆς Συρίας καὶ ἐβαπτίσθη αὐτὸς καὶ οἱ μετ' αὐτοῦ πάντες ὑπὸ τοῦ Ἁγίου Βαβύλα. Καὶ οὕτως ἀπῄεσαν εἰς τὴν Πέργην.

and loosed the chains of sins, and saved us from your father, Satan."

The soldiers said to him, "If you want to come with us, come; but if not, we can go and say to the emperor 'we didn't find him,' and you may retreat and go wherever you want." 8

The holy martyr of Christ replied, "No, but when I do come with you, I'll show you the grace of my Christ. Just wait for me a little."

The soldiers said to him, "Our provisions have been used up, and we can't wait for you."

Then he said to them, "*Listen to my* voice, *and you shall eat good things,* and you shall see the power of my Lord. Put down whatever leftovers you have here." And they obeyed eagerly and threw down the little food they had.

And he went down on his knees and prayed, saying, "Lord Jesus Christ, you who blessed the five loaves of bread and fed a large crowd, you are still the same, Lord Jesus Christ; listen to me at this hour, so that all these men may witness your miracles and so glorify you, the true God."

Immediately God sent his blessing, and their loaves were multiplied, and they had their fill as much as each one needed. And when they saw the miracles of God, they believed in God and followed the holy martyr. The athlete of Christ took them with him, and went to the city of Antioch in Syria, and there he himself and all those with him were baptized by Saint Babylas. And thus they went to Perge.

9   Ἐγγισάντων δὲ αὐτῶν ἐν τῇ πόλει, λέγει αὐτοῖς ὁ Ἅγιος Ῥέπρεβος, "Ἀδελφοί, δήσατέ με καὶ οὕτως προσαγάγετέ με τῷ βασιλεῖ ὑμῶν, ἵνα μή τις ἰδὼν κατηγορήσῃ ὑμῶν, καὶ μέλλετε τιμωρεῖσθαι δι᾽ ἐμέ· ἀλλ᾽ ἀπέλθετε καὶ σκέψασθε περὶ τῆς ὑμετέρας σωτηρίας καὶ τῆς μελλούσης αἰωνίου ζωῆς." Καὶ ταῦτα παρακαλέσας προσῆλθεν ἐνώπιον τοῦ βασιλέως.

Ἰδὼν δὲ τὸ πρόσωπον αὐτοῦ ὁ βασιλεὺς ἐταράχθη, καὶ ἤγγισε τοῦ καταπεσεῖν ἀπὸ τοῦ θρόνου αὐτοῦ. Εἶπεν δὲ πρὸς αὐτὸν ὁ ἀθλητὴς τοῦ Χριστοῦ, "Ὦ ἀτυχέστατον βασίλειον καὶ κατεφθαρμένον, εἰ ἐμὲ τὸν δοῦλον τοῦ Θεοῦ οὕτως ἐφοβήθης, τῷ Θεῷ πῶς ἀπολογήσῃ ὅτι ἀπώλεσας ψυχὰς τῶν ἀνθρώπων;"

Δέκιος εἶπεν, "Πόθεν ὁρμᾶσαι καὶ ποίου γένους ὑπάρχεις, ἢ τί τὸ ὄνομά σου;"

Ῥέπρεβος εἶπεν, "Θέλεις μαθεῖν ποίας θρησκείας εἰμί; Χριστιανός εἰμι. Τὸ δὲ ἐπιτεθέν μοι ὄνομα Ῥέπρεβος ἐκλήθην· μετὰ δὲ τὸ λαβεῖν με τὸ ἅγιον βάπτισμα, Χριστοφόρος ἐκλήθην. Τὸ δὲ γένος ἐὰν ἐρωτᾷς ἢ τὸ ἔθνος ἢ τὴν χώραν μου, εἰς τὸ πρόσωπόν μου βλέπε καὶ μανθάνεις τὸ ἔθνος μου."

Δέκιος εἶπεν, "Ἄκουσόν μου, Ῥέπρεβε, καὶ θῦσον τοῖς θεοῖς καὶ γράφω τοῖς πᾶσιν, ἵνα ἱερέα σε καταστήσω."

Ὁ δὲ ἀθλητὴς τοῦ Κυρίου εἶπεν πρὸς αὐτόν, "Τὸ ἀργύριόν σου καὶ τὸ χρυσίον σου, σὺν σοὶ εἴη εἰς ἀπώλειαν· θεοὶ γὰρ οἳ οὐκ ἐποίησαν τὸν οὐρανὸν καὶ τὴν γῆν, ἀπολέσθωσαν ὑποκάτω παντὸς τοῦ οὐρανοῦ (οὐ γάρ εἰσι θεοί)."

As they approached the city, Saint Reprebos said to them, 9
"Brothers, tie me up and thus present me to your emperor, so that no one, seeing me like this, may accuse you, for then you will be punished because of me; just go and think about your own salvation and the future eternal life." Having exhorted them in this way he came before the emperor.

When the emperor saw Reprebos's face, he was shaken and almost fell off his throne. The athlete of Christ said to him, "Most miserable, corrupt emperor, if you are so afraid of me, God's servant, how are you going to defend yourself in front of God for having destroyed people's souls?"

Decius said, "Where are you from and what's your race, or what's your name?"

Reprebos said, "Do you want to learn about my religion? I am a Christian. The name I was given was Reprebos; but since receiving holy baptism, I'm called Christopher. As for my race, people, or land, about which you ask, just look at my face and you may find out what my people is."

Decius said, "Listen to me, Reprebos, and sacrifice to the gods and I shall decree to everyone that I'm appointing you as a priest."

The athlete of the Lord said to him, "Your silver and your gold, can go to hell with you; *let gods who did not make the sky and the earth perish from the* entire *sky* (for they are not gods)."

Ἐκέλευσεν δὲ αὐτὸν ὁ βασιλεὺς κρεμασθῆναι ἀπὸ τῶν τριχῶν, καὶ λέγει αὐτῷ, "Θῦσον τοῖς θεοῖς ἵνα ζήσῃς."

Ὁ ἅγιος ἀπεκρίθη, "Μή σοι καλῶς, ἀσεβέστατε, ἵνα ἐγὼ λίθοις θύσω καὶ δαίμοσιν ὁμοίοις σοῦ;"

Ἐκέλευσε δὲ αὐτὸν σπαθίζεσθαι λέγων, "Μὴ μωρολόγει αἰσχρῶς, ἀλλὰ θῦσον τοῖς θεοῖς!"

Ῥέπρεβος εἶπεν, "Ἡ τοῦ κόσμου τούτου βάσανος πρόσκαιρός ἐστιν· ὃ δὲ μένει σοὶ τῷ ἀνόμῳ, πῦρ αἰώνιον."

10 Τότε χολέσας ὁ βασιλεὺς ἐκέλευσε τρεῖς λαμπάδας προσάψαι τῷ σώματι αὐτοῦ. Ἡ δὲ σύγκλητος καὶ πᾶσαι αἱ ἐξουσίαι λέγουσι τῷ βασιλεῖ, "Μηδαμῶς, κύριε, μὴ ἐν τοιαύταις βασάνοις ἀνάλισκε τὸν ἄνθρωπον ὅτι τερπνὸς ἡμῖν ἐστιν! Ἀλλὰ μετὰ ἠπιότητος χρῆσαι αὐτῷ."

Ὁ δὲ λέγει, "Κατενέγκατε αὐτὸν ἀπὸ τῶν δεσμῶν." Καὶ λέγει αὐτῷ ὁ βασιλεύς, "Δεῦρο, καλὲ ἄνθρωπε, ὁμολόγησον τοὺς θεούς· τερπνὸς γάρ μοι ἐφάνης καὶ θέλω σε στράτορα εἶναι τοῦ ἅρματός μου."

Ὁ δὲ ἀθλητὴς τοῦ Χριστοῦ εἶπεν πρὸς αὐτόν, "Εἰ τοῦτο θέλεις γενέσθαι, γενοῦ Χριστιανὸς ὡς ἐγώ, καὶ ἔσῃ ἐν οὐρανοῖς βασιλεύων καὶ ἐγὼ ἔσομαι στράτωρ τοῦ ἅρματός σου."

Λέγει οὖν αὐτῷ ὁ βασιλεύς, "Ἐγώ σε προετρεψάμην θύειν τοῖς θεοῖς, καὶ σύ με καταναγκάζεις καταλιπεῖν τοὺς θεούς;"

11 Ἡ τάξις εἶπεν, "Δεόμεθα τῆς θειότητός σου, θεωροῦμεν τὸν ἄνθρωπον ὅτι ἀλλόφυλός ἐστι· κέλευσον οὖν αὐτῷ ἐνεχθῆναι δύο γυναῖκας εὐμόρφους, ὅπως τῇ τούτων φιλίᾳ ἀγόμενος, θύσῃ τοῖς θεοῖς." Καὶ ἤρεσε τοῦτο τὸ ῥῆμα

The emperor ordered that he should be hung up by his hair, and he said to him: "Sacrifice to the gods so you may live."

The saint responded, "Are you out of your mind, you most ungodly man? Do you think that I'll sacrifice to stones and demons who are like you?"

Then Decius ordered that Reprebos should be struck with swords, saying, "Stop talking such insolent nonsense; sacrifice to the gods instead!"

Reprebos said, "Torture in this world is temporary, but what awaits you, you lawless man, is the eternal fire."

At that point, the emperor became very angry and or- 10 dered that three torches should be attached to Reprebos's body. But the senate and all the powerful people said to the emperor, "Please, lord, please, don't destroy this man with such tortures! We like him. Treat him with clemency instead."

The emperor said, "Release this man from his chains!" And he said to him, "Come on, my good man, confess your faith in the gods; I like you, and I want you to be the groom in charge of my chariot."

The athlete of Christ said to him, "If you want that, become a Christian like me, and you shall remain an emperor in heaven, and I shall become the groom in charge of your chariot."

The emperor said to him, "I just urged you to sacrifice to the gods, and are you now forcing me to abandon them?"

The army officers said, "Please, your godliness, we see 11 that the man is a foreigner; order two beautiful women to be brought for him, so that, driven by desire for them, he may sacrifice to the gods." These words pleased the emperor. So

τῷ βασιλεῖ. Ἐποίησε δὲ ζητηθῆναι αὐτῷ δύο γυναῖκας εὐμόρφους· καὶ ἱμάτια πολύτιμα ἐνέδυσεν αὐτὰς καὶ μύροις ἔχρισεν, καὶ οὕτως συναπέκλεισεν αὐτὰς ἐν οἰκίσκῳ μικρῷ σὺν τῷ μάρτυρι.

Ὁ δὲ μακάριος Ῥέπρεβος, πεσὼν ἐπὶ πρόσωπον, ἐδέετο τοῦ Θεοῦ ἐπὶ ὥρας πολλάς· καὶ ἀναπέμψας τὴν δέησιν καὶ εἰπὼν τὸ "Ἀμήν," ἀνέστη ἀπὸ τοῦ τόπου οὗ ἦν προσευχόμενος καὶ ἦν προσέχων αὐταῖς.

Αἱ δὲ ἰδοῦσαι τὸ πρόσωπον αὐτοῦ, ἐταράχθησαν ἀπὸ φόβου καὶ ἐκρύβοντο μία πρὸς τὴν μίαν πρὸς τὸν τοῖχον λέγουσαι, "Οὐαὶ ἡμῖν ταῖς πολυαμαρτωλοῖς, σκληρὸν ἡμῖν πρᾶγμα κατέφθασε τοῦτο· ἐὰν γὰρ ἐπιμείνῃ προσέχων ἡμῖν, ἀποθανούμεθα."

12 Εἶπεν δὲ αὐταῖς ὁ ἀθλητὴς τοῦ Χριστοῦ, "Τί ἐνταῦθα ἥκατε;" Αἱ δὲ οὐκ ἐτόλμων ἀνανεῦσαι καὶ προσέχειν αὐτῷ. Εἶπεν δὲ πρὸς αὐτάς, "Πείσθητέ μοι καὶ ὁμολογήσατε Θεὸν εἰς ὃν ἐγὼ πεπίστευκα."

Αἱ δὲ πρὸς ἑαυτὰς εἶπον, "Σκληρὸν ἡμῖν πρᾶγμα κατέφθασε τοῦτο· ἐὰν γὰρ εἴπωμεν ὅτι 'Οὔ,' ἀποκτενεῖ ἡμᾶς οὗτος· ἐὰν δὲ τούτῳ πεισθῶμεν, ἀποκτενεῖ ἡμᾶς ὁ βασιλεύς."

Μία δὲ ἐξ αὐτῶν ὀνόματι Ἀκυλίνα εἶπεν, "Μᾶλλον τούτῳ πεισθῶμεν, καὶ ζήσωμεν εἰς τὸν αἰῶνα χρόνον."

Καὶ ταῦτα εἰποῦσα, λέγουσιν αὐτῷ, "Δεόμεθά σου, πρόσευξαι μόνον ὑπὲρ ἡμῶν, ἵνα ἐπιλάθηται ὁ Θεὸς τὰς ἁμαρτίας ἡμῶν, ὅτι πολλαί εἰσιν σφόδρα."

Λέγει πρὸς αὐτάς, "Ἐν φόνῳ ἢ ἐν μαγείαις ὑπόκεισθε;"

he had them find two beautiful women for him; and he dressed them up in expensive clothes and perfumed them with fragrances, and in this way he shut them up in a very small cell with the martyr.

The blessed Reprebos fell on his face and began beseeching God for a long time; once he had completed his supplication and said "Amen," he got up from the spot where he was praying and started staring at the women.

When they saw his face, they were shaken with fear and hid behind each other facing the wall, saying, "Too bad for us women of many sins; we're in a tough situation here; if he goes on staring at us, we shall die."

The athlete of Christ said to them, "Why did you come 12 here?" But they did not dare look up and face him. He said to them, "Follow my advice and confess your faith to the God in whom I've believed."

The women said to each other, "We're in a tough situation here; for if we say 'No,' this man's going to kill us; and if we follow his advice, then the emperor's going to kill us."

The one of them, Akylina by name, said, "It would be better to follow his advice, and live *forever.*"

When she had said this, they appealed to him: "Please, just pray for us, so that God may overlook our sins, because there are very many of them."

He said to them, "Have you engaged in murder or magic?"

Λέγουσιν αὐτῷ, "Οὐχί, κύριε! Ἀλλ' εἰς ὃ ἐστρατεύθη-
μεν, τοῦτο καὶ ἐπράττομεν. Φονευομένους δὲ μᾶλλον ἐλυ-
τρωσάμεθα, ἐλευθέρους πιπρασκομένους ἐξηγοράσαμεν
ἐκ τοῦ αὐτοῦ χρυσίου."

Εἶπεν δὲ αὐταῖς, "Ὑμεῖς μόνον ἐξ ὅλης ψυχῆς πιστεύσατε τῷ Κυρίῳ, καὶ δέομαι ὑπὲρ ὑμῶν, ὅπως μὴ ἅψηται
ὑμῶν βάσανος τοῦ φθαρτοῦ βασιλέως."

13 Αὐτῶν δὲ αὐτὰ σκεπτομένων, εἰσῆλθεν ὁ δεσμοφύλαξ
καὶ λέγει αὐταῖς, "Ἀνάστητε! Καλεῖ ὑμᾶς ὁ βασιλεύς."

Καὶ ἐξελθοῦσαι, ἦλθον πρὸς τὸν βασιλέα καὶ λέγει αὐταῖς, "Ἐπείσατε τὸν ἄνδρα ἐλθεῖν πρὸς ἡμᾶς;"

Αἱ δὲ εἶπον, "Ἐπείσθημεν καὶ ἡμεῖς, ὡς οὐκ ἔστιν ἐν
ἄλλῳ ἢ σωτηρία ἡμῶν, εἰ μὴ ὡς λέγει ὁ τοῦ Θεοῦ παῖς."

Τότε λέγει αὐταῖς ὁ βασιλεύς, "Ἐμαγεύθητε καὶ ὑμεῖς
καὶ ἀπέστητε τῶν θεῶν;"

Ἀκυλίνα εἶπεν, "Εἷς Θεὸς ἐν οὐρανοῖς μόνος· οἱ γὰρ
θεοί σου τέφρα εἰσὶν καὶ οὐδὲν δύνανται ποιῆσαι, εἰ μή τι
εἰς χάος ἀπολέσαι τὰς ψυχὰς τῶν ἀνθρώπων τῶν πιστευ-
όντων αὐτοῖς."

Τότε θυμωθεὶς ὁ βασιλεύς, ἐκέλευσεν αὐτὴν ἀπὸ τριχῶν
κρεμασθῆναι· καὶ ἐποίησε δύο λίθους περιτεθῆναι αὐτῇ,
ἕνα ἀφ' ἑνός. Καὶ ἐκ τοῦ βάρους τῶν λίθων τὰ σπλάγχνα
αὐτῆς ἐτέμνοντο. Ἐνέβλεψέν τε ἐπὶ τὸν μακάριον Ῥέπρεβον καὶ λέγει αὐτῷ, "Δέομαί σου, πρόσευξαι περὶ ἐμοῦ ὅτι
κάμνω πολύ."

Ὁ δὲ ἀναβλέψας εἰς τὸν οὐρανὸν εἶπεν, "Σοὶ τῷ Πατρὶ
τοῦ Χριστοῦ προσκυνῶ· ἵλεως γενοῦ τῇ δούλῃ σου Ἀκυλίνῃ." Καὶ ταῦτα αὐτοῦ προσευχομένου, ἡ δούλη τοῦ Θεοῦ

They said to him, "No, sir! We simply did what we were enlisted to do. In fact, we've ransomed some men who were about to be killed, and with the same money we've bought the freedom of some who were being sold into slavery."

He said to them, "Just believe with all your soul in the Lord, and I shall intercede on your behalf, so that no torture by the corrupt emperor may harm you."

While they were thinking about his words, the prison 13 guard came inside and said to them, "Get up! The emperor's calling for you."

So they left and came to the emperor, and he said to them, "Did you convince the man to come over to our side?"

They replied, "Actually we ourselves became convinced that there is no other salvation for us except the one which the servant of God preaches."

Then the emperor said to them, "Have you yielded to his magic too and strayed from the gods?"

Akylina said, "There is only one God in the heavens; your gods are mere ashes and they can do nothing, except lead the souls of the people who believe in them to utter destruction."

At that, the emperor became angry and ordered that she be hung up by her hair; and he had two rocks attached to her, one on either side. And the weight of the rocks was tearing her apart internally. She looked at the blessed Reprebos and said to him, "Please, pray for me as I'm really exhausted."

So he looked up to heaven and said, "I bow before you, Father of Christ; bring mercy on your servant Akylina." And once he said this prayer, the servant of God Akylina reposed

ἐκοιμήθη ἐν εἰρήνῃ. Ἐκέλευσε δὲ ὁ βασιλεὺς φυλάττεσθαι αὐτῆς τὸ σῶμα ἵνα κατακαύσῃ αὐτό.

14   Καὶ κελεύει προσαχθῆναι αὐτῷ Καλλινίκην· καὶ λέγει αὐτῇ, "Ἐλέησον σεαυτὴν ἵνα μή, ὡς ἡ ἄλλη κακὸν τέλος τοῦ βίου ἔδωκεν, οὕτως καὶ σύ. Φεῖσαι οὖν σεαυτῆς, καὶ προσελθοῦσα θῦσον τοῖς θεοῖς ἵνα μὴ ποιήσῃς με ἐπενεγκεῖν τὰς χεῖράς μου ἐπὶ σέ· εὐλαβοῦμαι γὰρ ἀφανίσαι σου τὸ κάλλος μὴ λιθασθῶ ὑπὸ τῆς πόλεως. Τοῦτο οὖν ποίησον καὶ θῦσον τοῖς θεοῖς καὶ εἰκόνα σοι χρυσῆν ποιήσω κατὰ πόλιν στῆναι."

     Ἡ δὲ εἶπεν, "Ποίοις με θεοῖς κελεύεις θύειν;"

     Ὁ δὲ λέγει, "Θῦσον τῷ Διὶ καὶ τῷ Ἀπόλλωνι καὶ τῷ Ἡρακλεῖ."

     Ἡ δὲ εἶπεν, "Προτραπεῖσα ὑπὸ τοῖς θεοῖς, σεμνῶς ὀφείλω θῦσαι τοῖς θεοῖς."

     Περιχαρὴς δὲ γενάμενος ὁ βασιλεύς, ἐκέλευσεν αὐτὴν ἀπιέναι ἐπὶ τὸν ναόν. Ἀπελθούσης δὲ τῆς ἁγίας, ἔστησαν κήρυκες προσφωνοῦντες καὶ λέγοντες, "Καλλινίκη ἡ φίλη τῶν θεῶν θύει." Ἐχάρησαν οὖν οἱ ἱερεῖς νομίζοντες ὅτι ὄντως τοῖς εἰδώλοις προσκυνεῖ. Ἀτενίσασα δὲ τοῖς ἱερεῦσι καὶ πᾶσι τοῖς ἑστῶσιν εἶπεν, "Ἐμβλέψατε εἰς ἐμέ, καὶ ἀτενίσατε εἰς τὴν θυσίαν ὅτι θύω τῷ μεγάλῳ Θεῷ μου." Καὶ ἀπελθοῦσα εἰς τὸ βῆμα τῶν εἰδώλων, ἔστη πρὸς τὴν εἰκόνα τοῦ Διός, καὶ ἀτενίσασα εἰς αὐτὸν εἶπεν, "Εἰ θεὸς εἶ σύ, λάλησον ὅτι δούλη σοι προσηνέχθην καὶ τί θέλεις ποιήσω σοι." Καὶ οὐκ ἦν φωνὴ οὐδὲ ἀκρόασις ἐν αὐτοῖς.

     Ἡ δὲ εἶπεν, "Οὐαί μοι τῇ ἁμαρτωλῷ, οἱ θεοὶ ἐν ὀργῇ μοί εἰσι διότι ἠθέτησα αὐτοὺς καὶ οὐκ ἀκούουσί μου. Ἄρα

in peace. And the emperor ordered that her body should be guarded so that he could burn it to ashes.

He then ordered Kallinike to be brought to him; and he 14 said to her, "Take pity on yourself so that you don't come to a bad end like the other woman. Save yourself, and come and sacrifice to the gods, so that you don't force me to lay my hands on you; for I'm afraid to destroy your beauty in case the people of the city throw stones at me. So do as I say and sacrifice to the gods, and I shall have a golden image of you set up in the city."

She said, "To which gods are you ordering me to sacrifice?"

He said, "Sacrifice to Zeus, Apollo, and Herakles."

She said, "If the gods exhort me, it is my duty to sacrifice to the gods with reverence."

The emperor was overjoyed, and ordered her to go to the temple. When the saint left, heralds took up their positions and made the following announcement: "Kallinike, the friend of the gods, is about to perform sacrifices." So the priests rejoiced thinking that she was actually going to venerate the idols. But looking at the priests and at everyone standing there, she said, "Watch me, and look at the sacrifice I shall make to my great God." She thus went to the pedestal of the idols, stood in front of the statue of Zeus and, looking at him, said, "If you are a god, speak, as I have been brought to you as a servant, and I shall do for you whatever you want." And there was *neither sound nor hearing* from the idols.

She said, "Alas for me, the sinner, the gods are angry at me because I rejected them, and they're not listening to me.

μὴ ὕπνῳ κατέχονται;" Καὶ προσελθοῦσα πάλιν, ἔκραξε λέγουσα, "Οἱ θεοὶ τῶν Ἑλλήνων, εἰσακούσατέ μου. Εἰ δὲ οὔκ ἐστε θεοί, τί ἐν πλάνῃ ἑστῶτες φαντάζετε πολλούς;" Καὶ περὶ Δία κινήσασα τὴν τράπεζαν αὐτῶν, ἀναβλέψασα εἰς τὸν οὐρανὸν εἶπεν, "Ὁ πάσης ἀγαθότητος δωτὴρ καὶ τῶν ψυχῶν ἡμῶν σωτήρ, βοήθησόν μοι ἐν ταύτῃ τῇ ὥρᾳ." Καὶ ἀποδυσαμένη τὸ σουδάριον αὐτῆς καὶ τὴν ζώνην, ἐν πολλοῖς εἰλήσασα, περιέθηκε τῷ ἀγάλματι τοῦ Διός· καὶ ἑλκύσασα, κατέστρεψεν αὐτόν, καὶ ἐγένετο ὡς ἡ ἄμμος. Ὁμοίως δὲ καὶ τὸν Ἀπόλλωνα καθεῖλεν καὶ εἶπεν, "Ἀνά-στητε, οἱ θεοί, καὶ βοηθήσατε ἑαυτοῖς καὶ τοῖς πεποιθόσιν ἐφ' ὑμᾶς."

15   Ἐπιλαβόμενοι δὲ οἱ ἱερεῖς, ἐκράτησαν αὐτὴν καὶ προσ-ήγαγον τῷ βασιλεῖ λέγοντες, "Ταύτην τὴν μαινομένην ἡμῖν ἐπήγαγες, καὶ τοὺς θεοὺς καθελοῦσα ἐλέπτυνεν. Καὶ εἰ μὴ αὐτὴν ἐκρατήσαμεν, οὐκ ἂν εἴασεν ἕνα τῶν θεῶν."

Δέκιος εἶπεν, "Οὐχὶ συνέθου θύειν τοῖς θεοῖς; Πῶς οὖν σὺ τοῦτο τετόλμηκας καὶ ἀντὶ τοῦ θῦσαι αὐτοῖς καὶ μύρα προσενεγκεῖν, καθελοῦσα ἐλέπτυνας;"

Ἡ δὲ εἶπεν, "Ἐγὼ λίθους ἐκίνησα πρὸς οἰκοδομήν· τοι-οῦτοι γάρ εἰσιν οἱ θεοὶ ὑμῶν ὅτι ὑπὸ γυναικὸς ἐκινήθησαν. Ἐγὼ δὲ Θεὸν ὁμολογῶ καὶ προσκυνῶ, ὅστις ὑπ' οὐδενὸς νικᾶται."

Τότε χολέσας ὁ βασιλεύς, ἐκέλευσεν γενέσθαι σούβλαν καὶ ἐμβληθῆναι ὑπὸ τὴν πτέρναν ἕως τοῦ ὤμου αὐτῆς, καὶ ἐμβληθῆναι ἔνθα καὶ ἔνθα αὐτὴν διὰ κρικίων, καὶ κρε-μασθῆναι πλαγίαν· καὶ λίθον ἐποίησεν ἐνεχθῆναι ὑπὸ τὸν

Could it be that they are fast asleep?" So she approached them again and shouted the following words: "Gods of the Hellenes, listen to me. If you are not gods, why are you falsely standing there and deceiving the masses?" She then shook the plinth of the idols near Zeus, looked up to heaven, and said, "Giver of every good and savior of our souls, help me at this hour." Then she took off her scarf and her belt, wound them up carefully, and put them around the statue of Zeus; she then pulled and toppled it, and it became like sand. After she destroyed Apollo in the same way, she said, "Get up, gods, and help yourselves and those who believe in you."

The priests grabbed her and, when they had seized her, 15 brought her to the emperor, saying, "You sent us this mad woman, who toppled the gods and reduced them to dust. If we hadn't seized her, she wouldn't have left a single one of the gods."

Decius said, "Didn't you agree to sacrifice to the gods? So how did you dare do this and, instead of sacrificing to them and of offering them perfumed oil, you toppled them and reduced them to dust?"

She said, "All I did was move stone building blocks; for that's what your gods are if they could be moved by a woman. As for me, I confess and venerate a God who cannot be defeated by anyone."

Then the emperor became very angry and ordered that they should take a spit and that she should be put on it from her heels to her shoulders, and that links of chain be put on her on either side, and she should be hung horizontally; then

μηρὸν αὐτῆς, ὁμοίως καὶ ἐπὶ τὸν βραχίονα ὅπως δια-
σπασθῇ.

Ἐπιβλέψασα δὲ ἐπὶ τὸν ἅγιον Ῥέπρεβον εἶπεν, "Δέομαί
σου, δοῦλε τοῦ Θεοῦ τοῦ Ὑψίστου, πρόσευξαι περὶ ἐμοῦ
ὅτι κάμνω."

Ἀναβλέψας δὲ ὁ μακάριος εἰς τὸν οὐρανόν, προσηύξατο
λέγων, "Ὁ Θεὸς τῶν ἁγίων πάντων, πρόσδεξαι τὴν δούλην
σου καὶ λόγισαι τὸν κάματον αὐτῆς, ὅτι σὺ μόνος οἰκτίρ-
μων καὶ φιλάνθρωπος ὑπάρχεις." Προσευξαμένου δὲ αὐτοῦ ἐτελειώθη ἐν εἰρήνῃ ἡ Ἁγία Καλλινίκη. Ἐκέλευσεν ὁ
βασιλεὺς καὶ αὐτῆς φυλάττεσθαι τὸ ἅγιον σῶμα, σὺν τῇ
ἀδελφῇ αὐτῆς Ἀκυλίνῃ, ἕως ἂν προσέλθῃ καὶ ὁ ἀθλητὴς
τοῦ Θεοῦ Χριστοφόρος.

16   Καὶ κελεύει προσαχθῆναι τὸν μακάριον Ῥέπρεβον, καὶ
λέγει αὐτῷ, "Κακώνυμε καὶ κακόβιε καὶ κακοπρόσωπε,
προέκειτο σὲ μᾶλλον ἀναλωθῆναι, καὶ μὴ τὴν περικρότησιν
τῆς πόλεως <ἣν> ἐκ μαγείας ἀπέστησας καὶ ἀπέκτεινας. Τί
οὖν λέγεις λοιπόν; Κἂν νῦν θύῃς τοῖς θεοῖς, ἢ ἐμμένεις τῇ
μανίᾳ ταύτῃ;"

Γελάσας δὲ ὁ μακάριος Ῥέπρεβος, εἶπεν, "Δικαίως ἐκλή-
θης Δέκιος· δοκὸς γὰρ εἶ τοῦ διαβόλου, σύνδεσμος εἶ τοῦ
πατρός σου τοῦ Σατανᾶ, καὶ ἀληθῶς τῇ ἐκείνου ἐνεργείᾳ
περιελαυνόμενος, καὶ οὔπω ἐπείσθης μοι ἀναίσθητος ὢν
καὶ μωρός· εἶπον γάρ σοι πλειστάκις, εἰ δυναίμην καὶ σὲ
κλῖναι εἰς τὸ ἀγαθὸν ἔργον· ἀλλ' οὐκ ἄξιος εἶ γνῶναι τὴν
γνῶσιν ταύτην. Πλὴν ἑτοίμως ἔχε! Πολλοὺς γὰρ ἐργάτας
ἔχω σοι παραστῆσαι διὰ τοῦ Κυρίου ἡμῶν Ἰησοῦ Χριστοῦ."

he had rocks placed under her thighs as well as on her arms so that she would be torn apart.

She looked at Saint Reprebos and said, "Please, I beg you, servant of God the Highest, pray for me because I'm exhausted."

The blessed man looked up to heaven and prayed thus: "God of all the saints, receive your servant and consider her labors, since you alone are merciful and compassionate." When he prayed, Saint Kallinike died in peace. The emperor ordered that her holy body be guarded as well, together with her sister Akylina, while Christopher, the athlete of God, was also brought to him.

So he ordered that the blessed Reprebos should be 16 brought, and he said to him, "You, with the evil name, the evil life, and the evil face, *you* should have rather been destroyed, and not those whom the entire city applauded, and whom you've misled and killed through magic. So what do you say? Will you sacrifice now to the gods, or will you stay stuck in this madness of yours?"

The blessed Reprebos laughed and said, "You've rightly been called Decius, because you're the tie beam of the devil, the one that holds the house of your father Satan together, and indeed, because it's his energy that you're being driven by you've yet to listen to me, since you're senseless and stupid. I've told you many times that, if I could, I would make even you turn to doing good; but you're not worthy of that kind of understanding. Still, beware! I can present to you many who work for me through our Lord Jesus Christ."

17   Αὐτοῦ δὲ ταῦτα ἀπολογουμένου, ἰδοὺ οἱ διακόσιοι στρατιῶται ὡς ἐξ ἀποδημίας παρεγένοντο. Καὶ ῥίψαντες τὰ ἱμάτια αὐτῶν καὶ τὸ ἅρμα, προσπεσόντες τῷ Ἁγίῳ Ῥεπρέβῳ πάντες, ἠσπάσαντο αὐτὸν λέγοντες, "Φῶς ἡμῶν γέγονας ἔκπαλαι· οὐ φοβούμεθα κακὰ ὅτι ὁ Θεὸς διὰ σοῦ μεθ' ἡμῶν ἐστιν."

    Ἰδὼν δὲ ὁ βασιλεὺς αὐτοὺς προσκυνοῦντας, ἔκραξε λέγων, "Ἀντάρτης μου γέγονας;"

    Τότε οἱ στρατιῶται εἶπαν, "Οὐδείς σοι ἀνταίρει. Ἡμεῖς Χριστιανοί ἐσμεν· ἀφ' οὗ γὰρ ἔπεμψας ἡμᾶς <ἐπὶ τ>ὸν ὅσιον τοῦ Χριστοῦ δοῦλον, οὐράνιον ἄρτον λαμβάνομεν μέχρι τῆς σήμερον. Καὶ οὐκ ἀρνούμεθα τὸν Θεὸν ἡμῶν, ἔχοντες τὸν ὁδηγὸν ἡμῶν καὶ *καλὸν ποιμένα* τὸν κύριον ἡμῶν Χριστοφόρον."

    Λέγει αὐτοῖς ὁ βασιλεύς, "Μὴ ἀννόναι ὑμῶν ἔλειψαν ἢ τὰ βέστια ἢ οἱ ἵπποι ὑμῶν ἠστόχησαν; Ἐάν τι ὑστέρησα, παρακαλῶ, ἑπταπλάσια ἀποδίδωμι ὑμῖν. Μόνον μὴ ἐγκαταλίπητέ με!"

    Εἶπαν δὲ πρὸς αὐτὸν οἱ στρατιῶται, "Τὴν ἐπίνοιάν σου σὺν σοὶ ἔχε. Καὶ ἐπὶ τῶν ἵππων ἡμῶν σὺ καθέζου· καὶ τὰ βέστια ἡμῶν συντεθήσονταί σοι ἐν τῷ ταρτάρῳ τῷ μέλλοντί σε ὑποδέχεσθαι."

    Ταῦτα ἀκούσας ὁ βασιλεὺς ἐκέλευσεν αὐτοὺς κατασφαγῆναι εἰς ἕν, καὶ γενομένης καμίνου, βληθῆναι τὰ σώματα αὐτῶν ἐν τῷ πυρί.

18   Ἐκέλευσεν δὲ προσαχθῆναι αὐτῷ τὸν Ἅγιον Χριστοφόρον, καὶ λέγει αὐτῷ, "Ἀπονενοημένε καὶ ἐχθρὲ τῆς τῶν

As he gave this retort, lo and behold the two hundred sol- 17
diers arrived, as if from a long journey. And laying down
their military garments and their attire, they all fell at
Reprebos's feet, and greeted him, saying, "You became our
light a long time ago; we're not scared of any evil, since God
is with us through you."

When the emperor saw them kneeling in respect before
Reprebos, he shouted out and said, "Have you mounted a
rebellion against me?"

Then the soldiers said, "No one is rebelling against you.
We are Christians; from the moment you sent us to the holy
servant of Christ until today, we've been receiving bread
from heaven. We cannot reject our God, as our lord Christopher is our guide and *good shepherd*."

The emperor responded to them, "Did you not have
enough provisions or clothes, or were your horses not good
enough? If what I gave you was insufficient, please, I shall
bestow it upon you seven time over. Just don't abandon me!"

The soldiers said to him, "Keep your plans to yourself.
You can ride on our horses; and our clothes will be put on
you in the nether world which is awaiting you in the future."

When the emperor heard this, he ordered that they be
slaughtered at once, and that their bodies be thrown into
the fire, in a furnace made for this purpose.

He also ordered that Saint Christopher be brought be- 18
fore him, and he said to him, "You conceited man, you en-

θεῶν εὐμενείας! Τίς ἡ τηλικαύτη σου τόλμα, ἢ ἡ τοσαύτη σου παρρησία, ὅτι ἀστρατόπεδόν με ἐποίησας;"

Εἶπεν δὲ πρὸς αὐτὸν ὁ ἀθλητὴς τοῦ Χριστοῦ, "Ἐγὼ αἴτιος τοῦ πράγματος τούτου οὔκ εἰμι, ἀλλ᾽ ὁ Χριστός ἐστιν ὁ ἐκλεγόμενος τὸν χρυσὸν ἐκ τῆς κόπρου καὶ στρατεύων εἰς τὸ ἴδιον τάγμα, καὶ σώζων τοὺς ἐπ᾽ αὐτὸν ἐλπίζοντας· σοὶ γὰρ πρόκειται κόλασις αἰώνιος, ἄνομε καὶ πάσης ἐπινοίας τοῦ διαβόλου μεστέ! Ἀνδρίζου οὖν ἵνα δυνηθῇς ἀπαντῆσαι τοῖς ἐρχομένοις ἐπὶ τὸν Κύριόν μου Ἰησοῦν Χριστόν· ἐὰν ἐπιμείνῃ ἡ ζωή μου, πολλοὺς προσάγει δι᾽ ἐμοῦ ὁ Θεὸς εἰς τὴν ἑαυτοῦ ἐπίγνωσιν."

Τότε χολέσας ὁ βασιλεὺς ἐκέλευσε γενέσθαι χαλκοῦν συμψέλιον καὶ καθηλωθῆναι αὐτὸν ἐκεῖ· καὶ ἐκέλευσεν ἐνεχθῆναι ὕλην ξύλων πολλήν· καὶ ἐποίησε κύκλῳ θημωνίαν γενέσθαι καὶ καλυφθῆναι αὐτὸν ὑπὸ τῶν ξύλων ὥσπερ σκηνήν· καὶ προσέταξεν ἐνεχθῆναι ἔλαιον πολὺ καὶ βληθῆναι ἐπάνω τῶν ξύλων· καὶ ἐκέλευσεν ἀφθῆναι εἰς τρεῖς ἀρχάς. Καὶ ἀνήφθη πυρὰ σφοδροτάτη.

19 Τοῦ δὲ χαλκώματος στίλβοντος ὑπὲρ τὴν φλόγα τοῦ πυρός, πάντων τῶν Χριστιανῶν ἅμα καὶ τῶν Ἑλλήνων ἑστώτων, τῶν μὲν Χριστιανῶν τηρούντων καταξιωθῆναι ἐπιλαβέσθαι τῶν ἁγίων αὐτοῦ λειψάνων, τῶν δὲ Ἑλλήνων ἰδεῖν τὸν θάνατον αὐτοῦ, ὁ μακάριος Χριστοφόρος ἀναστάς, ἐκάθητο ἐπὶ τοῦ σκαμνίου καὶ ἐξηγεῖτο τοῖς ἑστῶσι λέγων:

"Ἐθεώρουν ἐν τῇ ὥρᾳ ταύτῃ μέσον τῆς ἀγορᾶς τῆς πόλεως ἄνδρα ὑψηλὸν τῷ εἴδει καὶ ὡραῖον τῷ κάλλει οὗ τὸ πρόσωπον ἔλαμψεν ὡς ἥλιος, τὰ δὲ ἱμάτια αὐτοῦ ὡς χιών,

emy of the gods' benevolence! What great audacity of yours is this? What is this great boldness of yours, that you have stripped me of my army?"

The athlete of Christ said to him, "It wasn't me who caused this, but Christ who sorts out the gold from the filth, and then enlists such people into his own brigade and saves those who place their hope in him; for eternal damnation awaits you, you lawless man, full of every wicked plan of the devil! You'll need to be brave if you're going to be able to face all those who are joining my Lord Jesus Christ; for if I go on living, through me, God will bring many to knowledge of him."

Then the emperor was enraged and he ordered a bronze rack to be made and Christopher nailed to it; and he ordered that a lot of logs should be brought; and he had them made into a heap all around him and so that he was covered with the logs as if by a tent; and he ordered much oil to be brought and poured over the wood; and he ordered that it should be set on fire at three different spots. And an inferno broke out.

When the bronze was glowing more brightly than the 19 fire's flames, and all the Christians as well as the Hellenes were standing around it, the former watching so as to become worthy to take Christopher's holy relics, and the latter waiting to see his death, the blessed Christopher got up and sat on the bench, and started recounting the following to the bystanders:

"*I saw* at this very moment, in the middle of the city's marketplace, a man who was tall in stature and striking in his beauty, whose *face shone like the sun, and his garments like*

καὶ ὁ στέφανος αὐτοῦ ὑπέρκαλος σφόδρα. Καὶ ἄλλον ἐθεώρουν μελανὸν ἐν μελανίᾳ πολλῇ, καὶ πολλοὶ στρατιῶται ὅμοιοι αὐτοῦ μελανιῶντες· οὗ ἡ θρὶξ ὥσπερ ἁλύσεις πεπλεγμέναι, καὶ πολλὴ πανοπλία μετ᾽ αὐτῶν. Συνέρρηξε δὲ πόλεμον ὁ ἔνδοξος καὶ αὐτός· καὶ κατεπράξατο οὗτος τὸν ἔνδοξον καὶ τὸν στρατὸν αὐτοῦ ἀπέκτεινεν· καὶ ἐνεκαυχήσατο ἐπὶ τοῦ θρόνου αὐτοῦ χρόνον τινά. Μετὰ τοῦτο δὲ ἀπεστράφη ὁ ἔνδοξος ἐν θυμῷ καὶ ὀργῇ, καὶ ἐδιχοτόμησε τὸν στρατὸν αὐτοῦ, καὶ τὸν βασιλέα αὐτῶν κρατήσας, ἔδησεν αὐτὸν ἁλύσεσι πεπυρωμέναις, καὶ ἐγένετο ὁ ἔνδοξος καταλύων τὰς οἰκίας ἐκείνου τοῦ μέλανος, καὶ τὴν κοίτην αὐτοῦ κατέσκαψεν."

20   Οἱ δὲ ἀκούσαντες ὄχλοι ὅτι μετὰ τηλικαύτην τιμωρίαν ζῇ καὶ ἡ θρὶξ τῆς κεφαλῆς αὐτοῦ οὐκ ἐφλογίσθη οὐδὲ ὀσμὴ πυρᾶς εὑρέθη ἐν αὐτῷ, ἔκραξαν λέγοντες: "Δόξα σοι, ὁ Θεὸς Ῥεπρέβου! Δόξα σοι, βασιλεῦ οὐράνιε, ὁ Θεὸς τῶν Χριστιανῶν! Καὶ ἡμεῖς σοὶ πιστεύομεν ὅτι σὺ εἶ ὁ Θεὸς μόνος ὁ ποιῶν μεγάλα θαυμάσια· ὁ Θεὸς τῶν θεῶν, βοήθησον ἐν τῇ ὥρᾳ ταύτῃ." Καὶ ἐμβάντων αὐτῶν εἰς τὸ πῦρ, ἐξέβαλον τὸν ἀθλητὴν τοῦ Χριστοῦ· καὶ πάντες ὑφ᾽ ἓν ἔκραξαν λέγοντες: "Αἰσχύνθητι, Δέκιε· Χριστὸς γὰρ νικᾷ σε· πᾶσα γάρ σου ἡ ἐπίνοια κατήργηται."

    Ἀκούσας δὲ τὴν κραυγὴν ταύτην ὁ βασιλεὺς καὶ θροηθεὶς σφόδρα, καὶ ἀναχωρήσας τοῦ σεκρέτου, ἦλθεν εἰς τὸ παλάτιον.

21   Πρωίας δὲ γενομένης, ἐκέλευσεν θυσίαν γενέσθαι τοῖς θεοῖς ἑστώτων τῶν κηρύκων καὶ προσφωνούντων ἐπὶ τῶν

snow, and the crown he wore was exceptionally beautiful. And I also saw another man, a dark man steeped in great darkness, along with many soldiers all just as dark as him; their hair was like chains all bound up, and they were heavily armored. The glorious one and that other one engaged in a battle with each other; and that one overpowered the glorious one and killed his army; and he sat all puffed up on the throne of the glorious one for some time. But then, the glorious one returned in anger and rage, and he cut the dark man's army to pieces, and captured their king, and bound him with fiery chains; and the glorious one destroyed the houses of that dark man, and razed his lodgings to the ground."

When the crowds heard this and realized that after such 20 torture Christopher was still alive, his hair had not caught on fire, and there was not even any smell of burning on him, they shouted out the following words: "Glory to you, God of Reprebos! Glory to you, heavenly king, God of the Christians! We too believe that *you alone are the God who works great wonders*; God of gods, help us at this time." And they went into the fire and took out the athlete of Christ; and all together they shouted out the following words: "You have been put to shame, Decius; Christ has defeated you and all your plans have been brought to nothing."

When the emperor heard this shout, he was deeply disturbed, left the court room, and went into the palace.

When morning came, the emperor ordered that sacri- 21 fices should be performed to the gods; so the heralds stood

ὑψηλῶν, "Θυσία τοῖς θεοῖς! Πάντες συνέλθετε! Ὅστις δὲ μὴ συνέλθῃ, τῇ τοῦ ξίφους τιμωρίᾳ ὑποπεσεῖται."

Πάντων δὲ συντρεχόντων ἐπὶ τὴν ἀσεβῆ θρησκείαν, ὁ μακάριος Ῥέπρεβος μετὰ πάντων τῶν Χριστιανῶν ὅπου τὸ καμινεῖον, ἤρξατο ψάλλειν οὕτως· "Λαμπρὸς ὁ στέφανος τῆς ἐπαγγελίας, λαμπρὸς ὁ Παράδεισος σφόδρα· μικρὸν ὑπομείνωμεν, ἵνα στεφανωθῶμεν." Καὶ οὕτως ὑπέψαλλον πάντες, ὡς ἀπὸ τῆς φωνῆς πολλοὺς τῶν Ἑλλήνων ἐλθεῖν πρὸς αὐτούς.

Τινὲς δὲ τῶν φλυάρων ἐμήνυσαν τῷ βασιλεῖ λέγοντες, "Ἡ θρησκεία ἡμῶν ἦρται. Ἐὰν μὴ σεαυτῷ βοηθήσῃς νυνί, κακῶς ἀποθάνῃ." Ἀκούσας δὲ ταῦτα καὶ ἐπιπηδήσας, ἐκάθισεν ἐπὶ τοῦ ἄρματος μετὰ πλήθους στρατιωτῶν. Καὶ ἀναλαβόντες τὸ ἄρμα ἑαυτῶν, ἐκύκλωσαν τοὺς ἁγίους εἰς τρεῖς ἀρχὰς καὶ ἤρξαντο τέμνειν αὐτούς. Ὁ δὲ μακάριος Χριστοφόρος ἔλεγεν αὐτοῖς, "Ὑπομείνατε! Ἡ ζωὴ τοῦ Παραδείσου ἡμετέρα ἐστίν· ἡ γέεννα ἡ αἰώνιος ἐκείνοις ἐστίν."

Οἱ δὲ ἀκούσαντες τὸν λόγον τοῦ ἁγίου, ἔστησαν προθύμως καὶ αὐτοὶ ἀλλήλους ἠξίουν. Ἐκόπησαν δὲ οὕτως ἀνελεημόνως· οὐ γὰρ ἀπεκεφάλισεν αὐτούς, ἀλλ᾽ ὥσπερ λύκος εἰς μάνδραν προβάτων εἰσελθὼν μὴ ἐχόντων ποιμένα ταῦτα διαρρήγνυσιν, οὕτως πάντας ἀνῆρε.

Τούτων δὲ οὕτως ἀναλωθέντων ἐννάτῃ τοῦ μηνὸς Ἰουλίου, ἡμέρᾳ Κυριακῇ, ἐμαρτύρησαν τῷ λόγῳ τοῦ ἁγίου μάρτυρος μύριοι διακόσιοι τρεῖς.

22   Συλλαβόμενος δὲ τὸν Ἅγιον Χριστοφόρον, ἀπῄει εἰς τὸ παλάτιον, καὶ ἐκέλευσε κυλισθῆναι λίθον παμμεγέθη ὃν

on the high places and proclaimed, "Sacrifices to the gods! All must come! Whoever does not, shall be subjected to capital punishment by the sword."

As everyone was rushing to perform the impious religious rites, the blessed Reprebos together with all the Christians who were where the furnace was, began to chant the following: "Brilliant is the promised crown, extremely brilliant is Paradise; let us persevere for a little while so we may receive the victory crown." And everyone chanted the same words, so that many Hellenes came to them because of their voices.

Some snitches reported the following to the emperor: "Our religion has been destroyed. If you don't help yourself now, you'll die a bad death." When he heard this, the emperor jumped up and sat in his chariot with a crowd of soldiers. And taking up their weapons, they surrounded the saints in three groups, and began slaughtering them. The blessed Christopher said to them, "Don't give up! The life of Paradise is ours; theirs is eternal hell."

When they heard the words of the saint, they eagerly stood fast, and they themselves encouraged each other. They were mercilessly cut to pieces; for the evil one did not have them decapitated, but killed them like a wolf who enters the fold of sheep without a shepherd and tears them apart.

These men were killed in this way on the ninth of July, on a Sunday; there were ten thousand two hundred and three who became martyrs at the word of the holy martyr.

The emperor had Saint Christopher arrested, went into 22 the palace, and ordered a huge rock to be rolled up, which it

ἤνεγκαν ὀνόματα τριάκοντα, καὶ τρυπηθῆναι τὸ ἓν μέρος τοῦ λίθου καὶ βληθῆναι ἄλυσιν καὶ περιτεθῆναι εἰς τὸν τράχηλον τοῦ Ἁγίου Χριστοφόρου. Καὶ ἦν φρέαρ ξηρὸν μὴ ἔχον ὕδωρ· καὶ ἐκέλευσε ριφῆναι αὐτὸν ἐκεῖ λέγων, "Οὐ μὴ ποιήσω εὑρεθῆναι αὐτοῦ ὀστοῦν."

Ἐμβληθέντος δὲ αὐτοῦ, περιφερόμενος ὁ λίθος ἔνθα καὶ ἔνθα, ἐγένετο ὡσεὶ κονιορτός· αὐτὸς δὲ ὑπὸ ἀγγέλων ἀναληφθείς, ἦλθεν ἔμπροσθε τοῦ παλατίου. Ἐμηνύθη δὲ τῷ βασιλεῖ καὶ ἐκέλευσεν εὐθέως ἀναρτηθῆναι αὐτὸν καὶ λέγει αὐτῷ, "Διὰ τί ἄληπτος εἶ ταῖς μαγείαις σου, Ῥέπρεβε;"

Ὡς δὲ οὐκ ἀπεκρίνατο λόγον, ἐκέλευσε γενέσθαι καράκαλλον χαλκοῦν καὶ ἐπύρωσεν αὐτὸν εὐτόνως καὶ ἐνέδυσεν αὐτὸν καὶ οὐδὲ ὅλως ἐτιμωρεῖτο ὁ τοῦ Θεοῦ παῖς.

Πάλιν δὲ εἰρωνείᾳ χρησάμενος ὁ τύραννος, εἶπεν πρὸς αὐτόν, "Κἂν νῦν θύῃς τοῖς θεοῖς;"

Ὁ δὲ μακάριος ἔφη, "Κύριε Παντοκράτορ Ἰησοῦ Χριστέ, πρόσδεξαι τὸ πνεῦμά μου λοιπόν, ὅπως κἀγὼ ἀναπαύσωμαι τῇ δόξῃ σου." Καὶ ταῦτα εἰπὼν κύψας προσηύξατο.

23 Ἰδὼν δὲ ὁ βασιλεὺς ὅτι οὐδὲν ὠφελεῖ αἰκιζόμενος αὐτόν, ἀπόφασιν ἔδωκεν κατ' αὐτοῦ οὕτως· "Ῥέπρεβος ἀθετήσας τοὺς θεούς, καὶ τὰ προστάγματά μου, κεφαλικῇ τιμωρίᾳ κολασθήσεται."

Καὶ λαβὼν τὴν ἀπόφασιν ἐξῆλθεν ἀπὸ τοῦ παλατίου, καὶ ἦλθεν ἐπὶ τὸν προκείμενον τόπον. Ἰδὼν δὲ πολλοὺς Χριστιανοὺς ἀκολουθοῦντας καὶ δακρύοντας, εἶπεν τῷ κατέχοντι αὐτὸν στρατιώτῃ, "Μεῖνον, ὅπως προσεύξωμαι."

took thirty men to move, and for a hole made in it in one place, and chains attached to it, and for it to be hung around the neck of Saint Christopher. And there was a dry well there, without water; and he ordered that they throw the saint into it, saying, "I'll make sure they don't find even a single bone of his."

But when Christopher was thrown into it, the rock was dragged here and there, and became *like dust;* meanwhile, the saint, who had been raised up by angels, came right in front of the palace. The news reached the emperor and immediately he ordered that Christopher be captured, and he said to him, "Why do you keep escaping with your magic tricks, Reprebos?"

As the saint said nothing in reply, the emperor ordered a hood to be made from bronze, and he had it heated up intensely by fire and put it on him, but God's servant suffered no torture whatsoever.

Again, the tyrant said to him sarcastically, "Perhaps now you might sacrifice to the gods?"

But the blessed man said, "Lord Almighty Jesus Christ, receive now my spirit, so that I too may rest in your glory." Having said that, he went down on his knees and prayed.

Realizing that there was no use in torturing Christopher, 23 the emperor gave out the following final verdict for him: "Reprebos, who negated the gods and my commands, shall receive capital punishment."

After he had received the verdict, Christopher went out of the palace and came to the place of the execution. When he saw many Christians following him in tears, he said to the soldier who had hold of him, "Wait for me to pray."

Ἑστὼς δὲ προσηύξατο οὕτως· "Κύριε Ἰησοῦ Χριστέ, ὁ βοηθήσας μοι πολλάκις, ἀπόδος τὸν μισθὸν τῷ βασιλεῖ, ὅπως ὑπὸ δαίμονος τιμωρούμενος ἐσθίων τὰς ἑαυτοῦ σάρκας ἀντὶ ἄρτου, οὕτως ἀναλωθῇ. Κύριε Παντοκράτορ, ἀχειροποίητε βασιλεῦ, σωτὴρ τῶν σὲ φιλούντων, τὸ αἴτημα ὃ αἰτῶ σε, τοῦτο παράσχου μοι. Βοήθησον τοῖς Χριστιανοῖς· δὸς χάριν τῷ σώματί μου, ἵνα πᾶς ἄνθρωπος ὁ ἔχων βραχύ τι λείψανόν μου, δύναμις ἔσται σὺν αὐτῷ ὥστε φανερῶς διώκειν δαίμονας· μὴ γράψῃς αὐτῷ ἁμαρτίαν, μὴ καταδικάσῃς ἐν σφάλματι ἁμαρτίας· ἀλλὰ δὸς χάριν τῷ σώματί μου, ἐπειδὴ πολλοὶ ζητοῦσί με ἁρπάσαι εἰς πόλιν ἢ χώραν ἢ ὄρος· μὴ ἐπέλθῃ χάλαζα ἐν αὐτοῖς, μηδὲ θυμὸς σός, μηδὲ ἀφορία ἀμπέλων, μήτε αὐχμὸς γεννημάτων· ἀλλ' εἰ καί ποτε ἠδικοῦντο, ἐμοῦ ἐπελθόντος, φύλαξον τοὺς τόπους ὅπου καὶ ὑπομνήματά μου κατάκεινται, ὅπως οἱ κατοικοῦντες ἀφθόνως ἔχοντες τὰς ἐκ τῶν σῶν δωρεῶν τροφάς, καὶ ἐμὲ τιμῶσιν, καὶ σὲ δοξάζωσιν εἰς τοὺς αἰῶνας τῶν αἰώνων, ἀμήν."

Καὶ ἦλθε φωνὴ ἐκ τῶν οὐρανῶν λέγουσα, "Κατὰ τὸ αἴτημά σου οὕτως ἔσται καὶ οὐ μή σε λυπήσω ἕως τοῦ αἰῶνος. Ἀλλὰ καὶ ἐν τούτῳ θαυμαστωθήσῃ ὅτι ἐμερίμνησας περὶ τούτου. Σὺ οὖν λοιπὸν ἀπόρριψον τὸ σῶμά σου τοῖς θέλουσιν. Πλὴν λέγω σοι ὅτι ἐν ἀνάγκῃ πολλῇ ἐάν τις ᾖ, καὶ μνημονεύσῃ ἀξίως τοῦ ὀνόματός σου ἐπικαλούμενος πρεσβείαν, φεύξεται τὴν ἀνάγκην."

Καὶ τοῦτο ἀκούσας ὄπισθεν ἑαυτὸν ἔδωκεν, καὶ λέγει τῷ σπεκουλάτορι, "Δεῦρο, τέκνον, ποίησον τὸ κελευσθέν σοι ὑπὸ τοῦ βασιλέως." Ὁ δὲ προσελθὼν καὶ ποιήσας τὴν

Standing there, he made the following prayer: "Lord Jesus Christ, you who have helped me many times, give the emperor his retribution: let him be punished by a demon so that he eats his own flesh instead of food, and thus perish. Lord Almighty, king not made by human hands, savior of those who love you, grant me the request I am making to you. Help the Christians; give divine grace to my body, so that anyone who has even a small piece of my relic, may have the power to openly drive demons away; do not hold him responsible for any sin, nor condemn him for any sinful mistake; but grant divine grace to my body, when many seek to take me away to some city or land or mountain; may neither hail, nor your wrath, nor barrenness of grapevines, nor dearth of produce befall them; and if they are ever in harm's way, may my coming protect those places where my memory is preserved, so that those who live there may receive abundant nourishment from your gifts, and may honor me, and also glorify you unto the ages of ages, amen."

And *a voice* came *from heaven, saying,* "As you request, so it shall be, and I shall not disappoint you until the end of time. Rather, you will also be admired because you cared about this. So, go now and throw your body to those who want it. And I am telling you that if anyone finds himself in great trouble, and reverently mentions your name, and calls for your intercession, he shall escape that trouble."

When he heard this, he turned back, and said to the executioner, "Come, child, do what you have been ordered by the emperor." The executioner came near, made the sign of

ἐν Χριστῷ σφραγῖδα ἀπέτεμεν τὸν τράχηλον αὐτοῦ· καὶ εὐθέως ὁ σπεκουλάτωρ ἑαυτὸν ἐπάταξεν, καὶ ἐτελεύτησεν ἐπάνω τοῦ Ἁγίου Χριστοφόρου. Ἐτελειώθη δὲ μηνὶ Μαΐῳ ἐννάτῃ.

24   Παραγενάμενος δὲ ὁ ἐπίσκοπος Πέτρος πόλεως Ἀτταλείας συνορούσης Πισιδίᾳ ἐν Ἀντιοχείᾳ, ἀπέδοτο ἀργύρια ἱκανά· καὶ λαβὼν τὸ σῶμα τοῦ ἁγίου μάρτυρος καὶ ἐν ὀθονίοις καὶ μύροις εἰλήσας, καὶ ἄλλα πολλὰ σώματα, ἐσκέπασε τὸν μακάριον Χριστοφόρον καὶ ἐκόμισεν ἐν τῇ πόλει αὐτοῦ.

Ἦν δὲ ποταμὸς ἐπερχόμενος τῇ πόλει κατ' ἐνιαυτὸν καὶ ἠφάνιζεν τὴν πόλιν. Οὗτος ποιήσας εἰς τὴν ἀπόρροιαν τοῦ ποταμοῦ τὸ μαρτύριον, ἐκεῖ τὸν ἅγιον κατέθετο· καὶ ἔστι πεφυλαγμένη ἕως τῆς ἡμέρας ταύτης ἐν Κυρίῳ, ᾧ ἡ δόξα καὶ τὸ κράτος εἰς τοὺς αἰῶνας τῶν αἰώνων, ἀμήν.

25   Μετὰ δὲ τὸ τὸν Ἅγιον Χριστοφόρον ἀποδοῦναι τὴν καλὴν ὁμολογίαν, ἐξεπέμφθη ὀργὴ Κυρίου οὐρανόθεν ἐπὶ τὸν βασιλέα Δέκιον κατὰ τὴν αἴτησιν τοῦ μακαρίου Χριστοφόρου· καὶ τὸ σῶμα αὐτοῦ διελύετο ὡς χιὼν ὑπὸ νότου. Καὶ ἤρξατο λέγειν, "Οὐαί μοι, τῷ παρανόμῳ, ὅτι τὸν ἄνθρωπον τοῦ Θεοῦ πικρῷ θανάτῳ ἀνεῖλον!"

Ἡ δὲ γυνὴ αὐτοῦ παρεστῶσα ἔλεγεν, "Οὐαί μοι, τῇ ἀνελπίστῳ! Ἔλεγόν σοι καὶ οὐκ ἤκουσάς μου! Νῦν τί ποιήσω ἐγὼ ἡ ταπεινή, ὅτι ἐστέρημαι τῆς θειότητός σου; Οἱ θεοί σου μὴ δύνανται μετὰ τοῦ Χριστοῦ εἰπεῖν καὶ ῥύσασθαί σε ἀπὸ βασάνου πικρᾶς καὶ φοβερᾶς;"

Christ's cross, and cut through Christopher's neck; and right after that turned the sword against himself and fell dead on Saint Christopher. Christopher's death took place on the ninth of the month of May.

Peter, the bishop of the city of Attaleia, which borders on   24 Pisidia, came to Antioch and offered a lot of money; so he obtained the body of the holy martyr, wrapped it (along with many other bodies) in linen cloths and perfumed oils. He thus protected the blessed Christopher and brought him back to his own city.

There was a river which would rush through the city every year, and it used to destroy the city. Peter built the martyrion in the riverbed and placed the saint there. And since then, down to the present day, the city has thus been protected by the Lord, to whom belongs the power and the glory unto the ages of ages, amen.

After Saint Christopher had made his confession of faith   25 so well, the Lord's wrath was sent down from heaven upon the emperor Decius, just as the blessed Christopher had requested; and the emperor's body began to dissolve like snow when the south wind blows. Decius started saying, "Alas for me, lawless man that I am, because I killed the man of God with such a cruel death!"

His wife who was there would also say, "Alas for me, hopeless woman that I am! I told you so, but you did not listen! What am I to do now, wretch that I am, since I'm bereft of your godliness? Can't your gods speak with Christ and save you from this bitter and terrible torture?"

Ὁ δὲ βασιλεὺς Δέκιος λέγει τοῖς στρατιώταις, "Δράμετε, παρακαλῶ! Καὶ ἐὰν εὕρητε τὸ σῶμα αὐτοῦ, ἢ κράσπεδον τοῦ ἱματίου αὐτοῦ, μόνον ἅψωμαι αὐτοῦ καὶ ἀποθάνω."

Οἱ δὲ ἀπελθόντες ὅπου εἱστήκει τιμωρούμενος, καὶ λαβόντες γῆν ἤνεγκαν· καὶ λύσαντες ὕδατι, ἐπότισαν αὐτόν. Καὶ οὕτως ἀπέδωκεν ἐν κρίσει τὴν ψυχὴν αὐτοῦ καὶ ἐδοξάσθη τὸ ὄνομα τοῦ Θεοῦ ἐν Χριστῷ Ἰησοῦ τῷ Κυρίῳ ἡμῶν σὺν τῷ Παναγίῳ Πνεύματι, νῦν καὶ ἀεὶ καὶ εἰς τοὺς αἰῶνας τῶν αἰώνων, ἀμήν.

The emperor Decius said to his soldiers, "Please, go! And if you find his body or *the fringe of his garment,* perhaps I might *only* touch it, and die at last."

So they went to where Christopher had stood while he was being tortured, and took earth from there and brought it back; then they dissolved it in water and gave it to him to drink. In this way Decius justly paid with his life and God's name was glorified in Jesus Christ our Lord, together with the Holy Spirit, now and forever and unto the ages of ages, amen.

GEORGE,
THE GREAT MARTYR

Μαρτύριον τοῦ Ἁγίου
μεγαλομάρτυρος Γεωργίου

Κατ' ἐκεῖνον τὸν καιρόν, τῆς ἀσεβεστάτης καὶ βδελυρᾶς κατακρατούσης θρησκείας, βασιλεύοντος δὲ Δαδιανοῦ τοῦ παραβάτου, δόγμα ἐξέθετο κατὰ πᾶσαν πόλιν καὶ χώραν, περιέχον οὕτως· "Βασιλεὺς Δαδιανὸς τῇ οἰκουμένῃ πάσῃ χαίρειν. Εἴ τις γὰρ εὑρεθῇ τοῖς ἀθανάτοις θεοῖς θυσίαν ἀπονέμων καὶ τιμῶν αὐτούς, πολλὰς τιμὰς καὶ δωρεὰς ἀπονέμω· καὶ εἴ τις ἀνὴρ εὑρεθῇ <ἐν> τοῖς μὴ προσκυνοῦσιν, ἀλλὰ σέβονται τὸν Χριστόν, ὃν οἱ Ἰουδαῖοι ἐσταύρωσαν ὡς κατάδικον, δειναῖς τιμωρίαις καὶ πικρῷ θανάτῳ παραδώσω." Κατὰ πάντα δὲ τόπον ταῦτα ἐξέθετο· καὶ φρίκη συνεῖχε μεγάλη τοὺς Χριστιανούς.

Ἔδειξε δὲ καὶ κολαστήρια φοβερά, γομφιστῆρας, καταπέλτας, καὶ νευρολύτας· καὶ πᾶσαν ὅσην εἶχεν τῶν παλαιῶν κατασκευὴν ἔθηκεν. Ἔλεγε τοιγαροῦν ὁ βύθιος δράκων, ὅτι· "Ἐὰν εὕρω ἄνδρα τὸν στασιάζοντα τοῦ μὴ θύειν τοῖς θεοῖς, τότε δικαίως ἀλλάξω τὴν πατρικήν μου περὶ αὐτὸν διάθεσιν, καὶ βάψω τὴν ποικίλων ὀργάνων κατασκευήν. Φίλτατον τέκνον οὐ φείσομαι· κεφαλὴν κατεάξω, καὶ λικμήσω ἐγκέφαλον, πύργον τῆς αἰσθήσεως· θύλακα ἀποδείρω· κοιμίσω κόρας ὀφθαλμῶν· ἐκκεντήσω εἰς πίδακας τοὺς τῶν φλεβῶν ὀχετούς· πρίσω τὰ νεῦρα, τοὺς

Passion of Saint George, the great martyr

At that time, when the most impious and loathsome religion prevailed, and Dadian the apostate was king, a decree was issued to every city and land. It contained the following: "King Dadian, to the world, greetings! If someone is found sacrificing to the immortal gods and honoring them, I will grant them many honors and gifts. If, however, any person should be found not venerating them but revering Christ, the one whom the Jews crucified as a convict, I will hand them over to terrible tortures and bitter death." This decree was published everywhere; and great horror overtook the Christians.

Dadian also put on display terrifying instruments of torture, devices with nails, catapults, and sinew cutters; and he set out every sort of contraption inherited from the ancients. And so the abysmal dragon would say, "If I find any man who rebels by not sacrificing to the gods, then I will justly change my fatherly attitude toward him, and I will dye the array of various torture instruments with his blood. I will not spare even a dearest child; I will smash his head, and crush his brains, the tower of his senses; I will make a bag out of his skin; I will put the pupils of his eyes to sleep; I will make the streams of his veins spurt out in jets; I will saw

στήμονας τῶν ποδῶν· λογοθετήσω τῶν ἐντέρων τὴν σύνθεσιν· τὸ δὲ ὑπόλοιπον σῶμα, σκωληκόβρωτον τῇ γῇ παραδώσω." Ὅσοι γὰρ εἶχον προθύμως τοῦ μαρτυρῆσαι, ἀπὸ τῆς ὁράσεως τῶν βασάνων ἐκόπτοντο· ἕκαστος γὰρ εἰς ἑαυτὸν ὑπενόει τὸ ἔγκλημα, ὥστε μηδένα λέγειν ὅτι "Χριστιανός εἰμι."

2 Τούτων δὲ οὕτως πραττομένων, ἰδοὺ Γεώργιός τις ὀνόματι, ὢν ἐτῶν εἴκοσι δύο, ὁ γενναῖος καὶ τέλειος ἀθλητὴς ἐν μάρτυσιν, τὸ ἄστρον τὸ τίμιον, τὸ μέσον οὐρανοῦ καὶ γῆς λάμπον, γένους μὲν ὑπάρχων τῶν Καππαδόκων, στρατευθεὶς δὲ ἐν νουμέρῳ τινί, καλῶς διαπραξάμενος τὴν κομητατοῦρα, ἔπειτα λαβὼν χρήματα οὐκ ὀλίγα, ἀνέδραμε πρὸς τὸν Βασιλέα Δαδιανόν, τοῦ ζωσθῆναι ἔπαρχον. Ἰδὼν δὲ ὅτι Χριστὸς παρυβρίζεται, καὶ δαίμονες θεραπεύονται, τὰ προσόντα αὐτῷ χρήματα δέδωκε τοῖς πτωχοῖς, ἔπειτα τὴν ἑαυτοῦ ἐσθῆτα· ἔλεγε γὰρ ἐν ἑαυτῷ, "Ἐκείνων τετύφλωκεν ὁ Σατανᾶς τοὺς ὀφθαλμούς, τοῦ μὴ ὁρᾶν με γυμνόν"· γυμνὸς γὰρ ἔστη εἰς τὸ μέσον κράζων καὶ λέγων, "Τὰς μὲν ἀπειλὰς καταστεῖλαι σπουδάσατε, τοὺς δὲ μὴ ὄντας θεοὺς μὴ ὀνομάζετε· θεοὶ οἳ τὸν οὐρανὸν καὶ τὴν γῆν οὐκ ἐποίησαν, ἀπολέσθωσαν (ὥς φησιν ὁ προφήτης)."

3 Ἀτενίσας δὲ εἰς αὐτὸν ὁ βύθιος δράκων, ἔφη, "Ὅσοι τὰς τῶν θεῶν εὐεργεσίας τετρυγήκαμεν, ἅπαντες τὴν ὑφήλιον νεμόμεθα. Αὐτὸς οὖν ἐλάνθανες ἡμᾶς ὢν μεγαλόψυχος· <καὶ ἡμᾶς> οὐ μετρίως ἐνυβρίσας· καὶ τοὺς θεοὺς μικροποιήσας, ἐθριάμβευσας. Αὐτοὶ δὲ οἴδασι τοῖς φιλουμένοις συγγνώμην χαρίσασθαι. Λοιπὸν οὖν πρόσελθε καὶ θῦσον

through his sinews, the threads of his legs; I will examine the composition of his entrails; and the rest of his body I will deliver to the earth for the worms to eat." Anyone who had been ready to become a martyr was struck by the sight of these tortures; for each supposed the charges were directed at them, so that no one would say "I am a Christian."

As this was going on, lo and behold, a man called George 2 approached King Dadian so as to be appointed eparch. The brave and perfect athlete among the martyrs, the precious star that shines between the sky and the earth, was twenty-two years of age; his family was from Cappadocia, he had enlisted in an army unit, had deservedly earned for himself the position of count, and had then been paid a great deal of money. But when he saw that Christ was being disgraced, and demons were being worshipped, he gave his money to the poor, and then his own clothes, for he said to himself, "Satan has blinded their eyes so that they won't see that I am naked." So he stood naked in public, shouting and saying, "Hurry up and withdraw your threats, and don't call gods those who are not! *Let those gods who did not create the heavens and the earth perish* (as the prophet says)."

The abysmal dragon stared at him, and said, "All of us reap 3 the bounty of the gods and live under the sun. Anyhow, I had not noticed that you were arrogant; you have both insulted me greatly, and you have flaunted your ridicule of the gods. But they know how to pardon those whom they love. So,

τῷ μεγάλῳ θεῷ Ἀπόλλωνι, τῷ τὴν οἰκουμένην διασώζοντι·
ἢ τίς ἡ χρεία ἡ καταλαβοῦσά σε μέχρις ἐνταῦθα;"

Ἀποκριθεὶς δὲ ὁ γενναῖος μάρτυς τοῦ Χριστοῦ Γεώργιος, ἔλεγε, "Τὸ μὲν πρῶτον καὶ ἐξαίρετον ὄνομά μου,
Χριστιανός εἰμι· τὸ δὲ ἐν ἀνθρώποις, Γεώργιος λέγομαι.
Γένος μὲν τῶν Καππαδόκων, θρεπτὸς δὲ καὶ τιθηνὸς τῆς
Παλαιστινῶν χώρας· στρατεύομαι δὲ ἐν νουμέρῳ τινί,
καλῶς διαπραξάμενος τὴν κομητατοῦρα. Ποίοις δὲ ἀναγ-
κάζεις με θῦσαι θεοῖς, ὦ βασιλεῦ;"

Ὁ βασιλεὺς λέγει, "Τῷ Ἀπόλλωνι, ὃς ἐκρέμασε τὸν
οὐρανόν."

Γεώργιος λέγει, "Ἀλλ' εἰ μὲν Ἀπόλλων ἐκρέμασε τὸν
οὐρανόν, καλῶς λέγεις ὅτι θεός ἐστιν. Οὐκ αἰσχύνῃ, βύθιε
δράκον, θεοὺς ὀνομάζειν τοὺς δαίμονας; Ἐγὼ δὲ οὐ διὰ σέ,
οὐδὲ διὰ τοὺς συγκαθεζομένους σοι βασιλεῖς, ἀλλὰ διὰ
τὸν παρεστῶτα λαόν, λέξω τὰ ὀνόματα τῶν δικαίων· τοὺς
πολλοὺς παρεάσω λόγους· μνημονεύσω καὶ λέξω τὰ κατορ-
θώματα τῶν δικαίων μου, καὶ τὴν ἀπώλειαν τῶν θεῶν σου.

"Τίναν οὖν ἴσόν μοι διακρίνεις, ὦ βασιλεῦ, Πέτρον τὸν
κορυφαῖον τῶν ἀποστόλων, ἢ Ἀπόλλωνα τὴν τοῦ κόσμου
ἀπώλειαν; Εἰπέ, βασιλεῦ, τίνα μοι ἴσον διακρίνεις, Ἠλίαν
τὸν Θεσβίτην, τὸν ἐπίγειον ἄγγελον καὶ οὐράνιον ἄνθρωπον, τὸν χαμαὶ βαδίσαντα καὶ εἰς τὰς οὐρανίας ἀψίδας
ἱστάμενον, ἢ Σκάμανδρον τὸν γόητα, τὸν γοητεύοντα τὸ
πῦρ, τὸν μοιχὸν τῆς Μηδείας, ἥτις ἐγέννησε τὸν Ἀρὰθ καὶ
τὸν Ζαρὲθ τοὺς Ποντικοὺς πολεμήτορας, οἵτινες διὰ τὰ
ἔργα αὐτῶν κατεποντίσθησαν, ἐν τῷ πελάγει τῆς θαλάσσης; Τί οὐκ ἀποκρίνῃ, βασιλεῦ; <Εἰπέ, ὦ βασιλεῦ, τίνα

come and sacrifice to the great god Apollo, who sustains the world! In any case, what other need brought you all the way here?"

George, the brave martyr of Christ, responded, "Christian is my principal and most distinctive name; but among people, I am called George. My family is from Cappadocia, but I was raised and brought up in the land of Palestine; I am a soldier, and I have deservedly earned for myself the position of count. But who are the gods to whom you are forcing me to sacrifice, my king?"

The king said, "To Apollo, he who suspended the heavens above."

George said, "If it were indeed Apollo who suspended the heavens, then you would be right to say that he is a god. But aren't you ashamed, abysmal dragon, to call the demons gods? Not for your sake, nor for that of the kings who sit beside you, but for the sake of the people who are present, I shall list the names of the righteous; I shall set aside lengthy speeches; I shall recall and list the feats of my righteous men and the destruction of your gods.

"So whom do you judge as equals, my king: Peter, the chief of the apostles, or Apollo, the perdition of the world? Say, my king, whom do you judge as equals: Elijah the Tishbite, the earthly angel and heavenly human, who walked this earth and who also stands on the vaults of heaven, or Skamandros the sorcerer, who bewitches fire, the adulterer of Medea, who gave birth to Arath and Zareth, the Pontic fighters, who were swallowed up by the waters of the sea because of their deeds? Why don't you respond, my king? Tell me, my king, what do you judge superior: the bouts of

μείζονα διακρίνεις, τὰ παλαίσματα> Ἀνταίωνος καὶ Ἡρα-
κλέους, ἢ τῶν μαρτύρων τοὺς ἀγῶνας καὶ στεφάνους; Ἰε-
ζάβελ τὴν τῶν προφητῶν φονεύτριαν, ἢ Μαρίαν τὴν θεο-
τόκον; Αἰσχύνθητι λοιπόν· οὐ γάρ εἰσι θεοί, ἀλλὰ δαίμονες,
εἴδωλα κωφά."

4   Τότε ὀργισθεὶς ὁ βασιλεύς, ἐκέλευσεν ἀνατεθῆναι αὐτὸν ἐπὶ τὸ ἅρμα, καὶ ξέεσθαι εὐτόνως, ὥστε τὰ ἔγκατα
αὐτοῦ ῥιφῆναι, καὶ ὅλῳ τῷ σώματι αὐτοῦ μολυνθῆναι τῷ
αἵματι. Ὡς δὲ ταύτην τὴν πληγὴν γενναίως ὑπήνεγκεν,
ἐκέλευσεν ἐκβληθῆναι αὐτὸν ἔξω τῆς πόλεως, καὶ διὰ τεσσάρων μαγκάνων ἀποταθῆναι, καὶ βουνεύροις ἀφειδῶς
τὰς σάρκας ξέεσθαι, καὶ ἅλατι καταπάσασθαι τοὺς μώλω-
πας, καὶ ζιβύναις ἀποξέεσθαι τὰ πεπηγότα αὐτοῦ αἵματα.

5   Ὡς δὲ καὶ ταύτην τὴν πληγὴν γενναίως ὑπήνεγκεν, κελεύει πάλιν ἐνεχθῆναι αὐτὸν ἐπὶ τὴν πόλιν, καὶ γενέσθαι
βωμὸν ὑψηλόν, καὶ καθηλωθῆναι τοὺς πόδας αὐτοῦ· καὶ
προστάττει γενέσθαι ὀγκινίσκους ἓξ μακρούς, καὶ ἐν αὐτοῖς βολισθῆναι τὰς σάρκας τοῦ δικαίου. Ὡς δὲ καὶ ταύτην
τὴν τιμωρίαν γενναίως ὑπήνεγκεν, ἐκέλευσε πάλιν κατενεχθῆναι αὐτόν, καὶ βληθῆναι αὐτὸν ἐν λεκάνῃ, καὶ κό-
ρακι σιδηρῷ κατενεχθῆναι.

6   <Καὶ καθίσας, κελεύει πρόσταγμα γενέσθαι περιέχον
τὸν τύπον τοῦτον· "Βασιλεὺς μέγας [Δαδιανὸς] πάσῃ ὑφη-
λίῳ χαίρειν. Εἴ τις μάγος μέγας ἐστὶν δυνατὸς εἰς τὸ λῦσαι
τὰς μαγείας τῶν Χριστιανῶν, ἐλθάτω πρός με, καὶ δώσω
αὐτῷ κτήματα, ὅσα ἂν αἰτήσηταί με, καὶ δεύτερος ἔσται
ἐν τῇ βασιλείᾳ μου." Τῶν δὲ γραμμάτων ἐκπεμφθέντων
κατὰ πάσης τῆς οἰκουμένης, παραγίνεται αὐτῷ ἐπίσημος

Antaios and Herakles, or the contests and crowns of the martyrs? Jezebel, the prophets' murderess, or Mary, the mother of God? You should be ashamed. Yours are not gods, but demons, deaf idols."

Then the king became angry, and he ordered that George 4 be placed on a chariot and flogged intensely, so that his guts would be flung out and his whole body soiled with blood. But as George valiantly endured this torture, the king ordered that he be exposed outside the city, and be stretched by four winches, and have his flesh flogged mercilessly with ox tendon whips, his wounds sprinkled with salt, and his coagulated blood scraped off with pikes.

As George valiantly endured this torture also, the king 5 ordered that he should be brought back into the city again, and that they should make a high platform, and that his feet should be nailed to it; and he also commanded that there should be six long hooks, and that the flesh of the righteous man should be pierced with these. As George valiantly endured this torture also, the king ordered that he should be taken down and thrown into a pan, and be tortured with an iron pointed hook.

The king took his seat once more, and ordered that a 6 mandate be released with the following text: "Great King Dadian, to the whole earth greetings! If there is any magician able to undo the magic of the Christians, let him come to me, and I shall give him as many possessions as he may request of me, and he shall be second in command in my kingdom." After these letters had been sent out to the entire world, a renowned man by the name of Athanasios came

ἀνήρ, ὀνόματι Ἀθανάσιος, καὶ λέγει τῷ βασιλεῖ, "Βασιλεύς, εἰς τοὺς αἰῶνας ζῆθι! Εἰ τολμήσει τις ἐπ᾽ ἐμοῦ ποιῆσαί
τι, κἀγὼ διαλύσω αὐτοῦ τὰς μαγείας." Περιχαρὴς δὲ γενάμενος ὁ βασιλεὺς εἶπεν πρὸς αὐτόν, "Καὶ τί ἔχεις ποιῆσαι,
ἵνα λύσῃς τὰς μαγείας τῶν Χριστιανῶν;" Εἶπεν ὁ Ἀθανάσιος πρὸς αὐτόν, "Κέλευσον, βασιλεύς, ἐνεχθῆναί μοι
ταῦρον."> Τότε προστάττει βοῦν ἕνα μελισθέντα <ἄγε-
σθαι>, καὶ τὸν μελισθέντα ταῦρον εἰς δύο ταύρους ἀπεκα-
τέστησεν.

7   Τότε κελεύει τὸν Ἅγιον Γεώργιον ἐπὶ τὸ βῆμα ἀχθῆναι·
καὶ λέγει αὐτῷ ὁ Βασιλεὺς Δαδιανός, "Γεώργιε, τούτου
χάριν, ἐκάλεσα τὸν μάγον τοῦτον ἐν τῇ βασιλείᾳ μου· ἢ
λῦσον αὐτοῦ τὰς μαγείας, ἢ ἀναιρεῖ σέ, ἢ ἀναιρεῖται ὑπὸ
σοῦ." Ὁ δὲ Ἅγιος Γεώργιος βλέψας πρὸς τὸν νεανίσκον
λέγει, "Σπεῦσον, τέκνον, ὃ ἂν ἔχῃς ποιῆσαι, τάχιον ποίη-
σον· θεωρῶ γὰρ καταλαβοῦσά σε ἡ χάρις τοῦ Θεοῦ μου."
Λαβὼν δὲ ὁ Ἀθανάσιος ποτήριον, <καὶ> προσμίξας τῇ
αὐτοῦ εἰκόνα, καὶ ἐπικαλεσάμενος δαιμόνων ὀνόματα,
ἔδωκεν αὐτῷ πιεῖν· καὶ οὐδὲν ἄτοπον ἦν αὐτῷ. Εἶπε δὲ
Ἀθανάσιος πρὸς τοὺς βασιλεῖς, "Ἄλλον ἕν ἐστιν ὃ ἔχω
ποιῆσαι· ἐὰν δὲ μηδὲν πάθῃ πορεύσομαι κἀγὼ πρὸς τὸν
ἐσταυρωμένον." Καὶ λαβὼν ἕτερον ποτήριον, <καὶ> προσμίξας τῇ ἑαυτοῦ εἰκόνα, καὶ ἐπικαλεσάμενος δαιμόνων
ὀνόματα (χείρονα τῶν πρώτων), ἔδωκεν αὐτῷ πιεῖν· καὶ
οὐδὲν ἄτοπον ἦν ἐν αὐτῷ.

Καὶ λέγει ὁ Ἀθανάσιος πρὸς τὸν Ἅγιον Γεώργιον, "Ὁ
λύχνος τῆς ἀληθείας, ὁ ὁδηγὸς τῶν ἐπικαλουμένων τὸ
ὄνομα τοῦ Χριστοῦ τοῦ ἐλθόντος εἰς τὸν κόσμον σῶσαι

to him and said to the king, "My king, may you live forever! Let anyone dare to do some trick in front of me, and I shall put an end to his magic." The king became overjoyed and said to him, "What can you do to put an end to the magic of the Christians?" Athanasios said to him, "My king, order a bull to be brought to me." Then the king commanded that they bring a dismembered bull, and the magician restored the dismembered bull into two bulls.

Then King Dadian ordered Saint George to be brought 7 to the tribunal and said to him, "George, this is why I summoned this magician into my royal presence; for sure you must undo his magic, or he will kill you, or he will be killed by you." Saint George looked toward the young man and said, "Hurry, child! Do quickly whatever you can; for I see that the grace of my God is upon you." Athanasios took a cup, mixed George's effigy in it, invoked the names of demons, and gave it to George to drink; and nothing bad happened to him. Athanasios said to the kings, "I only have one more trick; if he suffers nothing, I too will join the crucified one." He then took another cup, mixed George's effigy in it, invoked the names of demons (even worse than the previous ones), and gave it to him to drink; and nothing bad happened to him.

And Athanasios said to Saint George, "You are the lamp of truth, the guide of those who invoke the name of Christ who came into this world so as to save all those in error.

πάντας τοὺς πεπλανημένους, ἐλέησόν με, καὶ δός μοι τὸ σωτήριον βάπτισμα, ὅπως ἀνοίξει μοι ὁ θυρωρὸς τῆς ἀληθείας, καὶ εἰσδέξεταί με ἐν τῇ μονῇ τῶν ἁγίων αὐτοῦ τῶν ἀπ᾽ αἰῶνος αὐτῷ εὐαρεστησάντων." Ἰδὼν δὲ ὁ βασιλεὺς τὸ γεγονός, ἐκέλευσεν ἐκβληθῆναι αὐτὸν μηνὶ Ἰαννουαρίῳ κγ᾽· καὶ ἐτελειώθη ἡ αὐτοῦ μαρτυρία ἐν καλῇ ὁμολογίᾳ· καὶ παρεγένετο ἔνδοξος πρὸς τὸν Κύριον ἡμῶν Ἰησοῦν Χριστόν. Τότε κελεύει ὁ βασιλεὺς τὸν μακάριον Γεώργιον ἀπενεχθῆναι ἐν τῇ φυλακῇ.

8 Πρωΐας δὲ γενομένης, προστάττει γενέσθαι τροχὸν παμμεγέθη, καὶ ἐν τῷ τροχῷ ἐμπαγῆναι ἥλους καὶ τρυπανίσκους. Καὶ ἀπαρτίσθη ὁ τροχὸς ὡσεὶ τεκτονικὸν πριστήριον κατεσκευασμένον, ὑπεράνω μὲν ἔχον ξίφη, ὑποκάτω δὲ διστόμους μαχαίρας· καὶ κελεύει ἄγεσθαι αὐτὸν ἐπὶ τὸν τροχόν. Ἡνίκα δὲ ἦλθεν ὁ Ἅγιος Γεώργιος ἐπὶ τὸν τροχόν, καὶ ἰδὼν αὐτὸν κατεσκευασμένον, εἶπεν, "Οὐ μὴ διασωθῶ ἐκ τοῦ μαγκάνου τούτου." Ἔπειτα ἀποκινήσας τὸν ἑαυτοῦ λογισμὸν λέγει, "Γεώργιε, ἐννόησον τὸν καταλαβόντα σε κλῆρον καὶ γνῶθι, ὅτι ὁ Κύριος ἡμῶν Ἰησοῦς Χριστὸς οὐκ ἐγκαταλείψει σε, ἀλλὰ βοηθήσει ἐν πᾶσι· καὶ τί οὕτως ἐδειλίασας, ἵνα εἴπῃ ὁ ἐχθρὸς Ἴσχυσα πρὸς αὐτόν;"

Ἔπειτα ἀνανεύσας πρὸς τὸν ἑαυτοῦ εὐεργέτην, λέγει, "Ἄναρχε, ἀδιάδοχε, σταδιάρχα τῶν φοβουμένων σε, νικηφόρε τῶν πολεμίων ἐχθρῶν, στέφανε τῶν ἀγωνιζομένων διὰ τὸ ὄνομά σου, Κύριε ὁ Θεός· ὃς πρὸ τοῦ τὸν οὐρανὸν καὶ τὴν γῆν γενέσθαι, ἐπὶ τῶν ὑδάτων ἀναπέπαυσαι· οὗ γένος ἀνθρώπων οὐκ ἔγνω τὴν σὴν ἀνάπαυσιν· ὅταν δὲ ἐν αἰσθήσει ἐκαμάρωσας τὸν οὐρανόν, ὀμβροτόκους νεφέλας

Have mercy on me and grant me the salvific baptism, so that the gatekeeper of truth may open the door for me and receive me into the dwelling of his saints, who have pleased him since the beginning of time." When the king saw what happened, he ordered that Athanasios be exposed, on the twenty-third of January. His martyrdom was completed in good confession of faith, and he appeared in glory in front of our Lord Jesus Christ. Then the king ordered that the blessed George should be taken to jail.

When morning came, the king commanded that a huge 8 wheel should be constructed, and nails and gimlets fixed upon it. And the wheel was put together, made like a carpenter's saw, with swords on top, and double-edged knives below; and he ordered George to be led to the wheel. When Saint George came near the wheel and saw how it was made, he said, "I hope I shall survive this contraption." Then he fought off his own thought and said, "George, you should understand the lot that has fallen to you and be certain that our Lord Jesus Christ will not abandon you, but will help you in everything; so why did you show such fear, allowing *the enemy to say, 'I overpowered him'?*"

Then, raising his eyes toward his benefactor, he said, "You, without beginning or succession, you who are the superintendent of the arena for those who fear you, the victor over their opposing enemies, and the crown of those who fight on behalf of your name, Lord God! You who, before heaven and earth were made, rested upon the waters; you, whose repose the human race has never comprehended, and when you created the vault of the perceptible heaven, you

ἐνετείλω γεμίζειν ὑετόν, ὥστε βρέχειν ἐπὶ δικαίους καὶ ἀδί-
κους· Κύριε Παντοκράτορ, ὁ στήσας τὰ ὄρη σταθμῷ καὶ τὰς
νάπας ζυγῷ, ὁ ἐπιτιμήσας τῷ ὄγκῳ τῶν ἀνέμων καὶ τὰ κύ-
ματα γαληνιάσας, καὶ τοὺς ἀπειθήσαντας ἀγγέλους βυθῷ
Ταρτάρου παραδώσας—καὶ οὗτοι ὦσιν ὑπὸ τὰ θυρώματα
τῆς ἀβύσσου τῶν μοχλευμάτων, ὑπὸ δρακόντων κολαζόμενοι, τῷ δὲ προστάγματι τῷ σῷ ἀντειπεῖν οὐ δύνανται.
Κύριε ὁ Θεός, ὁ ἐν ὑστέροις καιροῖς ἐξαποστείλας τὸν
μονογενῆ σου παῖδα, καὶ ἐν λαγόσι παρθένου ἐνοικίσας
ὡς ἠθέλησας, οὗ γένος ἀνθρώπων οὐδεὶς δύναται περιερ-
γάζεσθαι τοῦ μονογενοῦς σου τὴν γέννησιν. Ὁ ἐπὶ τοῖς
κύμασι τῆς θαλάσσης περιπατήσας καὶ πόδας μὴ μολύνας,
ὁ ἀνέμοις καὶ θαλάσσῃ ἐπιτιμήσας (πάντα γὰρ ὑπήκουσάν
σου ἐν τρόμῳ), Κύριε Ἰησοῦ Χριστέ, ἐλθὲ ἵλεως καὶ εὐμενὴς
ἐμοὶ τῷ ἁμαρτωλῷ, καὶ κούφισόν με ἀπὸ τῶν αἰκισμῶν καὶ
πόνων τῶν περιεχόντων με, ὅτι δεδοξασμένον ἐστὶ τὸ
ὄνομά σου εἰς τοὺς αἰῶνας, ἀμήν."

9   Τελέσαντος δὲ τὴν εὐχὴν αὐτοῦ ταύτην, ἐβλήθη ἐν τῷ
τροχῷ· καὶ μεγάλως πιεσθείς, εἰς δέκα μέρη ἐρράγη. Ἧιρε
δὲ ὁ βασιλεὺς Δαδιανὸς εἰς ὕψος τὴν φωνὴν αὐτοῦ, καὶ
λέγει πρὸς τοὺς βασιλεῖς, "Ἴδετε, πῶς οὐκ ἔστιν ἄλλος
θεός, εἰ μὴ Ἀπόλλων, καὶ Σκάμανδρος, καὶ Ἡρακλῆς, καὶ
Ποσειδῶν, οἵτινες τὰ τρία κλίματα τοῦ οὐρανοῦ συνεκρότησαν, δι᾽ ὧν βασιλεῖς βασιλεύουσι, καὶ δυνάσται κρατοῦσι
γῆς. Ποῦ ἐστιν ὁ θεὸς Γεωργίου, Ἰησοῦς ὁ ἐσταυρωμένος;
Διὰ τί οὐκ ἦλθεν καὶ ἐρρύσατο αὐτὸν ἐκ τῶν χειρῶν μου;"
Κελεύει δὲ ὁ βύθιος δράκων τὰ ὀστᾶ τοῦ ἁγίου ἀκον-
τισθῆναι εἰς λάκκον ξηρόν, εἰπὼν ἐν ἑαυτῷ, "Μή τις τῶν

ordered the rain-bringing clouds to be filled with moisture, so as *to rain on the just and on the unjust.* All-sovereign Lord, *you who have weighed the mountains with a scale and the valleys with a balance,* you who rebuked the swollen mass of the winds, and calmed the waves, and delivered the angels who disobeyed you to the depths of Tartaros—may they remain there behind the bolted gates of the abyss, punished by dragons, where they are unable to oppose your command. Lord God, who in later times sent your only begotten son, and had him dwell, as you wished, in the womb of a virgin; your only begotten son, into whose birth no one of the human race can inquire. You who *walked upon* the waves of *the sea* without polluting your feet, who *rebuked the winds and the sea* (for everything has yielded to you in terror), Lord Jesus Christ, full of mercy and compassion come to me the sinner, and relieve me from the tortures and pains that surround me, because your name is glorified forever, amen."

When George completed this prayer, he was thrown onto 9 the wheel; and being severely crushed, he was broken into ten pieces. King Dadian raised his voice, and he said to the kings, "You see? There is no other god than Apollo and Skamandros and Heracles and Poseidon, who established the three regions of the heavens, and through whom kings reign, and tyrants *rule the earth.* Where is George's god, Jesus, the crucified one? Why did he not come and deliver him from my hands?" Then, the abysmal dragon ordered the bones of the saint to be thrown into a dry cistern, saying to himself,

Χριστιανῶν λάβῃ τῶν μελῶν αὐτοῦ, καὶ ἀναστήσῃ μαρτύριον αὐτοῦ, καὶ ἐπαγάγῃ τὸ *αἷμα αὐτοῦ ἐπὶ τὰς κεφαλὰς ἡμῶν.*"

Ἦν δὲ ὥρα τοῦ ἀρίστου, καὶ ἐπορεύθησαν οἱ βασιλεῖς εἰς τὸ ἀριστῆσαι. Ἐγένετο δὲ μετὰ τὸ ἀπελθεῖν τοὺς βασιλεῖς, γίνεται ἀὴρ συνεχής, καὶ ἦχος μέγας, ὥστε τοὺς οὐρανοὺς λυγισθῆναι, καὶ τὴν γῆν ἀναπηδῆσαι, καὶ τὴν θάλασσαν κοπάσαι ἐπὶ πήχεις δεκαπέντε. Ἐσάλπισε δὲ Μιχαὴλ ὁ ἀρχιστράτηγος τῇ κερατίνῃ σάλπιγγι, καὶ ἦλθεν ὁ Κύριος ἐπὶ ἄρματος χερουβίμ, καὶ ἔστη ἐπὶ τοῦ στόματος τοῦ λάκκου, καὶ συνέζευξε τὰ ὀστᾶ τοῦ Ἁγίου Γεωργίου, λέγων, "Ἐπειδὴ εἶπεν Γεώργιος ἐν τῇ ζωῇ αὐτοῦ, ὅτι 'Οὐ μὴ διασωθῶ ἐκ τοῦ μαγκάνου τούτου,' ἵνα πεισθῇ καὶ γνώσει ὅτι ἐγώ εἰμι κύριος τῆς ζωῆς αὐτοῦ." Καὶ εἶπεν, "Γεώργιε, ἰδοὺ ἡ χεὶρ ἡ πλάσασά σε ἐξ ἀρχῆς"· καὶ δίδωσι πνεῦμα ζωῆς, "Νῦν πάλιν ἀναπλάττει σε, πρὸς ἔλεγχον τῶν παρανόμων βασιλέων." Καὶ ἐνεφύσησεν *εἰς αὐτὸν* ὁ Κύριος, καὶ ἔδωκεν αὐτῷ *πνεῦμα ζωῆς,* καὶ ἔζησεν· καὶ ἀσπασάμενος αὐτὸν ὁ Κύριος, ἀνῆλθεν εἰς τοὺς οὐρανούς, μετὰ τῶν ἁγίων ἀγγέλων αὐτοῦ.

Ἀνέστη δὲ ὁ Ἅγιος Γεώργιος ἐκ τῶν νεκρῶν καὶ περιεπάτει· καὶ ἐζήτει τοὺς βασιλεῖς, καὶ εὗρεν αὐτοὺς ἐν τῇ πλατείᾳ ἱεροσυλοῦντας καὶ δικάζοντας· καὶ προσδραμὼν ἔστη ἔμπροσθεν αὐτῶν, καὶ λέγει αὐτοῖς, "Ἐπιγινώσκετέ με, βασιλεῖς;" Ἀτενίσας δὲ εἰς αὐτὸν ὁ βασιλεύς, λέγει, "Τίς εἶ σύ;" Καὶ εἶπεν ὁ μάρτυς τοῦ Χριστοῦ, "Ἐγώ εἰμι Γεώργιος, ὁ ἀφ' ὑμῶν κατακοπεὶς καὶ ῥιφεὶς ἐν τῷ λάκκῳ. Διὰ τί οὐκ ἐπιγινώσκετε τὸ ὄνομα τοῦ Θεοῦ μου;"

"So that one of the Christians does not take his body parts, and set up a martyr's monument for him, and bring *his blood upon* our *heads.*"

It was lunchtime, and the kings went to eat. Just after they left, the following occurred: there was a constant movement of the air and a loud noise, so that the heavens were distorted, and the earth leaped up, and the sea stood still fifteen cubits high. And the archangel Michael blew his horn trumpet, and the Lord came on a chariot of cherubim, and stood at the mouth of the cistern, and joined the bones of Saint George together, saying, "Since George, when he was alive, said 'I shall not survive this instrument of torture,' let him be persuaded and learn that I am the master of his life." And he said, "George, here is the hand that fashioned you originally," and upon giving him the breath of life continued, "Now again it fashions you anew, for the refutation of the lawless kings." And the Lord *breathed into* him, and gave him the breath *of life,* and he lived. And after the Lord had greeted him, he ascended into the heavens, along with his holy angels.

Saint George thus rose from the dead and was walking about. He looked for the kings, and found them in the square committing sacrilege and passing judgments; he ran up and stood in front of them, and he said to them, "Do you recognize me, kings?" And the king stared at him and said, "Who are you?" And the martyr of Christ said, "It's me, George, the one whom you had cut into pieces and thrown into a cistern. Why don't you acknowledge the name of my

Ἀτενίσας δὲ εἰς αὐτὸν ὁ βύθιος δράκων, λέγει, "Τὸ εἴδωλον αὐτοῦ ἐστιν." Μαγνέντιος εἶπεν, "Ὅμοιος αὐτοῦ
ἐστιν."

Ἰδὼν δὲ Ἀνατόλιος ὁ στρατηλάτης ὅτι ὁ Ἅγιος Γεώργιος ἀνέστη ἐκ τῶν νεκρῶν, ἐπίστευσε μεθ᾽ ὅλης τῆς τά-
ξεως αὐτοῦ· καὶ ἐγένοντο πᾶσαι αἱ ψυχαὶ αἳ ἐπίστευσαν
πρὸς τὸν Κύριον ἡμῶν Ἰησοῦν Χριστὸν ἐν τῇ ἡμέρᾳ
ἐκείνῃ, τρισχίλιαι ἐνενήκοντα ἐννέα καὶ μία γυνὴ ἐκ τοῦ
ὄχλου. Ἐκέλευσε δὲ Δαδιανὸς ὁ βασιλεύς, ἐκβληθῆναι
αὐτοὺς ἔξω τῆς πόλεως, καὶ γενέσθαι εἰς ἀρχὰς δεκαπέντε,
καὶ οὕτως αὐτοὺς τῷ ξίφει τελειωθῆναι. Ἐτελειώθη αὐτῶν
ἡ μαρτυρία ἐν καλῇ ὁμολογίᾳ, μηνὶ Φεβρουαρίῳ, εἰκοστῇ
τρίτῃ.

10   Καὶ μετὰ ταῦτα κελεύει ἀχθῆναι τὸν Ἅγιον Γεώργιον
ἐπὶ τοῦ βήματος. Καὶ προστάττει γενέσθαι κράββατον
χαλκοῦν, καὶ ἐν αὐτῷ τανυθῆναι τὸν ἅγιον. Καὶ πάλιν κελεύει ἐνεχθῆναι τρῶγλαν σιδηρᾶν, καὶ ἐν αὐτῇ λυθῆναι
μόλυβδον, καὶ ἀνοῖξαι τὸ στόμα αὐτοῦ, καὶ καταχυθῆναι
τὸν μόλυβδον εὐτόνως· καὶ τούτου γενομένου, οὐχ ἥψατο
αὐτοῦ ὁ μόλυβδος. Καὶ κελεύει λυθῆναι αὐτὸν ἀπὸ τοῦ
κραββάτου, καὶ ἑξήκοντα ἥλους κρουσθῆναι κατὰ τῆς
κεφαλῆς αὐτοῦ, καὶ λίθον μέγαν γλυφθῆναι καὶ ἐμβληθῆναι τὴν κεφαλὴν αὐτοῦ, καὶ μολύβδῳ ἀσφαλισθῆναι τὰς
ῥαγμάς, καὶ οὕτως κυλισθῆναι τὸν λίθον ἐπὶ ἱκανοῦ, ὥστε
κυλιομένου τοῦ λίθου, διασπασθῆναι τὰ ἄρθρα τῶν μελῶν
αὐτοῦ. Ὡς δὲ καὶ ταύτην τὴν τιμωρίαν γενναίως ὑπ-
ήνεγκε, εἶτα κελεύει λυθῆναι αὐτόν, καὶ κατὰ κεφαλῆς
κρεμασθῆναι, καὶ δεθῆναι λίθον παμμέγεθον περὶ τὸν

God?" The abysmal dragon stared at him and said, "It's his ghost." Magnentios said, "It looks like him."

But when the general Anatolios saw that Saint George had risen from the dead, he believed, together with his whole army unit; the entire number of souls who believed that day in our Lord Jesus Christ was three thousand and ninety-nine, as well as one woman from the crowd. King Dadian ordered for them to be taken out of the city, be divided in fifteen groups, and thus be killed by the sword. Their martyrdom in good confession of faith was completed on the twenty-third of the month of February.

After this, he ordered Saint George to be brought to the tribunal. And he commanded that a brazen bed be constructed, and the saint stretched upon it. Then he ordered an iron funnel to be brought, and lead be melted in it, and his mouth be opened and the lead forcibly poured into it; when this was done, the lead had no effect on him. And he ordered him to be untied from the bed, and sixty nails to be hammered into his head, and a large rock to be hollowed out and put on his head, and the openings to be secured with lead, and in this way for the rock to be rolled enough for the joints of his limbs to be torn apart by the rolling of the rock. But as George valiantly endured this torture also, the king ordered that he should be released and hung head down, and an immense rock should be tied around his neck, and

τράχηλον αὐτοῦ, καὶ καπνῷ δριμυτάτῳ καπνίζειν αὐτὸν εὐτόνως. Καὶ μετὰ τοῦτο κελεύει γενέσθαι βοῦν χαλκοῦν, ὥστε καὶ τὰ ἔγκατα αὐτοῦ λικμᾶσθαι ὡσεὶ κονιορτόν.

Ὡς δὲ καὶ ταύτην τὴν τιμωρίαν γενναίως ὑπήνεγκεν, κελεύει πάλιν ἀχθῆναι αὐτὸν ἐν τῇ φυλακῇ, καὶ εἰς τὸ ξύλον ἀσφαλισθῆναι αὐτόν, ἕως οὗ σκέψηται, ποίᾳ κολάσει ἀναλώσῃ τὴν ὁρωμένην νεότητα αὐτοῦ· ἦν γὰρ ὡραῖος σφόδρα. Καὶ ἐπιφανεὶς αὐτῷ ὁ Κύριος τῇ νυκτὶ ἐκείνῃ εἶπεν αὐτῷ, "Ἀνδρίζου, Γεώργιε, καὶ μὴ ἐκλύου, *μηδὲ δειλιάσῃς, ὅτι ἐγώ εἰμι μετὰ σοῦ.* Ἰδοὺ τοῦτο ἅπαξ ἀνέστησά σε· ἔτι δεύτερον ἀποθανῇ, καὶ πάλιν ἀναστήσω σε· τὸ δὲ τέταρτον ἐγὼ αὐτὸς ἐλεύσομαι διὰ τῶν νεφελῶν, καὶ παραλήψομαι τὴν παρακαταθήκην ἣν παρεθέμην ἐν τῷ ἁγίῳ σου σκηνώματι· ἔστι γὰρ ἡ μαρτυρία σου ἐν τοῖς βασιλεῦσι τούτοις, ἔτη ἑπτά. Ἴσχυε οὖν καὶ μὴ ἐκλύου." Καὶ ἀσπασάμενος αὐτὸν ὁ Κύριος, ἀνῆλθεν εἰς τοὺς οὐρανούς· αὐτὸς δὲ ἄυπνος διετέλει ἐπὶ τῇ προτροπῇ τοῦ Κυρίου.

11 Πρωΐας δὲ γενομένης, κελεύει ἀχθῆναι αὐτὸν ἐπὶ τοῦ βήματος· καὶ λέγει αὐτῷ ὁ Βασιλεὺς Μαγνέντιος, "Γεώργιε, ἓν αἴτημα αἰτοῦμαι παρὰ σοῦ, ὅπερ ἐὰν παράσχῃς μοι, μὰ τὸν δεσπότην Ἥλιον, καὶ τοὺς ἑβδομήκοντα ὀκτὼ θεούς, καὶ τὴν μητέρα τῶν θεῶν Ἄρτεμιν, πιστεύω εἰς τὸν θεόν σου."

Εἶπε δὲ αὐτῷ ὁ Ἅγιος Γεώργιος, "Αἴτησαι εἴ τι ἂν θέλῃς." Εἶπε δὲ ὁ Βασιλεὺς Μαγνέντιος, "Εἰσὶ παρ' ἐμοὶ δεκατέσσαρεις θρόνοι βασιλικοί, καὶ ἕκαστος θρόνος ἔχει σανίδας, τὰς μὲν ἐγκάρπους, τὰς δὲ ἀκάρπους. Ἐὰν οὖν διὰ τῆς προσευχῆς σου λυθῶσιν οἱ δεκατέσσαρεις θρόνοι,

that he should be forcibly subjected to the densest smoke. After this, he ordered a brazen bull to be made, so that his innards would be scattered *like dust.*

As George valiantly endured this torture also, the king ordered that he should be taken to the prison once more, and secured in the stocks until he could think up the kind of torture by which he might destroy George's youthful appearance; for George was extremely good looking. That night, the Lord appeared to George, and said to him, *"Be manly,* George, and do not lose your courage *or be frightened,* because I am with you. Look, I have resurrected you once already; you shall die a second time, and I will resurrect you again; but the fourth time I myself will come through the clouds, and claim the deposit which I have entrusted to your holy body; for your martyrdom will last seven years under these kings. So *be strong,* and do not lose your courage." And when the Lord had embraced him, he ascended to the heavens; meanwhile George remained sleepless following the Lord's exhortation.

When morning came, the king ordered him to be brought 11 to the tribunal; and King Magnentios said to him, "George, I have one request for you; if you grant me this, by the lord Sun, and by the seventy-eight gods, and by Artemis, the mother of the gods, I shall believe in your god."

Saint George said to him, "Request whatever you want." And King Magnentios said, "I have fourteen royal thrones, and each throne has panels, some made from fruit-bearing trees, others from those which do not bear fruit. So, if with your prayer the fourteen thrones are taken apart, and the

καὶ ῥιζώσουσιν αἱ σανίδες, καὶ γένωνται δένδρα, τὰ μὲν ἔγκαρπα ἔχοντα καρπόν, τὰ δὲ ἄκαρπα ὡς ἄκαρπα, πιστεύω εἰς τὸν θεόν σου."

Ὁ δὲ Ἅγιος Γεώργιος κλίνας τὰ γόνατα ἐπὶ ὥρας δύο αἰτούμενος καὶ παρακαλῶν, καὶ ἐπὶ τὸ τέλος τῆς εὐχῆς, εἶπε τὸ "Ἀμήν." Καὶ ἐγένετο πνεῦμα Κυρίου ἐπὶ τοὺς θρόνους, καὶ ἐλύθησαν οἱ δεκατέσσαρες θρόνοι, καὶ ἐρριζώθησαν αἱ σανίδες αὐτῶν, καὶ ἐγένετο τὰ μὲν ἔγκαρπα ὡς ἔχοντα καρποὺς πεπείρους, τὰ δὲ ἄκαρπα ὡς ἄκαρπα. Τότε λέγει ὁ Βασιλεὺς Μαγνέντιος, "Μέγας εἶ βασιλεὺς καὶ θεὸς Ἡράκλειος καὶ Ἀπόλλων, ὅτι καὶ ἐν τοῖς ξηροῖς ξύλοις τὰς δυνάμεις αὐτῶν δεικνύουσι. Γεώργιον δὲ τὸν μύστην τῶν Γαλιλαίων, οἶδα πῶς αὐτὸν ἀναλώσω."

Καὶ κελεύει ὁ Βασιλεὺς Δαδιανὸς γενέσθαι μέγα πρίονα, καὶ ἐν αὐτῷ διχοτομηθῆναι τὸν ἅγιον εἰς δύο· καὶ οὕτως ἀπέδωκε τὴν ψυχήν. Καὶ προστάττει γενέσθαι λέβητα μέγα, καὶ ἐν αὐτῷ βληθῆναι τὰς σάρκας τοῦ ἁγίου, καὶ μόλυβδον καὶ πίσσαν καὶ στέαρ καὶ ἄσφαλτον ὑποκαίεσθαι τὸν λέβητα, ὥστε τὰ ἀπορραντίσματα τοῦ λέβητος, ἀποτρέχειν ἐπὶ δεκαπέντε πηχῶν. Καὶ μὴ δυνάμενοι φέρειν τὸν κόπον οἱ ὑπηρέται τῆς ἀδικίας διὰ τὰ ἀπορραντίσματα τοῦ λέβητος, ἀνήγγειλαν τῷ βασιλεῖ, ὅτι· "Ἐξεκαύθη ὁ τρισόλβιος κατὰ κράτος. Κέλευσον οὖν σὺν τῷ λέβητι χυθῆναι αὐτὸν ἐν τῷ ἐδάφει, ἵνα μή τις τῶν Χριστιανῶν λάβῃ τῶν ὀστέων αὐτοῦ, καὶ ἀναστήσῃ μαρτύριον αὐτοῦ."

Ὡς δὲ ἀπήγγειλαν ταῦτα τῷ βασιλεῖ οἱ ὑπηρέται, γίνεται ταραχὴ μεγάλη, ὥστε τὸν ἥλιον μὴ φαίνειν, καὶ τὰ ἄστρα σκοτισθῆναι· *καὶ γίνεται σεισμὸς μέγας· καὶ ἦλθεν*

panels grow roots and turn into trees, those from fruit-bearing having fruit, and those from trees which do not bear fruit being without fruit, I shall believe in your god."

Saint George knelt down and for two hours implored and entreated, and at the end of his prayer he said "Amen." And the Lord's spirit came down on the thrones, and the fourteen thrones were taken apart, and their panels grew roots, and those from fruit-bearing trees turned into trees bearing ripe fruits, and those from trees which do not bear fruit became trees without fruit. At that point King Magnentios said, "You are a great king and god, Herakleios, as well as you Apollo, since you display your power even on dry wood. As for George, the initiate of the Galileans, I know how I will destroy him."

And King Dadian ordered a large saw to be made, and the saint to be cut in two with it; in this fashion George gave up his soul. And the king commanded a large cauldron to be made, and to have the corpse of the saint thrown into it, and lead, pitch, fat, and tar to be heated up in the cauldron, so that the splashes from the cauldron would reach as far as fifteen cubits. As the servants of this wrongdoing could not bear the labor, due to the splashes from the cauldron, they announced to the king, "The thrice blessed man has been entirely burned up. So please order that he be poured out on the ground together with the contents of the cauldron, so that none of the Christians may take his bones and set up a martyr's monument for him."

But when the servants reported this to the king, there was a great commotion, so that the sun stopped shining and the stars became dark; *and there was a great earthquake;* and

αὐτὸς ὁ Κύριος *ἐπὶ τῶν νεφελῶν μετὰ τῶν ἀγγέλων αὐτοῦ ἐπὶ τὸν λέβητα·* καὶ εἶπε τῷ ἀρχαγγέλῳ Γαβριήλ, "Κάτελθε ἐπὶ τὴν γῆν εἰς τὸν λέβητα, καὶ δέξαι τὰς ρανίδας τὰς ἐκφυγούσας ἐκ τοῦ λέβητος." Καὶ ἐποίησεν ὁ ἀρχάγγελος Γαβριήλ, καθὼς συνέταξεν αὐτῷ ὁ Κύριος, καὶ ἔλαμψεν αὐτῇ τῇ ὥρᾳ, ὥστε μὴ φέρειν τοὺς παρεστῶτας. Πάντων δὲ ὁμοῦ καταπεσόντων, ἐφώνησεν αὐτῷ ὁ Κύριος λέγων, "Γεώργιε, ἐγώ εἰμι ὁ Θεός σου, ὁ ἐγείρας Λάζαρον ἐκ νεκρῶν· καὶ σοὶ λέγω: Ἔξελθε ἐκ τοῦ ἀδήλου τόπου τούτου." Καὶ αὐτῇ τῇ ὥρᾳ ἀνέστη ὁ Ἅγιος Γεώργιος, ὡς μηδενὸς πειρασθεὶς πειρατηρίου· καὶ ἐθαύμασαν οἱ παρεστῶτες. Καὶ εἶπεν αὐτῷ ὁ Κύριος, "*Ἀνδρίζου καὶ ἴσχυε,* Γεώργιε, ὅτι πολλὴ χαρὰ γίνεται ἐν τῷ οὐρανῷ ἐπὶ τῇ σῇ ἀθλήσει, ὅτι τὸ τρίτον ἐγὼ ἐλεύσομαι πάλιν καὶ ἀναπλάσω σε, καὶ ἔσῃ μετὰ Ἀβραὰμ καὶ Ἰσαὰκ καὶ Ἰακώβ, τῶν συγκληρονόμων μου. *Ἴσχυε καὶ ἀνδρίζου, ὅτι ἐγώ εἰμι μετὰ σοῦ.*" Καὶ ἀσπασάμενος αὐτὸν ὁ Κύριος, ἀνῆλθεν εἰς τοὺς οὐρανούς. Ὁ δὲ ἅγιος Γεώργιος ἀνέστη καὶ περιεπάτει.

12   Ἐδηλώθη δὲ τῷ βασιλεῖ, ὅτι Γεώργιος ὁ εἰς τὸν λέβητα βληθείς, ἐν τῇ πόλει διάγει. Καὶ ἐκέλευσεν ὁ βασιλεὺς αὐτῇ τῇ ὥρᾳ, ἁρπαγῆναι αὐτὸν καὶ ἀχθῆναι ἐπὶ τοῦ βήματος. Ἰδὼν δὲ ὁ Δαδιανὸς ἐξεπλάγη, καὶ πάντες οἱ συνόντες αὐτῷ· ἐλθὼν δὲ ὁ ἅγιος ἐπὶ τὸ βῆμα, λέγει, "Βῆμα, βῆμα, κατὰ σοῦ ἦλθον· σὺ μετὰ τοῦ Ἀπόλλωνος, ἐγὼ μετὰ τοῦ Κυρίου μου Ἰησοῦ Χριστοῦ."

Καί τις γυνὴ ὀνόματι Σχολαστική, ἐβόησε πρὸς τὸν Ἅγιον Γεώργιον, λέγουσα, "Κύριέ μου Γεώργιε, ἰδοὺ ὁ υἱός μου ἔζευξεν τὸν βοῦν ὃν εἴχομεν, καὶ ἀροτριῶν

the Lord himself came *upon the clouds,* together with his angels, above the cauldron. And he said to his archangel Gabriel, "Go down to the earth into the cauldron, and collect the drops as they are spilling out of the cauldron." And the archangel Gabriel did as the Lord had commanded him, and he became so blazing at that very moment, that those present could not bear it. And, as everyone fell to the ground, the Lord cried out to George and said, "George, I am your God, who raised Lazaros from the dead; and I say to you: Come out from this obscure place." And at that very moment, Saint George rose from the dead, as if he had experienced nothing whatsoever, and those present were amazed. And the Lord said to him, "*Be manly and strong,* George; for there is great joy in heaven over your contest, for the third time I come again and make you anew, you shall join Abraham and Isaac and Jacob, my heirs. *Be strong and manly,* for I am with you." And the Lord embraced him, and ascended into the heavens. And George, had risen and was walking about.

The king was informed that the George who had been 12 thrown into the cauldron, was alive in the city. And at that very moment the king ordered that he should be arrested and taken to the tribunal. When Dadian saw him, he was beside himself, as were all those with him. The saint approached the tribunal and said, "Tribunal, tribunal, I have come against you; you are with Apollo, I am with my Lord Jesus Christ."

Then a woman called Scholastike called out to Saint George, saying, "George, my lord, look, my son yoked the bull we had, and while he was plowing, it became ill, fell to

ἐμαλακίσθη, καὶ πεσὼν ἐτελεύτησεν. Ἀλλ' εἴ τι δύνασαι βοήθησον ἡμῖν ἐν τῇ ταπεινώσει ἡμῶν, ὅτι οὐκ ἔστιν ὑπόστασις ἐν τῷ οἴκῳ μου." Εἶπε δὲ πρὸς αὐτὴν ὁ ἅγιος, "Δέξαι τὴν βακτηρίαν μου, καὶ ἐπίθες ἐπὶ τὸν τράχηλον τοῦ βοός, καὶ εἰπέ, 'Τάδε λέγει ὁ δοῦλος τοῦ Θεοῦ Γεώργιος· ἐν τῷ ὀνόματι <τοῦ> Κυρίου μου Ἰησοῦ Χριστοῦ, ἀνάστηθι ἐπὶ τοὺς πόδας σου.'" Καὶ ἐποίησεν ἡ γυνή, καθὼς εἶπεν αὐτῇ ὁ ἅγιος· καὶ ἀνέστη αὐτῇ τῇ ὥρᾳ ὁ βοῦς· καὶ <ἡ γυνὴ> ἐδόξασε τὸν Θεόν.

13   Τότε ὁ βασιλεὺς Τρακυλῖνος λέγει πρὸς τὸν Ἅγιον Γεώργιον, "Γεώργιε, εἰς τοὺς θρόνους οὓς ἔλυσας, οὐκ οἶδα εἰ ὁ θεός <σου> ἐποίησεν, ἢ οἱ θεοὶ ἡμῶν προσετάξαντο. Καὶ ἰδού ἐστιν παρ' ἡμῖν λάρναξ λελατομημένη, καὶ οὐδεὶς τῶν ἀνθρώπων οἶδεν τὴν εἴσοδον αὐτῆς ἢ τὴν ἔξοδον. Ἐὰν οὖν διὰ τῆς προσευχῆς σου ἀναστῶσιν οἱ ἐν τῇ λάρνακι, πιστεύομεν εἰς τὸν θεόν σου."

Εἶπε δὲ ὁ ἅγιος Γεώργιος, "Ἔχω τὴν αὐτόλεκτον φωνὴν τοῦ εὐαγγελίου τὴν λέγουσαν, ὅτι *Ἐὰν ἔχετε πίστιν ὡς κόκκον σινάπεως, ἐρεῖτε τῷ ὄρει τούτῳ, Μετάβηθι ἐντεῦθεν, ἐκεῖ καὶ μεταβήσεται, καὶ οὐδὲν ἀδυνατήσει ὑμῖν·* πάντα γὰρ δυνατὰ παρὰ τῷ θεῷ μου." Εἶπε δὲ πρὸς τοὺς βασιλεῖς, "Ἀπελθόντες ὑμεῖς ἀποστεγάσατε τὴν λάρνακα, καὶ ἐὰν εὕρητε ὀστέα τεθνηκότων, ἀγάγετέ μοι ἐνταῦθα."

Καὶ ἀνέστησαν οἱ βασιλεῖς, καὶ ἐπορεύθησαν ἐπὶ τὴν λάρνακα· καὶ ἀπεστέγασαν αὐτήν, καὶ οὐχ εὗρον οὐδὲν τῶν ὀστέων αὐτῶν· τὸν δὲ ἐγκείμενον χοῦν, ξύσαντες καὶ κοσμήσαντες, ἤνεγκαν αὐτῷ. Αὐτὸς δὲ θεὶς τὰ γόνατα, ἐπὶ

the ground and died. If you are able, help us in our wretchedness, since my household has no assets." The saint said to
her, "Take my staff, and place it on the bull's neck, and say,
'These are the words of George, the servant of God: in the
name of my Lord Jesus Christ, stand on your feet.'" And the
woman did as the saint told her to do; and at that very moment the bull was resurrected; and the woman glorified
God.

Then the king Trakylinos said to Saint George, "George, 13
regarding the thrones which you took apart, I do not know
if your god did this, or if it was our gods who commanded it.
But look, we have a sarcophagus hewn out of a rock, and
nobody knows the way in, or the way out of it. So, if those in
the sarcophagus are made to rise from the dead through
your prayer, we shall believe in your god."

Saint George said, "I have the voice of the gospel that
says word for word that '*If you have faith as a grain of mustard
seed, you shall say to this mountain, Move from here to there, and it
shall move, and nothing shall be impossible for you*'; for *everything
is possible for* my *God*." Then he said to the kings, "Go and re-
move the lid of the sarcophagus, and if you find any bones of
dead people inside, bring them to me here."

The kings got up and went to the sarcophagus; they re-
moved its lid, and found no bones of the dead whatsoever;
but they scraped up and arranged the dust that was in it
and brought it to him. George knelt and prayed for a long

ὥραν ἱκανὴν ηὔξατο· καὶ μετὰ τὸ τελεσθῆναι τὴν εὐχήν, εἶπε τὸ "Ἀμήν." *Καὶ γίνεται σεισμὸς μέγας καὶ ἀστραπὴ πυρός, καὶ ἔλαμψεν εἰς τὸν ἐγκείμενον χοῦν· καὶ ἐξῆλθον ἐκ τοῦ χοὸς ἄνδρες πέντε, καὶ γυναῖκες ἐννέα, καὶ τρία παιδία.*

Ἰδὼν δὲ ὁ βασιλεὺς Θεόγνιος, μετεκαλέσατο ἕνα τῶν ἀνισταμένων νεκρῶν, καὶ λέγει αὐτῷ, "Τί τὸ ὄνομά σου;" Ὁ ἀνιστάμενος ἐκ τῶν νεκρῶν λέγει, "Ἰούβης καλοῦμαι." Λέγει αὐτῷ ὁ βασιλεύς, "Πόσα ἔτη εἰσίν, ἀφ᾽ οὗ ἐτελεύτησας;" Λέγει αὐτῷ, "Τετρακόσια πλεῖον ἢ ἔλαττον." Λέγει αὐτῷ ὁ βασιλεύς, "Χριστὸς ἐπεδήμει, ἢ οὔ;" Εἶπε δὲ αὐτῷ ὁ ἀνιστάμενος, "Οὐδὲ ἦν ὄνομα Ῥχριστοῦ." Λέγει αὐτῷ ὁ βασιλεύς, "Τί οὖν σεβόμενος, διέδραμες τὸ κάλλος τοῦ βίου τούτου;"

Εἶπε δὲ ὁ ἀναστὰς ἐκ τῶν νεκρῶν, "Μὴ ἀναγκάσῃς με, βασιλεῦ, εἰπεῖν τὸ ῥῆμα τοῦτο· ἐγὼ γὰρ ἐσεβόμην τὸ εἴδωλον τοῦ Ἀπόλλωνος, τὸ κωφὸν καὶ τυφλὸν καὶ μωρὸν καὶ ἀναίσθητον. Ἡνίκα δὲ ἐκ τοῦ βίου τοῦ ἀδίκου τούτου ἐξεβλήθημεν, γεγόναμεν ὑποβρύχιοι· ἐκεῖ γὰρ ἐπῆρεν ἡμᾶς ὁ πύρινος ποταμός, καὶ σκώληξ ὁ ἀκοίμητος. Ἆρα οὐκ ἤκουσας τῆς φωνῆς τῶν Χριστιανῶν; Ἐννοήσομεν τὴν ἡμέραν ἐκείνην τὴν φοβεράν. Οὐκ ἔστιν οὖν ἡμῖν <οὐδὲ> μικρὰ βοήθεια, ἀλλὰ ποταμοὶ πύρινοι, καὶ καχλάζοντες, καὶ ἀπειλὴ φοβερὰ ὀργῆς, καὶ βῆμα φοβερόν, καὶ δικαστήριον ἀδυσώπητον· καὶ ἑκάστου τὰ πεπραγμένα πρὸ ὀφθαλμῶν ἵστανται· ἐπιφωνεῖ γὰρ ὁ ἀρχάγγελος Μιχαὴλ λέγων, "Δείξατε τὰ ἔργα καὶ λάβετε τὸν μισθόν." Ἄκουσον, βασιλεῦ, καὶ διηγοῦμαί σοι. Πᾶς ἄνθρωπος ὃς

time; once he finished his prayer, he said "Amen." *And there was a great earthquake,* and fiery lightning, and it lit up the dust that was in it; and five men, nine women, and three children came out of the dust.

When the king Theognios saw this, he summoned one of dead men who had been resurrected, and said to him, "What's your name?" The resurrected man said, "I'm called Juves." The king said to him, "How many years is it since you died?" He said to him, "Four hundred, more or less." The king said to him, "Had Christ come to dwell among people, or not?" The resurrected man said to him, "Not even the name 'Christ' existed." The king said to him, "So what did you worship as you experienced the beauty of this life?"

The man who had been resurrected from the dead replied, "My king, don't force me to say this; for I venerated the idol of Apollo, that mute, blind, stupid, senseless thing. And when we were cast out of this wicked life, we went down into the depths; that's where the river of fire and the sleepless worm received us. Haven't you heard the words of the Christians, 'We shall perceive that awful day, when there will not be even some small help for us, but, rather, boiling rivers of fire, and the terrible threat of wrath, and the awful tribunal, and merciless court; and what everyone has done will be publicly exposed; for the archangel Michael exclaims, "Show your deeds, and receive your reward"'? Listen, king, to what I am telling you. Everyone who is born on

γεννηθῇ ἐπὶ τῆς γῆς, ὁμολογήσῃ δὲ τὸν ἐσταυρωμένον (κἂν πολλαῖς ἁμαρτίαις περιπέσῃ αὐτοῦ τὸ σῶμα), ἐξέλθῃ δὲ ἐκ τοῦ ἀδίκου βίου τούτου, καὶ ὑποβρύχιος γένηται, κἂν τῆς ἡμέρας τῆς ἁγίας Κυριακῆς, ἀνέσεως τυγχάνει διὰ τὸ ἐπιβλέπειν Κύριον ἐπὶ τὰς κολάσεις. Ἐγὼ δὲ οὐδὲ ἐν ἡμέρᾳ ἁγίας Κυριακῆς, ἀνέσεως ἔτυχον, διότι τὴν κυριότητα οὐχ ὡμολόγησα."

Εἶπε δὲ αὐτῷ ὁ βασιλεύς, "Ληρεῖς σύ, πολλὰ ἔτη ἔχων ἐν τῷ Ἅιδῃ." Ἀναβλέψας δὲ ὁ ἀναστὰς πρὸς τὸν Ἅγιον Γεώργιον, λέγει αὐτῷ, "Δέομαί σου, τὸν λύχνον τῆς ἀληθείας, ἐλέησον τὴν ψυχήν μου, καὶ πάντας τοὺς ἀναστάντας σὺν ἐμοί. Δὸς ἡμῖν τὴν ἐν Χριστῷ σφραγῖδα, καὶ μὴ ἐάσῃς ἡμᾶς ἀπελθεῖν εἰς ὑποβρύχιον τόπον." Ἰδὼν δὲ ὁ ἅγιος τὴν πίστιν τοῦ ἀνδρός, ἐλάκτισεν εἰς τὸ πρόσωπον τῆς γῆς, καὶ εὐθέως ἐξῆλθεν πηγὴ ὕδατος, καὶ ἐβάπτισεν αὐτοὺς εἰς τὸ ὄνομα τοῦ Πατρὸς καὶ τοῦ Υἱοῦ καὶ τοῦ Ἁγίου Πνεύματος, λέγων αὐτοῖς, "Πορεύεσθε, καὶ πληρώσατε τὴν οἰκονομίαν ὑμῶν." Καὶ εὐθέως ἀφανεῖς ἐγένοντο, καὶ οὐκέτι ἐθεωροῦντο.

14　　Ἐννεὸς δὲ γενόμενος ὁ βασιλεὺς Δαδιανὸς ἐπὶ ὥραν μίαν, λέγει πρὸς τοὺς βασιλεῖς, "Οὐκ εἶπον ὑμῖν, ὅτι γόης ἐστὶν καὶ φαρμακός; Ἰδοὺ λόγῳ προβάλλεται· δαίμονας παρέστησεν ἡμῖν. Ἀλλ' ἐγὼ ἀτιμάσω ἄρτι τὸ γένος τῶν Γαλιλαίων." Καὶ εἶπεν, "Ἐπιλέξασθέ μοι χήραν ἥτις οὐκ ἄλλη πενιχροτέρα οὐκ ἔστιν ἐν τῇ πόλει ταύτῃ." Καὶ ἐξελέξαντο χήραν πενιχρὰν σφόδρα, καὶ κατέκλεισαν αὐτὸν ἐκεῖ πρὸς αἰσχύνην τῶν Γαλιλαίων.

Ἡνίκα δὲ εἰσῆλθεν ὁ ἅγιος εἰς τὸν οἶκον τῆς χήρας,

earth, who confesses faith in the crucified one (even if his body should fall into many sins), when he leaves this wicked life and goes down into the depths, gets some respite, at least on the day of holy Sunday, as the Lord supervises the punishments. But I, did not get any respite, even on the day of holy Sunday because I did not confess faith in his lordship."

The king said to him, "You're talking nonsense, because you've spent too many years in Hades." But the resurrected man turned his eyes toward Saint George, and said to him, "I implore you, lamp of truth, have mercy on my soul, and on all those who were raised from the dead with me. Grant us the seal in Christ, and do not let us return to that place in the depths." And as the saint saw the man's faith, he kicked the face of the earth, and immediately a fountain of water came forth, and he baptized them in the name of the Father and of the Son and of the Holy Spirit; and he said to them, "Go and fulfill God's plan for you." And they disappeared at once, and were seen no more.

King Dadian was dumbfounded for an hour, and then 14 said to the kings, "Didn't I tell you that he is a sorcerer and a wizard? Look how he conjures with words and has presented demons to us. But I will now disgrace the race of the Galileans." And he said, "Find me the poorest widow in this city." And they found a widow who was extremely poor, and they shut George up there so as to put the Galileans to shame.

When the saint entered the house of the widow, he said

λέγει πρὸς αὐτήν, "Δός μοι ἄρτον ὅτι πεινῶ." Ἡ δὲ εἶπεν αὐτῷ, "Οὐκ ἔστιν ἐν τῷ οἴκῳ μου ἄρτος." Εἶπε δὲ ὁ ἅγιος πρὸς αὐτήν, "Ποίῳ θεῷ λατρεύεις;" Λέγει αὐτῷ ἡ γυνή, "Τῷ μεγάλῳ θεῷ Ἀπόλλωνι, καὶ τῷ Ἡρακλεῖ." Λέγει αὐτῇ ὁ ἅγιος, "Δικαίως οὐκ ἔστιν ἄρτος ἐν τῷ οἴκῳ σου, διότι τοιούτους θεοὺς σέβῃ." Ἡνίκα δὲ εἶδεν ἡ γυνὴ τὸ πρόσω-πον αὐτοῦ ὡσεὶ πρόσωπον ἀγγέλου, εἶπεν αὐτῷ, "Ἰδοὺ θεωρῶ ἄνδρα, ὡς εἴ τις τῶν Γαλιλαίων θεωρεῖ ἄγγελον. Νῦν ἐξελεύσομαι πρὸς τοὺς γείτονάς μου, εἰ εὕρω χάριν ἐνώπιον αὐτῶν, καὶ λήψομαι ἄρτον καὶ εἰσελεύσομαι τῷ ἀνδρὶ τούτῳ· καὶ φάγῃ αὐτὸς καὶ ἐγὼ μετὰ τῶν τέκνων μου, καὶ ἀποθανοῦμαι τῇ ἐπιούσῃ ἡμέρᾳ."

Ἡνίκα δὲ τοῦ ἐξελθεῖν τὴν γυναῖκα, ἐκάθισεν ὁ Ἅγιος Γεώργιος παρὰ τὴν βάσιν τοῦ ξύλου, καὶ εὐθέως ἐρρίζωσεν ὁ στῦλος, καὶ κλάδους ἀπέλυσεν, καὶ διέβη τὸ δένδρον ἐπάνω τοῦ δώματος, καὶ ηὐξήθη ἐπὶ πήχεις δεκαπέντε. Καὶ ἤνεγκεν αὐτῷ ὁ ἀρχιστράτηγος Μιχαὴλ <ἄρτον>· καὶ ἔφαγεν, καὶ *ἐνίσχυσεν.* Ἦλθε δὲ ἡ γυνὴ εἰς τὴν οἰκίαν αὐ-τῆς, καὶ βλέπει τὸν στῦλον ῥιζωθέντα καὶ εἶπεν, "Ὁ θεὸς τῶν Γαλιλαίων ἐπεῖδεν ἐπὶ τὸ γένος τῶν Χριστιανῶν, ὅτι ἐν κακοῖς ὑπάρχοντας ἡμᾶς, σαρκὶ παραγέγονεν εἰς τὸν οἶκον τῆς χήρας, τοῦ βοηθῆσαι αὐτῇ"· καὶ ἔπεσεν εἰς τοὺς *πόδας αὐτοῦ.* Εἶπε δὲ πρὸς αὐτὴν ὁ ἅγιος, "Ἀνάστα, γύναι, καὶ στῆθι ἐπὶ τοὺς πόδας σου· οὐκ εἰμὶ ἐγὼ ὁ Θεὸς τῶν Χριστιανῶν, ἀλλὰ αὐτοῦ δοῦλος."

Καὶ εἶπεν ἡ γυνή, "Δέομαί σου, κύριε· εἰ εὕρω χάριν ἐνώπιόν σου, λαλήσω εἰς τὰ ὦτά σου, καὶ μὴ ὀργισθῇς τῇ δούλῃ σου." Εἶπε δὲ ὁ ἅγιος, "Λάλησον, ὦ γύναι." Λέγει

to her, "Give me some bread, because I'm hungry." She said to him, "There's no bread in my house." The saint said to her, "Which god do you worship?" The woman said to him, "The great god Apollo, and Herakles." The saint said to her, "Deservedly there is no bread in your house, because you venerate such gods." When the woman saw that his face was like the face of an angel, she said to him, "Look, I'm seeing a man just as one of the Galileans sees an angel; I'll go out right now to my neighbors, and if I find favor with them and get some bread, I shall come back to this man, and he as well as I and my children shall eat, and I shall die tomorrow."

When the woman went out, Saint George sat next to the base of a wooden pillar, and straightaway it sprouted roots, and put out branches, and the tree went through the roof over the house, and grew fifteen cubits high. And Michael, the chief of the angelic host, brought him bread; and he ate and *felt stronger.* The woman came back to her house, and she saw that the pillar had taken root, and she said, "The god of the Galileans looks after the race of the Christians, since, while we were in dire straits, he came in the flesh to the house of a widow so as to help her"; and *she fell* upon *his feet.* And the saint said to her, "Get up, woman, and stand on your feet; I am not the God of the Christians, but rather his slave."

And the woman said, "I implore you, my lord; if I find favor in your sight, may I speak to you, and please do not get angry with me, your slave." The saint said to her, "Speak,

αὐτῷ ἡ γυνή, "Ἰδοὺ ἔστι μοι παιδίον τριετῆ, καὶ τοῦτό ἐστι κωφὸν καὶ τυφλὸν καὶ χωλόν, καὶ αἰσχύνομαι ἐπιδεῖξαι αὐτὸ τοῖς γείτοσί μου. Ἐὰν οὖν διὰ τῆς προσευχῆς σου ἀνορθωθῇ ὁ υἱός μου, πιστεύω εἰς τὸν Θεόν σου." Ὁ δὲ ἅγιος λέγει πρὸς τὴν γυναῖκα, "Ἔνεγκέ μοι ὧδε τὸ παιδίον σου." Καὶ ἤνεγκεν αὐτὸ πρὸς αὐτόν· καὶ ἐκοίμισεν αὐτὸ εἰς τὰ γόνατα αὐτοῦ. Καὶ κλίνας τὴν κεφαλὴν αὐτοῦ ὁ ἅγιος, ἐπεκαλέσατο τὸν ἑαυτοῦ δεσπότην. Ἐπὶ δὲ τὸ τέλος τῆς εὐχῆς εἶπε τὸ "Ἀμήν," καὶ ἐνεφύσησεν εἰς τοὺς ὀφθαλμοὺς αὐτοῦ. Καὶ ἔπεσαν ἀπὸ τῶν ὀφθαλμῶν αὐτοῦ δάκρυα, καὶ εὐθέως ἀνέβλεψεν. Εἶπε δὲ ἡ γυνὴ πρὸς τὸν μάρτυρα, "Κύριε, τὰ ὦτα αὐτοῦ ἀκούσωσιν;" Εἶπε δὲ αὐτῇ ὁ Ἅγιος Γεώργιος, "Τέως τοῦ παρόντος ἀρκέσῃ τούτῳ· καὶ ὅταν αὐτὸν καλέσω, τότε καὶ τοῖς ὠσὶν ἀκούσει, καὶ τοῖς ποσὶν περιπατήσει καὶ διακονήσει μοι λόγους." Ἡ δὲ γυνὴ δοξάσασα τὸν Θεὸν ἡσύχασεν.

15 Ἀναστάντες δὲ οἱ βασιλεῖς ἀπὸ τῆς στιβάδος, περιεπάτουν ἐπὶ τὴν πόλιν, ἱεροσυλοῦντες καὶ δικάζοντες. Καὶ ἀτενίσας ὁ Βασιλεὺς Δαδιανός, εἶδε τὸ δένδρον ἱστάμενον ἐπάνω τοῦ δώματος· καὶ λέγει τοῖς βασιλεῦσιν, "Τίς ἡ ξένη αὕτη τοῦ δένδρου θέα;" Ἀπήγγειλαν δὲ αὐτῷ, ὅτι Γεώργιος, ὁ μύστης τῶν Γαλιλαίων, ἐκεῖ κατακέκλεισται. Κελεύει δὲ αὐτῇ τῇ ὥρᾳ ἐκβληθῆναι αὐτὸν ἐκ τοῦ οἰκήματος, καὶ ἄγεσθαι ἐπὶ τὴν δημοσίαν, καὶ βουνεύροις ἀφειδῶς τὰς σάρκας αὐτοῦ καταξέεσθαι. Καὶ κασσίδαν πυρώσαντες, ἔθηκαν ἐπὶ τὴν κεφαλὴν αὐτοῦ. Καὶ προστάττει αὐτὸν ὁ βασιλεύς, τῷ ἄμβωνι προσελθεῖν, καὶ ξέεσθαι αὐτοῦ τὰς πλευράς, καὶ κανδήλας προσάπτεσθαι τῷ σώματι αὐτοῦ,

woman." The woman said to him, "Look, I have a three-year-old child, and he is deaf, blind, and lame, and I am ashamed to show him to my neighbors. If my son is made well through your prayer, I shall believe in your God." The saint said to the woman, "Bring your child here to me." And she brought the child to him, and he had him fall asleep on his knees. And the saint bent his head, and called upon his own master. At the end of his prayer, he said "Amen" and breathed into the child's eyes. Tears *fell from his eyes,* and *he was immediately able to see again.* The woman said to the martyr, "My lord, will his ears also be able to hear?" But Saint George said to her, "For now, you should be content with this; when I summon him, then he will also hear with his ears, and walk on his feet, and will serve on my commands." The woman glorified God and was at peace.

In the meantime, the kings got up from their couches, 15 and walked about the city, committing their sacrileges and presiding over court cases. King Dadian caught sight of the tree that stood above the house, and said to the other kings, "What's this strange spectacle of the tree?" People reported to him that George, the initiate of the Galileans, was confined there. Dadian ordered that he should be taken out of the building that very moment and be led to the public hall, and that his flesh should be lacerated mercilessly with ox-tendon whips. They also heated up a helmet and placed it on the saint's head. And the king commanded that he should be brought to the pulpit, and his rib cage should be lacerated, and torches attached to his body, so that he would be unable

ὡς μηκέτι φέρειν τὰς ὀδύνας. Ἐβόησε δὲ ὁ ἅγιος Γεώργιος, <καὶ ἀπέδωκε τὸ πνεῦμα>. Καὶ κελεύει ὁ ἄνομος βασιλεύς, ἀπενεχθῆναι αὐτὸν εἰς ὄρος ὑψηλόν, καὶ ῥιφῆναι
αὐτὸν ἐκεῖ· ἔλεγε γὰρ ὁ βύθιος δράκων, ὅτι· "Καταβήσεται
τὰ πετεινὰ τοῦ οὐρανοῦ, καὶ καταφάγωσι τὰς σάρκας αὐτοῦ,
ἵνα μή τινες τῶν Χριστιανῶν ὄψονταί τι τῶν μελῶν, καὶ
ἀναστήσωσιν αὐτῷ μαρτύριον."

Ἡνίκα ἀνηνέχθη ὁ Ἅγιος Γεώργιος εἰς τὸ ὄρος καὶ
ἐρρίφη ἐκεῖ, κατήρχοντο δὲ οἱ ὑπηρέται· καὶ κατελθόντων
αὐτῶν ἀπὸ τοῦ ὄρους ὡς ἀπὸ σταδίων τριάκοντα, γίνεται
βροντὴ μεγάλη καὶ ἀστραπή, ὥστε καὶ τὸν οὐρανὸν σα-
λευθῆναι. Καὶ ἐλθὼν ὁ Κύριος *ἐπὶ τῶν νεφελῶν,* ἐφώνησε
τῷ ἁγίῳ λέγων, "Δεῦρο, παῖς μου ἀγαπητέ· ἐγέρθητι ἀπὸ
τοῦ ὕπνου σου!" Καὶ ἀνέστη ὁ ἅγιος ἀπὸ τῶν νεκρῶν, ὡς
ἀπὸ ὕπνου. Καὶ κατεδίωξεν ὀπίσω τῶν ὑπηρετῶν, κράζων
καὶ λέγων, "Ἐκδέξασθέ με." Ἐπιστραφέντες δὲ οἱ ὑπηρέται, καὶ ἰδόντες τὸν Ἅγιον Γεώργιον, ἔπεσον εἰς τοὺς πόδας αὐτοῦ, λέγοντες αὐτῷ, "Κύριε, δὸς ἡμῖν τὴν ἐν Χριστῷ
σφραγῖδα, ὁ ἀγαπητὸς τοῦ Θεοῦ!" Καὶ αὐτῇ τῇ ὥρᾳ ἐβάπτισεν αὐτούς, εἰς τὸ ὄνομα τοῦ Πατρὸς καὶ τοῦ Υἱοῦ καὶ
τοῦ Ἁγίου Πνεύματος. Ἐπορεύθησαν δὲ ἀμφότεροι καὶ
ἦλθον πρὸς τοὺς βασιλεῖς· καὶ ἀπεκρίθησαν πάντες ὁμοῦ
λέγοντες, "Πάντες ἡμεῖς Χριστιανοί ἐσμεν, καὶ τοῖς θεοῖς
ὑμῶν οὐ προσκυνοῦμεν, τυφλοὺς καὶ κωφοὺς καὶ ἀναι-
σθήτους." Καὶ ἐν ἐκστάσει γενόμενοι οἱ βασιλεῖς, κελεύει
ὁ Βασιλεὺς Δαδιανός, τὸν μὲν Ἀείκονα κρεμασθῆναι κατὰ
κεφαλῆς, τὸν δὲ Γλυκάδην καὶ Λαστηρῖνον, τῷ ξίφει

to bear the pains any longer. Saint George let out a loud cry and gave up his spirit. The lawless king ordered that the saint should be taken up to a high mountain, and thrown off there; for the abysmal dragon said that "The *birds of the air* will descend, and will devour his flesh, so that no Christian will ever see any of his body parts and then set up a martyr's monument for him."

After Saint George had been taken up to the mountain and thrown off from there, the king's servants began their descent. When they had climbed down about thirty stades, there was great thunder and lightning, so that even the sky trembled. And the Lord came *upon the clouds,* and called to the saint the following words: "Come, my dear child; wake from your sleep!" And the saint rose from the dead, as if from sleep; and he ran after the servants, shouting and saying, "Wait for me!" When the servants turned round and saw Saint George, they fell upon his feet, saying to him, "Lord, beloved of God, give us the seal in Christ!" And he baptized them at that very moment, in the name of the Father and of the Son, and of the Holy Spirit. Then they went on their way together and came to the kings, and with one voice declared, "All of us are Christians, and we do not venerate your gods, those blind, deaf, and senseless things." The kings were flabbergasted, and King Dadian ordered that Aeikon should be hung with his head down, while Glykades and Lasterinos should be given to the sword. Their

παραδοθῆναι. Καὶ ἐτελειώθη αὐτῶν ἡ μαρτυρία ἐν καλῇ ὁμολογίᾳ, μηνὶ Μαρτίῳ θ΄.

16 Ὁ δὲ βασιλεύς, βουληθεὶς διὰ λόγου κολακευτικοῦ πεῖσαι τὸν ἅγιον, λέγει, "Μὰ τὸν δεσπότην Ἥλιον, καὶ τοὺς ἑβδομήκοντα ὀκτὼ θεούς, καὶ τὴν μητέρα τῶν θεῶν Ἄρτεμιν, ἀνέχομαί σου ὡς τέκνον ἴδιον. Ἄκουσόν μου ὡς πατρὶ συμβουλεύοντί σοι καλὴν συμβουλήν, καὶ θῦσον τῷ μεγάλῳ θεῷ Ἀπόλλωνι τῷ διασώζοντι τὴν οἰκουμένην." Εἶπε δὲ αὐτῷ ὁ ἅγιος, "Καὶ ποῦ ἦσαν οἱ λόγοι σου οὗτοι; Ἰδοὺ ἑξαετίαν ἔχω τιμωρούμενος ὑπὸ σοῦ, καὶ τρίτον ἐμελίσθην, καὶ πάλιν ἀνέστησέ με ὁ Χριστός· καὶ οὐδέποτε ἤκουσα τοιαῦτα ῥήματα κολακευτικὰ οἷα νῦν ἀκούω. Ἢ οὐκ ἤκουσας, βασιλεῦ, <ὅτι τὸ γένος τῶν Χριστιανῶν δυσθάνατόν ἐστιν, καὶ πρὸς πάντα τὰ ἔργα τοῦ διαβόλου ἀντερίζει; Ἄρτι δὲ προτραπεὶς σεμνῶς ὑπὸ τῆς θεότητός σου, θύσω τῷ μεγάλῳ Ἀπόλλωνι."

Περιχαρὴς δὲ γενάμενος ὁ βασιλεύς>, ἤρξατο φιλεῖν τὴν κεφαλὴν αὐτοῦ. Ἀπωσάμενος δὲ τὸν βασιλέα ὁ ἅγιος, λέγει αὐτῷ, "Μή, βασιλεῦ, οὐκ ἔστιν ἔθος τοῖς Γαλιλαίοις τοῦτο ποιεῖν· ἐὰν μὴ πρῶτον θύσω τῷ Ἀπόλλωνι καὶ τοῖς λοιποῖς θεοῖς, οὐ φιλήσεις μου τὴν κεφαλήν." Καὶ πάλιν ὁ ἅγιος, "Ἰδοὺ ἡ ἡμέρα ἤχθη πρὸς δυσμάς, κέλευσόν μοι ἀσφαλισθῆναι ἐν τῷ δεσμωτηρίῳ· καὶ γενομένης τῆς πρωΐας, θύσω τοῖς θεοῖς ἐπὶ πάντων ὑμῶν." Εἶπε δὲ ὁ βασιλεὺς πρὸς τὸν μάρτυρα, "Μὴ γένοιτο, Γεώργιε, εἰς κόλασίν σε παραδοῦναι· ἀλλὰ καὶ ἃς ἐπήνεγκά σοι πληγάς,

martyrdom in good confession of faith was completed on March 9.

The king now wanted to persuade the saint through flat- 16 tering words, and so he said to him, "By the lord Sun, and by the seventy-eight gods, and by Artemis, the mother of the gods, I accept you as my own child. Listen to me as a father giving you good advice, and sacrifice to the great god Apollo, the preserver of the world." The saint said to him, "Where were such words from you before? For six years I've been punished by you, and I've been dismembered three times, and every time Christ has raised me from the dead. I've never ever heard such flattering words as the ones I now hear. Or is it news to you that the race of the Christians does not die easily, but rather fights back against all the devil's works? But since your highness has now asked me politely, I shall sacrifice to the great Apollo."

The king became overjoyed, and started kissing George's head. The saint however pushed him away, and said, "No, don't, my king, it's not customary for Galileans to do this; until I sacrifice to Apollo and the rest of the gods, you shall not kiss my head." And then the saint added, "Look, the day has turned to dusk; order me to be shut safely in the prison and when the morning comes, I shall sacrifice to the gods in front of you all." The king said to the martyr, "God forbid, George, that I should send you to be tortured; indeed, please forgive me as your father for the abuse I

ὡς πατρὶ συγχώρησόν μοι. Νῦν δὲ εἴσελθε εἰς τὸ παλάτιον πρὸς τὴν Ἀλεξάνδραν· καὶ ἐκεῖ ἀναπαύου πρὸς αὐτὴν ἐν τῷ κλιναρίῳ."

17 Ὁ δὲ ἅγιος μὴ καταδεξάμενος ἐπὶ κλίνης ἀνατεθῆναι, ἔθηκεν ἑαυτὸν χαμαί. Καὶ περὶ ἕκτην ὥραν τῆς νυκτός, ἤρξατο ψάλλειν τὸν ψαλμὸν τοῦτον: "*Τίς Θεὸς μέγας ὡς ὁ Θεὸς ἡμῶν; Σὺ εἶ ὁ Θεὸς ἡμῶν, ὁ ποιῶν θαυμάσια μόνος*"· καὶ "*Ἵνα τί ἐφρύαξαν ἔθνη καὶ λαοὶ ἐμελέτησαν κενά; Παρέστησαν οἱ βασιλεῖς τῆς γῆς καὶ οἱ ἄρχοντες συνήχθησαν ἐπὶ τὸ αὐτό, κατὰ τοῦ κυρίου καὶ κατὰ τοῦ Χριστοῦ αὐτοῦ*" καὶ τὰ ἑξῆς. Ἐπὶ δὲ τὸ τέλος τῆς εὐχῆς εἶπε τὸ "Ἀμήν."

Καὶ λέγει αὐτῷ ἡ βασίλισσα Ἀλεξάνδρα, "Κύριέ μου, Γεώργιε, εἰπέ μοι, τίνες ἐφρύαξαν ἔθνη, καὶ οἱ λαοὶ ἐμελέτησαν κενά; Καὶ τίς ἐστιν ὁ Χριστός, δίδαξόν με· ἡδέως σου γὰρ ἀκούω." Εἶπε δὲ ὁ ἅγιος, "Ἄκουσον, βασίλισσα. Ὁ Θεὸς μέγας ἐστίν, ὃς ἐποίησε λόγῳ τὸν οὐρανὸν καὶ τὴν γῆν, καὶ τὸν ἄνθρωπον ἔπλασε, τὸ περισπούδαστον ζῷον τοῦ Θεοῦ, δι' ὃν οὐρανὸς ἐτανύσθη, καὶ ἥλιος φαίνει, καὶ σελήνη τρέχει, καὶ τὰ στοιχεῖα σχηματίζονται."

Εἶπε δὲ αὐτῷ ἡ βασίλισσα, "Καὶ πῶς λέγουσιν ὅτι ὁ θεὸς τῶν Χριστιανῶν ἄνθρωπός ἐστιν;" Λέγει ὁ ἅγιος, "Ἄκουσον, βασίλισσα, τῶν προφητῶν τῶν λεγόντων. Ὁ μὲν Δαυὶδ λέγει, '*Ὁ καθήμενος ἐπὶ τῶν χερουβὶμ ἐμφάνηθι· ἐξέγειρον τὴν δυναστείαν σου, καὶ ἐλθὲ εἰς τὸ σῶσαι ἡμᾶς.*' Καὶ Σολομὼν εἶπε, '*Πρὸ τοῦ ἡλίου διεθέμην σε, καὶ πρὸ πάντων βουνῶν ἐγέννησά σε.*' Τὸ αὐτὸ δὲ πρὶν καὶ Μωϋσῆς ἔλεγεν, '*Καταβήσεται ὡς ὑετὸς ἐπὶ πόκον.*' Καὶ πάλιν

already brought upon you. Instead, go into the palace now, to Alexandra, and sleep on the little bed near her."

The saint refused to lie on a bed, and lay down on the ground. Around the sixth hour of the night, he began chanting the following psalm: "*Who is as great as our God? You are our God, the only one who works wonders,*" and "*Why did nations grow insolent, and peoples contemplate vain things? The kings of the earth stood side by side, and the rulers gathered together, against the Lord and against his anointed,*" and so on. And at the end of his prayer, he said "Amen." 17

And the queen, Alexandra, said to him, "My lord, George, tell me which nations grew insolent, and peoples contemplated vain things? Teach me who is this Anointed one, for I'm listening to you with pleasure." The saint said, "Listen, my queen. That God is great, who created heaven and earth by his word, and fashioned humans, God's most admirable living creature, for whom heaven has been stretched out, and the sun shines, and the moon runs its course, and the elements take their shape."

The queen said to him, "How is it then that they say the god of the Christians is human?" The saint said, "Hear, my queen, the words of the prophets. David says, '*You who sit upon the cherubim, reveal yourself; stir up your strength, and come to save us.*' And Solomon said, 'Before the sun I brought you forth, and *before all mountains* I gave birth to you.' Moses too had said the same thing before that: '*He shall come down like rain upon the mown grass.*' And again Habbakuk

Ἀββακοὺμ εἶπεν, ʻΚύριε, εἰσακήκοα τὴν ἀκοήν σου καὶ ἐφο-
βήθην· κατενόησα τὰ ἔργα σου καὶ ἐξέστην.ʼ"

Λέγει αὐτῷ ἡ βασίλισσα, "Τί ἤκουσαν οἱ προφῆται, καὶ
ἐφοβήθησαν; Ἢ τί κατενόησαν καὶ ἐξέστησαν;" Λέγει
αὐτῇ ὁ ἅγιος, "Ἄκουσον, βασίλισσα. Ὁ προφήτης καλῶς
εἶπεν· ἤκουσε γὰρ ὅτι ὁ Δεσπότης ἔρχεται, καὶ ἐφοβήθη·
κατενόησε δὲ ὅτι μετὰ τῶν ἀνθρώπων συναναστραφήσε-
ται, καὶ ἐξέστην."

Καὶ λέγει αὐτῷ ἡ βασίλισσα. "Ἀληθῶς καλῶς λέγεις·
πάντα ἡδέως σου ἀκούω. Ἀλλ᾽ εὖξαι ὑπὲρ ἐμοῦ, ἵνα φύγῃ
ἀπ᾽ ἐμοῦ ἡ τῶν εἰδώλων πλάνη." Εἶπε δὲ αὐτῇ ὁ ἅγιος,
"Πίστευσον εἰς τὸν Ἰησοῦν τὸν ἐσταυρωμένον, καὶ οὐ μή
σου κυριεύσει κνῆσις δαιμόνων." Εἶπε δὲ αὐτῷ ἡ βασίλισσα, "Πιστεύω, κύριέ μου." Εἴασε δὲ αὐτὴν ὁ ἅγιος, καὶ
οὐκέτι ἐλάλει πρὸς αὐτήν. Κλίνας δὲ τὰ γόνατα πρὸς τὸν
ἑαυτοῦ εὐεργέτην, διετέλει ἕως ὄρθρου.

18   Πρωΐας δὲ γενομένης, κελεύει ἄγεσθαι αὐτὸν ἐν τῷ
ναῷ πρὸς τὸν βασιλέα. <Ὁ δὲ ἅγιος εἶπεν,> "Ἐπὶ ἑνὸς βασιλέως πρόοδος γίνεται πολλή· ἐπὶ δὲ τοσούτων βασιλέων,
πλείονα γίνεται ὡς νομίζω ἐγώ. Ἄκουσον οὖν, βασιλεῦ.
Εἰσέλθατε ὑμεῖς ἐν τῷ παλατίῳ· ἐγὼ δὲ καὶ οἱ ἱερεῖς καὶ οἱ
στρατιῶται τοῦ ἱεροῦ πορευθῶμεν εἰς τὸν ναόν, καὶ θύσω
αὐτῷ." Καὶ οἱ κήρυκες ἐβόων ἐν ἰσχύι, "Πάντες δράμετε!
Ἰδοὺ ὁ μύστης τῶν Γαλιλαίων προσέρχεται πρὸς τὸν
Ἀπόλλωνα θῦσαι."

Ἤκουσε δὲ ἡ γυνὴ τοῦ βασιλέως καὶ ἐλυπήθη. Ἤκουσε
δὲ καὶ ἡ γυνὴ ἧς ὁ υἱὸς ἀνέβλεψεν τῆς φωνῆς τοῦ κήρυκος
ἐπιβοῶντος· καὶ εὐθέως ἄρασα τὸν υἱὸν αὐτῆς ἐπὶ τῶν

said, '*Lord, I have heard of your renown and feared; I considered your works and was astonished.*'"

The queen said to him, "What did the prophets hear and feared? Or what is it that they considered and were astonished?" The saint said to her, "Listen, my queen. The prophet spoke well; for he heard that the Lord was coming, and he became fearful; and he considered that he was going to live among humans, and he was astonished."

And the queen said to him, "Indeed, you speak well; I hear everything you say with pleasure. But please pray on my behalf, that the error of the idols may leave me." The saint said to her, "Believe in Jesus who was crucified, and the temptations of the demons will not overpower you." The queen said to him, "I believe, my lord." The saint left her, and said nothing more to her. Then he knelt before his benefactor and continued until dawn.

When morning came, she ordered him to be led into the 18 temple to the king. And the saint said, "For one king, a great entrance is performed; but for so many kings, I think it should be greater. So listen, my king. All of you go into the palace; and I, together with the priests and the soldiers of the sanctuary, shall walk into the temple, and I shall sacrifice to him." And the heralds shouted in a strong voice, "Everyone, come quickly! See, the initiate of the Galileans is about to sacrifice to Apollo."

The wife of the king heard this and was saddened. And the woman whose son had regained his eyesight also heard the voice of the herald who was calling out; and, immediately, she raised her son in her arms, and began to shout

ἀγκαλῶν, ἐβόα εἰς τὸν ὄχλον: "Ὦ Γεώργιε, ὁ τοὺς νεκροὺς
ἐγείρας, καὶ τυφλοὺς ποιήσας περιβλέπειν, ὁ τοὺς χωλοὺς
ποιήσας περιπατεῖν, καὶ τὰ σεσηπωμένα ξύλα τοῦ οἴκου
μου ῥιζώσας καὶ δένδρα ποιήσας, καὶ τὴν τράπεζάν μου
γεμίσας ἀγαθῶν, ὁ μυρίων ἀγαθῶν κατορθωμάτων ἐπιδει-
ξάμενος κατὰ τοῦ διαβόλου, ἄρτι προσέρχῃ τῷ Ἀπόλλωνι,
καὶ ὄνειδος καταλίπῃς τοῖς μέλλουσιν; Οὐαὶ τῷ διαβόλῳ
καὶ τοῖς σὺν αὐτῷ!" Μειδιάσας δὲ ὁ ἅγιος, εἶπε πρὸς τὸ
γύναιον, "Ἀπόθου τὸ παιδίον σου ἀπὸ τῶν ἀγκαλῶν σου."
Ἐφώνησε δὲ ὁ Ἅγιος Γεώργιος, "Σοὶ λέγω, παιδίον, ἐν τῷ
ὀνόματι Ἰησοῦ Χριστοῦ, τοῦ φωτίσαντός σε ἀπὸ τοῦ σκότους εἰς φῶς, στῆθι ἐπὶ τοὺς πόδας σου, ἵνα μοι διακο-
νήσῃς λόγον." Καὶ αὐτῇ τῇ ὥρᾳ ἐξαλλόμενον τὸ παιδίον,
ἔδραμε καὶ εἰσῆλθε πρὸς τὸν μάρτυρα, καὶ κατεφίλει τὰ
ἴχνη τῶν ποδῶν αὐτοῦ.

Εἶπε δὲ ὁ ἅγιος πρὸς αὐτό, "Σοὶ λέγω, παιδίον· εἴσελθε
εἰς τὸν ναὸν τῶν εἰδώλων, καὶ εἰπὲ τῷ ἀγάλματι τοῦ Ἀπόλλωνος, ''Έξελθε ταχέως· καλεῖ σε ὁ δοῦλος τοῦ Θεοῦ Γεώργιος.'" <Τὸ δὲ παιδίον κωφὸν ὄντα καὶ παραλυτικόν,
αὐτῇ τῇ ὥρᾳ ἤκουσεν καὶ ἔστη εἰς τοὺς πόδας αὐτοῦ. Καὶ
ἀπελθὸν ἐν τῷ ναῷ τῶν Ἑλλήνων εἶπεν τῷ ἀγάλματι τοῦ
Ἀπόλλωνος, "Σοὶ λέγω, κωφὲ καὶ ἀναίσθητε· ἔξελθε ταχέως, καλεῖ σε ὁ παῖς τοῦ Θεοῦ Γεώργιος."> Τὸ δὲ παραμένον πνεῦμα τῷ ἀγάλματι, ἐβόησε λέγον, "Ὦ Ἰησοῦ Να-
ζαρηνέ, πάντας εἵλκυσας· κατ' ἐμοῦ πάλιν τοὺς παῖδάς σου
ὁπλίζεις; Πόθεν αὐτὸν ἀνέστησας κατ' ἐμοῦ, οὐκ οἶδα."

Ἐξῆλθε τὸ πνεῦμα τοῦ Ἀπόλλωνος, καὶ ἦλθε πρὸς τοὺς
πόδας Γεωργίου. Καὶ λέγει αὐτῷ ὁ ἅγιος, "Σὺ εἶ ὁ θεὸς

toward the crowd: "George, who raised the dead, and made the blind see, and the lame walk; who made the rotten wood of my house grow roots and turned it into trees, and filled my table with good things, you who performed a myriad of noble feats against the devil, do you intend now to turn to Apollo, and leave a legacy of disgrace for the future? Woe to the devil and those with him!" But the saint smiled, and said to the woman, "Let your child down from your arms." Then Saint George shouted, "I am talking to you, child, in the name of Jesus Christ, the one who gave light to you and brought you from darkness into light, stand on your feet, so that you may carry out my commands." And at that very moment the child leaped down and came running to the martyr, and began kissing his footsteps.

The saint said to him, "I am speaking to you, child; go into the temple of the idols, and say to the statue of Apollo, 'Come out of there quickly! George, the servant of God, summons you.'" The child, who was deaf and paralyzed, at the very moment he heard these words, stood up on his feet. And he went into the temple of the Hellenes and said to the statue of Apollo, "I'm talking to you, you deaf, senseless thing! Come out of there quickly! George, the servant of God, summons you." And the spirit that dwelled in the statue shouted out the following words: "O Jesus Nazarene, you have drawn everyone to your side; do you now again arm your children against me? I have no idea from where you raised this one against me."

The spirit of Apollo came out, and came to George's feet. And the saint said to it, "Are you the god of the Hellenes?"

τῶν Ἑλλήνων;" Τὸ δὲ παραγενόμενον πνεῦμα τῷ ἀγάλματι εἶπεν, "Ἄνες μοι, Γεώργιε, ἄνες μοι, καὶ διηγήσομαί
σοι, τίς εἰμι ἐγώ. Ὅτε ὁ Θεὸς ἐποίησε τὸν οὐρανὸν καὶ τὴν
γῆν ἐθεμελίωσε, καὶ ἐποίησε παράδεισον ἐν Ἐδὲμ κατὰ ἀνατολάς, τότε ἤμην ἀρχάγγελος αὐτοῦ πρῶτος τῶν ἀγγέλων.
Ὠργίσθη δέ μοι ὁ Θεὸς καὶ ἐξώρισέ με ἐκ τῆς δόξης μου·
καὶ κατηνέχθην ὡς ἀετὸς ἐπὶ πέτραν. Καὶ νῦν κάθημαι εἰς
τὰ ξόανα ταῦτα. Καὶ ὅσους ἐὰν δυνηθῶ πλανῆσαι, τοῦτο
εἰς κέρδος ἡγοῦμαι. Ἀναβαίνω δὲ ἕως τρίτου οὐρανοῦ, καὶ
ἀκροῶμαι τὴν ἀπόφασιν τὴν ἐκβαίνουσαν κατὰ τῶν ἀν-
θρώπων· καὶ προσλαμβάνω καὶ συνέχω πυρετοὺς κατ' αὐ-
τῶν· ἄλλους δὲ ἐν ποταμοῖς πνιγμῷ αὐτοῖς ποιῶ. Ὑπάγω
δὲ ἐν τῇ ἐκκλησίᾳ τοῦ Θεοῦ, καὶ παραστήκω εἰς τὰς εὐχὰς
τοῦ λαοῦ, καὶ ἀκροῶμαι· καὶ ὅτε ὁ ἱερεὺς ἀφορίζει τινὰς ἐξ
αὐτῶν, ἐκπέμπω τὰς χεῖράς μου, καὶ λαμβάνω αὐτοὺς πρὸς
ἐμαυτόν, καὶ ἐὰν χρονίσῃ ὁ ἱερεὺς τοῦ δέξασθαι αὐτούς,
τρέπομαι αὐτοὺς εἰς ἄλλας ἀθλήσεις."

Εἶπε δὲ αὐτῷ ὁ ἅγιος, "Ταλαίπωρε, ἑαυτὸν ἐξώρισας τῇ
προαιρέσει· ἵνα τί καὶ τὰς ψυχὰς τῶν Χριστιανῶν θέλεις
ἀποσπᾶν;" Τὸ δὲ παραμένον πνεῦμα εἶπε, "Μὰ τὰ ἑπτὰ
στερεώματα τοῦ οὐρανοῦ, καὶ τὰς ἀκτῖνας τοῦ ἡλίου, καὶ
τὸ κέρας τῆς σελήνης, εἰ εἶχον ἐξουσίαν, διὰ πολλοῦ ἀπώλεσα τὴν ψυχήν σου." Εἶπε δὲ αὐτῷ ὁ ἅγιος, "Ταλαίπωρε,
καὶ ἐπ' ἐμὲ ἀσχολεῖς; Ἔκδεξαι, καὶ ὄψῃ τάχει τὴν τιμωρίαν
σου." Καὶ ποιήσας τὴν ἐν Χριστῷ σφραγῖδα ὁ ἅγιος,
ἐλάκτισεν εἰς τὴν γῆν· καὶ ἤνοιξεν ἡ γῆ τὸ στόμα αὐτῆς·
καὶ λέγει πρὸς τὸν Ἀπόλλωνα ὁ ἅγιος, "Κάτελθε εἰς τὰ

And the spirit that had resided in the statue replied, "Leave me alone, George, leave me alone, and I will tell you who I am. At the time when God created heaven, and laid the foundations of the earth, and created *paradise in Eden toward the east,* I was his archangel, first among the angels. But God became angry with me, and expelled me from my glory; and I tumbled down like an eagle to a rock. Now I live in these carved images. And as many people as I am able to lead astray, I consider to be my gain. And I go up *to the third heaven,* and I eavesdrop on the decision being made about people; and I take hold of them, and afflict them with fevers, and I make others drown in rivers. I also go to the church of God, and stand by while the congregation is praying, and I eavesdrop; and when the priest excommunicates some of them, I stretch out my hands, and take them for my own, and if the priest delays their reacceptance, I turn them toward other temptations."

The saint said to him, "Wretched creature, you expelled yourself by your own free choice; why do you also want to drag away the souls of Christians?" The resident spirit responded, "By the seven firmaments of heaven, and the rays of the sun, and the horn of the moon, if I had the power, I would have destroyed your soul a long time ago." The saint said to him, "Wretched creature, you want to cause trouble for me as well? Just wait; you'll soon face your punishment." The saint then made the sign of Christ's cross, and kicked the ground; and the earth opened up its mouth; and the saint said to Apollo, "Go down into the underworld of the

καταχθόνια τῆς ἀβύσσου, ἕως τῆς μεγάλης ἡμέρας, ἧς δώ-
σεις λόγον περὶ τῶν ψυχῶν ὦν ἀπώλεσας."

19   Καὶ λύσας τὴν ἑαυτοῦ ζώνην, καὶ ποιήσας τὴν ἐν Χριστῷ
σφραγῖδα, εἰσῆλθε εἰς τὸν ναὸν τῶν εἰδώλων, καὶ ἐπέθη-
κεν αὐτὴν τῷ ἀγάλματι τοῦ Ἡρακλέος, καὶ κατέαξεν αὐτὸ
ἐπὶ τὴν γῆν. Εἶπε δὲ πρὸς τοὺς λοιποὺς θεούς, "Φύγετε ἀπ'
ἐμοῦ οἱ θεοὶ τῶν Ἑλλήνων· ἐγὼ γὰρ ἐν θυμῷ καὶ ὀργῇ
ἦλθον τοῦ ἀπολέσαι ὑμᾶς." Εἰπόντος δὲ αὐτοῦ ταῦτα, ἐγένετο σεισμὸς μέγας ἐν τῷ ναῷ· καὶ τρομάξαντες οἱ θεοὶ
κατέπεσαν, καὶ ἄλωσις ἐγένετο εἰς αὐτούς. Ἰδόντες δὲ οἱ
ἱερεῖς τὴν ἀπώλειαν τῶν θεῶν αὐτῶν, ἐπιλαβόμενοι τὸν
ἅγιον, ἔδησαν αὐτόν, καὶ ἤγαγον πρὸς τοὺς βασιλεῖς, καὶ
διηγήσαντο τὰ συμβεβηκότα αὐτῶν καὶ τοῖς θεοῖς αὐτῶν,
ἐξαιρέτως δὲ τὸν μέγιστον θεὸν αὐτῶν τὸν Ἀπόλλωνα.

Καὶ λέγει ὁ βασιλεὺς πρὸς τὸν ἅγιον, "Κακὴ κεφαλή,
οὐ συνέθου μοι θύειν τοῖς θεοῖς; Καὶ ἀντὶ τοῦ θῦσαι αὐτοῖς,
τοιαῦτα κατ' αὐτῶν ἐτόλμησας; Ἢ οὐκ οἶδας ὅτι τὸ αἷμά
σου ὑπὸ τὴν κραταιά<ν> μου χεῖρά ἐστιν;" Εἶπε δὲ ὁ Ἅγιος
Γεώργιος, "Ἐμοὶ τοὺς λαχόντας θεοὺς ἔθυσα. Ἐὰν δὲ μὴ
πιστεύῃς, βασιλεῦ, ὕπαγε καὶ ἄγαγέ μοι τὸν Ἀπόλλωνα,
καὶ ἐνώπιόν σου θύσω αὐτῷ." Εἶπε δὲ αὐτῷ ὁ βασιλεύς,
"Ὡς ἔμαθα παρὰ τῶν ἱερέων ὅτι εἰς τὰς λαγόνας τῆς γῆς
κατέβαλες αὐτόν, κἀκεῖ με πέμπεις ζῶντα;" Εἶπε δὲ ὁ
ἅγιος, "Ταλαίπωρε, εἰ ἑαυτῷ οὐ δύναται βοηθῆσαι, σὲ πῶς
δυνήσεται βοηθῆσαι; Ὅταν δὲ ἔλθῃ ὁ Κύριος Ἰησοῦς
Χριστὸς τῇ ἡμέρᾳ ἐκείνῃ, ἀλλάξαι τὸν οὐρανὸν καὶ τὴν
γῆν, τί ποιήσεις τότε;"

Θυμωθεὶς δὲ ὁ βασιλεύς, διέρρηξε τὴν ἑαυτοῦ ἐσθῆτα·

abyss, until that great day when you shall have to account for the souls you have destroyed."

George then untied his belt, made the sign of Christ's 19 cross, entered the temple of the idols, placed his belt on the statue of Herakles, and smashed it on the ground. He said to the rest of the gods, "Go away from me, gods of the Hellenes; for I have come, in anger and wrath, to destroy you." When he said these words, *there was a great earthquake* in the temple; the gods were terrified, fell to the ground, and were obliterated. When the priests saw the destruction of their gods, they seized the saint, tied him up, led him to the kings, and recounted to them everything that happened to them and their gods, and especially to their greatest god, Apollo.

The king said to the saint, "Wicked man, did you not agree with me to sacrifice to the gods? And instead of sacrificing to them you have dared to do such things against them? Don't you know that your blood is in my powerful hands?" Saint George said to him, "I sacrificed the gods that were allotted to me. If you don't believe me, my king, go and bring Apollo to me, and I shall sacrifice to him in front of you." The king replied, "As I have learned from the priests that you consigned him to the bowels of the earth, are you also now sending me there while I'm still alive?" The saint said to him, "Wretched man, if Apollo cannot help himself, how will he be able to help you? When the Lord Jesus Christ arrives on that day to transform the heaven and the earth, what will you do then?"

The king became angry and tore his garment apart; and

καὶ εἰσεπήδησεν εἰς τὸ ἐσώτερον παλάτιον, ὅπου ἦν ἡ Ἀλεξάνδρα· καὶ λέγει αὐτῇ, "Οὐαί μοι, βασίλισσα, ἐξεκάκησα πρὸς τὸ γένος τῶν Γαλιλαίων, ἐξαιρέτως μετὰ τοῦ λυμεῶνος τούτου." Εἶπε δὲ ἡ βασίλισσα, "Οὐκ ἔλεγόν σοι, λυμεὼν καὶ σαρκοφάγε; Ἀπόστα ἀπὸ τὸ γένος τῶν Χριστιανῶν· μέγας γάρ ἐστιν ὁ Θεὸς αὐτῶν, ὅστις καθελεῖ σου τὴν ἀλαζονείαν ταύτην." Εἶπε δὲ ὁ βασιλεύς, "Οὐαί μοι, Βασίλισσα Ἀλεξάνδρα, τί σοι γέγονε τοῦτο; Τάχα καὶ σὲ κατέλαβον αἱ μαγεῖαι τῶν Χριστιανῶν;" Ἡ δὲ βασίλισσα εἶπεν αὐτῷ, "Ἐμὲ μαγεῖαι οὐ κατέλαβον, ἀλλ' ἡ δόξα εἰς τοὺς αἰῶνας, ἀμήν· ἐπὶ δὲ τῆς ἐνθυμήσεώς μου, ἑτοίμως ἔχω τοῖς παναγίοις αὐτοῦ οἰκτιρμοῖς."

Ἀκούσας δὲ ὁ βασιλεὺς τὸ ἀμετάθετον τῆς ὁμολογίας αὐτῆς, κρατήσας αὐτὴν ἤγαγε καὶ ἤκουσε πάντα τὰ συμβεβηκότα αὐτῇ. Τότε κελεύουσιν αὐτὴν οἱ βασιλεῖς, Μαγνέντιος, καὶ Θεόγνιος, καὶ Στραγκυλῖνος, ἀπὸ τῶν μασθῶν κρεμασθῆναι καὶ σπαθίζεσθαι. Σπαθιζομένης δὲ αὐτῆς, οὔτε φωνὴ ἐξήρχετο ἐξ αὐτῆς, εἰ μὴ μόνον εἰς τὸν οὐρανὸν ἀτενίσασα, εἶπε πρὸς τὸν μάρτυρα, "Ἅγιε τοῦ Θεοῦ Γεώργιε, ἐπικάλεσαι τὸν Θεόν σου, ἵνα βοηθήσῃ μοι, ὅτι κάμνει μου ὁ λογισμός." Ὁ δὲ μάρτυς τοῦ Χριστοῦ λέγει αὐτῇ, "Ὑπόμεινον μικρὸν χαίρουσα, καὶ ὄψῃ τὴν δόξαν τοῦ Θεοῦ."

Ἐκέλευσεν δὲ ὁ βασιλεύς, κατενεχθῆναι αὐτήν, καὶ γενέσθαι σοῦβλαν σιδηρᾶν ὡς πηχῶν δύο, καὶ πυρωθῆναι αὐτήν, καὶ οὕτως διαπαρῆναι τὴν σοῦβλαν εἰς τοὺς λαγόνας αὐτῆς· καὶ κελεύει μαχαίρᾳ κοπῆναι τοὺς μασθοὺς αὐτῆς. Μὴ φερούσης δὲ <τὰς ἀλγηδόνας, λέγει τῷ

he ran into the inner palace where Alexandra was; and he said to her, "Alas, my queen, I'm sick and tired of the race of the Galileans, especially of this destructive man." The queen responded, "Did I not tell you, you destructive and flesh-eating man, to stay away from the race of the Christians? Their God is great; it is he who will put an end to this arrogance of yours." The king said, "Alas, Queen Alexandra, what's happened to you? Has the Christians' magic perhaps taken hold of you too?" The queen said to him, "It is not magic that has taken hold of me, but eternal glory, amen; his all-holy mercies are constantly on my mind."

When the king heard how unwavering her confession of faith was, he grabbed her, led her away, and heard everything that had happened to her. Then the kings Magnentios, Theognios, and Strangulinos ordered that she should be hung by her breasts and beaten with a sword. While she was being beaten in this way, she uttered no sound, but only raised her eyes toward the heavens, and said to the martyr, "Saint of God, George, please ask your God to come and help me, because my mind is growing weary." The martyr of Christ said to her, "Be patient and remain joyful for a little longer, and you shall see the glory of God."

The king ordered that she should be brought down, and that they should make an iron stake, about two cubits long, heat it, and then drive the stake through her flanks; he also ordered that her breasts should be cut off with a knife. As she could not bear the pain, she said to the martyr,

μάρτυρι>, "Ὦ μάρτυς τοῦ Χριστοῦ, τί ποιήσω, ὅτι οὐκ
εἴληφα τὸ ἅγιον βάπτισμα; Πῶς ἀνοίξει μοι τὰς θύρας τῆς
ἀληθείας καὶ τῆς μετανοίας;" Ὁ δὲ μάρτυς τοῦ Χριστοῦ
λέγει αὐτῇ, "Ὁ τύπος τοῦ σταυροῦ, ὅς ἐστιν Ἰησοῦς Χριστός, ἐσφράγισέ σε διὰ τῆς πίστεώς σου. Δέξαι δὲ καὶ τὸ
βάπτισμα διὰ τοῦ αἵματός σου τῆς διὰ ξίφους τελειώσεως·
καὶ προσδέξεταί σε εἰς τὴν αὐτοῦ βασιλείαν."

Καὶ ἐκέλευσαν οἱ βασιλεῖς δοθῆναι αὐτῇ τὴν ἀπόφασιν
τοῦ ξίφους. Ἡ δὲ λαβοῦσα τὴν ἀπόφασιν, λέγει πρὸς τοὺς
κρατοῦντας αὐτήν, "Ἐκδέξασθέ μοι μικρόν, ἵνα ἀποβλέψω
πρὸς τὰ ὑπερῷα τοῦ παλατίου." Ἐάσαντες δὲ αὐτήν, ἀτενίσασα εἰς τὸν οὐρανόν, εἶπεν, "Κύριε Ἰησοῦ Χριστέ, ἰδοὺ
τὸ παλάτιόν μου διὰ σὲ ἀνεῳγμένον ἀφιεῖσα, οὐκ ἔκλεισα
αὐτό. Σὺ δέ, Κύριέ μου, μὴ κλείσῃς ἔμπροσθέν μου τὰς
θύρας τοῦ Παραδείσου, ἀλλὰ ἄνοιξόν μοι αὐτάς, ἵνα πο-
ρευθῶ κἀγώ, ἐν τῇ μονῇ τῶν ἁγίων σου, καὶ σὺν αὐτοῖς
δοξάσω σε εἰς τοὺς αἰῶνας, ἀμήν." Καὶ ταῦτα εἰπούσης
αὐτῆς, ἐκρούσθη ὑπὸ τοῦ ξίφους, μηνὶ Ἀπριλίῳ πεντεκαι-
δεκάτῃ. Ἐτελειώθη δὲ ἡ μαρτυρία αὐτῆς ἐν καλῇ ὁμολο-
γίᾳ· καὶ ἀπηνέχθη ἐν τῷ Παραδείσῳ ὑπὸ τῶν ἁγίων ἀγγέ-
λων· καὶ πρεσβεύει ὑπὲρ πάντων ἁμαρτωλῶν.

20   Μετεκαλέσατο δὲ ὁ βασιλεὺς τὸν ἅγιον, καὶ λέγει αὐτῷ,
"Γεώργιε, διὰ τὰς μαγείας σου ἀπώλεσας καὶ τὴν Βασίλισ-
σαν Ἀλεξάνδραν, καὶ ἄλλους πολλοὺς πλανήσας, τῷ θανάτῳ παρέδωκας· καὶ λοιπὸν δὲ καὶ περὶ ἡμῶν ἀσχολεῖσαι."
Ἀποκριθεὶς δὲ καὶ ὁ Βασιλεὺς Μαγνέντιος, λέγει, "Δέομαι
οὖν κατ' αὐτοῦ τὴν ἀπόφασιν, ἐπεὶ οὐ παύσηται ἐνυβρίζων
τοὺς θεούς, καὶ πᾶσιν ἀνθρώποις προξενεῖ θάνατον."

"O martyr of Christ, what am I to do, since I have not yet received holy baptism? How will he open the gates of truth and repentance for me?" The martyr of Christ said to her, "The sign of the cross, which stands for Jesus Christ, has baptized you through your faith. Now also receive the baptism through your blood and death by the sword; and he will accept you into his kingdom."

And the kings ordered that she be sentenced to the sword. She heard their sentence, and said to her captors, "Wait for me a little bit, so that I may turn my gaze to the upper floors of the palace." They let her, and she looked up to heaven and said, "Lord Jesus Christ, see, I have left my palace open for you, and I did not shut it. You in turn, my Lord, do not close the gates of Paradise before me, but open them to me, so that I too can walk into the dwellings of your saints, and glorify you together with them forever, amen." When she said these words, she was struck by the sword, on April the fifteenth. She completed her martyrdom in good confession of faith, and was led into Paradise by the holy angels, and now she intercedes on behalf of all the sinners.

The king then summoned the saint, and said to him, 20 "George, with your magic, you have even led Queen Alexandra to perdition, and you have deceived many more people, causing their death; and now you make trouble for us too." In response, King Magnentios also spoke: "So I ask for sentence to be passed on him since he will not stop insulting the gods, and he continues to bring death to everyone."

Ἤρεσε δὲ ὁ λόγος οὗτος τῷ Βασιλεῖ Δαδιανῷ· καὶ καθίσας ἔγραψε, ἀποφηνάμενος οὕτως κατ᾽ αὐτοῦ· "Γεώργιον,
τὸν μύστην τῶν Γαλιλαίων, ἀθετήσαντα τῷ δόγματί μου,
καὶ μὴ προσκυνήσαντα τοῖς ἀηττήτοις θεοῖς, ἀλλὰ τῇ
βασιλικῇ ἀντηλλαξάμενον φωνῇ, κελεύει τὸ ἡμέτερον
κράτος τοῦ παραδιδόσθαι ξίφει." Ὁ δὲ μέγας μάρτυς τοῦ
Χριστοῦ Γεώργιος, λαβὼν τὴν ἀπόφασιν, ἔσπευδε χαίρων
ὁμοῦ τε καὶ ψάλλων, "Ὡς ἐμεγαλύνθη τὰ ἔργα σου, Κύριε·
πάντα ἐν σοφίᾳ ἐποίησας."

Ἡ δὲ μήτηρ αὐτοῦ ἀκούσασα ὅτι ἔλαβε τὴν ἀπόφασιν,
ἀτενίσασα εἰς τὸν οὐρανόν, ηὔξατο οὕτως λέγουσα, "Ὁ
Θεὸς ὁ προσδεξάμενος Ἀβραὰμ τὴν θυσίαν εἰς ὁλοκάρπω-
σιν τοῦ υἱοῦ αὐτοῦ Ἰσαάκ, προσδέξεταί σε εἰς τὴν βασιλείαν αὐτοῦ τὴν ἐπουράνιον." Καὶ ταῦτα αὐτῆς εὐξαμένης,
εἶπε πρὸς τὸν υἱὸν αὐτῆς, "Μακάρια τὰ ἔργα σου, τέκνον,
ὅτι ἠκολούθησας τοῖς διδάγμασι τοῦ Κυρίου Ἰησοῦ Χρι-
στοῦ· προσδέξεταί σε ὡς Ἄβελ τὰ δῶρα· ἠγάπησέ σε ὡς
Ἐνὼχ τὸν οἰκεῖον αὐτοῦ. Ἀλλ᾽ εὖξαι ὑπὲρ ἐμοῦ, τέκνον·
πρώτη γάρ σου τελειοῦμαι."

Ὁ δὲ βασιλεὺς θεασάμενος αὐτήν, προσκαλεσάμενος
αὐτὴν λέγει, "Εἰπέ μοι, γύναι, τί καλεῖται τὸ ὄνομά σου;"
Ἡ δὲ λέγει αὐτῷ, "Πολυχρονία καλοῦμαι· Χριστιανὴ δὲ
εἶμαι, καθάπερ καὶ ὁ υἱός μου Γεώργιος, ὃν ἐτιμώρησας,
στεφανοῦται δὲ παρὰ τοῦ βασιλέως Χριστοῦ." Λέγει αὐτῇ
ὁ βασιλεύς, "Σὺ ἐδίδαξας αὐτὸν ἐνυβρίζειν τοὺς θεούς;" Ἡ
δὲ λέγει αὐτῷ, "Ἐγὼ ἐδίδαξα αὐτόν, Θεὸν ἀληθινὸν σέ-
βειν." Ὁ δὲ βασιλεὺς λέγει αὐτῇ, "Πολυχρονία, παῦσαι
τῆς φλυαρίας σου ταύτης· ὁ γὰρ ἀπονενοημένος σου υἱὸς

These words pleased King Dadian, and he sat down and wrote, pronouncing the following verdict against George: "Our majesty commands that George, the initiate of the Galileans, who renounced my decree, and did not venerate the invincible gods, but objected to the imperial order, should be given over to the sword." George, the great martyr of Christ, when he received the sentence, rushed toward them, rejoicing as well as singing: "*How great are your works, Lord! In wisdom you have created them all.*"

When his mother heard that he had received the sentence, she gazed toward heaven and began to pray with the following words: "God, who accepted Abraham's sacrifice for offering his own son Isaac, will accept you into his heavenly kingdom." After she had prayed in this way, she said to her son, "Blessed are your works, child, because you have followed the teachings of our Lord Jesus Christ; he will thus accept you as he accepted Abel's gifts, and he has loved you, as he loved Enoch, his servant. But pray for me, child; as I shall die before you."

When the king saw her, he summoned her; and he said, "Tell me, woman, what is your name?" She said to him, "I'm called Polychronia, and I am a Christian, just like my own son George, whom you have punished, but who will be crowned by Christ the king." The king said to her, "So it's you who taught him to insult the gods?" She said to him, "I taught him to venerate the true God." The king said to her, "Polychronia, stop this nonsense of yours; for this crazy son

οὗτος ἀντιλέγων, ἔλαβε τὴν ἀπόφασιν τοῦ ἀναιρεθῆναι ὑπὸ τοῦ ξίφους." Πολυχρονία δὲ εἶπεν αὐτῷ, "Ἐγὼ (ὡς ἔφην) Χριστιανή εἰμι, καὶ δαίμοσιν οὐ θύω, ἀλλὰ τὸ σῶμά μου θυσίαν προσφέρω τῷ Θεῷ."

Τότε ὁ βασιλεὺς θυμοῦ μεγάλου πλησθείς, ἐκέλευσε τανυθῆναι αὐτὴν ἐπὶ τοῦ ἐδάφους, καὶ τύπτεσθαι αὐτὴν βουνεύροις ἀφειδῶς. Πάλιν δὲ κελεύει αὐτὴν κρεμασθῆναι ἐπὶ τοῦ ξύλου, καὶ ξέεσθαι τὰς πλευρὰς αὐτῆς, καὶ λαμπάδας προσάπτεσθαι αὐτήν, καὶ ὑποδήματα σιδηρᾶ πεπυρωμένα ὑποδεθῆναι τοὺς πόδας αὐτῆς. Ἡ δὲ μάρτυς τοῦ Χριστοῦ κάμνουσα ἐν ταῖς βασάνοις, ἐπεκαλέσατο τὸν δεσπότην Χριστόν, καὶ ἀπέδωκε τὸ πνεῦμα αὐτῆς τῷ Κυρίῳ. Καὶ λαβόντες ἄνδρες Χριστιανοὶ τὸ σῶμα αὐτῆς, λάθρα τῶν Ἑλλήνων ἔθαψαν.

Ὁ δὲ μάρτυς τοῦ Χριστοῦ Γεώργιος ἀπελθών, λέγει πρὸς τοὺς κρατοῦντας αὐτόν, "Δέομαι οὖν ὑμῶν, ἐκδέξασθέ με μικρόν· ἰδοὺ γὰρ ἑπτὰ ἔτη ἔχω τιμωρούμενος διὰ τὸ ὄνομα τοῦ Κυρίου Θεοῦ. Μείνατε μικρόν, ἵνα εὐχὰς καταλείψω ταῖς μελλούσαις γενεαῖς· θεωρῶ γὰρ τὸ πλῆθος τοῦτο, μήποτε οὐκ ἀρκέσει τὸ σῶμά μου." Βλέψας δὲ ὁ ἅγιος εἰς τὸ ὑψηλότατον κύτος τοῦ οὐρανοῦ εἶπεν, "Κύριε ὁ Θεός, ὁ τῇ ἀνεξικάκῳ σου καὶ φιλανθρώπῳ θεότητι παριδὼν πάντα τὰ ἁμαρτήματά μου, καὶ σεμνῶς τὸν βίον μου οἰκονομήσας, χάρισαί μοι ὑπομονὴν τῇ σῇ θεότητι· καὶ καταίσχυνον τοὺς ἀντικειμένους τῇ ἀληθείᾳ· καὶ φαίδρυνον ἐν ἐμοὶ τὸ ὄνομά σου, καὶ τοῦ μονογενοῦς σου υἱοῦ· καὶ καταίσχυνον Δαδιανὸν καὶ τὴν ἀλαζονείαν αὐτοῦ.

of yours, has been sentenced to be executed by the sword for contradicting me." Polychronia said to him, "I am Christian, as I told you, and I do not sacrifice to demons; rather, I offer my body as a sacrifice to God."

Then the king was filled with immense anger, and he ordered that she should be stretched out on the ground, and be beaten mercilessly with ox-tendon whips. Again, he ordered that she should be hung from a beam, and have her sides lacerated, and torches attached to her, and heated iron shoes be put on her feet. The martyr of Christ, worn out from the tortures, invoked Christ, her master, and gave up her spirit to the Lord. And some Christian men took her body and buried it, secretly from the Hellenes.

George, the martyr of Christ, went and said to his captors, "Please, wait for me a moment; for see, I have been tortured for seven years for the name of my Lord God. Delay a little, so that I may bequeath prayers for future generations; for I see this crowd, and my body may not be enough for them." Then the saint looked up to the highest vault of heaven and said, "Lord God, who in your divine forbearance and love of humanity have disregarded all my sins, and have reverently arranged my life, give me the power to endure for your divinity; put the enemies of the truth to shame; and make your name and the name of your only begotten son shine more brightly through me; and put Dadian and his arrogance to shame.

"Κύριε ὁ Θεός, ὁ συντρίψας τῇ εἰκόνι τῇ χρυσῇ, καὶ τὸν κακόφρονα βασιλέα ἀπὸ τῶν ἀνθρώπων ἐκδιώξας, καὶ μετὰ θηρίων ἀγρίων τὴν μερίδα αὐτοῦ παραθέμενος, ἕως οὗ ἑπτὰ καιροὶ παρηλλάγησαν, ἕως ἔγνω σε τὸν Δεσπότην Χριστὸν τὸν Θεόν· ὁ τὸν υἱὸν αὐτοῦ μονοήμερον τῆς βασιλείας καθελών· ὁ τὴν προσευχὴν τοῦ ἀγαπητοῦ λαοῦ σου ὑπακούσας, καὶ τὸν ἀλάστορα Ὀλοφέρνην καθελών· ὁ τοῦ προφήτου Ἐλισσαίου ὑπακούσας, καὶ τὸν υἱὸν τοῦ φονευτοῦ ὑπὸ χεῖρας αὐτοῦ ποιήσας, καὶ τῆς τῶν Ἀλλοφύλων ἐκδιώξας ματαιότητος, καὶ τοῖς φοβουμένοις σε τὴν σωτηρίαν χαρισάμενος.

"Δέσποτα, Θεὲ ἐπουράνιε, πάσης κτίσεως ὁρωμένης τε καὶ οὐχ ὁρωμένης, ἔφιδε ἐπὶ τῇ ταπεινώσει μου, καὶ τέλειον τὸν ἀγῶνά μου ἀνάδειξον. Κύριε ὁ Θεός, ἐπάκουσόν μου τῆς φωνῆς, καὶ παράσχου μοι τὴν αἴτησιν ταύτην. Καὶ δός, Κύριε, τῷ ὀνόματί μου χάριν, ἵνα πᾶς ὅστις γένηται ἐν ὑπνίῳ φοβερῷ, καὶ μνησθῇ τοῦ δούλου σου Γεωργίου, γενέσθω εἰς ἀγαθόν. Κύριε ὁ Θεὸς ἡμῶν, δὸς τῷ ὀνόματί μου καὶ τῷ σώματί μου χάριν, ἵνα πᾶς τις γενόμενος ἐν δικαστηρίῳ φοβερῷ, καὶ μνησθῇ τοῦ ὀνόματός μου, ἐξέλθῃ ἄνευ πειρασμοῦ. Κύριε ὁ Θεός, δὸς τῷ ὀνόματί μου καὶ τῷ σώματί μου χάριν, ἵνα ἐν τῷ συσκευάζειν τὸν οὐρανὸν ὥστε βρέχειν ἐπὶ τὴν γῆν χάλαζαν διὰ τὰς ἁμαρτίας τῶν ἀνθρώπων, ἐάν τις μνησθῇ τοῦ ὀνόματος Γεωργίου τοῦ δούλου σου, μὴ ἐπέλθῃ ἀὴρ κακὸς ἐν τῷ τόπῳ ἐκείνῳ, ἀλλ᾽ ἡ δρόσος ἡ παρὰ σοῦ, ἵαμα αὐτοῖς ἔστω. Κύριε ὁ Θεὸς Ἀβραὰμ καὶ Ἰσαὰκ καὶ Ἰακώβ, δὸς τῷ δούλῳ σου Γεωργίῳ χάριν, ἵνα πᾶς ὅστις μνημονεύσει τοῦ δούλου σου

"Lord God, who crushed the golden image, and chased the wicked king away from people, and set his lot to be with the wild beasts, until seven years came and went, until he recognized you Lord Christ as God; who brought down his son after a single day of kingship; who listened to the prayer of your beloved people, and brought down Holofernes the destroyer; who listened to the prophet Elisha, and subjected the murderer's son to him, and chased away the vanity of the Philistines, and granted salvation to those who fear you.

"Master, heavenly God, God of all creation, visible and invisible, watch over my humble self, and bring my struggle to completion. Lord God, hearken to my voice, and grant me this favor. Lord, give grace to my name, so that for anyone who may experience a nightmare and who calls to mind your slave George, things will turn out well. Lord our God, give grace to my name and my body, so that anyone who may find himself at a fearful place of judgment and who calls my name to mind shall come out of it without trouble. Lord God, give grace to my name and my body, so that when the heavens get ready to pour hail upon the earth because of people's sins, if anyone may call to mind the name of George your slave, no bad weather may fall upon that place, but rather let your dew be healing for them. Lord, *God of Abraham, Isaac, and Jacob,* give grace to your slave George, so that whoever calls your slave to mind and

καὶ τὴν ἡμέραν τῆς ἀθλήσεως καὶ τῆς ὑπομονῆς μου, μὴ γένηται ἐν τῷ οἴκῳ αὐτοῦ λεπρὸς ἢ κωφός, ἢ μογγίλαλος, ἢ τυφλός, ἢ ξηρός, ἢ παραλυτικός· μηδὲ μνησθῇς τῶν ἀνομιῶν αὐτῶν, ἀλλ' ἐξαγόρασον τὰς ἁμαρτίας αὐτῶν ὡς εὔσπλαγχνος σωτήρ, ὅτι δεδόξασταί σου τὸ ὄνομα εἰς τοὺς αἰῶνας ἀμήν."

Ἡνίκα δὲ ἐπαύσατο ὁ Ἅγιος Γεώργιος προσευχόμενος, ὁ Κύριος ὑπὸ νεφελῶν εἶπε πρὸς τὸν ἅγιον, "Δεῦρο, παῖς μου ἀγαπητέ, ἀνάβαινε εἰς τὰ ταμιεῖα τοῦ Πατρός μου, οὗ ἡ δρόσος ἡ τιμία καὶ στέφανος ἀμαράντινος, καὶ ζωὴ ἀτελεύτητος, ἡτοιμάσθη σοι παρὰ τοῦ Πατρός μου. Κατ' ἐμαυτοῦ ὀμνύω, καὶ κατὰ τῶν ἁγίων μου ἀγγέλων, ὅτι πᾶς ἄνθρωπος ὅστις γένηται ἐν ἀνάγκῃ καὶ μνησθῇ τοῦ ὀνόματός μου καὶ τοῦ ὀνόματος Γεωργίου, ῥύσομαι αὐτὸν ἀπὸ πάσης ἀνάγκης, καὶ τῶν ἀνομιῶν αὐτῶν οὐ μὴ μνησθῶ ἐν ἡμέρᾳ κρίσεως, διότι Θεὸς τῶν μετανοούντων εἰμὶ ἐγώ." Ἐγένετο δὲ σύναξις ἀγγέλων πολλῶν καὶ δικαίων πατέρων, καὶ μαρτύρων ἀγαλλομένων εἰς ἀπάντησιν Γεωργίου.

Ὁ δὲ μάρτυς τοῦ Χριστοῦ λέγει πρὸς τοὺς κρατοῦντας αὐτόν, "Ἐάσατέ με μικρόν, ἵνα εὐχὴν καταλείψω τῷ Βασιλεῖ Δαδιανῷ, καὶ τοῖς σὺν αὐτῷ βασιλεῖς." Οἱ δὲ εἶπον πρὸς αὐτόν, "Εὖξαι ὡς θέλεις." Καὶ ἀναβλέψας τοῖς ὀφθαλμοῖς αὐτοῦ εἰς τὸν οὐρανόν, εἶπε, "Κύριε ὁ Θεὸς ὁ Παντοκράτωρ, ὁ τῆς αἰωνίου βασιλείας συνέχων τὰ πάντα, καὶ τῆς δικαιοκρισίας ὢν ἀρχηγός, ὁ ἀποστείλας πῦρ ἐν τῇ πενταπόλει Σοδόμων, καὶ ἕως τῆς ἡμέρας ταύτης ἐπ' αὐτοὺς ἡ ὀργή σου, ὁ ἀποστείλας πῦρ διὰ τοῦ προφήτου Ἠλία, καὶ τοὺς δύο πεντηκοντάρχας ἀπολέσας, καὶ νῦν

the day of my martyrdom and endurance, there may never be a leper or deaf or mute or blind or lame or paralyzed person in his household, and may you also forget their iniquities, but redeem their sins as a merciful savior, since your name is glorified forever, amen."

When Saint George stopped praying, the Lord through the clouds said to the saint, "Come, my dear child, ascend to the innermost chambers of my Father, where precious dew, an unfading crown, and eternal life have been prepared for you by my Father. I swear by myself, and by my holy angels, that every person who may be in distress and calls to mind my name and the name of George, I shall rescue from all distress, and I shall forget their iniquities on judgment day, because I am the God of those who repent." Then many angels and righteous fathers and rejoicing martyrs gathered to welcome George.

The martyr of Christ said to his captors, "Allow me a moment to bequeath a prayer for King Dadian, and for the kings that are with him." They responded, "Pray as you wish." So he raised his eyes toward heaven, and said, "Lord God Almighty, you who maintain all things in the eternal kingdom, you who are the leader of righteous judgment, you who sent down fire onto the five-city league of Sodom, and whose anger continues upon them to this very day, you who sent down fire through your prophet Elijah and consumed the two captains of fifty men, you, Lord, are still the same,

αὐτὸς εἶ, Κύριε· κατάπεμψον αὐτὸ τὸ πῦρ, καὶ ἀνάλωσον τὸν Βασιλέα Δαδιανόν, καὶ τοὺς σὺν αὐτῷ βασιλεῖς, διὰ τὴν αὐτῶν ἀπιστίαν καὶ ἀνταρσίαν ἣν ποιοῦσιν εἰς τοὺς δούλους σου."

Καὶ οὕτως ποιήσας τὴν ἐν Χριστῷ σφραγῖδα, λέγει τῷ σπεκουλάτορι, "Δεῦρο, πλήρωσον, τέκνον, τὸ κελευσθέν σοι." Καὶ ἐκτείνας τὴν χεῖρα, ἀπέτεμε τὴν ἁγίαν αὐτοῦ κεφαλήν, μηνὶ Ἀπριλίῳ, εἰς τὰς εἴκοσι τρεῖς, εἰς δόξαν Πατρὸς καὶ Υἱοῦ καὶ Ἁγίου Πνεύματος, ᾧ ἡ δόξα καὶ τὸ κράτος εἰς τοὺς αἰῶνας τῶν αἰώνων, ἀμήν.

so send down that fire, and kill King Dadian, and the kings that are with him, because of the faithless and rebellious things they do to your slaves."

He then made the sign of Christ's cross and said to the executioner, "Go on, child, carry out your orders." So the executioner stretched out his hand and cut off George's holy head, on the twenty-third of the month of April, for the glory of the Father and the Son and the holy Spirit, to whom be glory and power for ever and ever, amen.

Θαῦμα τοῦ Ἁγίου μεγαλομάρτυρος Γεωργίου, περὶ τοῦ δράκοντος

Ἐκ τῶν θαυμάτων εἰς θαῦμα ἀκούσαντες, τοῦ μεγαλομάρτυρος καὶ θαυματουργοῦ Γεωργίου, δῶμεν δόξαν τῷ
Θεῷ, τῷ μεγαλύναντι αὐτόν, καὶ δόντι τοιαύτην χάριν τῷ
πανενδόξῳ μάρτυρι Γεωργίῳ. *Τίς ἤκουσεν ἐξ αἰῶνος, ἢ τίς
ἑώρακεν πώποτε τὸ τοιοῦτον θαῦμα, ὃ ὁ παμμακάριστος
ἐποίησεν;*

2   Κατὰ τοὺς καιροὺς ἐκείνους, ἐγένετο πόλις ὀνόματι
Λασία· καὶ ἐβασίλευεν ἐπ᾽ αὐτὴν βασιλεὺς ὀνόματι Σέλ-
βιος· καὶ αὐτὸς ἦν πονηρὸς εἰδωλολάτρης, παράνομος,
ἀσεβής, μὴ ἐλεῶν, ἢ οἰκτείρων τοὺς εἰς τὸν Χριστὸν πιστεύοντας. *Κατὰ δὲ τὰ ἔργα αὐτῶν ἀνταπέδωκεν αὐτοῖς ὁ
Κύριος.*

Ἐγγὺς γὰρ τῆς πόλεως ἦν λίμνη ἔχουσα ὕδωρ πολύν.
Καὶ ἐγεννήθη ἐν τῷ ὕδατι τῆς λίμνης πονηρὸς δράκων·
καὶ καθ᾽ ἑκάστην ἐξερχόμενος, κατέσθιεν αὐτούς. Καὶ
πολλάκις ὁ βασιλεὺς συναγαγὼν πάντα τὰ στρατεύματα
αὐτοῦ εἰς πόλεμον ἐξῆλθον κατὰ τοῦ θηρίου· καὶ ταραχθέν-
τος τοῦ ὕδατος, οὐκ ἴσχυσαν οὔτε τῷ τόπῳ προσεγγίσαι·
ὡς δὲ κατῆσθιεν αὐτούς, κατεπείγοντο πονηρῶς.

3   Συναχθεῖσα ἡ πόλις, ἐβόησαν πρὸς τὸν βασιλέα λέγοντες, "Βασιλεῦ, ἰδοὺ ἡ κατοίκησις τῆς πόλεως ἡμῶν καλὴ
καὶ ἀγαθή, καὶ ἡμεῖς ἀπολλόμεθα κακῶς."

Καὶ λέγει ὁ βασιλεύς, "Δότε ἀπογραφὴν πάντες ὑμεῖς,

MIRACLES

Miracle of Saint George the great martyr: about the dragon

Having listened to one miracle after another of George, the great martyr and miracle worker, let us glorify God, who made him great, and who gave such grace to the all-glorious martyr George. Since the beginning of time, *who has heard of,* or *who has seen such* a miracle as the one the all-blessed George performed?

At that time, there was a city called Lasia, and a king 2 called Selvios ruled over it. This man was a wicked idolater, a lawless and impious man, showing neither mercy nor pity for those who believed in Christ. Yet the Lord *repaid* them *according to* their deeds.

Near the city, there was a lake containing a lot of water. And a wicked dragon had been born in the water of the lake, and every day he would come out and devour them. Many times the king gathered all his troops and went out to fight the beast, but as the water would be stirred up, they could not even get near the place; and since the dragon continued to devour them, they were cruelly oppressed.

The people of the city gathered and called out to the 3 king, "King, living in our city is all well and good, yet we are being miserably destroyed."

And the king said, "You must all register a name, so that

καὶ δοθῇ ἑνὶ ἑκάστῳ ἡμῶν λαχμός. Κἀγὼ ἔχω ἓν θυγά-
τριον μονογενῆ, καὶ δίδωμι αὐτὴν ὡς καὶ ὑμεῖς, ἐν τῷ
λαχμῷ μου· καὶ μὴ ἐκτριβώμεθα ἐκ τῆς πόλεως ἡμῶν."

4   Καὶ ἤρεσεν ὁ λόγος τοῖς πᾶσιν· καὶ ἤρξατο δίδειν
ἕκαστος ἡμέρᾳ τῇ ἡμέρᾳ τὰ νήπια αὐτῶν, ἕως οὗ ἦλθεν
ὁ λαχμὸς τοῦ βασιλέως. Ὁ δὲ βασιλεὺς ἐνέδυσεν τὴν
θυγατέρα αὐτοῦ *πορφύραν καὶ βύσσον,* κοσμήσας αὐτὴν
διὰ χρυσοῦ καὶ λίθου καὶ μαργαριτῶν. Κρατήσας πο-
θεινῶς, κατεφίλει αὐτὴν ὡς νεκράν, ὀδυρόμενος μετὰ δακρύων καὶ ἔλεγεν, "Ὕπαγε μονογενῆ καὶ γλυκύτατόν μου
τέκνον, τὸ φῶς τῶν ἐμῶν ὀφθαλμῶν. Τίνα, γλυκύτατόν
μου τέκνον, περιβλέψομαι, ἵνα μικρὸν εὐφρανθῶ; Πότε
γάμον σοι ποιήσω; Πότε θάλαμον ὄψομαι; Πότε λαμπάδας
ἀνάψω; Πότε μελῳδήσω; Πότε *καρπὸν κοιλίας σου* ὄψομαι;
Οἴμοι, γλυκύτατόν μου τέκνον, πορεύου, οὗ δίχα ἦν ὁ
θάνατος· χωρίζομαί σου." Καί φησιν ὁ βασιλεὺς πρὸς τὸν
λαόν, "Λάβετε χρυσίον καὶ ἀργύριον καὶ τὴν βασιλείαν
μου, καὶ ἄφετε τὸ θυγάτριόν μου." Καὶ οὐδεὶς αὐτῷ συν-
εχώρησεν, διὰ τὸ δόγμα ὃ ἐκεῖνος νενομοθέτηκεν. Τότε ὁ
βασιλεὺς βρύξας πικρῶς, ὥρμησεν αὐτὴν πρὸς τὴν λίμνην.
Συνέδραμεν δὲ πᾶσα ἡ πόλις ἀπὸ μικροῦ ἕως μεγάλου
πρὸς θεωρίαν τῆς κόρης.

5   Ὁ δὲ φιλάνθρωπος Θεός, καὶ εὔσπλαγχνος, *ὁ μὴ θέλας
τὸν θάνατον τοῦ ἁμαρτωλοῦ, ὡς τὸ ἐπιστρέψαι καὶ ζῆν
αὐτόν,* θέλας δεῖξαι σημεῖον, διὰ τοῦ πανενδόξου μεγαλομάρτυρος Γεωργίου.

6   Κατὰ τὸν καιρὸν ἐκεῖνον, ἦν ὁ Ἅγιος Γεώργιος, ὅστις
εἶχεν ἀξίαν κόμης· ἐγένετο δὲ ἀπολυθῆναι τὸν στρατόν·

each one of us may be given a lot. I too have but one daughter, and, like you, I will give her name on my lot. And in this way let us hope we shall not be wiped out from our city."

Everyone was pleased by his words. Day after day, each 4 one offered to give their children, until the king's lot came up. The king dressed his daughter *in purple and fine linen,* and adorned her with gold, gems, and pearls. Holding her tenderly, he kissed her as if she were dead and, lamenting her with tears, he said, "Go, my only and sweetest child, light of my eyes! At whom, my sweetest child, shall I gaze so as to gain a little happiness? When shall I arrange your wedding? When shall I see your bridal chamber? When shall I light the candles? When shall I sing the wedding song? When shall I see *the fruit of your womb?* Alas, you must go, my sweetest child, you for whom death was supposed to be far away, and yet now I am separated from you." And the king said to the people, "Take gold and silver, take my kingdom, but let my little girl live." But no one gave him their consent, because of the decree he himself had issued. Then the king, howling bitterly, sent her to the lake. The entire city, young and old alike, flocked together to watch the girl.

Yet God, who loves mankind and is merciful, and who 5 does *not wish the death of the* sinner, *rather than for him to turn back and live,* wanted to show a sign through the most glorious and great martyr George.

At that time, Saint George was alive and held the rank of 6 count. When his army was released, he too was traveling to Cappadocia, to his own fatherland. And by God's design the

ἤρχετο δὲ καὶ αὐτὸς ἐπὶ τὴν Καππαδόκων χώραν, πρὸς τὴν ἰδίαν πατρίδα. Κατ᾽ οἰκονομίαν δὲ τοῦ Θεοῦ, κατήντησεν ὁ ἅγιος ἐν τῷ τόπῳ ἐκείνῳ· καὶ ἐξένευσεν ἐν τῇ λίμνῃ, ποτίσαι τὸν ἵππον αὐτοῦ. Καὶ θεωρεῖ τὴν κόρην καθεζομένην, καὶ τοῖς δάκρυσιν βρέχουσαν τοῖς γόνασιν, καὶ περιβλέπουσαν ὧδε κἀκεῖσε, καὶ ὀλολύζουσαν.

7   Ὁ δὲ ἅγιος πρὸς αὐτὴν εἶπεν, "Γύναι, τίς εἶ σὺ καὶ τίς ὁ λαὸς ὁ ἀπὸ μακρόθεν ἑστώς, καὶ ὁρῶντες μεγάλως θρηνοῦσιν;" Ἡ δὲ κόρη φησίν, "Πολλὴ ἡ ἀφήγησις τοῦ λόγου, καὶ οὐ δύναμαί σοι λέγειν· ἀλλὰ φύγε πρὶν κακῶς ἀποθάνῃς." Καὶ λέγει αὐτὴν ὁ ἅγιος, "Εἰπέ μοι, γύναι, τὴν ἀλήθειαν· ἐπεί, μὰ τὸν Δεσπότην Θεόν, σὺν σοὶ ἀποθανοῦμαι, ὅτι οὐ μή σε ἐγκαταλείπω."

8   Τότε ἡ κόρη στενάξασα πικρῶς εἶπεν, "Κύριέ μου, ἡ κατοίκησις τῆς πόλεως ἡμῶν καλὴ καὶ ἀγαθή· καὶ ἐγεννήθην ἐν τῷ ὕδατι τῆς λίμνης πονηρὸς δράκων. Καὶ καθ᾽ ἑκάστην ἡμέραν ἐξερχόμενος, κατήσθιεν τὸν λαὸν τῆς πόλεως. Καὶ ἔδωκεν δόγμα ὁ πατήρ μου· καὶ ἀπέστειλέ με εἰς βρῶσιν τοῦ θηρίου. Νῦν ἰδοὺ εἶπόν σοι πάντα. Ἔξελθε ἐν τάχει."

9   Ἀκούσας δὲ ταῦτα ὁ ἅγιος, λέγει τῇ κόρῃ, "Μὴ φοβοῦ ἀπὸ τοῦ νῦν, ἀλλὰ θάρσει." Καὶ ἠρώτησεν αὐτὴν λέγων, "Ποῖον σέβας ἔχει ὁ πατήρ σου καὶ οἱ μετ᾽ αὐτοῦ;" Ἡ δὲ κόρη φησὶν πρὸς αὐτόν, "Ἡράκλην καὶ Σκάμανδρον, Ἀπόλλωνα καὶ τὴν μεγάλην θεὰν Ἄρτεμιν." Ὁ δὲ ἅγιος λέγει τῇ κόρῃ, "Σὺ δὲ πιστεύεις εἰς τὸν ἐμὸν Θεόν; Μὴ φοβοῦ ἀπὸ τοῦ νῦν, ἀλλὰ θάρσει."

10   Καὶ ἦρεν τὴν φωνὴν αὐτοῦ ὁ μακάριος πρὸς τὸν Θεόν,

saint ended up at that place, and made a detour to the lake to water his horse. And he saw the girl sitting there, soaking her knees with tears, looking here and there, and wailing.

The saint said to her, "Woman, who are you, and who are the people standing at a distance, who are looking this way and lamenting so much?" And the girl said, "It's a long story, and I can't tell you. Just go, before you come to a sticky end." And the saint said to her, "Tell me the truth, woman. For, by the Lord God, I shall die along with you, because I shall not abandon you." 7

Then the girl, sighed bitterly and said, "My lord, living in our city was well and good, but a wicked dragon was born in the water of the lake. And every day, he would come out and devour the people of the city. And my father issued a decree, and sent me as food for the beast. So there, I have told you everything. Go away quickly!" 8

When he had heard these words, the saint said to the girl, "From now on, don't be afraid, but take courage." And he asked her, "What is the religion of your father and his people?" And the girl said to him, "That of Herakles and Skamandros, Apollo and the great goddess Artemis." And the saint said to the girl, "Do you believe in my God? From now on, don't be afraid, but take courage." 9

And the blessed man raised his voice toward God, and he said, "My God, *enthroned upon the cherubim and the seraphim,* 10

καὶ εἶπεν, "Ὁ Θεὸς ὁ καθήμενος ἐπὶ τῶν χερουβίμ καὶ ἐπὶ τῶν σεραφὶμ καὶ ἐπιβλέπων ἀβύσσους, ὁ ὢν καὶ διαμένων ἀληθινὸς Θεός, αὐτὸς γινώσκεις τὰς καρδίας τῶν ἀνθρώπων, ὅτι εἰσὶν μάταιαι· ὁ δείξας τὰ φρικτὰ σημεῖα τῷ θεράποντί σου Μωσῇ, δεῖξον καὶ ἐπ' ἐμοὶ τὰ ἐλέη σου, καὶ ποίησον μετ' ἐμοῦ σημεῖον εἰς ἀγαθόν, καὶ ὑπόταξον τὸ δεινὸν θηρίον ὑπὸ τοὺς πόδας μου, ἵνα γνώσουσιν <ὅτι> πάντοτε μετ' ἐμοῦ εἶ." Καὶ ἦλθεν φωνὴ ἐκ τοῦ οὐρανοῦ λέγουσα, "Εἰσηκούσθη σου ἡ δέησις εἰς τὰ ὦτα Κυρίου· ποίει ὃ βούλει."

11   Καὶ εὐθέως ἡ κόρη ἐβόησεν λέγουσα, "Οἴμοι, κύριέ μου, ἔξελθε, ὅτι ἔρχεται τὸ δεινὸν θηρίον." Καὶ δραμὼν ὁ ἅγιος εἰς ἀπάντησιν τοῦ δράκοντος, ἐποίησεν τὸν τύπον τοῦ σταυροῦ εἰπών, "Κύριε ὁ Θεός μου, μετάβαλε τὸ δεινὸν θηρίον τοῦτον, εἰς ὑπακοὴν πίστεως, τοῦ ἀπίστου λαοῦ τούτου." Καὶ τοῦτο εἰπὼν συνεργίᾳ τοῦ αὐτοῦ Θεοῦ καὶ τῇ εὐχῇ τοῦ ἁγίου ἔπεσεν ὁ δράκων εἰς τοὺς πόδας τοῦ ἁγίου.

12   Καὶ λέγει ὁ ἅγιος τῇ κόρῃ, "Λῦσον τὴν ζώνην σου καὶ τὸ σκοινίον τοῦ ἵππου <μου καὶ φέρε μοι ὧδε." Καὶ λύσασα ἡ κόρη> δέδωκεν αὐτὰ τῷ ἁγίῳ. Καὶ κατ' οἰκονομίαν τοῦ Θεοῦ, ἔδησεν τὸν δράκοντα, καὶ παρέδωκεν αὐτὸν τῇ κόρῃ λέγων, "Ἄγωμεν αὐτὸν τῇ πόλει." Καὶ λαβοῦσα τὸν δράκοντα, ἤρχοντο ἐν τῇ πόλει. Ἰδὼν δὲ ὁ λαὸς τὸ παράδοξον θαῦμα καὶ ἐν φόβῳ αὐτῶν γενομένων, ἔμελλον φεύγειν, διὰ τὸν φόβον τοῦ δράκοντος. Ὁ δὲ Ἅγιος Γεώργιος ἐβόησεν πρὸς αὐτοὺς λέγων, "Μὴ φοβεῖσθε, ἀλλὰ στήκετε, καὶ ὁρᾶτε τὴν δόξαν τοῦ Θεοῦ, καὶ πιστεύσατε εἰς

watching over the depths, you who are and remain the true God, you know that the hearts of men are vain. You who showed awesome signs through Moses your servant, show also your mercy upon me, and *make with me a sign for good* by making this terrible beast submit beneath my feet, so that they may learn that you are always by my side." And a voice came down from heaven, saying, "Your request has been heard by the ears of the Lord; do as you wish."

And straightaway the girl cried out, "Alas, my lord, go 11 away, because the terrible beast is coming." But the saint ran to meet the dragon, made the sign of the cross, and said, "Lord my God, transform this terrible beast, calling this faithless people to faithful obedience." And when he had said this, with his God's help and by the saint's prayer, the dragon fell at the saint's feet.

And the saint said to the girl, "Untie your belt and the 12 bridle of my horse, and bring them here to me." And the girl untied them and gave them to the saint. And by God's design he bound the dragon and handed him over to the girl, saying, "Let us take him to the city." And she took the dragon and they came into the city. When the people saw the incredible miracle, they became afraid and were about to flee because of their fear of the dragon. But Saint George shouted to them, "Do not be afraid, but stay and see the glory of God; believe in our Lord Jesus Christ the true God,

τὸν Κύριον ἡμῶν Ἰησοῦν Χριστὸν τὸν ἀληθινὸν Θεόν, καὶ ἀποκτενῶ τὸν δράκοντα." Καὶ ἐβόησεν ὁ βασιλεὺς καὶ πᾶσα ἡ πόλις, "Πιστεύομεν εἰς Πατέρα καὶ Υἱὸν καὶ Ἅγιον Πνεῦμα, εἰς Τριάδα ὁμοούσιον καὶ ἀχώριστον." Καὶ ταῦτα ἀκούσας ὁ ἅγιος, ἐξενέγκας τὴν ῥομφαίαν αὐτοῦ, ἀπέκτεινε τὸν δράκοντα, καὶ παρέδωκεν τὴν κόρην τῷ βασιλεῖ. Τότε συνήχθη τὸ πλῆθος τοῦ λαοῦ καὶ κατεφίλει τοὺς πόδας τοῦ ἁγίου δοξάζοντες τὸν Θεόν.

13 Μετακαλεσάμενος δὲ ὁ ἅγιος Γεώργιος τὸν ἀρχιεπίσκοπον Ἀλεξανδρείας, ἐβάπτισεν τὸν βασιλέα καὶ τοὺς μεγισ[τάνους αὐ]τοῦ καὶ πάντ[α τὸν λα]ὸν ἐπὶ ἡμέρας [δεκαπέν]τε ὡσεὶ χιλι[άδας] σμ´· καὶ ἐγένετο χαρὰ μεγάλη τῷ τόπῳ ἐκείνῳ. Τότε Λασία ἡ πόλις ἀνήγειρεν πάνσεπτον ναὸν εἰς τὸ ὄνομα τοῦ Ἁγίου Γεωργίου· καὶ ὅτε ᾠκοδομεῖτο ὁ ναός, ἑστὼς ὁ ἅγιος ἐν ἑνὶ τόπῳ καὶ ἐπευξάμενος, ἐξῆλθεν πηγὴ ἁγιασμοῦ. Τότε ἐπίστευσαν ὑπὸ τὸν Κύριον· πολλά τε θαύματα καὶ σημεῖα ἐποίησεν ὁ Ἅγιος Γεώργιος, διὰ τῆς δοθείσης αὐτοῦ χάριτος.

<Περὶ τοῦ δαίμονος>

14 Ἐξερχομένου δὲ τοῦ Ἁγίου Γεωργίου ἐκ τῆς πόλεως Λασίας, ἀνήρχετο ἐπὶ τὴν ἰδίαν αὐτοῦ πατρίδα. Καὶ ὑπήντησεν αὐτὸν πονηρὸς δαίμων, τεταπεινωμένος, κρατῶν βακτηρίας δύο ἐν ταῖς χερσίν· καὶ λαλῶν εἰρηνικὰ [μετὰ τὸ συν]αντῆσαι τῷ Ἁ[γίῳ Γεω]ργίῳ, λέγει αὐ[τῷ, "Εἰρήν]η σοι, Γεώργιε."

and I shall kill the dragon." And the king and the entire city shouted, "We believe in the Father, and the Son, and the Holy Spirit, in the Trinity of one essence and undivided." And when the saint heard these words, he drew his sword, and killed the dragon, and handed over the girl to the king. Then the crowd of people gathered and began kissing the feet of the saint, glorifying God.

Saint George summoned the archbishop of Alexandria, 13 and he baptized the king and his nobles and all the people, some two hundred and forty thousand souls, over fifteen days. And there was great joy in that place. Then the city of Lasia built a most holy church in the name of Saint George; and while the church was being built, the saint stood in a certain place and prayed, and a fountain of sanctified water sprang forth. Then they believed in the Lord; and Saint George performed many miracles and signs by the grace that had been granted to him.

About the Demon

When Saint George left the city of Lasia, he went on his way 14 to his own fatherland. And he met an evil demon, who looked humiliated and who was holding two sticks in his hands; when he encountered Saint George, the demon said to him, speaking peaceably, "Peace be with you, George."

Ὁ ἅγιος λέγει αὐτῷ, "Πῶς ἐ[κά]λεσας τὸ ὄνομά μου; εἰ γὰρ ὑπῆρχες πονηρὸς δαίμων, οὐκ ἂν ἐγίνωσκες τὸ ὄνομά μου."

Ὁ δὲ δαίμων λέγει, "Πῶς ἐτόλμησας τοιαῦτα εἰπεῖν, καὶ τοὺς ἀγγέλους τοῦ Θεοῦ ἐνυβρίζεις; Σκόπησον ὃ ἐλάλησας."

Ὁ ἅγιος εἶπεν, "Εἰ σὺ εἶ ἄγγελος φωτός, δεῖξον τὴν δύναμίν σου." Καὶ ποιήσας τὸν τύπον τοῦ τιμίου σταυροῦ, περιέφραξεν τὸν δαίμονα. Καὶ λέγει αὐτῷ, "Ἐπὶ τῷ ὀνόματι τοῦ Κυρίου ἡμῶν Ἰησοῦ Χριστοῦ, δεῦρο ἀκολούθει μοι, εἰ σὺ εἶ ἄγγελος φωτός."

Καὶ εὐθέως ἐβόησεν ὁ δαίμων λέγων, "Οὐαί μοι, Γεώργιε, εἰς σὲ κατήντησα."

Ὁ δὲ ἅγιος λέγει αὐτῷ, "Ὁρκίζω σε, πονηρὲ δαῖμον, ἵνα μοὶ εἴπῃς τίς εἶ σύ, καὶ τί μοι ἐβούλου ποιῆσαι."

15   Ὁ δὲ δαίμων λέγει, "Ἐγώ, Γεώργιε, πρῶτος συνεργὸς τοῦ Σατανᾶ· ἐγώ, Γεώργιε, ὅταν ὁ Θεὸς τὴν ἄβυσσον ἄγων ὑδάτων, ἐκεῖ παρήμην, φοβερὰν ἀστραπὴν σὺν βρονταῖς ἐγὼ ἐπεῖχον, ἐγὼ τὰς νεφέλας ἐδέσμευον· ἐμέ, Γεώργιε, ἀνθρώπων φύσις ὁρᾶν <οὐ δύναται>· ἐμὲ οἱ λεγεῶνες τῶν ἀγγέλων δεδοίκασιν· καὶ ἄρτι διὰ τὴν ὑπερηφανίαν μου, πατοῦσιν οἱ πόδες μου τὴν γῆν, ἀλλ' οὖν μᾶλλον, ὅτι καὶ σώματα γηίνων ἀνθρώπων ἡμᾶς μίγουσιν. Ἐγώ, Γεώργιε, ἐφθόνησα τὴν δοθεῖσάν σοι χάριν, καὶ ἠβουλήθην ἀπαντῆσαί σοι, ἵνα με προσκυνήσῃς, ὅτι πολλοὺς τοῦ Θεοῦ ἐχώρισα ἐκ τῆς δόξης αὐτοῦ. Ταῦτα πάντα εἶπόν σοι. Μνήσθητι, Γεώργιε, τὴν προτέραν μου δόξαν, καὶ τὴν δευτέραν μου ἀθλιότητα· μὴ ἐπιτρέψῃς με

And the saint said to him, "How did you call me by my name? For you could not know my name if you were an evil demon."

And the demon said, "How dare you use such words, and thus insult God's angels? Think what you said."

The saint said, "If you are indeed an *angel of light,* show your power." Then he made the sign of the cross, encircling the demon. And he said to him, "In the name of our Lord Jesus Christ, *come follow me,* if you are an *angel of light.*"

And immediately the demon shouted and said, "Woe is me, George, for having met with you."

The saint said to him, "I adjure you, evil demon, to tell me who you are and what you wanted to do to me."

The demon said, "I, George, am the first collaborator of Satan; I was there, George, when God produced the abyss of the waters, and I possessed the power of terrifying lightning with thunders, I bound up the clouds. Humans could not look at me, George; the *legions of the angels* were scared of me. Yet now, because of my pride my feet tread upon the earth, and indeed, even worse, the bodies of earthly humans commingle with us. I, George, envied the grace that has been given to you, and I wanted to meet you, so that you might bow before me, because I have separated many people of God from his glory. So I've told you all this. Remember, George, my previous glory, and my later wretchedness. Do not command me to go into the abyss, because those

ἀπελθεῖν εἰς τὴν ἄβυσσον, ὅτι οἱ ἐν τῷ ἀβύσσῳ ὄντες πρῶτοί εἰσιν παραβάσεως, καὶ οὐ μὴ εἰσέλθω ἐκεῖ εἰς τὸν αἰῶνα."

16 Τότε ὁ μέγας Γεώργιος, ἦρεν τὴν φωνὴν αὐτοῦ πρὸς <τὸν> τῶν ὅλων Θεὸν λέγων, "Κύριε ὁ Θεός μου, εἰσάκουσον τῆς δεήσεώς μου, διότι πάντοτέ μου ἀκούεις· σὺ γὰρ εἶπας, Κύριε, ὅτι 'τὸν ἐρχόμενον πρός με, οὐ μὴ ἐκβάλω ἔξω'· σὺ γάρ, Κύριε καρδιογνῶστα, ὁ δήσας καὶ δεσμεύσας ἐν τῇ χειρί μου τὸν πονηρὸν δράκοντα, καὶ τοῦτον τὸν δαίμοναν τὸν μὴ ποιήσαντα τὸ θέλημά σου, καὶ μὴ φυλάξαντα τὰ προστάγματά σου, ἀλλὰ μείναντα εἰς τὴν ἑαυτοῦ πονηρίαν, καὶ μὴ ἐπιστρέψαντα πρὸς σὲ τὸν μόνον ἀληθινὸν Θεόν, κατάβαλε εἰς τόπον φοβερὸν ἵνα κολάζεται, καὶ τὴν εἰκόνα ἣν ἐπλαστούργησας μὴ πειράζῃ."

17 Καὶ ἦν ἐκεῖ πέτρα παμμεγέθης, καὶ ἐσφράγισεν αὐτὴν ὁ μέγας Γεώργιος λέγων, "Ἐν ὀνόματι τοῦ Κυρίου ἡμῶν Ἰησοῦ Χριστοῦ, ἀνοίχθητι πέτρα, καὶ ὑπόδεξαι τὸν πονηρὸν δαίμονα τοῦτον." Καὶ παραχρῆμα ἐσχίσθη ἡ πέτρα, καὶ ἐξῆλθεν πῦρ ἐξ αὐτῆς· καὶ κρατήσας τὸν δαίμονα, ἔρριψεν αὐτὸν ἐν τῷ χάσματι ἐν μέσῳ τοῦ πυρός· καὶ πάλιν ἐπέστρεψεν τὴν πέτραν ὡς ἦν ἀπαρχῆς. Καὶ ἦν ἐκεῖ κολαζόμενος ὑπὸ τοῦ πυρός, ἕως τῆς συντελείας τοῦ αἰῶνος.

18 Δοξάσωμεν πάντες τὸ θαυμαστὸν ὄνομα τοῦ Ἁγίου μεγαλομάρτυρος Γεωργίου, καὶ ἡμεῖς τῷ Θεῷ <δόξαν> ἀναπέμψωμεν· ὁμοῦ αὐτῷ πρέπει πᾶσα δόξα, τιμὴ καὶ προσκύνησις, τῷ Πατρὶ καὶ τῷ Υἱῷ, καὶ τῷ Ἁγίῳ Πνεύματι, νῦν καὶ ἀεὶ καὶ εἰς τοὺς αἰῶνας τῶν αἰώνων, ἀμήν.

that are in the abyss are the first among the transgressors, and may I never, ever go there."

Then, the great George raised his voice toward the God 16 of all and said, "Lord my God, hearken to my petition, since you always hear me; for it is you, Lord, who said, '*I shall not cast out the one who comes to me*'; for it is you, Lord, *who knows hearts,* who bound and tied the wicked dragon in my hand. Now, this demon too, who did not do your will and did not keep your commandments, but rather persisted in his own evil and did not turn back to you, the only true God, send him down into a terrible place so that he may be punished, and thus not tempt the image of yours which you fashioned."

And there was an extremely large rock right there, and 17 the great George made the sign of the cross over it and said, "In the name of our Lord Jesus Christ, open up, rock, and receive this wicked demon." And straightaway, the rock was split open, and fire came out of it; and George took hold of the demon and threw him into the gap in the middle of the fire; and then he returned the stone to its original form. And the demon remained there punished by the fire until the end of time.

Let us all glorify the wondrous name of Saint George, the 18 great martyr, and let us give glory to God; to whom belongs all glory, honor and veneration, the Father, the Son, and the Holy Spirit, now and forever and ever, amen.

PASSION OF NIKETAS

Μαρτύριον τοῦ Ἁγίου καὶ ἐνδόξου μεγαλομάρτυρος καὶ θαυματουργοῦ Νικήτα

*Ἐ*ν ταῖς ἡμέραις ἐκείναις, ἐγένετο ἀνὴρ θεόφρων συγ-κλητικός, ὀνόματι <Νικήτας>, υἱὸς βασιλέως Μαξιμιανοῦ· ὅντινα ὁ Θεὸς ἠγάπησε καὶ ὁδήγησεν αὐτὸν εἰς τὴν ὁδὸν τῆς ζωῆς. Πληρωμένου δὲ χρόνου ἱκανοῦ, ἐγένετο ἀνὴρ πανεύφημος ἐν ὅλῃ τῇ πόλει ἐκείνῃ. Ἐν μιᾷ δὲ νυκτὶ περὶ ὥραν τοῦ μεσονυκτίου, κατῆλθεν ὁ ἀρχάγγελος Μιχαὴλ ἀπ᾿ οὐρανοῦ καὶ ἔστη πρὸς τὴν κεφαλὴν αὐτοῦ κρατῶν τὸν τύπον τοῦ τιμίου καὶ ζωοποιοῦ σταυροῦ. Καὶ λέγει αὐτῷ, "Προσκύνησον τοῦτο καὶ ζήσῃ εἰς αἰῶνας."

2 Διεγερθεὶς δὲ ὁ μακάριος Νικήτας τῷ πρωΐ, καὶ γυρεύ-σας πᾶσαν τὴν πόλιν ἐκ τρίτου, ἔλεγε, "Τίς δύναται ὑπο-δεῖξαί μοι τὸν τύπον ὃν ἑώρακα τῇ παρελθούσῃ νυκτί;"

Γυνὴ δέ τις πενιχρά, ὀνόματι Ἰουλιανή, φοβουμένη τὸν Θεόν, θαρρήσασα λέγει αὐτῷ: "Δέσποτα τῆς οἰκουμένης, υἱὸς βασιλέως τυγχάνεις καὶ πτοοῦμαί σου τὸν πατέρα, ἐπεὶ ἐγώ σοι εἶχον δεῖξαι τὸν τύπον ὃν ἑώρακας."

Λέγει αὐτῇ ὁ μακάριος Νικήτας, "Γῦναι, *μὴ δειλιάσῃς, ἀλλὰ μᾶλλον ἀνδρίζου,* καὶ πολλὰ χρήματα παρέξω σοι."

Ταῦτα ἀκούσασα ἡ μακαρία Ἰουλιανή, ἔβαλε τὴν χεῖρα εἰς τὸν κόλπον αὐτῆς καὶ ἐξέβαλε τὸν τίμιον σταυρὸν ὃν ὑπέδειξεν αὐτῷ ὁ ἄγγελος.

Passion of the great and glorious martyr and wonderworker Saint Niketas

In those days there lived a man, a pious consul, by the name of Niketas, the son of the emperor Maximian. God loved this man and led him on *the way of life*. In the fullness of time, he became a man who was praised by that entire city. One night, around midnight, the archangel Michael came down from heaven and stood by Niketas's head, holding the sign of the honorable and life-giving cross. And Michael said to him, "Venerate this, and you shall live forever."

When the blessed Niketas woke up in the morning, he searched the whole city three times over, saying, "Who can show me the sign that I saw last night?"

A destitute woman named Iouliane, a woman filled with the fear of God, took courage and spoke to him: "Master of the world, you are the son of an emperor and I fear your father, because I can indeed show you the sign which you saw."

The blessed Niketas said to her, "Woman, *do not be frightened,* but rather *be brave* and I shall give you a lot of money."

When the blessed Iouliane heard this, she placed her hand in her bosom and took out the holy cross which the angel had showed to him.

3　　Καὶ ἰδὼν αὐτόν, ἀπῆλθε πρὸς τὸν πατέρα αὐτοῦ καὶ λέγει αὐτῷ, "Πῶς θύομεν θεοὺς τῶν εἰδώλων καὶ οὐκ ἔγνωμεν ἕως ἄρτι τὸν ἀληθινὸν Θεόν;" Καὶ ἐξελθὼν ἔξω, ἀποδυσάμενος τὰ ἱμάτια αὐτοῦ, ἔδωκεν αὐτὰ πτωχοῖς. Καὶ προσκυνῶν τὸν Θεόν, ἔλεγε, "Κύριέ μου, Ἰησοῦ Χριστέ, καθοδήγησόν με εἰς τὴν ἐπίγνωσιν τῆς σῆς ἀληθείας."

　　Καὶ εὐθέως κατῆλθεν ὁ ἀρχάγγελος Μιχαήλ, <καὶ ἔστη μετὰ τοῦ ἁγίου. Καὶ λέγει αὐτῷ ὁ ἅγιος, "Τίς εἶ σύ;">

　　<Καὶ εἶπεν ὁ ἀρχιστράτηγος, "Ἐγώ εἰμι Μιχαὴλ ὁ ἀρχάγγελος Κυρίου>, καὶ ἀπεστάλη<ν> πρὸς σὲ κομίσαι σοι θησαυρὸν καὶ σοφίαν ἐκ Πνεύματος Ἁγίου."

　　Καὶ ὁ μακάριος Νικήτας κλίνας τὰ γόνατα προσεκύνησεν αὐτόν. Καὶ ἀνατείνας τὰς χεῖρας καὶ τὸ ὄμμα εἰς τὸν οὐρανόν, εἶπεν, "Εὐχαριστῶ σοι, Ταξιάρχα Μιχαήλ, γοργοπέταστε. Δόξα σοι, ὁ Θεός, ὁ ποιῶν τοὺς ἀγγέλους σου πνεύματα, καὶ τοὺς λειτουργοὺς αὐτοῦ πυρὸς φλόγα, διότι ὄντα με ἀνάξιον, προσελάβου πρὸς σέ."

4　　Καὶ ἰδοὺ παιδάριον μιαρόν, ὀνόματι Ἰουλιανὸς ὁ Παραβάτης, ἀπελθὸν πρὸς τὸν πατέρα τοῦ μακαρίου Νικήτα, λέγει αὐτῷ, "Δέομαί σου, δέσποτα, Βασιλεῦ Μαξιμιανέ, ὅτι ὁ γλυκύτατός σου υἱὸς θύει τὸν Θεὸν τῶν Χριστιανῶν, καὶ ἀπαρνεῖται τοὺς θεοὺς ἡμῶν, Ἀρτέμην καὶ Ἀπόλλωνα."

　　Καὶ ἀκούσας ταῦτα ὁ βασιλεύς, ἐζήτει αὐτὸν ἀπὸ τότε κρατῆσαι.

5　　Καὶ ἐξελθὼν εὗρεν αὐτὸν ἐν τῷ ναῷ τοῦ ἀρχιστρατήγου Μιχαὴλ προσευχόμενον. Καὶ ἰδὼν αὐτὸν λέγει αὐτῷ, "Ὦ τέκνον, ταῦτα ἤκουον καὶ οὐκ ἐπίστευον· ἀρτίως δὲ πεπίστευκα, ὅτι θύεις Θεὸν τῶν Χριστιανῶν τὸν

And when Niketas saw the cross, he went to his father 3
and said to him, "How is it that we keep sacrificing to the
gods of the idols and have not yet recognized the true God?"
And he went out, took off his clothes, and gave them to the
poor. And bowing toward God, he said, "My Lord, Jesus
Christ, guide me to the understanding of your truth."

And immediately the archangel Michael came down and
stood by the saint. And the saint said to him, "Who are
you?"

And the leader of the heavenly host said, "I am Michael,
the archangel of the Lord, and I have been sent to you to
bring you treasure and wisdom from the Holy Spirit."

And the blessed Niketas fell on his knees and bowed before him. And after he had raised his hands and eyes toward
the heaven, he said, "Thank you, Taxiarch Michael, you who
fly swiftly. Glory be to you, God, *who makes spirits his messen-
gers, and flaming fire his ministers,* because you accepted me to
your side, though I was unworthy."

And lo and behold, an abominable child, by the name of 4
Julian the Apostate, went to the blessed Niketas's father and
said to him, "If you please, master, Emperor Maximian! Your
most precious son is sacrificing to the God of the Christians, and renouncing our gods, Artemes and Apollo."

When the emperor heard these words, he sought, from
then on, to seize Niketas.

And he went out and found Niketas praying in the church 5
of the leader of the heavenly host, Michael. And when Maximian saw him, he said to him, "Child, I heard about this,
but I didn't believe it; now I believe that you are sacrificing
to the God of the Christians who was crucified under

σταυρωθέντα ἐπὶ Ποντίου Πιλάτου, καὶ ἀπαρνεῖσαι τοὺς μεγάλους θεούς, Ἀρτέμην καὶ Ἀπόλλωνα."

Ὁ δὲ λέγει αὐτῷ, "Τάχα ἐλήρησας καὶ διὰ τοῦτο φλυαρῶν τοιαῦτά μοι λέγεις· ἐγὼ γὰρ ἐπίστευσα καὶ πιστεύω εἰς τὸν Θεὸν τὸν ἀθάνατον ἵνα ῥύσεταί με ἀπὸ πάσης ὀργῆς καὶ ἀνάγκης."

Ταῦτα ἀκούσας ὁ βασιλεὺς λέγει αὐτῷ, "Ἐὰν οὐ θύσεις τοῖς μεγάλοις ἡμῶν θεοῖς, πολλῶν τιμωριῶν ἔνοχος εὑρεθήσῃ."

Καὶ ὁ μάρτυς λέγει αὐτῷ, "Κύον, τετυφλωμένε καὶ ἄπιστε τῆς ἀληθείας, ἄσπλαγχνε καὶ παράνομε, ὅσας βασάνους ἔχεις, ἐπάγαγέ μοι· ἐγὼ γὰρ τὸν ἀληθῆ Θεὸν οὐκ ἀρνοῦμαι, οὐδὲ θύω θεοῖς ἀψύχοις· *ὦτα γὰρ ἔχουσι καὶ οὐκ ἀκούουσι, χεῖρας ἔχουσι καὶ οὐ ψηλαφῶσι, πόδας ἔχουσι καὶ οὐ περιπατῶσι, ὀφθαλμοὺς ἔχουσι καὶ οὐ βλέπουσιν· ὅμοιοι αὐτῶν γένοιντο οἱ ποιοῦντες αὐτούς, καὶ πάντες οἱ πεποιθότες ἐπ' αὐτοῖς· πίπτουσι γὰρ καὶ οὐκ ἐγείρονται, καὶ ἑαυτοῖς βοηθῆσαι οὐ δύνανται· καὶ ὅταν ἑαυτοῖς οὐ δύνανται βοηθῆσαι, πῶς ἄλλοις βοηθήσωσιν;"*

6   Ὁ οὖν πατὴρ αὐτοῦ λέγει αὐτῷ, "Πείσθητί μοι, τέκνον, καὶ θῦσον τοῖς θεοῖς καὶ θεράπευσον τὴν ψυχήν μου."

Καὶ ὁ ἅγιος λέγει αὐτῷ, "Ἀπέλθωμεν εἰς τὸν ναὸν τῶν θεῶν, καὶ δός μοι τὸ ἐπιλαχόν μοι μέρος τῶν θεῶν, ἵνα ἔχω καὶ προσκυνεῖν αὐτοὺς κρυφίως."

Καὶ ὁ βασιλεὺς περιχαρὴς γενάμενος, ἔδωκεν αὐτῷ θεοὺς δώδεκα χρυσοῦς καὶ ἀργυροῦς. Ὁ δὲ μακάριος Νικήτας λαβὼν αὐτούς, *ἐποίησεν ὡσεὶ κονιορτόν.*

Pontius Pilate, and renouncing the great gods, Artemes and Apollo."

Niketas said to him, "Perhaps you have lost your mind, and because of that you speak such nonsense to me; for I have believed and I do believe in the immortal God who shall save me from all anger and need."

When the emperor heard these words, he said to him, "If you do not sacrifice to our great gods, you're going to be found liable for many punishments."

And the martyr said to him, "You dog, you've been blinded and are faithless toward the truth, you, you merciless and lawless man, may inflict upon me as many tortures as you can; yet I shall not renounce the true God, nor shall I sacrifice to lifeless gods. For *ears they have and do not hear, hands they have and do not feel, feet they have and do not walk, eyes they have and do not see. May those who make them become like them, and all who trust in them!* They fall down, but they cannot stand back up, and they are unable to help themselves; and when they cannot help themselves, how will they help others?"

His father said to him, "Listen to me, child, sacrifice to 6 the gods and do my soul a favor."

And the saint said to him, "Let's go to the temple of the gods, and give me those statues which belong to me, so that I can worship them privately."

And the emperor became overjoyed, and gave him twelve gods, made of gold and silver. The blessed Niketas took them, and turned them *into dust.*

Πρωίας δὲ γεναμένης εἶπεν αὐτῷ ὁ βασιλεύς, "Τέκνον, ἀκμὴ οὐχ ἑώρακά σε προσκυνοῦντα τοὺς θεούς."

Καὶ ὁ ἅγιος λέγει αὐτῷ, "Δεῦρο, λοιπόν, καὶ ἰδὲ τὴν δύναμιν τῶν θεῶν σου." Καὶ κρατήσας ἀπὸ τῆς χειρός, ἀπήγαγεν αὐτὸν ἐν τῷ ναῷ τῶν εἰδώλων.

Εἰσελθὼν δὲ ὁ βασιλεὺς καὶ μὴ εὑρὼν τοὺς θεούς, ἀνεβόησε λέγων, "Εἰπέ μοι, τέκνον, τίς ἐμάγευσέ σε; Μὴ Γεώργιος, ὃν ὁ ἀδελφός μου Δαδιανὸς ἐβασάνισεν, ἢ Κήρυκος ὁ νήπιος, ἢ Βλάσιος ὁ βουκόλος, ἢ ἄλλος μάγος τῶν Χριστιανῶν;"

Ὁ δὲ μάρτυς τοῦ Χριστοῦ λέγει αὐτῷ, "Ἐγὼ οὐκ ἐμαγεύθην, ἀλλ᾽ ἐπίστευσα εἰς τὸν ἀληθινὸν Θεὸν τῶν Χριστιανῶν."

7 Τότε κελεύει ὁ βασιλεὺς ἀχθῆναι αὐτὸν ἔξω καὶ δεθῆναι αὐτὸν ἐν μέσῳ δύο κιόνων, καὶ τύπτεσθαι αὐτὸν ὑπὸ δεκαπέντε στρατιωτῶν, μετὰ βουνεύροις ὠμοῖς· ἦσαν γὰρ εἰς ὄξος ἐγκεκυλισμένοι.

Ὁ δὲ μάρτυς τοῦ Χριστοῦ Νικήτας, ἐπάρας τὸ ὄμμα εἰς τὸν οὐρανόν, εἶπεν, "Εὐχαριστῶ σοι, Κύριε ὁ Θεός μου, πλὴν τάχυνον εἰς τὴν ἐμὴν βοήθειαν, καὶ ῥῦσαί με ἀπὸ τὸν κακοῦργον καὶ μισόκαλον καὶ βύθιον δράκοντα, ὅτι ἐνθυμήσεις πονηρὰς ἐξέγειρε κατ᾽ ἐμοῦ· ὁρῶ γὰρ τὰ τρυφερά μου μέλη ὑπὸ τῶν πληγῶν μελανούμενα καὶ τὴν λεπτήν μου ἡλικίαν ἀπολυμένην καὶ τὸ αἷμά μου χεόμενον ἐν τῇ γῇ, καὶ σκανδαλίζομαι ἐγκαταλεῖψαί σε τὸν ὄντως ὄντα Θεὸν ἀθάνατον καὶ ποιητὴν τῶν ἁπάντων. Ἀλλὰ σύ, Δέσποτα, μὴ ἐγκαταλίπῃς με."

8 Ταῦτα αὐτοῦ εὐχομένου, ἰδοὺ ἄγγελος Κυρίου ἔστη

When morning came, the emperor said to him, "Child, I still have not seen you worshiping the gods."

And the saint said to him, "Alright then, come and see the power of your gods." And holding him by his hand, he led him to the temple of the idols.

When the emperor went inside and could not find the gods, he shouted out these words: "Tell me, child, who bewitched you? Was it George, whom my brother Dadian tortured, or Kerykos the baby, or Blasios the shepherd, or some other magician from the Christians?"

The martyr of Christ said to him, "I haven't been bewitched; *I have believed* in the true God of the Christians."

Then the emperor ordered Niketas to be brought outside, and tied between two columns, and beaten by fifteen soldiers, with raw ox-tendon whips which had been dipped in vinegar. 7

Niketas, the martyr of Christ, raised his eyes to heaven and said, "Thank you, Lord my God, yet please be quick about coming to help me, and save me from this wicked and abysmal dragon who hates the good, because he has aroused evil thoughts in me; for I see my tender limbs bruised from the beatings, and the delicacy of my youth destroyed, and my blood gushing out upon the earth, and I am tempted to abandon you, who are truly the immortal God and creator of everything. Nevertheless, Lord, *may you not abandon me.*"

While he was praying like this, lo and behold an angel of 8

ἔμπροσθεν αὐτοῦ λέγων, "Χαίροις, τρισμακάριστε Νικήτα! Ἀνδρίζου καὶ ἴσχυε καὶ ἀγωνίζου· ἰδοὺ γὰρ στέφανός
σοι πλέκεται ὑπὸ ἁγίων ἀγγέλων. Χαίροις, φίλε Χριστοῦ
καὶ μάρτυς ἔνδοξε, τῶν δαιμόνων ὀλοθρευτὰ καὶ τοῦ Χριστοῦ γνήσιε δοῦλε. Ἀνάβλεψον εἰς τὸν οὐρανὸν καὶ ἴδε τὰ
ἡτοιμασμένα σοι ἀγαθά."

Ἀτενίσας δὲ ὁ ἅγιος, ἐθαμβήθη. Καὶ εἶπεν ὁ ἄγγελος
πρὸς αὐτόν, "Τί ὁρᾷς, ὦ μακάριε;"

Ὁ δὲ λέγει, "Ὁρῶ στέφανον, καὶ μέσον αὐτοῦ τὴν χεῖρα
τοῦ Κυρίου μου· καὶ ἐν αὐτῇ Πνεῦμα Ἅγιον ὡσεὶ περιστε-
ράν· καὶ βλέπω καὶ στύλον πυρὸς ἀπὸ τῆς γῆς ἕως εἰς τὸν
οὐρανόν· καὶ λογίζομαι ὅτι ὁ Θεός μού ἐστι."

Καὶ λέγει αὐτῷ ὁ ἄγγελος, "Ὁ μὲν Θεὸς ἡτοίμασέ σοι
ἃ βλέπεις· ταῦτα δέ εἰσιν ὑπὲρ τῶν ἀγώνων καὶ ἱδρώτων
σου στέφανος ἀμοιβῶν."

9   Ὁ δὲ βασιλεύς, πλέον ἐθυμοῦτο· καὶ λέγει πρὸς τὸν
ἅγιον, "Παῦσε φλυαρῶν ἔμπροσθέν μου."

Καὶ εὐθὺς κελεύει δεθῆναι αὐτοῦ χεῖρας καὶ πόδας. Καὶ
κελεύει ἀχθῆναι παρθένον εὔμορφην κόρην, καὶ τεθῆναι
ἐπάνω τοῦ ἁγίου ὅπως κινηθῇ πρὸς ἐπιθυμίαν, καὶ συγ-
γενῆ μετ' αὐτῆς, καὶ ὡς ἐκ τούτου θύσῃ τοῖς εἰδώλοις. Καὶ
προσηνέχθη ἡ κόρη μετὰ πασῶν ἀρωμάτων <ἐπὶ> τὰ ἱμάτια αὐτῆς, δι' ὧν ἤλπιζε ἐξαπατῆσαι τὸν ἅγιον· καὶ ἔθηκαν
αὐτὴν ἐπάνω αὐτοῦ.

Ὁ δὲ ἅγιος φυλαττόμενος ὑπὸ τοῦ Θεοῦ, ἔμεινεν ἐκτὸς
πάσης κακῆς ἐνθυμήσεως· πλὴν ἐμβριμώμενος πρὸς τὸ
ἀποστρέψαι ἀπ' αὐτοῦ τὴν κόρην, ἔκοψε τὴν γλῶτταν

the Lord stood in front of him and said, "Hail, thrice-blessed Niketas! *Be brave and strong* and keep up the fight. For behold, a crown is being plaited for you by holy angels. Hail, friend of Christ and glorious martyr, destroyer of demons and Christ's genuine servant. *Look up to heaven* and see the good things that have been stored up for you."

The saint looked and was amazed. And the angel said to him, "What do you see, blessed man?"

And he said, "I see a crown, and the hand of my Lord in the middle of it; and in the hand I see the Holy Spirit *like a dove;* and I also see a *pillar of fire,* reaching up from the earth to the heaven; and I think that it is my God."

And the angel said to him, "Indeed, God has prepared for you all that you see; these things are the crown rewarding all your struggles and labors."

The emperor became more enraged; and he said to the saint, "Stop talking nonsense in front of me." 9

And immediately he ordered that Niketas's hands and feet be tied up. And he ordered a beautiful virgin girl to be brought and be placed on top of the saint so that he might be moved to desire, and have sex with her, and might as a result sacrifice to the idols. And the girl was brought with her clothes all perfumed up, a device by which she hoped to lead the saint astray; and they placed her on top of him.

Yet the saint, guarded by God, remained unaffected by any evil thought; nevertheless, *deeply moved,* so that he might get the girl away from him, he bit off his tongue with his

αὐτοῦ μὲ τοὺς ὀδόντας αὐτοῦ. Καὶ ἔρριψεν αὐτὴν τοῦ κυνὸς λέγων, "Δέξαι, κύον, βρῶμα." Ἰδοῦσα δὲ ἡ κόρη τὸ αἷμα ῥέον ἀπὸ τοῦ στόματος αὐτοῦ σφοδρῶς, διέστη ἀπ᾽ αὐτοῦ· καὶ φυγοῦσα ἀπῆλθε πρὸς τὸν βασιλέα λέγουσα, "Βασιλεῦ, ὁ υἱός σου ἔκοψε τὴν γλῶτταν αὐτοῦ μετὰ τῶν ὀδόντων αὐτοῦ, καὶ ἔρριψεν αὐτὴν τοῦ κυνὸς λέγων 'Δέξου, κύον, βρῶμα.'"

Αὐτῆς γὰρ ἀπαγομένης πρὸς τὸν βασιλέα, εὐξάμενος ὁ ἅγιος ἀπεκατέστη ἡ γλῶττα αὐτοῦ ὑγιὴς ὡς τὸ πρότερον.

10 Καὶ κελεύσαντος τοῦ βασιλέως ἐλθεῖν τὸν ἅγιον πρὸς αὐτόν, προσέταξε τεθῆναι αὐτὸν ἐπὶ κλίνην σιδηρᾶν, καὶ βαλεῖν ἐπ᾽ αὐτὴν πῦρ καὶ ἄσβεστον· εἶχε δὲ ἡ κλίνη τροχοὺς τέσσαρας. Καὶ ἐκέλευσεν κυλισθῆναι ἐπὶ ὀξὺν κατήφορον ὅπως διασκορπισθῶσι τὰ μέλη αὐτοῦ. Ὁ δὲ ἅγιος ἰδὼν τὴν κλίνην, ἐσφράγισεν αὐτὴν τῷ τύπῳ τοῦ σταυροῦ, καὶ εὐθὺς διελύθησαν οἱ τροχοὶ καὶ ἀνέθαλε χόρτος· καὶ κοιμηθεὶς ἐπάνω αὐτῆς ἀνεπαύσατο ψάλλων οὕτως: "Εὐλογητὸς Κύριος ὁ Θεὸς ποιῶν μεθ᾽ ἡμῶν θαυμάσια."

Ἐκέλευσε δὲ ὁ βασιλεὺς στρατιώτας συναγαγεῖν τὰ σκορπισθέντα αὐτοῦ μέλη· ἤλπιζε γὰρ ὅτι σκορπισθῆναι ὄφειλεν ἀπὸ τοῦ μηχανήματος τούτου. Ἐλθόντες δὲ οἱ στρατιῶται, εὗρον αὐτὸν ἐν τοῖς χόρτοις ἀναπαυόμενον ἀβλαβήν. Καὶ προσκυνήσαντες αὐτόν, παρεκάλεσαν ἵνα δώσῃ αὐτοῖς τὴν ἐν Χριστῷ σφραγῖδα πιστεύοντες εἰς αὐτόν. Καὶ ἀναστὰς ὁ ἅγιος τοῦ Θεοῦ, ἐσφράγισεν αὐτοὺς ἐπὶ τῷ ὀνόματι τοῦ Πατρὸς καὶ τοῦ Υἱοῦ καὶ τοῦ Ἁγίου Πνεύματος.

own teeth. And he threw it to a dog, saying, "Take this, dog, and eat it!" When the girl saw the blood gushing freely from his mouth, she left him; she went running to the emperor and said, "Emperor, your son bit off his tongue with his own teeth, and threw it to a dog saying, 'Take this, dog, and eat it!'"

In the meantime, while she was on her way to the emperor, the saint prayed and his tongue was restored to its previous condition.

And then the emperor ordered the saint to come to him 10 and ordered him to be placed on an iron bed, and then fire and lime be put on it. The bed had four wheels; and he ordered it to be rolled down a steep incline so that Niketas's body parts would be scattered. But when the saint saw the bed, he made the sign of the cross upon it, and immediately the wheels disappeared and grass sprouted; and he lay on the bed and took a rest, while chanting, *"Blessed be the Lord God, who does wondrous things* for us."

Then the emperor ordered soldiers to gather Niketas's scattered body parts; for he was hoping that they would indeed be scattered about because of that instrument of torture. When the soldiers came, however, they found him unharmed and resting on the grass. And they fell on their knees before him, and they asked him to give them Christ's seal as they believed in Christ. And the saint of God stood up, and sealed them with the sign of the cross in the name of the Father and the Son and the Holy Spirit.

11 Καὶ ἀπελθὼν πρὸς τὸν βασιλέα λέγει αὐτῷ, "Ὁρᾷς, ἀσύνετε καὶ ἄσπλαγχνε, τὴν δύναμιν τοῦ Θεοῦ μου;"

Ἰδὼν δὲ αὐτὸν ὁ βασιλεὺς ἐθυμώθη λίαν, καὶ ἐκέλευσεν τεθῆναι εἰς τὸ στόμα αὐτοῦ ἀνθρακίαν πυρός, καὶ ἐπὶ τὰ χείλη αὐτοῦ δύο λαβράρια, καὶ σούβλαν πεπυρωμένην σιδηρᾶν πηχῶν τεσσάρων κόπτοντα ἐπὶ τὰ τέσσαρα μέρη τεθῆναι εἰς τὸ ὠτίον αὐτοῦ καὶ διαπερᾶσαι εἰς τὸ ἕτερον, καὶ ἄνθρακας καυστικοὺς βαλεῖν ἐν τοῖς ὑποδήμασιν αὐτοῦ. Καὶ ταῦτα ὑπομείνας ὁ τοῦ Χριστοῦ ἀθλητὴς Νικήτας, εὐχαρίστει τῷ Κυρίῳ λέγων, "Στεφάνωσόν μου τὴν ψυχήν, Κύριε· ἐγὼ γὰρ τὸ σῶμά μου οὐκ ἐλεήσω διὰ σέ· ἐκ γῆς ἐγένετο καὶ εἰς γῆν ἀπελεύσει."

12 Καὶ πάλιν κελεύει ὁ βασιλεὺς ἄνδρας δώδεκα ἐξονυχίσαι αὐτόν, καὶ τρεῖς ὀδοντάγρας ἐξοδοντίσαι, καὶ ἑτέρους δύο ἐξοφθαλμίσαι αὐτόν, καὶ μετὰ ταῦτα κρεμασθῆναι αὐτὸν ἐπὶ κεφαλῆς καὶ καπνισθῆναι ὑπὸ στυπίων. Ὁ δὲ μακάριος Νικήτας γενναίως ὑπομείνας καὶ ταύτην τὴν κόλασιν, ἔλεγε, "Κύριε, Κύριε, ἵνα τί με ἐγκατέλιπες; Διὸ δέομαί σου, μὴ ἐγκαταλίπῃς ἀλλ᾽ ἐπάκουσον τῆς δεήσεως τοῦ δούλου σου, καὶ ἀπόστειλον τὸν ἄγγελόν σου ἵνα δροσίσῃ μου τὸ στόμα ὅτι οὐ φέρω τὸν καύσωνα."

Καὶ εὐξαμένου αὐτοῦ, κατῆλθε δρόσος ἀπὸ τοῦ οὐρανοῦ καὶ ἐδρόσισεν αὐτόν, καὶ τοὺς ἀντικειμένους κατέπνιξε. Καὶ λαβὼν ἀναψυχὴν ὁ μακάριος, εὐχαρίστησε τῷ Κυρίῳ λέγων, "Δόξα σοι, ὁ Θεός, ὁ ταχύνας εἰς τὴν ἐμὴν βοήθειαν καὶ οὐκ ἐγκατέλιπές με τὸν δοῦλόν σου ἀφανισθῆναι."

13 Ἰδὼν δὲ ὁ βασιλεὺς ὅτι οὐχ ἅπτεται αὐτοῦ βάσανος

And Niketas went to the emperor and said to him, "You   11
stupid and merciless man, do you see the power of my God?"

But when he saw him, the emperor became very angry,
and ordered fiery coals to be placed in Niketas's mouth, and
two clips on his lips, and a spit, four cubits long and with
cutting edges on all four sides, to be heated up and placed in
one ear and driven through to the other, and burning coals
to be put into his shoes. And after the athlete of Christ
Niketas had endured these tortures, he thanked the Lord,
saying, "Crown my soul, Lord; for I shall not spare my body
on your behalf; from the earth it came into being and *to earth
it will return.*"

Once more, the emperor ordered twelve men to rip out   12
Niketas's nails, three teeth pullers to draw out his teeth, and
two other men to gouge out his eyes, and after that to hang
him, head down, and to smoke him with oakum. The blessed
Niketas also bravely endured this torture and said, "Lord,
Lord, *why have you forsaken me? I beg you, *do not abandon* me,
but *hear the petition* of your servant, and *send* your *angel* to
cool my mouth with dew as I cannot bear the *scorching heat.*"

When he had prayed, dew came down from heaven and
cooled him off, and drowned his opponents. And when the
blessed one obtained relief, he thanked the Lord, saying,
"Glory to you, God, who hastened to my aid and did not
forsake me your servant and let me perish."

Seeing that no torture could affect Niketas, but rather   13

ἀλλὰ μᾶλλον ἰσχυρότερος ἦν ἐν τῇ Χριστοῦ πίστει, ἐξ-
ίστατο καὶ διηπόρει, διαλογιζόμενος ποίῳ τρόπῳ αὐτὸν
ἀπολέσαι. Καὶ ἀναστάντες δύο μάγοι, Χαμὲλ καὶ Ἀβενα-
γώρ, εἶπον τῷ βασιλεῖ, "Δέσποτα, ἡμεῖς ἀποκτείνωμεν
αὐτόν."

Καὶ ἀποκριθεὶς ὁ βασιλεὺς εἶπεν αὐτοῖς, "Μὰ τοὺς μεγάλους θεοὺς Ἀρτέμην καὶ Ἀπόλλωνα, ἐὰν τοῦτο ποιή-
σετε, πολλὰ χρήματα ἔχω ὑμῖν δοῦναι."

Ὁ δὲ ἅγιος ἔφη πρὸς τὸν βασιλέα, "Τετυφλωμένε καὶ
ἀποστερημένε τῆς ἀληθείας! Οὐκ ἀκούεις κἂν τὰ ὀνόματα
τῶν θεῶν σου; Ὁ Ἀρτέμης ποιεῖ σε ἄρτι ἀποστερηθῆναι
ἀπὸ τῆς ζωῆς· ὁ Ἀπόλλων ἀπώλειαν προξενεῖ σοι καὶ σκότος αἰώνιον."

Τότε θυμωθεὶς ὁ βασιλεύς, λέγει τῷ πρώτῳ τῶν μάγων,
"Ἀπόκτεινον αὐτὸν καὶ πρῶτος ἔσῃ ἐν τῇ βασιλείᾳ μου."

Ἐνέγκας δὲ ὁ μάγος δράκοντος κεφαλὴν καὶ ὄφεως θηριακῆς ἄκρατον καὶ συγκεράσας <εἰς> ποτήριον, ἔδωκε
πιεῖν τῷ μάρτυρι. Ὁ δὲ πιὼν τὸ ποτήριον ἐν τῇ ἐπικλήσει
τοῦ Κυρίου ἡμῶν Ἰησοῦ Χριστοῦ, ἔμεινεν ἀβλαβὴς δοξά-
ζων καὶ εὐχαριστῶν τῷ Θεῷ τῷ εἰπόντι, "Ἐν τῷ ὀνόματί
μου κἂν θανάσιμόν τι πίωσιν, οὐ μὴ βλάψῃ αὐτοὺς πιστεύοντας εἰς ἐμέ."

Ἰδόντες δὲ οἱ μάγοι ὅτι οὐκ ἠδυνήθησαν βλάψαι τὸν
ἅγιον ἀπὸ τοῦ φαρμακοποσίου, λέγουσιν αὐτῷ, "Πῶς καλεῖται τὸ ὄνομά σου, ἅγιε δοῦλε τοῦ μεγάλου Θεοῦ;"

Ὁ δὲ λέγει αὐτοῖς, "Τὸ μὲν πρῶτόν μου ὄνομα, Χριστιανός εἰμι· τὸ δὲ κληθέν μοι ὑπὸ τοῦ ἀγγέλου, Νικήτας,
δοῦλος Χριστοῦ."

made him stronger in his faith in Christ, the emperor was at a loss and perplexed, unable to figure out a way to finish him off. Two magicians, Chamel and Abenagor, stood up and said to the emperor, "Master, let us kill him."

The emperor responded and said to them, "By the great gods, Artemes and Apollo, if you manage that, I shall give you lots of money."

The saint said to the emperor, "You blind man, deprived of the truth! Don't you even realize what the names of your gods mean? 'Artemes' makes you lose your life right now. 'Apollo' brings about your destruction and eternal darkness."

At that point the emperor became angry and said to the first of the magicians, "Kill him, and you shall become first in my kingdom."

The magician brought the head of a serpent and pure snake venom, mixed them up in a cup, and gave it to the martyr to drink. Niketas drank from the cup, but invoked the name of our Lord Jesus Christ, and remained unharmed, thus giving glory and thanks to God, who had said, "Whoever believes in me, if, *in my name, they drink any deadly thing, it will not hurt them.*"

When the magicians saw that they were unable to hurt the saint with the poisoned drink, they said to him, "What is your name, holy servant of the great God?"

He said to them, "Christian is my principal name; by the angel, I was called Niketas, servant of Christ."

Τότε προσεκύνησαν αὐτοῦ τοὺς πόδας λέγοντες, "Ἅγιε τοῦ Θεοῦ Νικήτα, βάπτισον ἡμᾶς, καὶ πιστεύομεν εἰς ὃν κηρύττεις Ἰησοῦν Χριστόν, τὸν Υἱὸν καὶ Λόγον τοῦ Θεοῦ."

Ὁ δὲ ἅγιος σφραγίσας αὐτοὺς τῷ τύπῳ τοῦ σταυροῦ, ἐρράντισεν αὐτοὺς τῷ ὕδατι τοῦ ἁγίου βαπτίσματος λέγων αὐτοῖς, "Βάπτισμα ἀναγεννήσεως λαβόντες πορεύεσθε."

Καὶ ὁ βασιλεὺς κελεύει σιδηρωθῆναι τοὺς πόδας αὐτοῦ καὶ ἀχθῆναι ἐν τῇ φυλακῇ. Μετασχηματισθεὶς δὲ ὁ διάβολος ὡς ἄγγελος φωτός, εἰσῆλθε πρὸς αὐτὸν καὶ λέγει αὐτῷ, "Χαίροις, Νικήτα μακάριε."

Ὁ δὲ λέγει αὐτῷ, "Τίς εἶ σύ, ὁ κομίζων μοι δωρεὰν τὸ 'Χαῖρε';"

Καὶ ὁ διάβολος λέγει, "Ἄγγελός εἰμι τοῦ Θεοῦ σου καὶ ἀπεστάλην παρ' αὐτοῦ πρὸς σὲ εἰπεῖν ἵνα εἰσακούσῃς τῷ βασιλεῖ καὶ θύσῃς τοῖς θεοῖς ἐν τῷ φανερῷ, καὶ ἐν τῷ κρυπτῷ θύσῃς τῷ Θεῷ σου, καὶ μὴ τιμωρῆσαι, ὅτι πολλὰς βασάνους κατὰ σοῦ ἑτοιμάζει."

Ὁ δὲ ἅγιος ἐν ὀλιγωρίᾳ γενόμενος, εἶπε, "Κύριε, ὁ Θεός μου, τίς ἐστιν οὗτος ὁ συμβουλεύων μοι οὕτως ποιῆσαι; Παράσχου μοι γνῶσιν καὶ δύναμιν, καὶ ὑπόδειξόν μοι τίς ἐστιν οὗτος ὁ λαλῶν μοι τὰ τοιαῦτα."

Εὐθέως δὲ κατῆλθεν ἄγγελος ἀπὸ οὐρανοῦ καὶ κρατήσας τὸν διάβολον, παρέδωκεν αὐτὸν εἰς τὰς χεῖρας τοῦ ἁγίου λέγων αὐτῷ, "Κράτησον αὐτόν, μάρτυς Χριστοῦ, καὶ μάθε τίς ἐστι."

Καὶ ὁ ἅγιος ῥίψας τὸν διάβολον χαμαὶ καὶ λαβὼν τὸ

Then, bowing down at his feet, they said, "Holy man of God, Niketas, please baptize us; we believe in Jesus Christ, the Son and Word of God, whom you preach."

The saint sealed them with the sign of the cross and sprinkled them with the water of the holy baptism, saying to them, "Now you have received a baptism of rebirth, go on your way."

And the emperor ordered Niketas's feet to be put in irons 14 that he be taken to prison. The devil transformed himself into an angel *of light,* and came to Niketas and said to him, "Hail, blessed Niketas."

He said to him, "Who are you, offering this 'Hail' to me so freely?"

And the devil said, "I am an angel of your God, and I've been sent by him to tell you to obey the emperor and sacrifice to the gods in public, and pray to your God in private; that way you will avoid punishment, since the emperor is preparing many tortures for you."

The saint became hesitant and said, "Lord, my God, who is this who is advising me to act this way? Grant me understanding and power, and show me who it is who is saying such things to me."

Immediately, an angel came down from heaven and grabbed hold of the devil and delivered him into the saint's hands, saying to him, "Hold on to him, martyr of Christ, and find out who he is."

And the saint threw the devil to the ground, took the

σίδηρον ὃ ἦν ὑπὸ τοὺς πόδας αὐτοῦ δεδεμένον, ἔτυπτεν αὐτὸν σφοδρῶς λέγων αὐτῷ, "Εἰπέ μοι τίς εἶ καὶ πόθεν ἔρχῃ;"

Καὶ ὁ δαίμων ἔφη αὐτῷ, "Ἀνάστειλον τὸν πόδα σου ἀπὸ τοῦ τραχήλου μου κἀγὼ σοὶ ἀναγγέλω πάντα."

15   Ἀναστείλας δὲ ὁ ἅγιος τὸν πόδα αὐτοῦ ἀπὸ τοῦ τραχήλου τοῦ δαίμονος, λέγει αὐτῷ ὁ δαίμων, "Ἀπέστειλέ με πρὸς σὲ ὁ πατήρ μου ὁ Σατανᾶς."

Καὶ ὁ ἅγιος λέγει, "Καὶ πῶς ἐτόλμησας ἐλθεῖν πρός με καὶ εἰς ποῖα ἔργα ἐπιτυγχάνεις;"

Ὁ δαίμων εἶπεν, "Πολλάκις ἐπιτυγχάνομεν, πολλάκις καὶ οὐκ ἐπιτυγχάνομεν, πολλάκις καὶ ἐμπαιζόμεθα ὡς καὶ ἄρτι."

Ὁ μάρτυς λέγει, "Πῶς καλεῖσαι;"

Ὁ δαίμων εἶπε, "Βεελζεβούλ. Καὶ εἰς τοὺς μεγιστάνους ἀνθρώπους ἐγὼ ἀποστέλλομαι. Ἐγὼ πολλῶν μοναχῶν κόπους ἀπώλεσα, εἰς ὀργὴν μετέβαλα. Ἐγὼ εἰσέρχομαι εἰς τὴν ἐκκλησίαν τοῦ Θεοῦ καὶ πάντας ποιῶ τοῦ ἁμαρτάνειν. Καὶ τοὺς μὲν ἀποστρέφω εἰς τὰ ὀπίσω, τοὺς δὲ διανεύεσθαι ἕτερος πρὸς τὸν ἕτερον· ἄλλους κινῶ πρὸς συντυχίας· ἑτέρους πρὸς γέλωταν. Τοὺς δὲ ἱερεῖς καὶ ἀρχιερεῖς πολλὰ σκανδαλίζω· ἐγὼ εἰσέρχομαι εἰς τὰς καρδίας αὐτῶν καὶ σκληρύνω αὐτοὺς πρὸς ἀλλήλους, καὶ ἐγείρω αὐτοὺς εἰς ἔχθραν καὶ φθόνον καὶ μῖσος καὶ καταλαλιάς, καὶ ἁπλῶς πρὸς πᾶν ὃ φιλεῖ ὁ εἰρημένος πατήρ μου ὁ Σατανᾶς, καὶ ὃ μισεῖ ὁ μόνος Θεὸς τῶν ὅλων. Ἐγὼ ταῖς γυναιξὶ παρασκευάζω λαλεῖν ἃ οὐκ ἀκούουσι· καὶ σοφίζω αὐταῖς ποιεῖν μάχας καὶ ἐπαοιδίας. Ἐγὼ ποιῶ τοὺς ἀνθρώπους

iron shackles with which his feet were fettered, and began to strike him fiercely, while saying to him, "Tell me who you are, and where you come from?"

And the demon said to him, "Get your foot off my neck and I'll tell you everything."

The saint lifted his foot off the neck of the demon, and the demon said to him, "My father, Satan, sent me to you." 15

And the saint said, "And how did you dare to come to me, and what are you successful at?"

The demon said, "Sometimes we succeed, sometimes we don't, and sometimes we're made fun of, as happened just now."

The martyr said, "What's your name?"

The demon said, "Beelzebul. And I'm the one who is sent to the powerful people. I'm the one who has made the labors of many monks go to waste, as I turned them to anger. I'm the one who enters the church of God and makes everyone sin. I make some turn round, and others nod to each other; I get others chatting, and others laughing. I trip up priests and archpriests in all sorts of ways; I enter into their hearts and harden them toward each other, and I provoke them to enmity, and envy, and hatred, and slander, and, simply put, to everything which my aforementioned father, Satan, loves and which the only God of all hates. I encourage women to say what they have not actually heard; and I teach them how to set up quarrels and cast spells. I make people

ἀκούειν τὸν κήρυκα τῆς ἐκκλησίας καὶ μὴ ἀπέρχεσθαι, ἀλλὰ λέγειν, ὅτι ὅλοι ἃς συναχθῶσιν καὶ τότε ὑπάγωμεν ἡμεῖς.’ Καὶ ὅσοι ἀπομείνουσι τοῦ ὄρθρου τῆς ἁγίας Κυριακῆς, φίλοι καὶ ἀδελφοί μού εἰσιν. Ἐγὼ ποιῶ τοὺς ἀνθρώπους ἐν ὁράμασιν ἁμαρτάνειν· καὶ τοὺς μὲν ποιῶ ἀζωσταρίους καὶ περιδεδεμένους τὰς ἑαυτῶν κεφαλὰς σουδαρίοις καταφρονητικῶς μεταλαμβάνειν. Ἐγὼ πολλοὺς τῶν ἀνθρώπων ἀπατῶ, καὶ πλανῶ.”

Ὁ δὲ ἅγιος βασανίσας αὐτὸν πολλά, ἔσυρε τὸν δαίμονα καὶ ἔρριψεν αὐτὸν ἔμπροσθεν τοῦ βασιλέως καὶ λέγει αὐτῷ, “Ἴδε ὁ πλάνος καὶ θεός σου.”

Καὶ ἀποκριθεὶς ὁ βασιλεὺς εἶπεν αὐτῷ, “Οὐκ ἔστιν θεὸς ἐμός.” Τότε ὁ ἅγιος ποιήσας τὴν ἐν Χριστῷ σφραγῖδα, <ὁ δαίμων> ἐγένετο ἄφαντος.

16 Καὶ ταῦτα ἰδὼν ὁ βασιλεύς, κελεύει δεθῆναι τὸν ἅγιον χεῖρας καὶ πόδας, καὶ τανυθῆναι αὐτὸν ἐπὶ τὴν γῆν καὶ ὑπὸ δέκα στρατιωτῶν ῥαβδισθῆναι. Ταῦτα δὲ αὐτοῦ πάσχοντος, ἰδοὺ ὁ δαίμων παρεγένετο πρὸς τὸν βασιλέα καὶ πρὸς τὸν ὄχλον λέγων, “Ναί, καλὰ τύψατε αὐτόν, ὅτι οὐδεὶς τῶν στρατιωτῶν ἢ ἐκ τῶν ἀρχόντων τῆς πόλεως τοιαῦτα σημεῖα ἐποίησεν. Αὐτὸς δὲ καὶ ἐπάτησε καὶ ἔτυψέ με, καὶ πάντας τοὺς θεοὺς ἡμῶν ἐξουδένωσε καὶ ἐσυνέτριψεν.”

Ὁ δὲ ἅγιος τοῦ Θεοῦ Νικήτας, ἐπάρας τὸ ὄμμα αὐτοῦ πρὸς τὸν δαίμονα, ἐθεώρει αὐτὸν ὡς λέων ἠγριωμένος. Καὶ ὁ δαίμων ὡς εἶδε τὸν ἅγιον ἐμβλέψαντα πρὸς αὐτὸν ἔλεγε, “Οἴμοι! Πάλιν πιάσαι με βούλη.” Καὶ εὐθέως ἐγένετο ἀφανής.

17 Καὶ πάλιν κελεύει ὁ βασιλεὺς λυθῆναι τὸν ἅγιον καὶ

not go when they hear the semantron of the church, but rather say 'let everyone else gather first, and then we'll go.' And all those who stay away from the matins of holy Sunday are my friends and brothers. I make people sin in their dreams. And I make some people receive the holy communion with contempt by not wearing a belt and by covering their heads with scarves. I deceive many people and lead them astray."

The saint tortured him a lot and then dragged the demon off and threw him in front of the emperor and said to him, "Here he is, the impostor, who is your god."

And the emperor responded and said to him, "He is not my god." Then the saint made the sign of the cross and the demon vanished.

And when the emperor saw all this, he ordered the saint 16 to be bound hand and foot, stretched out on the ground, and beaten by ten soldiers. While Niketas was subjected to this suffering, lo and behold the demon appeared before the emperor and the crowd, and he said, "Yes! Strike him well, because none of the soldiers or the noblemen of the city has ever performed such miracles. He both trampled on me and struck me, and turned all of our gods to nothing; he made them dust."

The saint of God Niketas raised his eyes to the demon and fixed his gaze upon him like an irate lion. And when the demon saw the saint staring at him, he said, "Oh dear! He wants to catch me again!" And he vanished immediately.

And again the emperor ordered the saint to be released 17

ἀγαγεῖν ἔξω τῆς πόλεως ἐν ἑνὶ τόπῳ, ἐν ᾧ ἵστατο κιόνιον ἕν, καὶ ἔγγιστα αὐτοῦ ἦν σώματα κεκοιμημένων νεκρῶν καὶ λέγει τῷ ἁγίῳ, "Ἐὰν τοὺς νεκροὺς τούτους ἀναστήσεις καὶ τὸν λίθον τοῦτον ποιήσεις εἰς ξύλον, πιστεύομεν εἰς τὸν Χριστὸν ὃν σὺ κηρύττεις."

Οὕτως ἀκούσας ὁ ἅγιος παρὰ τοῦ βασιλέως, κλίνας τὰ γόνατα αὐτοῦ πρὸς ἀνατολάς, ηὔξατο πρὸς Κύριον λέγων, "Κύριε, ὁ Θεὸς τοῦ Ἀβραὰμ καὶ Ἰσαὰκ καὶ Ἰακώβ, ὁ καταστήσας τὰ χερουβὶμ καὶ τὰ σεραφὶμ καὶ τὰ ἑξαπτέρυγα καὶ πολυόμματα βοῶντα, κεκραγότα, καὶ λέγοντα Ἅγιος, ἅγιος, ἅγιος, Κύριος Σαβαώθ, πλήρης ὁ οὐρανὸς καὶ ἡ γῆ τῆς δόξης σου,' ὁ ποιήσας τὸν ἥλιον καὶ τὴν σελήνην, ὁ στήσας τὴν θάλασσαν διὰ τεσσάρων στοιχείων καὶ πᾶσαν τὴν οἰκουμένην, ὁ ποιήσας τὸν ἄνθρωπον ἀπὸ τῆς γῆς καὶ πάλιν εἰς τὴν γῆν ἀποστρέφειν αὐτὸν ἐκέλευσας, ἐπάκουσον, Δέσποτα, καὶ ἐμοῦ τοῦ δούλου σου, καὶ ἀνάστησον τῇ δυνάμει σου καὶ *κραταιᾷ σου χειρὶ* τοὺς νεκροὺς τούτους, καὶ τὸν λίθον τοῦτον μεταποίησον εἰς ξύλον, ὅπως ἴδωσιν οἱ ἐν τῇ πόλει ταύτῃ καὶ πιστεύσωσιν εἰς σὲ τὸν κτίστην τῶν ἁπάντων· σὺ γὰρ εἶ *εὐλογητὸς εἰς τοὺς αἰῶνας, ἀμήν.*"

18 Καὶ ὡς ηὔξατο ταῦτα, ἤκουσε φωνῆς λεγούσης αὐτῷ, "Εἰσηκούσθη σου, Νικήτα, ἡ δέησις, καὶ γένηταί σοι ὡς ηὔξω." Καὶ εὐθέως κατελθὼν ἄγγελος ἀπὸ οὐρανοῦ ἀστράπτων τῇ μορφῇ, ἐξανέστησε τοὺς νεκρούς· καὶ τὸν κίονα μετεποίησε εἰς κλῆμα ἔχον βότρυας, καὶ ἐν τῇ ῥίζῃ αὐτοῦ ἔβλυσεν οἶνος ἡδύτατος ὡς μέλι.

and taken out of the city to a place where a column stood and near it lay the bodies of dead people, and he said to the saint, "If you raise these people from the dead and turn this stone into a tree, I shall believe in the Christ whom you preach."

When he heard these words from the emperor, the saint bent his knees toward the east and prayed to the Lord, saying, "Lord, God of Abraham, Isaac, and Jacob, you who set the cherubim and the seraphim and the six-winged and many-eyed creatures, exclaiming, crying out aloud, and saying 'Holy, holy, holy is the Lord of Sabaoth, heaven and earth are full of your glory,' you who created the sun and the moon, you who established the sea and the entire world with four elements, you who created man from the earth and have commanded that he shall return to the earth again, listen to me your servant, Lord, and by your power and *with your mighty hand* raise up these dead people and transform this stone into a tree, so that the inhabitants of this city may witness this and believe in you the creator of all; for you *are blessed forever, amen.*"

And when he had completed this prayer, he heard a voice 18 saying to him, "Your petition has been heard, Niketas, and what you requested will come about." And straightaway an angel came down from heaven with a dazzling face, and resurrected the dead people; and he transformed the column into a vine bearing grapes, and from its roots wine spouted, which was extremely sweet, like honey.

Ἰδόντες δὲ οἱ ἄνθρωποι τὰ τοιαῦτα σημεῖα καὶ τὸν ἄγγελον ἀστράπτοντα σφόδρα, ἐξέστησαν κράζοντες, "Ἀληθῶς εἷς Θεός, ὃν ὁ Νικήτας κηρύττει."

Καὶ ἐβόησαν ἅπαντες οἱ ὄχλοι, "Μέγας ὁ Θεὸς τῶν
Χριστιανῶν."

Προσελθόντες δὲ οἱ ἐγηγερμένοι νεκροί, προσεκύνησαν τῷ ἁγίῳ λέγοντες, "Εὐχαριστοῦμέν σε, ἅγιε μάρτυς
Χριστοῦ Νικήτα, ὅτι διὰ σοῦ ἔγνωμεν τὸ φῶς."

Ὁ δὲ λέγει αὐτοῖς, "Πῶς ἐπέγνωτε τὸ ὄνομά μου; Καὶ
πόσους χρόνους ἐνθάδε κεῖσθε;"

Οἱ δὲ νεκροὶ εἶπον αὐτῷ, "Ἀπὸ τοῦ αἰῶνος ἐνθάδε
ἤμεθα, καὶ εἰς σκότος ζοφερὸν ὑπήρχομεν κολαζόμενοι,
καὶ ἄρτι διὰ τῆς δυνάμεως τοῦ Κυρίου καὶ διὰ σοῦ, μακάριε, εἴδομεν τὸ φῶς τοῦ κόσμου. Καὶ πῶς οὐ μὴ ἐπεγνώ-
καμεν τὸ ὄνομά σου;"

Τότε σφραγίσας αὐτοὺς ὁ ἅγιος εἶπεν αὐτοῖς, "Πορεύεσθε καὶ ὁ Χριστὸς διατηρήσει ὑμᾶς ἵνα κληρονόμοι γέ-
νησθε τῆς αὐτοῦ βασιλείας, καὶ τῆς ἐν τῷ Παραδείσῳ
τρυφῆς ἀπολαύσετε."

19 Ἡ δὲ γυνὴ τοῦ βασιλέως καὶ πᾶς ὁ λαὸς τῆς πόλεως,
ὁμοθυμαδὸν ἐκραύγασαν πρὸς τὸν βασιλέα λέγοντες,
"Οὐ βλέπεις, ἄπιστε κύον, τὰς δυνάμεις τοῦ Χριστοῦ." Καὶ
κρατήσαντες αὐτὸν εἶπον, "Ἡμεῖς οὐ πειθόμεθά σου
πλεῖον, ἀλλὰ πιστεύομεν εἰς τὸν Θεὸν τὸν κηρυττόμενον
παρὰ τοῦ αὐτοῦ μάρτυρος Νικήτα." Καὶ λέγουσιν τῷ
ἁγίῳ, "Βάπτισον ἡμᾶς, ἅγιε τοῦ θεοῦ, ἐπὶ τῷ ὀνόματι τοῦ
Χριστοῦ, ὅτι πιστεύομεν διὰ σοῦ εἰς αὐτόν."

When the people saw such great miracles and how the angel was so dazzling, they were completely astonished, and they cried out aloud, "Truly there is one God, the one whom Niketas preaches."

And the entire crowd shouted, "Great is the God of the Christians."

The people who had risen from the dead came and knelt before the saint, saying, "We thank you, holy martyr of Christ, Niketas, because through you we have come to know the light."

He said to them, "How did you learn my name? And how many years have you been lying here?"

The resurrected ones said to him, "We've been lying here for ages, and we were being punished in deep darkness, and just now, through the power of the Lord and through you, blessed one, we saw *the light of the world.* How could we not know your name?"

Then the saint sealed them with the sign of the cross and said to them, "Go on your way, and may Christ preserve you so that you may become heirs *of* his *kingdom,* and enjoy the delight of Paradise."

The emperor's wife and all the people of the city, in one voice, shouted at the emperor, saying, "Don't you see, you faithless dog, the power of Christ?" And they seized him and said, "We're not obeying you anymore, but rather we believe in the God whom his martyr Niketas preaches." And they said to the saint, "Baptize us, holy man of God, in the name of Christ, because we believe in him through you." 19

Τούτων οὖν ταῦτα τῷ ἁγίῳ λεγόντων, εὐθὺς ἀνέβλυσεν
ἀπὸ τοῦ τόπου οὗ τὸ κιόνιον ἵστατο ποταμὸς συγκεκραμ-
μένος μύρον καὶ ἔλαιον, καὶ ἐβαπτίσθη σχεδὸν πᾶσα ἡ
πόλις, εἰς τὸ ὄνομα τοῦ Πατρὸς καὶ τοῦ Υἱοῦ καὶ τοῦ
Ἁγίου Πνεύματος, ἄνδρες τε καὶ γυναῖκες καὶ τὰ τέκνα
αὐτῶν, τὸν ἀριθμὸν χιλιάδες εἴκοσι πέντε, δοξάζοντες τὸν
Πατέρα καὶ Υἱὸν καὶ Ἅγιον Πνεῦμα ἐπὶ τῇ ἀναγεννήσει
καὶ τῇ εἰς Χριστὸν πίστει.

20 Ἐτελειώθη δὲ ὁ μάρτυς τοῦ Χριστοῦ Νικήτας ὑπὸ Ἀθαναρίχου ἄρχοντος τοῦ ἔθνους μηνὶ Σεπτεμβρίῳ πέντε καὶ
δεκάτῃ, ἡμέρᾳ Σαββάτῳ. Τὸ δὲ πολύαθλον καὶ ἅγιον
αὐτοῦ σῶμα, ἤρθη νεύσει Θεοῦ ὑπὸ ἁγίων ἀγγέλων, καὶ
μετετέθη εἰς τὴν ἁγίαν Πόλιν ἐν τῇ κρεμαστῇ πέτρᾳ, ἔνθα
ἀπόκεινται καὶ ἕτερα ἅγια λείψανα—τοῦ Ἁγίου Παφνουτίου καὶ Χαραλάμπους, Παρακλήτου καὶ Βονιφατίου,
Ἀλεξίου καὶ Εὐφημιανοῦ.

21 Καὶ ὅστις μετὰ φόβου Θεοῦ καὶ πίστεως ἐπακροάσεται
τὴν ἄθλησιν τῆς ἐναρέτου πράξεως τοῦ Ἁγίου μεγαλομάρτυρος Νικήτα, ἀφέονται τὰ ἁμαρτήματα αὐτοῦ ἡμέρας
ἑπτά, καὶ διώκονται καὶ οἱ δαίμονες ἀπ᾽ αὐτοῦ ἡμέρας
τεσσαράκοντα. Διὸ καὶ νῦν, Χριστὲ ὁ Θεὸς ἡμῶν, ταῖς
πρεσβείαις τοῦ Ἁγίου μεγαλομάρτυρος Νικήτα, ἀξίωσον
ἡμᾶς μετὰ φόβου δοξάζειν τὸ πανάγιον ὄνομά σου, καὶ τῆς
αἰωνίου ζωῆς ἀξιωθῆναι, ἧς γένοιτο πάντας ἡμᾶς ἐπιτυ-
χεῖν, χάριτι καὶ οἰκτιρμοῖς καὶ φιλανθρωπίᾳ τοῦ ἀνάρχου
σου Πατρὸς καὶ τοῦ παναγίου καὶ ἀγαθοῦ καὶ ζωοποιοῦ
σου Πνεύματος, νῦν καὶ ἀεὶ καὶ εἰς τοὺς αἰῶνας τῶν αἰώνων, ἀμήν.

As they were saying these things to the saint, immediately a river mixed with myrrh and oil spouted from the spot where the column stood, and almost the entire city was baptized, in the name of the Father and the Son and the Holy Spirit, men and women and their children, twenty-five thousand in number, glorifying the Father and the Son and the Holy Spirit for their rebirth and faith in Christ.

The martyr of Christ Niketas was killed by Athanarichos, 20 the ruler of a heathen nation, in the month of September, on the fifteenth, a Saturday. His holy body, which had gone through so many ordeals, was taken up by holy angels at God's command, and was transferred to the holy City, into the hanging stone, where also other holy relics are kept— those of Saints Paphnoutios and Charalampos, Parakletos and Boniphatios, Alexios and Euphemianos.

And whoever listens attentively to the passion and virtu- 21 ous deeds of the great martyr Saint Niketas, with the fear of God and with faith, his sins shall be forgiven for seven days, and the demons will also be driven away from him for forty days. For this reason, also now, Christ our God, by the intercessions of Saint Niketas the great martyr, deem us worthy to glorify in fear your all-holy name, and become worthy of the eternal life, which may we all obtain, through the grace and mercy and love of humankind of your Father who is without beginning and of your all-holy and good and life-giving Spirit, now and forever and unto the ages of ages, amen.

Abbreviations

AASS = *Acta Sanctorum,* 71 vols. (Paris, 1863–1940)

BHG = François Halkin, *Bibliotheca hagiographica Graeca,* 3rd ed. (Brussels, 1957); and François Halkin, *Novum auctarium bibliothecae hagiographicae Graecae* (Brussels, 1984)

BHL = *Bibliotheca hagiographica Latina,* 2 vols. (Brussels, 1898–1901)

BHO = Paul Peeters, *Bibliotheca hagiographica orientalis* (Brussels, 1910)

CPG = Maurice Geerard, F. Glorie, and J. Noret, eds., *Clavis patrum Graecorum,* 6 vols. (Turnhout, 1974–1998)

Ehr. 1, 2, 3 = Albert Ehrhard, *Überlieferung und Bestand der hagiographischen und homiletischen Literatur der griechischen Kirche, von den Anfängen bis zum Ende des 16. Jahrhunderts,* 3 vols. (Leipzig, 1937)

PG = Jacques-Paul Migne, ed., *Patrologiae cursus completus: Series Graeca,* 161 vols. (Paris, 1857–1866)

RGK = Ernst Gamillscheg, Dieter Harlfinger, and Herbert Hunger, *Repertorium der griechischen Kopisten 800–1600,* 3 vols. (Vienna, 1981–1997)

Synaxarion of Constantinople = Hippolyte Delehaye, *Synaxarium ecclesiae Constantinopolitanae e codice Sirmondiano nunc Berolinensi adiectis Synaxariis selectis,* Propylaeum ad Acta Sanctorum Novembris (Brussels, 1902)

Note on the Texts

The Greek texts edited in this volume are "open texts" in their manuscript transmission. That is, they show significant variation from manuscript to manuscript, as well as more or less freedom from "correct" linguistic usage as would be defined and demanded by learned Greek writers of the period. Each text is thus preserved in several *versions,* where variation is significant and affects the contents of the text. Each version is furthermore usually attested in several *redactions,* where variation is evident on a minor scale (only a few omissions or additions, different words or word forms, and the like). Finally, the Greek language used is often closer to spoken varieties of Medieval Greek (as much as these can be recovered), without fixity and with much irregularity in terms of syntax, morphology, and writing form.

Such openness in transmission requires special treatment in producing a critical edition. Even though families of versions and then families of redactions can be traced, no single, unified, and supposedly "original" or "final" version can be reconstructed and thus restored in the printed text. And even if more "correct" forms of words and syntax can be restored, the editor is forced to be hesitant in making such corrections, since these might hide the linguistic variety of Medieval Greek.

Accordingly, the editorial principles employed for the texts included in the present volume are the following:

1. Whenever, after studying the available manuscript evidence, a version can be reconstructed with some confidence and has never been edited previously, I present the text of this version, based on several manuscript witnesses, while still using a single manuscript redaction as my main guide; this is the case with the texts pertaining to Boniphatios, Alexios, and Makarios.

2. Whenever a redaction or a version of a text has already been published in printed form, I have tried to restore it further based on the manuscripts themselves; this is the case for Markos, Christopher, and George (*Passion* and *Miracles*).

3. For the last text in the collection, that pertaining to Niketas, which shows the most variation from redaction to redaction, I have chosen to present an unknown redaction of what I consider the earliest version, for whose reconstruction I consulted several manuscript witnesses.

In all cases, what is printed is a new, previously unedited text. Moreover, in all cases, I have tried to intervene as little as possible in producing the printed texts, often keeping or preferring an irregular or awkward form or syntax. I have also followed closely the punctuation and paragraphing of the manuscripts, observing principles that I have laid out elsewhere; see Stratis Papaioannou, ed., *Epistulae*, by Michael Psellus, 2 vols. (Berlin and Boston, 2019), vol. 1, pp. clvi–clix. Finally, as a rule, all clearly orthographical er-

rors have been corrected silently, and the accentuation of enclitics, which is somewhat inconsistent in the manuscripts, has been normalized.

PASSION OF BONIPHATIOS

Sigla

B = Vatican, Biblioteca apostolica Vaticana, Ottob. gr. 1, second half of the eleventh century, from southern Italy, fols. 321v–24v; Ehr. 1, pp. 293–98, 661, 715, and Ehr. 3, pp. 777 and 984; and Santo Lucà, "Scritture e libri in Terra d'Otranto fra XI e XII secolo," in *Bizantini, Longobardi e Arabi in Puglia nell'alto medioevo* (Spoleto, 2012), 487–548. Among many other hagiographical texts, the manuscript also contains a version of the *Life of Alexios.*

N = Milan, Ambrosiana, F 144 sup. (Martini-Bassi 377), twelfth century, from southern Italy, fols. 47v–50r; Ehr. 1, pp. 346–49 and 715.

T = Vatican, Biblioteca apostolica Vaticana, Vat. gr. 866, tenth or eleventh century, from southern Italy, fols. 193r–94v; scribe: Nikolaos (*RGK* vol. 3, p. 522); Ehr. 1, pp. 338–46; and Santo Lucà, "Esopo nel Mezzogiorno d'Italia di lingua greca: Una nuova testimonianza di riuso in contesto agiografico," Νέα Ῥώμη 16 (2019): 69–111. Among many other hagiographical texts, this important manuscript contains the "apocryphal" *Passion* of Marina (*BHG* 1165–1166c) as well as versions of the *Life of Alexios* and the *Passions* of George and Christopher.

U = Vatican, Biblioteca apostolica Vaticana, Barb. gr. 555, thirteenth century, from southern Italy, fols. 31v–32v; Ehr. 1, pp. 320–23.

Bigot = Émery Bigot, *Palladii episcopi Helenopolitani de vita s. Johannis Chrysostomi dialogus* (Paris, 1680), 310–24; and Thierry Ruinart, *Acta primorum martyrum sincera & selecta* (Amsterdam, 1713), 283–91. It is unclear on which manuscripts this edition is based; its version shows signs of "correction."

In the Notes to the Texts, I have noted only significant variants.

Life of the Man of God, Alexios

Sigla

H = Paris, Bibliothèque nationale de France, gr. 1538, tenth century, latter half, fols. 210r–14v. As attested by scribal notes, the manuscript belonged to the library of the Monastery of Saint George of Rhinia, in Kyzikos, in Asia Minor; see S. Kotzabassi, *Βυζαντινά χειρόγραφα από τα μοναστήρια της Μικράς Ασίας* (Athens, 2004), 89–91. However, the script comes certainly from an Italo-Greek environment; see Ehr. 2, p. 347 and, especially, Ehr. 3, pp. 776–77, against the later view of Santo Lucà, "Il Diodoro Siculo Neap. B.N. gr. 4* è italogreco?," *Bollettino della Badia greca di Grottaferrata* 44 (1990): 33–79, at 57. In my view, the manuscript was likely written by someone in the circle of Neilos of Rossano, if not copied by him himself. The manuscript contains also the *Life* of Mary of Egypt (*BHG* 1042) as well as the apocryphal *Passion* of Marina (BHG 1165–1166).

L = Vatican, Biblioteca apostolica Vaticana, gr. 2022, dated to 953/4, from Lucania, southern Italy, fols. 15r–19v; scribe: Markos (*RGK* vol. 3, p. 435); Ehr. 3, p. 923; and Santo Lucà, "La *Parva Catechesis* di Teodoro Studita in Italia meridionale: Un nuovo testimone ritrovato a Melfi, in Basilicata," *Rivista di Studi Bizantini e Neoellenici* 52 (2015): 93–164, at 103 and 137–39. Notably, the text of Alexios follows the *Life* of Mary of Egypt (*BHG* 1042).

Manuscript L, used as the main witness for the present edition, is the earliest dated manuscript of the *Life of the Man of God, Alexios* and was previously not taken into consideration in any editions of the *Life*. It is, nevertheless, close to (though it offers better readings and a more complete redaction than) manuscript H.

H was utilized but not preferred by Francisco Maria Esteves Pereira in his edition of the text, "Légende grecque de l'Homme de Dieu, Saint Alexis," *Analecta Bollandiana* 19 (1900): 243–53. That edition was based primarily on Vati-

can, Biblioteca apostolica Vaticana, Vat. gr. 866, from southern Italy (ms. T in the edition of Boniphatios above), with supplementary variants provided from the fifteenth-century manuscript Oxford, Bodleian Library, Baroccianus 146.

Manuscript L contains some corrections by a later hand (not always correct), some of which have been adopted silently. Similarly, I do not record the many different variants as well as mistakes of the previous edition, which indeed presents a different redaction. However, those correct variants adopted from H are noted, while additions (words or short phrases) based on H are indicated with angle brackets in the main text.

Life of Markos the Athenian

Sigla

R = Paris, Bibliothèque nationale de France, gr. 1547, dated to 1286, fols. 249v–58r; Ehr. 1, p. 641, and Ehr. 3, pp. 924 and 948; Charles Astruc et al., *Les Manuscrits grecs datés des XIIIe et XIVe siècles conservés dans les bibliothèques publiques de France, I: XIIIe siècle* (Paris, 1989), 53–56. The manuscript contains also the *Lives* of saints Basil the Younger (*BHG* 263–264f), Paisios (BHG 1402–1403), and Andrew the Fool (*BHG* 115z–117q), which precede Markos's story, the last complete text in the manuscript. The codex is concluded with *stichêra* troparia annotated with Byzantine musical notation, hymns in honor of Meletios the Younger and Loukas the Younger, both Middle Byzantine saints of central Greece.

Angelidi = Christine Angelidi, "Ὁ Βίος τοῦ Μάρκου τοῦ Ἀθηναίου (*BHG* 1039–1041)," Σύμμεικτα 8 (1989): 33–59 (Greek text at 45–59), where another ten further witnesses and their variant readings are presented and discussed.

NOTE ON THE TEXTS

The Greek text is based on the edition by Christine Angelidi, with minor revisions, including punctuation. Following the editorial principles of the present volume, these revisions, which are listed in the Notes to the Texts, restore all
viable readings of a *single* manuscript, R. That manuscript is
among the earliest witnesses of the text. More important,
its redaction of the story of Markos is a redaction of the
likely *earliest* version of the tale, as far as we can recover it in
the Greek tradition, as rightly argued by Angelidi. Angelidi
also used R as the primary witness (designated by the siglum
P in her edition), but did not retain all its readings throughout.

It should be added that, in 2006, Chrestos I. Kazilas prepared an edition (with extensive introduction) of the *Life* of
Markos, submitted as a Masters Thesis for the School of
Theology of the University of Athens, Greece. The work is
available on www.academia.edu under the title Κριτικὴ
ἔκδοση τοῦ Βίου τοῦ ὅσ. Μάρκου τοῦ Ἀθηναίου (Εἰσαγωγὴ—
Κείμενο—Πίνακες) (Argyroupoli, 2006). Kazilas's edition
was based on seven manuscripts from Athenian library collections—five of these manuscripts are post-Byzantine in
date, and none of them was utilized by Angelidi. Since, however, the Greek text produced in this otherwise useful study
is based on an arbitrary selection of manuscript witnesses
and thus does not assist much in recovering the earliest redaction of the text, it has not been taken into consideration
for the present edition.

A full survey of all the manuscript witnesses, and an edition of all the versions of the Greek *Life* of Markos, remains
a desideratum.

LIFE OF MAKARIOS THE ROMAN

Sigla

D = Vatican, Biblioteca apostolica Vaticana, Vat. gr. 824, eleventh century, a *Menologion,* fols. 259r–73r; Ehr. 3, pp. 743–44.

E = Athens, National Library of Greece, MS 1027, twelfth century (second half?), probably from Epirus, fols. 268r–78r; Ehr. 1, pp. 155–59. Among many other hagiographical texts, the manuscript contains also a version of the *Passion* of George.

S = Moscow, State Historical Museum, Sinod. gr. 364 (Vladimir 397), sixteenth century, fols. 268r–96r; Ehr. 3, pp. 593–94. This is the single manuscript on which the edition of *BHG* 1005 is based in Afanasii Vassiliev, *Anecdota Graeco-Byzantina* (Moscow, 1893), 135–65 (right column). In this manuscript the text of Makarios is preceded by a redaction of the *Life* of Markos the Athenian, while at the end of the volume we find the "apocryphal" *Acts* of the apostles Andrew and Matthew, who visit the "land of the Anthropophagi" (*BHG* 109–110c).

Y = Rome, Biblioteca Nazionale Centrale Vittorio Emanuele II, gr. 03, late eleventh or early twelfth century, fols. 45v–58r.

Since the Greek text of the legend is transmitted widely (see "Hagiographica, Macarius Romanus anach. (S.), Vita," Pinakes, http://pinakes.irht.cnrs.fr/notices/oeuvre/16821/) and with considerable variation, I have opted to present a better text of what I consider to be the earliest preserved version, namely *BHG* 1005 (*BHG* 1004 is, in my view, a later reworking). A post-Byzantine redaction of *BHG* 1005 was edited by Afanasii Vassiliev, *Anecdota Graeco-Byzantina,* in 1893, based on a single, sixteenth-century manuscript (S).

For the new text edited here, I consulted the text of S and

a few other witnesses (access to these manuscripts was provided to me by Christine Angelidi, to whom I am most grateful) but have used as my main witness manuscript D, which is the likely earliest Greek manuscript with the full text of *BHG* 1005 (or 1005d, according to the *BHG*, whose identifying numbers require revision). For the sake of comparison, I have also collated manuscript E, in which the *Life of Makarios* served as a reading during Lent, likely on the fourth Sunday, an indication of the ambivalent generic nature of the text, situated between a saint's *Life* and a beneficial tale. For some key and somewhat problematic passages, I have also consulted another early manuscript, Y, which however preserves a very mutilated text of the *Life*.

In the Notes to the Texts, I signal either significant variants or those variants from E, S, and Y that I have adopted against the readings of D. All other differences (and they are many) between the text transmitted in D and those in E, S, and Y are not noted. Finally, the text was checked also against one of the Latin versions of the story, edited in *AASS* October, vol. 10, pp. 566–71.

PASSION OF CHRISTOPHER

Sigla

Q = Paris, Bibliothèque nationale de France, gr. 1470, dated to 890 and copied from a manuscript, itself copied in Rome, fols. 19r–25r; Ehr. 1, pp. 258–266. Among many other hagiographical texts, the manuscript contains the "apocryphal" *Passion* of Marina (*BHG* 1165–1166c).

Usener = Hermann Usener, "Acta S. Marinae et S. Christophori," in *Festschrift zur fünften Säcularfeier der Carl-Ruprechts-Universität zu Heidelberg*, ed. Hermann Usener (Bonn, 1886), 56–76.

My research has indicated that the text of Q is in fact unique, and not preserved in other manuscripts as suggested in the relevant entry of Pinakes ("Hagiographica, Christophorus m. in Lycia (S.), Passio," https://pinakes.irht .cnrs.fr/notices/oeuvre/14898/). The many manuscripts that are there said to preserve *BHG* 309 actually transmit *BHG* 310c (or further redactions of it, such as *BHG* 310). Notably, *BHG* 310c remains unedited, even if it happens to be the earliest in manuscript attestation, as fragments from it are preserved in a palimpsest manuscript dated to the late eighth century (Cambridge, University Library, Add. 4489).

The edition is based on Usener, adopting silently his many corrections, although I fixed a few errors and restored the punctuation and paragraphing of the manuscript, as well as some readings that were considered ungrammatical by Usener and were placed by him in the critical apparatus.

George the Great Martyr

Passion

Sigla

A = Athens, National Library of Greece, 422, dated to 1546, fols. 277v–91r; scribe: Theodoros Arologos (from Chania). See further Karl Krumbacher, *Der heilige Georg in der griechiscehn Überlieferung,* ed. A. Ehrhard (Munich, 1911), 124; Ehr. 3, p. 229; and François Halkin, *Catalogue des manuscrits hagiographiques de la Bibliothèque nationale d'Athènes* (Brussels, 1983), 51–52.

K = Edition of A in Krumbacher, *Der heilige,* 3–16.

O = Seventh-century parchment fragment preserved in Oxford (Bodleian, MS Greek theol. f. 6), as edited in Ehr. 1, p. 73; see further

Joseph van Haelst, *Catalogue des papyrus littéraires juifs et chrétiens* (Paris, 1976), 256–57 (no. 706).

X-lat = The likely earliest (fifth-century?) Latin translation/version, ed. Wolfgang Haubrichs, *Georgslied und Georgslegende im frühen Mittel-alter: Text und Rekonstruktion* (Konigstein, 1979), 406–73.

Nub. = The ancient Nubian version of the *Passion,* as preserved in a twelfth-century codex, ed. G. M. Browne, *The Old Nubian Martyrdom of Saint George* (Leuven, 1998).

All textual additions (cited in angle brackets) and corrections introduced or suggested by Krumbacher have been adopted, several silently. I have, however, made a few additional corrections, incorporated omissions, retained in some instances the awkward "vulgar" Greek of the manuscript, fixed the punctuation so as to follow the manuscript, and added numbers to indicate separate paragraphs, replicating in this respect, for convenience, the paragraph numbers of the edition of the Latin version.

Miracles

Sigla

G = Paris, Bibliothèque nationale de France, gr. 770, dated to 1315, fols. 72r–75v; scribe: Georgios Kalospites (*presbyter* and *taboularios*); Ehr. 3, p. 761; and Henricus Omont, *Catalogus codicum hagiographicorum Graecorum bibliothecae nationalis Parisiensis* (Brussels and Paris, 1896), 33–35. G is used here only for the edition of the miracle regarding the demon (section 14 onward).

Z = Rome, Biblioteca Angelica, gr. 46, twelfth century, fols. 189r–91v (the end is missing: τὴν γῆν, ἀλλ᾿ οὖν μᾶλλον onward); Ehr. 3, pp. 209–10 and 898.

Aufhauser = Edition of Z for sections 1–13 and of G for sections 14–18: Johannes B. Aufhauser, *Miracula S. Georgii* (Leipzig, 1913), 113–29 and 129–35; compare also Johannes B. Aufhauser, *Das Drachenwunder des*

Heiligen Georg in der griechischen und lateinischen Überlieferung (Leipzig, 1911), 52–69 and 70–71 (where Aufhauser utilizes also further witnesses, each with slightly different text).

Following Aufhauser, I gave primacy, for the text of the first miracle (*BHG* 687), to a redaction attested in Z, the earliest of the surviving Greek witnesses. In style and expression, this is a rather bare and rough redaction, and possibly (though not necessarily) close to the earliest Greek version; see the Introduction to the present volume and also the apparatus in Aufhauser's editions for further insignificant variants not recorded in the Notes to the present edition. Unlike Aufhauser, I have followed Z also for the second miracle (*BHG* 687k), namely, sections 14–18 of the continuous text of the two miracles as edited in this volume; since, however, Z is mutilated, I have used (as Aufhauser does) G from the point that Z ends abruptly in section 15.

PASSION OF NIKETAS

Sigla

M = Munich, Bayerische Staatsbibliothek, gr. 219, a miscellaneous collection, dated to circa 1410–1420, fols. 147v–54v; Ehr. 3, p. 849; and Kerstin Hajdú, *Katalog der griechischen Handschriften der Bayerischen Staatsbibliothek München,* vol. 4, *Codices graeci Monacenses 181–265* (Wiesbaden 2012), 213–18.

A = Athens, National Library of Greece, 422, dated to 1546, fols. 197–203v (version: *BHG* 1346d). The manuscript contains also the "apocryphal" version of the *Passion* of George edited in the present volume (see above).

C = Milan, Ambrosiana, D 092 sup. (Martini-Bassi 259), second half of the tenth century, from southern Italy, fols. 8r–11r (version: *BHG* 1343); among numerous hagiographical texts, it contains also versions of the *Passions* of Christopher and George; Ehr. 3, pp. 782–83; and (for

the dating) Santo Lucà, "Γεώργιος Ταυρόζης copista e protopapa di Tropea nel sec. XIV," in *Bollettino della Badia greca di Grottaferrata* 53 (1999), 284–347, at 299.

F = Paris, Bibliothèque nationale de France, gr. 769, thirteenth or fourteenth century, fols. 111v–23v (version: *BHG* 1346); Ehr. 3, pp. 745–46.

J = Jerusalem, Πατριαρχική Βιβλιοθήκη, Timiou Staurou 35, fifteenth or sixteenth century, fols. 256v–60r (version: *BHG* 1346d); among numerous homilies and hagiographical texts, it contains also a version of the *Life of Alexios;* Ehr. 3, pp. 845–46.

P = Paris, Bibliothèque nationale de France, suppl. gr. 162, fourteenth century, fols. 139v–46v (version: *BHG* 1345). The *Passion of Niketas* is preceded by a redaction of the *Passion* of George, while the manuscript ends with the *Life of Alexios,* here notably titled *Life and Conduct of the Man of God Alexios, and His Father Euphemianos.*

V = Vienna, Österreichische Nationalbibliothek, hist. gr. 126, fourteenth century, fols. 3r–10v (version: *BHG* 1344); Ehr. 3, pp. 748–49.

W = Vienna, Österreichische Nationalbibliothek, hist. gr. 57, thirteenth century, fols. 10r–14v (version: *BHG* 1343); Ehr. 3, pp. 99–101.

Manuscript M is the main witness used for the present edition. The additional witnesses listed above and mentioned in the Notes to the Translation are those that have been used for important variations, additions, or corrections of the text preserved in M.

Notes to the Texts

PASSION OF BONIPHATIOS

title   Κύριε εὐλόγησον *added* B, εὐλόγησον δέσποτα *added* U

1   Ὁ θεὸς ὁ φιλάνθρωπος . . . τῇ ὑμετέρᾳ ἀγάπη: *the entire paragraph is missing from* T *and* U

χρήζων BN: προνοῶν *Bigot*

πλούσιος BN: πολὺς *Bigot*

ἐπιστραφεὶς BN: ἀποστραφεὶς *Bigot*

ὑποδείγματα σωτηρίας BN: ὑποδείγματος σωτηρίαν *Bigot*

εἰς B *Bigot*: πρὸς N

αὐτὸς τῇ οἰκείᾳ ἀγαθότητι προνοούμενος B: αὐτὸς τῇ ἀφάτῳ αὐτοῦ φιλανθρωπίᾳ προνοῶν τοῦ γένους τῶν ἀνθρώπων N, τῇ οἰκείᾳ αὐτοῦ ἀγαθότητι προνοούμενος ἡμῶν *Bigot*

δίδωσιν σωτηρίας BN: ἡμῖν δίδωσιν εἰς σωτηρίαν *Bigot*

πρὸς τὸ N *Bigot*: ὥστε B

ἀπαγορεύειν BN: ἀπογνῶναι *Bigot*

ἑαυτῶν N *Bigot*: ἡμᾶς B

ὑπὸ τοῦ ἐχθροῦ παγιδευθῶμεν N: σαγινευθῶμεν B, παγιδευθῶμεν ὑπὸ τοῦ ἀλλοτρίου *Bigot*

ἐπὶ τὴν ἄφατον αὐτοῦ ἀγαθότητα, καὶ ἐπὶ τὸ ἄμετρον πέλαγος τῆς αὐτοῦ εὐσπλαχνίας N: ἐπὶ τὸ ἄφατον πέλαγος τῆς αὐτοῦ εὐσπλαχνίας B, ἐπὶ τὸ ἄφατον πέλαγος τῆς αὐτοῦ ἀγαθότητος, καὶ ἐπὶ τὸ ἄμετρον ἔλεος τῆς αὐτοῦ εὐσπλαχνίας *Bigot*

καὶ περιπλακέντες BN: *omitted Bigot*

ἐπὶ τέλει ἀνανήψαντες N: ἔπειτα μετανοήσαντες *Bigot*, τελευταῖον ἀνανήψαντες B

ἀπηνέγκαντο B *Bigot*: παρὰ Κυρίου ἐκομίσαντο N

ὑπάρχει Β: ἐστίν Ν, αὐτῶν γέγονεν *Bigot*

ἡμέτερος στεφανίτης ὁ μακάριος Β: μακάριος μάρτυς τοῦ Χριστοῦ Ν, *omitted Bigot*

νυνί διηγήσομαι τῇ ὑμετέρᾳ ἀγάπῃ Ν: νῦν κατὰ μέρος διηγήσομαι Β, ὑμῖν νῦν διηγήσομαι *Bigot*

2   γυνὴ μεγάλη ΒΤU *Bigot*: περιφανεστάτη καὶ πρώτη τῶν εὐγενίδων Ν

πάντων ΒΝU: αὐτῶν Τ *Bigot*

συνεκοινώνει ΒΝU: ἐκοινώνει Τ *Bigot*

φιλόξενος ΒΝΤU: φιλόξενος ἦν καὶ *Bigot*

δέοντα ΒΝΤU: *omitted Bigot*

3   ὅστις ΒΝΤU: εἴ τις *Bigot*

σώματα ΒΝΤU: σώματα εἰς κόλασιν *Bigot*

ἀξίους ΒΝΤU: ἀξίως *Bigot*

4   τῶν ΒΝΤU: *omitted Bigot*

5   Δέσποτα . . . ἀμήν: Ν *marks this section in the margin as "prayer"*
     (εὐχή)

εὐόδωσον ΒΝU *Bigot*: κατευόδωσον Τ

τοῦ δούλου σου, καὶ κατευόδωσον τὴν ὁδόν μου ΝΤU *Bigot*:
     omitted Β

τὸ ὄνομά σου τὸ ἅγιον ΝΤU *Bigot*: τὸ πανάγιον ὄνομά σου Β

6   ἀθληταὶ ΝΤU: μάρτυρες καὶ ἀθληταὶ Β *Bigot*

ἄλλον ἠκρωτηριασμένον τὰς ὄψεις ΝΤU: *omitted* Β *Bigot*

ἄλλον ξεόμενον ΒΤU *Bigot*: *omitted* Ν

7   κολάσει ΝΤU: τῇ κολάσει Β ταῖς κολάσεσι *Bigot*

μάρτυρες ΒΝΤU: τοῦ Χριστοῦ, καὶ μάρτυρες *Bigot*

σῶμα ΒΝU: σῶμα ὑμῶν Τ *Bigot*

8   ὄνομα ΒΝΤU: ὄνομά μου *Bigot*

9   κατακέφαλα ΒΝΤU: κατὰ κεφαλῆς *Bigot*

ἀνεθῆναι ΝΤU *Bigot*: λυθῆναι Β

ὡσεὶ ΒΝ *Bigot*: *omitted* ΤU

ὁ ἄρχων ΒΝU: *omitted* Τ

σεαυτόν ΝΤ *Bigot*: ἑαυτόν ΒU

λέγων ΒΝΤU: λέγων μοι *Bigot*

10   ἐκχέαι αὐτῷ ΝΤU: ἐκχεῖσαι αὐτῷ Β αὐτῷ ἐπιχεθῆναι *Bigot*

Εὐχαριστῶ . . . πάσχω: Ν *marks this section in the margin as "prayer"*
     (εὐχή)

ἔκραξεν BNTU: ἔκραζεν *Bigot*

σοί BNTU: εἰς σὲ *Bigot*

11 ἔωθεν BNTU: ἐπιούσῃ *Bigot*

Χριστὸς BNTU: Ἰησοῦς Χριστὸς *Bigot*

παρεστηκότων BNTU: ὑπηρετηκότων *Bigot*

12 Κύριε . . . ἀμήν: N *marks this section in the margin as "prayer"* (εὐχή)

πονηρίᾳ αὐτοῦ, καὶ μὴ ἀπατήσῃ ἐν τῇ ἀπάτῃ NTU: πονηρίᾳ
αὐτοῦ B ἀπάτῃ *Bigot*

αὐτὴν BNTU: με *Bigot*

13 Ὁ δὲ εἶπεν . . . ἐστίν BNT *Bigot: omitted* U

μεθυστὴς BNTU: μεθυστὴς, καὶ εἰς τὸ μαρτυρῆσαι οὐ ποιεῖ
Bigot

ἱκανοῖς BNTU: *omitted Bigot*

14 καὶ ἄνδρας: *a proposal by Pio Franchi de' Cavalieri, "Dove fu scritta
la leggenda di S. Bonifazio?," Nuovo bullettino di archeologia cristiana
6 (1900): 217; compare also the Latin versions*

πέντε B, *so also in the Latin versions*: πεντήκοντα NTU *Bigot, as
well as versions BHG 280a, 280b, and 281–82*

οἰκοδομήσασα BNTU: εὐκτήριον οἰκοδομήσασα *Bigot*

15 θεραπεύειν BNT *Bigot*: φυγαδεύειν καὶ θεραπεύειν U

LIFE OF THE MAN OF GOD, ALEXIOS

2 ἐτίθεντο *Papaioannou*: ἐπετίθοντω L *(most of the text of sections 2
and 3 are omitted in* H)

ὑπὲρ *Papaioannou*: περὶ L

6 φθέγξῃ *Papaioannou*: φθέγξασθαι L *(likely infinitive of indirect
speech, governed by* εἶπεν), H *offers a revised text here* (καὶ μυστήριά
τινα ἐφθέγξατο αὐτῇ)

11 εἰς τὸν ναόν H: *omitted* L *(the word* ἔσω *was added by a later hand)*

14 αὐτῷ H: αὐτοῦ L

16 ἕτεροι δὲ H: οἱ δὲ L

24 τὸ πῶς L: *could be corrected to* τό<πον ὅ>πως *(compare* δότωσαν
δὴ τόπον πάντες ἵνα H)

ἣν *added Papaioannou*

25 προτεθῆναι H: προστεθῆναι L

Life of Markos the Athenian

1 & emskip; ἐμέ R: με *Angelidi*
  ἐν τῷ ὄρει ὄντα R: ὄντα ἐν τῷ ὄρει *Angelidi*
3   αὐτὴν R: *omitted Angelidi*
  τραχυτέρᾳ R: τραχυτάτῃ *Angelidi*
  ἐκείνῃ R: *omitted Angelidi*
  ἐκείνας R: *omitted Angelidi*
8   ἐχθές R: χθές *Angelidi*
  μου R: σου *Angelidi. The same correction applies to this word, repeated throughout the paragraph.*
  ἐπιλανθάνου: ἐπιλανθάνων R ἐπιλανθάνον *Angelidi*
  λυπῇ R: λυπεῖς *Angelidi*
9   ὡς R: *omitted Angelidi*
10   Θεοῦ R: τοῦ θεοῦ *Angelidi*
11   Ἀθήνας R: Ἀθηνῶν *Angelidi*
12   οὖν R: δὲ *Angelidi*
  σώματος *Angelidi*: σωμάτου R
15   οὐκ *supplemented Angelidi (based on other witnesses of the text)*
18   ψαλμούς R: ὕμνους *Angelidi*
19   παθητὸν R: ποθητὸν *Angelidi*
20   Σώζοισθε R: Σώζεσθε *Angelidi. The same correction applies to this word, repeated throughout the paragraph.*
  πάννυχοι R: παννύχιοι *Angelidi*
  Χριστοῦ R: Κυρίου *Angelidi*
21   καὶ R: *omitted Angelidi*
  τοῦ Χριστοῦ τοῦ υἱοῦ R: *omitted Angelidi*
23   τὸν Θεὸν γενέσθαι μοι *Papaioannou*: γενέσθαι μοι τὸν Θεὸν R, τὸν σταυρὸν γενέσθαι *Angelidi*
25   ἐπεὶ R: ἐνῷ *Angelidi*
  αὐτοῦ R: *omitted Angelidi*
  σκεπάσαι R: σκεπάσει *Angelidi*
  ὁδηγῆσαι R: ὁδηγήσει *Angelidi*

Life of Makarios the Roman

2	ἀσκήσεως DYS: δεήσεως E
3	ἐμέ DY: *the correct form should be* ἐμοῦ *as in* E
	Θεόφιλε DYS: Θεόδουλε E
5	Κτησιφῶν DYS: Πλησιφῶν E
6	πόλιν DYS: τόπον E
7	φοροῦντα DY: φορῶντα E, φορούντων S
	στεφάνων DYS: στέφανον E
10	ἔχιδνες EYS: ἔγχεις D
	βουβάλους ... λεοπάρδους DYS: πλὴν ὀλίγα ἐξ αὐτῶν E
11	ἴχνος DYS: χνοὺς E
12	οʹ DS: ροʹ E
15	ἄλλαι E: *omitted* DS
16	βόθυνος DYS: βόρβορος E
18	ἔχιδνες ES: ἔγχεις D
20	καθὰ πνέουσιν οἱ ἄνεμοι E: *omitted* D, καθὼς πνέουσιν S
	ὅμοιαν βαλάνου S: καλήν DE
24	πλῆρες *Papaioannou*: πλήρης DE, *omitted* S
28	ἑπτὰ ES: δέκα D
31	ἰδὼν ὁ ὄναγρος: *in the previous sentence the* ὄναγρος *is a feminine noun, a not uncommon inconsistency, hence it has not been corrected here*
33	σκύμνα DS: κυνάρια E
35	δώδεκα DS: ιʹ E
	ἑαυτὸν ES: *omitted* D
37	δάκρυα DS: δελεάσματα E
	πεῖναν DS: ἀσθένειαν E
40	ὤρυξαν τοῖς ὄνυξιν ἑαυτῶν D: ὀρύξαντες τοῖς ὄνυξιν αὐτῶν ἐποίησαν τὸ ὄρυγμα βάθος ἀνδρομήκου E, ὤρυξαν τοῖς ὄνυξιν αὐτῶν βάθος ἀνδρομήκου S
	βάλλοντες S: βάλλοντα D *is perhaps to be retained, as this manuscript shows some instability in participle forms, which likely points to vernacular usage rather than erroneous transcription; see also section 7, above, and the relevant note in the Notes to the Translations,* *omitted* E

42   ἐχούσας S: ἔχοντας D *is again perhaps to be retained*, ἔχοντα E
πυρὸς SD: φωτὸς E

43   ἑβδομήκοντα ἢ καὶ πλεῖον S: ρο΄ E

45   πεσόντες ES: πεσόντα D. *Compare the note on section 40, above.*

48   πεντήκοντα D: δέκα E, τεσσαράκοντα S

PASSION OF CHRISTOPHER

1   Ταύτης *Papaioannou (compare BHG 310c)*: Τοίν[..] Q *(the letters in the introductory paragraph are rewritten by a later hand)*, Τοίνυν *Usener*

        <ὁ> ἀπαίδευτος . . . κατήνεγκεν *Papaioannou*: ἀπαίδευτος εἰς ἄκραν· διὰ οὖν τῶν ἀρχόντων κατήνεγκαν Q, ἀπὸ Δεκίου σάκραν διὰ τῶν ἀρχόντων κατήνεγκαν *Usener*

        πάντα τὸν θρησκεύοντα: *I retain here the awkward reading of the manuscript, which does not agree in number with the participle* ἀπογευσαμένους *that follows*

4   θεοῖς *Papaioannou, compare BHG 310*

6   σοι πάντων Q: συμπάντων *Usener*

7   τισίν Q: γείτοσιν *Usener*

9   μέλλετε Q *compare BHG* 310c *etc.*: μέλλητε *Usener*
ἢ Q: καὶ *Usener*
ὁ δὲ *Papaioannou*: διὸ Q *Usener*

12   αἰῶνα Q: αἰώνιον *Usener*

13   ἡμᾶς Q: ὑμᾶς *Usener*
ὡς *Usener in critical appratus*: καὶ Q

16   ἦν *Usener in critical apparatus*
εἰ δυναίμην *Usener*: εἴθυσδυναίμην Q. *The passage is corrupt; as the Syriac version suggests (Popescu, Die Erzählung, 40), some phrase like* ὅτι οὐ θύω τοῖς θεοῖς *has fallen out.*

19   αὐτός Q: <ὁ> ἄτιμος *Usener*

21   ἅρματος Q: βήματος *Usener*

23   ἀχειροποίητε Q: ἀχειρότευητε *Usener*

24   Ἀτταλείας συνορούσης Πισιδίᾳ *Usener*: Ἰταλείας σύνοδαούσης (συνορευούσης?) Περσίδος Q

George, the Great Martyr

Passion

1 θύλακα *Albert Ehrhard, in Karl Krumbacher, Der heilige Georg in der griechischen Überlieferung, ed. Albert Ehrhard (Munich, 1911), 126:* φύλακα AK

εἰς πίδακας *Papaioannou:* σκύλακας AK

3 ἐλάνθανες . . . μεγαλόψυχος *Papaioannou:* ἐλάνθανεν ἡμᾶς, ὤν, μεγαλοψύχως A, ἐλάνθανες . . . μεγαλοψύχους K. *The passage is corrupt, and another likely correction may be* Αὐτὸς οὖν ἐλάνθανες. Ἡμᾶς ὄντας μεγαλοψύχους, οὐ μετρίως *etc. Compare BHG 1544c, Passion of Photios and Aniketos 2.9–10.*

καὶ ἡμᾶς: *added Papaioannou (compare X-lat 38–39)*

ἐνύβρισας K: ἐνύβρισεν A

ἔλεγε K: λέγων A

θρεπτὸς . . . χώρας *is placed after* κομητατοῦρα *in* AK

κομητατοῦρα A: κομητοῦρα K

ἴσον μοι A, *compare X-lat 53:* μείζονα K

μοι ἴσον A: μείζονα K

Μηδείας *Papaioannou following the suggestion in Krumbacher, Der heilige, 127–28 and the text of X-lat 58:* Δίας AK

4 ὅλῳ τῷ σώματι A: ὅλον τὸ σῶμα K

ἀποταθῆναι K: ἀποτεθῆναι A

καταπάσασθαι A: καταπάσσεσθαι K

6 Καὶ καθίσας . . . μοι ταῦρον: *the missing passage has been added from another early version (BHG 679), preserved in Paris. gr. 770 (dated to 1315), and edited in Krumbacher, Der heilige, 18–30, at 21*

7 καταλαβοῦσά σε ἡ χάρις A: καταλαβοῦσάν σε τὴν χάριν K

προσμίξας τῇ *Papaioannou:* προσμήξας τῇ A προσμήξας τὴν K. *I have also retained the problematic* τῇ . . . εἰκόνα, *which is repeated twice in the manuscript; see a few lines below.*

εἶπε δὲ Ἀθανάσιος . . . ἐν αὐτῷ *was mistakenly omitted by* K, *though Krumbacher adds it in his commentary (Der heilige, 111)*

8   πριστήριον *Papaioannou*: πριαστήριον A πιαστήριον K

ἡνίκα δὲ . . . τροχόν *also mistakenly omitted by* K

Ἔπειτα ἀνανεύσας . . . ὁ ἐπιτιμήσας: Ἔπειτα ἀνανεύσας πρὸς
τὸν ἑαυτοῦ εὐεργέτην, ἔλεγεν· "Ἀδιάδοχε, ἄναρχε, νικηφόρε,
μαρτύρων στέφανε, διὰ τὸ ὄνομά σου, οὐρανὸν καὶ γῆν ποιήσας, αὐτὸς ἐπὶ τῶν ὑδάτων ἀναπέπαυσαι· οὗ γένος ἀνθρώπων οὐκ ἔγνω τὴν σὴν ἀνάπαυσιν· ὅτε δὲ ἐν αἰσθήσει ἐκαμάρωσας τὸν οὐρανόν, τὰς ὀμβροτόκους νεφέλας ἐγέμισας
ὑδάτων, τοῦ βρέχειν ἐπὶ δικαίους καὶ ἀδίκους· Κύριε, ὁ
στήσας τὰ ὄρη σταθμῷ καὶ τὰς νάπας ζυγῷ, ὁ ἐπιτιμήσας O.
See Notes to the Translations; for μαρτύρων στέφανε, *compare co-
rona martyrum in* X-lat *158 and* μαρτύρων στέφανε *in the related
Passion of Barbara, ed. A. Wirth, Danae in christlichen Legenden (Vienna, 1892), p. 110, line 133.*

ταρτάρου K: ταρτάρῳ A

γένος ἀνθρώπων οὐδεὶς: *retaining once more the awkward syntax
of the Greek*

ἀνέμοις καὶ θαλάσσῃ *Papaioannou, compare Matthew 8:26*:
ἀνέμους καὶ θαλάσσης A, ἀνέμοις τῆς θαλάσσης K

9   συνεκρότησαν K: συνεκράτησαν A

γνώσει A: γνωρίσῃ K

10   λικμᾶσθαι A: λικμασθῆναι K

ἔστι K: ἔστη A, *perhaps to be retained*

11   εἴ τι A: ὅτι K

δεκατέσσαρεις K: δεκατέσσαροι A

φέρειν *Papaioannou, compare* Nub., *p. 11*: φαίρειν A φαίνειν K

τὸ τρίτον K: μετὰ τρία ἔτη A

13   ἐστὶν A: ἔστιν K

οὐδὲ *added Papaioannou*

καὶ *Papaioannou*: κἂν AK

14   ἄρτον *added Papaioannou, compare* X-lat: ἄρτους K

ἐνίσχυσεν K: ἡσύχασεν A

ἀρκέσῃ τούτῳ A: ἀρκέσει τοῦτο K

15   καὶ ἀπέδωκε τὸ πνεῦμα *added Papaioannou, compare* X-lat: καὶ
ἀπέθανε K

τῶν ὑπηρετῶν K: αὐτῶν A

16 πάντα τὰ ἔργα τοῦ διαβόλου ἀντερίζει *Papaioannou, compare*
X-lat: τὰ λεγόμενα ἀνταρίζει K
17 κνῆσις A *(I thank Alexandros Alexakis for this correction)*: κνῖσα K
ἐλάλει A: ἐλάλησε K
18 Ὁ δὲ ἅγιος εἶπεν *added Papaioannou*: Ὁ ἅγιος Γεώργιος εἶπεν
added K but placed after the phrase Ἐπὶ ἑνὸς ... νομίζω ἐγώ
Ἐπὶ ἑνὸς ... νομίζω ἐγώ: *this admittedly strange statement is excised*
in K
Ἤκουσε δὲ ἡ γυνὴ τοῦ βασιλέως καὶ ἐλυπήθη: *also excised in* K
Τὸ δὲ παιδίον ... τοῦ θεοῦ Γεώργιος: *the missing passage has again*
been added from BHG 679, as edited in Krumbacher, Der heilige
Georg, 18–30, at 26, with the sole correction of κωφὸν ὄντα *to*
κωφὸν ὄν
Πόθεν αὐτὸν ἀνέστησας K: τὸν πόθεν ἀνέστησεν A
Ὅτε K: ὅτι A
πνιγμῷ A: πνιγμὸν K
δέξασθαι K: μὴ δέξεται A
19 τὸν θεόν σου *omitted* K
20 ἀσχολεῖσαι K: χολῆσαι A
κατ' K *in the apparatus*: καὶ A
ἀπονενοημένος K: ἀπονεμισμένος A
οἰκονομήσας K: οἰκοδομήσας A
ὑπνίῳ A: ἐνυπνίῳ K
ἐάν τις *Papaioannou, compare* Nub. *page 26*: καὶ AK
τοῦ ὀνόματός μου καὶ A: *omitted* K
αὐτῶν A: αὐτοῦ K

Miracles

7 ὁρῶντες Z: <τί> ὁρῶντες *Aufhauser*
11 λέγουσα *Papaioannou*: λέγων Z *Aufhauser*
14 εἰ *Papaioannou*: οὐ Z
δεῖξον *Aufhauser*: δεῖξον σου ZG
15 παρήμην *Papaioannou*: πάρειμι Z
ἀστραπὴν *Papaioannou*: ἀστραπὴν κοιλίδος Z
βρονταῖς *Papaioannou*: βροντῆς Z

οὐ δύναται: *added Papaioannou based on* G

πόδες μου Z *breaks off here. From the start of section 14 to this point,* G, *followed by Aufhauser, offers a slightly different text.*

16 ἀλλὰ μείναντα εἰς *Papaioannou*: ἀλλ᾽ ἐμίανεν G *Aufhauser,* ἀλλ᾽ ἔμεινεν εἰς *André-Jean Festugière, Sainte Thècle, saints Côme et Damien, saints Cyr et Jean (extraits), saint Georges: Traduits et annotés (Paris, 1971)*

PASSION OF NIKETAS

1 πληρωμένου: *I retain the demotic form here*
2 ὑποδεῖξαι *Papaioannou*: ὑποδείξῃ M
3 γοργοπέταστε *Papaioannou*: γοργοπέτασθε M
   αὐτοῦ *Papaioannou*: σου M
4 Παραβάτης *compare* AJ: παμκράτης M
5 ἐλήρησας *Papaioannou*: ἐλήρινας M
   ἐπάγαγέ *Papaioannou*: ἀπάγαγέ M
   αὐτοῖς *Papaioannou*: αὐτούς M
6 ἑαυτοῖς *Papaioannou*: ἑαυτῶν M
   ἀκμὴ: *retaining the demotic form as opposed to* ἀκμὴν
   ὃν ὁ ἀδελφός μου Δαδιανὸς ἐβασάνισεν *compare* JAV: ὁ ἀδελφός σου, ἢ Δαδιανὸς M
   ὁ: ἢ M
7 κιόνων *Papaioannou*: κιωνίων M
8 ἀμοιβῶν *Papaioannou*: ἀμοιβέον M
9 ἐπὶ: *added Papaioannou*
   μὲ τοὺς ὀδόντας: *instead of* μετὰ τῶν ὀδόντων
10 ἀβλαβήν: *I retain again the awkward form*
11 λαβράρια *compare* λαυράρια JA: λαύρια M
   κόπτοντα: *the correct form would be* κόπτουσα (*modifying* σούβλαν, *which reads as* σουβλίον *in other redactions*)
   ἐλεήσω *Papaioannou*: ἠλεήσω M
   ἀπελεύσει: *the correct form would be* ἀπελεύσεται
12 εὐχαρίστησε: *the correct form would be* ηὐχαρίστησε
13 θηριακῆς *Papaioannou*: θύρικος M

εἰς: *added by Papaioannou*
πιστεύοντας *Papaioannou*: πιστεύοντες M
15 Πολλάκις ἐπιτυγχάνομεν, πολλάκις καὶ οὐκ ἐπιτυγχάνομεν JA:
   Πολλάκις ἐπιτυγχανόμενος, ἐπιτυγχάνομεν πολλάκις M
   Βεελζεβούλ *Papaioannou*: Βελζεβούλ M
   σκληρύνω *Papaioannou*: σκληρινῶ M
   ἐγείρω *Papaioannou*: ἐγέρω M
   ἐπαοιδίας *Alexakis*: ἐπαίδείας MAJ, ἀναιδείας V
   ἀζωσταρίους M: ἀζώστους AJ
16 ἐπὶ *Papaioannou*: ὑπὸ M
   ἐσυνέτριψεν: *the correct form would be* συνέτριψεν
17 κεκραγότα *Papaioannou*: καὶ κραγῶτα M
18 ηὔξω *Papaioannou*: ηὔξησας M
   πόσους *Papaioannou*: πῶς M
20 Ἀθαναρίχου *Papaioannou*: Ἀθανιρίχου M
   κρεμαστῆ *Papaioannou*: κρεμασθῇ M
   Χαραλάμπους *Papaioannou*: Χαραλαμπίου M
   Βονιφατίου *Papaioannou*: Βονηφαντίου M
   Ἀλεξίου καὶ Εὐφημιανοῦ M: Ἀλεξίου καὶ Εὐθυμίου V, Ἀλεξάνδρου καὶ Εὐφημιανοῦ JA, *omitted* P
   τοῦ Ἁγίου Παφνουτίου . . . Εὐφημιανοῦ: τῶν Ἁγίων μαρτύρων
   Χαραλαμπίου Φωτίου καὶ Τρύφωνος Ϝ, *passage absent in* CW
21 ἐπακροάσεται *Papaioannou*: ἐπακροάσαντο M

Notes to the Translations

PASSION OF BONIPHATIOS

1 *who desires the salvation*: Compare the *Acts* of Paul and Thecla, section 17 (*BHG* 1713), ed. Ricardus A. Lipsius, *Acta apostolorum apocrypha,* vol. 1 (Leipzig, 1891), 235–71.

I do not . . . living: See Ezekiel 18:23, 33:11; see also the *Miracle* of George, section 5.

I did . . . repentance: See Luke 5:32.

swift . . . mercies: A common phrase in Byzantine discourse of prayer.

When you turn back . . . shall be saved: See Isaiah 30:15.

Boniphatios: A name of Latin origin, which could be interpreted as "man of good fortune" or "doer of good deeds."

I shall now recount to you: The purported author-narrator of our story, a typical feature of early Byzantine *Passions* (compare the *Passion* of George, section 21), remains here anonymous.

2 *great woman*: 2 Kings 4:8.

Aglaïs: A name of Greek origin, which literally means "brilliant, noble"; compare the male character Aglaïdas, who erotically pursues the virgin Ioustine in the *Acts* of Kyprianos and Ioustine (*BHG* 452, etc.); see Stratis Papaioannou, ed. and trans., *Christian Novels from the Menologion of Symeon Metaphrastes,* Dumbarton Oaks Medieval Library 45 (Cambridge, MA, 2017), 284–85. The name, we should add, is borrowed in the Greek versions of the *Life of the Man of God, Alexios,* and used for the mother of the saint: see the next text in this volume.

Akakios: Also of Greek origin: "without evil."

Three times she sponsored . . . served as prefect: The same exact
phrase is used in the *Passion* of Eleutherios, section 1 (*BHG*
570), ed. Pio Franchi de' Cavalieri, *I martirii di S. Teodoto e di S.
Ariadne* (Rome, 1901), 149–61; see also the *Passion* of Sebastiane
(*BHG* 1619), ed. E. Kourilas Korytsas, "Ἅγιοι μάρτυρες Ἡρα-
κλείας: Μαρτύριον τῆς ἐνδόξου ὁσιομάρτυρος Σεβαστιανῆς,"
Θρακικά 26 (1957): 198–213, at 204. That Aglaïs, a woman, would
serve as a prefect in Rome is a historical impossibility, one
among the several distortions of reality on which the text is
built.

joined with her in sin: A curtailed euphemism for their sexual relations (compare the *Life of Makarios,* section 38); versions *BHG*
280a and 280b, as well as Symeon Metaphrastes, *Passion of Boniphatios,* section 2 (*BHG* 281–282), make the reference more
explicit, though the latter author proclaims his "shame" in
mentioning sex. Byzantine law punished harshly illicit affairs
of such a kind; see Spyros N. Troianos, "Τύποι ἐρωτικῆς 'ἐπι-
κοινωνίας' στὶς βυζαντινὲς νομικὲς πηγές," in *Ἡ ἐπικοινωνία
στὸ Βυζάντιο: Πρακτικὰ τοῦ Β΄ Διεθνοῦς Συμποσίου, 4–6 Ὀκτω-
βρίου 1990,* ed. N. G. Moschonas (Athens, 1993), 237–73, at 242.

addicted to drinking and sex: Compare Proverbs 23:21 with 1 Corinthians 6:9–10.

look after: In Greek the verb διηκόνει is reminiscent of the *diaconia* of Saint Boniface in Rome, the charitable institution that
offered solace to travelers and the poor, at whose basis lay the
veneration of Saint Boniphatios.

4 *jokingly*: The likely assumption here is that Boniphatios is
"drunk"; compare section 5. His jesting personality (along with
the sexual tension with his mistress) may, in any case, have reminded Byzantine listeners of Aesop. Compare also the relevant note to section 13, below.

took the form of a slave: Philippians 2:7.

send his angel in front of you: See Exodus 23:20 and 33:2.

direct your steps: See Psalms 36(37):23 and 118(119):133.

satisfy my desire: See Psalms 126(127):5.

6 *In a few days*: An impossible time frame, perhaps explained by

either the miraculous world in which the narrative takes place or some ignorance or indifference regarding geography.

a terrible darkness: 2 Samuel 1:9.

7   *began to kiss*: Luke 7:38, the story of the sinful woman kissing the feet of Jesus.

kissed their fetters: A common image; the archetype is in the *Acts* of Paul and Thecla, section 18 (*BHG* 1713).

8   *fairest court of law*: Compare the *Passion* of Probos, Tarachos, and Andronikos, section 1 (*BHG* 1574); notably, the first part of that *Passion*'s story unfolds also in Tarsos.

if you want to learn my common name: Compare the *Passion* of George, section 3, and also the *Passion* of Probos, Tarachos, and Andronikos, sections 1, 5, and 7 (*BHG* 1574).

Before I lay my hands upon your sides: Compare the *Passion* of Probos, Tarachos, and Andronikos, section 8 (*BHG* 1574).

Here is my body: Compare the *Passion* of Probos, Tarachos, and Andronikos, section 9 (*BHG* 1574). The phrasing echoes the words of Jesus at the last supper: see Matthew 26:26, Mark 14:22, Luke 22:19.

10   *as though from one mouth*: Daniel 3:51; compare also the *Acts* of Paul and Thecla, section 38 (*BHG* 1713).

11   *crucified as a criminal*: Compare the *Passion* of Probos, Tarachos, and Andronikos, section 37 (*BHG* 1574).

Shut your mouth: Compare the *Passion* of Probos, Tarachos, and Andronikos, section 38 (*BHG* 1574).

who has grown old in wicked days: Susanna 52.

as wax melts when it smells fire: See Psalms 67(68):3.

12   *and there was a great earthquake*: Revelation 11:13; see also Matthew 8:24 and Revelation 6:12. Compare the *Life of Makarios*, section 43, and the *Passion* of George, sections 11 and 13.

13   *kommentaresios*: Latin *a commentariis*, the official in charge of public records.

square . . . tunic: The somewhat unflattering appearance of Boniphatios might again remind one of Aesop. Symeon Metaphrastes, *Passion of Boniphatios*, section 11 (*BHG* 281–282), evades such connotations and writes: "his body was short, his hair blond."

laughed: This is another poignant detail that is transformed greatly and, in a sense, disappears in the version of Metaphrastes (*BHG* 281–282, section 11).

wept bitterly: Matthew 26:75 and Luke 22:62.

anointed . . . and wrapped . . . with . . . cloth: Compare the *Passion* of Probos, Tarachos, and Andronikos, section 29 (*BHG* 1574).

14   *devout men*: Acts 8:2.

five stades: The Greek *stadion*, or stade, measured around six hundred feet, so the distance envisaged here is, very roughly, half a mile—the distance also given in the Latin versions of our story. Most Greek manuscripts and versions of Boniphatios's *Passion* cite fifty stades (around five and a half miles); see the relevant Note to the Texts and also Albrecht Berger, *Life and Works of Saint Gregentios, Archbishop of Taphar: Introduction, Critical Edition, and Translation,* with a contribution by Gianfranco Fiaccadori (Berlin and New York, 2006) 35–36.

she built . . . martyr: For such matrons of faith in early Christianity (with an emphasis on Rome), see Nicola Denzey, *The Bone Gatherers: The Lost Worlds of Early Christian Women* (Boston, 2007). It should also be noted that according to one version of the *Synaxarion* of Boniphatios, preserved in a manuscript (Florence, Biblioteca Medicea Laurenziana, San Marco 787) dated to the year 1049/50 and likely from Palestine, the relic of the saint was brought later "into the middle of the city" of Rome "in a magnificent church"; see *Synaxarion of Constantinople,* col. 327, lines 40–44. This provides a remarkable testimony to the continued Byzantine contacts between Italy and Syro-Palestine.

15   *thirteen years*: Fifteen years according to versions *BHG* 280a, 280b, and 281–282.

LIFE OF THE MAN OF GOD, ALEXIOS

title   *the Man of God*: A frequent biblical expression, first in reference to Moses (compare, for example, Deuteronomy 33:1 or Psalms 89:1), but used elsewhere, especially in the Septuagint, but also in the New Testament (1 Timothy 6:11).

Alexios: Notably, the other two main early manuscripts of *BHG* 51 (Par. gr. 1538 [ms. H in the present edition] and Vat. gr. 866) do not mention the name Alexios in their titles; the full title of the Vatican manuscript indeed reads: "Life and conduct of the Man of God, whose name has not been found upon the earth." The name of Alexios is similarly absent in the best witnesses of the earliest Latin version, edited by Ulrich Mölk, "Die älteste lateinische Alexiusvita (8./10. Jahrhundert): Kritischer Text und Kommentar," *Romanistisches Jahrbuch* 27 (1976): 293–315, and of course in the original Syriac legend (see the Introduction). Thus the name, which appears only in the title of the manuscript (dated to 953/4) followed for the present edition, must be an addition, having occurred because the Man of God was by that time usually identified as Alexios; for this reason, I have marked "Ἀλεξίου" as excisable in the Greek text.

1 *Honorius and Arcadius*: Sons of emperor Theodosius I (347–395 CE); Honorius reigned over the Western Roman empire (393–423), and Arcadius over the Eastern (393–408).

   Euphemianos: Literally, a man of good reputation.

   slaves, gold girdled and silk wearing: The phrase is taken verbatim from the medieval *Life* of Alexander the Great, the so-called *Alexander Romance,* where it is used to describe the legendary king's retinue; see Ursula von Lauenstein, ed., *Der griechische Alexanderroman: Rezension γ, Buch I* (Meisenheim am Glan, 1962), chapter 26.

2 *the ninth hour*: Midafternoon; compare also the relevant note to the *Life of Makarios,* section 2.

   God's land: See Isaiah 14:2.

3 *Aglaïs*: The name is apparently borrowed from the *Passion of Boniphatios;* see the relevant note to that text. Neither this, nor the name of Euphemianos, nor the name Alexios appear in the Syriac version of the present tale; see the relevant discussion in the Introduction.

   Remember me . . . offspring: Inspired by (and partly citing) 1 Samuel 1:9–11.

   she conceived . . . bore a son: Compare Genesis 29:32, etc.

4 *school age*: The third manuscript utilized by Francisco Maria Es-

teves Pereira, "Légende grecque de l'Homme de Dieu, Saint
Alexis," *Analecta Bollandiana* 19 (1900): 243–53 (Oxford, Bodle-
ian Library, Barocci 146, fifteenth century), specifies that
Alexios was "six years old" at this time.

ecclesiastical education: The relevant Greek phrase, ἐκκλησια-
στική ἱστορία, could allude also to the title of a series of early
Byzantine historiographical texts (by Eusebius of Caesarea and
others), which founded what we now call "Church history," as
well as to an important text on Christian ritual, attributed to
Patriarch Germanos I (ca. 655–before 754 CE), patriarch of
Constantinople (715–730). Yet the meaning here seems to be
less specific; thus, I take it to refer to basic Christian learning
(from the study of the *Psalter* to hymnography, the writings of
the Church fathers, and the like).

5   *legal marital age*: Fourteen years old, by usual Byzantine standards.
6   *come to know your consort*: In other words, "make love to her."

the golden ring . . . purple headscarf: This sentence makes little
sense in Greek, while it also uses words nowhere else attested,
such as πασμάνην and ῥένδα (which is glossed wrongly as
"belt" in the twelfth-century *Lexikon* of Zonaras). As Aza Vladimirovna Paikova has shown, the Greek phrase is simply an
awkward translation from the original Syriac legend, in which
the relevant passage refers to the Man of God's giving up the
"wedding ring and scarf, while they were dressed in clothes
made of purple silk"; Aza Vladimirovna Paikova, "Легенды и
сказания в памятниках сирийской агиографии," *Palestiniskii
Sbornik* 30[93] (1990): 41–42 and 85.

God . . . between me and you: Genesis 16:5; compare 17:2 and elsewhere.

7   *Capitolium*: A somewhat confused reference to (likely) a small
port on the river Tiber at the bottom of the Capitoline Hill.

the acheiropoietos icon . . . lifetime: This reference to an image of
Christ "not made by human hands" and given to Abgar, legendary king of Edessa, is to the famous *Mandylion*, or Holy Towel,
a cloth with an imprint of Christ's face, Christ's alleged first
portrait; the relevant story had a wide circulation in Byzantium and beyond, starting from the sixth century onward (see

BHG 1704.i–ii, 1704a–d, 793–796m). In 944, the *Mandylion* was brought from Edessa to Constantinople and deposited in the Pharos chapel in the Great Palace, an event celebrated thereafter on August 16. On the *Mandylion,* see, for example, Andrea Nicolotti, *From the Mandylion of Edessa to the Shroud of Turin: The Metamorphosis and Manipulation of a Legend* (Leiden, 2014).

8   *He chose . . . to the next*: For this type of ascetic feat, see, for instance, the *Life* of Saint Luke the Stylite 5.39 (*BHG* 2239). The Greek is awkward here, using the participle μεταλαμβάνων instead of the correct infinitive form μεταλαμβάνειν, likely the result of translation from the Syriac. As elsewhere in this volume, I have retained the "problematic" form in the Greek text.

10   *sackcloth and ashes*: Isaiah 58:5, Esther 4:3, etc.

        she flung herself: The Greek ῥιγμένη (from ῥίχνω), retained in the edition here, is a vernacular form; in the *Thesaurus Linguae Graecae* it is attested only in post-Byzantine texts.

11   *seventeen years*: The same amount of time that Saint Mary of Egypt (*BHG* 1042) was said to have spent first as prostitute and then again in temptation while in the wild desert.

        pleased the Lord: Sirach 44:16.

        Bring inside the Man of God: Notably, it is the Virgin Mary who gives the saint his designation.

        an odor of fragrance: Genesis 8:21.

        like the sun shining on: See Sirach 50:7.

        took him by the hand: Compare Jeremiah 38:32, Hebrews 8:9, and elsewhere.

12   *Tarsos in Cilicia*: The city of Boniphatios's martyrdom, as well as the city of origin of Paul the Apostle.

13   *As the Lord my God lives*: Psalms 17:47(18:46), and elsewhere.

        the crumbs . . . table: Matthew 15:27; compare Mark 7:28.

14   *As the Lord my God lives*: See the previous section.

        Place a pallet . . . hall: Reminiscent of the parable of Lazaros and the rich man; Luke 16:19–31.

15   *the turtledove . . . single mate*: Part of medieval folklore, cited in various texts; see, especially, the relevant chapter in the *Physiologos* tradition in, for instance, F. Sbordone, ed., *Physiologus* (Milan, 1936), 285.

16   *seventeen years*: See the note to section 11, above.

17   *his golden ring ... purple headscarf*: For this phrase, see the note to section 6, above.

18   *archbishop Markianos ... present*: No Markianos is known among the bishops of Rome; it is also ahistorical for both Honorius and Arcadius to be present in the city.

       Come ... rest: See Matthew 11:28.

       Astonishment and fear overtook everyone: Compare Mark 16:8, for the reaction of the myrrh-bearing women at the sight and voice of the youth in Christ's tomb.

       fell face down: Genesis 17:17, etc.

       he will have departed ... entrusted him: It is unclear from the Greek text whether the voice prophesized Alexios's death (as some of the versions imply, and as I take it here) or if the event is presented as a later fact (as a literal translation of the passage would have it).

19   *As the Lord my God lives*: See above, section 13.

21   *neither sound nor hearing*: See 2 Kings 4:31.

       his face ... angel: Acts 6:15.

22   *chartoularios*: A high-ranking official in the Church administration with chancery-related, archival, and also recital duties.

24   *you were*: The "incorrect" form ὤν of the Greek (as opposed to ὄντα) has been retained in the text.

25   *the blind received their sight, lepers were cleansed*: Matthew 11:5, Luke 7:22.

27   *on the seventeenth of the month of June*: Our version is somewhat particular for giving this date instead of March 17, common in the Byzantine cult of Alexios; the possibility exists that June is a lapse from July, since July 17 was the feast date of Alexios in the Latin tradition and in the environment where the present version first appeared.

       anyone asked, God gave: Compare Matthew 7:8, Luke 11:10.

LIFE OF MARKOS THE ATHENIAN

1   *Abba Serapion*: This Serapion was likely intended to be identified with the Abba Serapion or Sarapion who was the purported

author of ascetic texts (*CPG* 2501–2504) and a character in several "beneficial tales" circulating in Byzantium. See *BHG* 1618–1618c; John Wortley, *The Anonymous Sayings of the Desert Fathers: A Select Edition and Complete English Translation* (Cambridge and New York, 2013), 382–85; and Christine Angelidi, "Ὁ Βίος τοῦ Μάρκου τοῦ Ἀθηναίου (BHG 1039–1041)," Σύμμεικτα 8 (1989): 33–59, at 36–37. See also, for example, *BHG* 999j and the Coptic *Life of Makarios the Egyptian,* ed. Emile Amélineau, *Histoire des monastères de la Basse-Égypte* (Paris, 1894), 113. I have retained the Coptic word "abba" (which means "father") used in the Greek.

Abba John, the great elder: Another common name of Egyptian ascetics; see Angelidi, "Ὁ Βίος," 36–37.

Abba Markos: A common name in the ascetic literary tradition of Egypt; see Angelidi, "Ὁ Βίος," 34–35.

the mountain of Thrace in Ethiopia: For most of the Greek-speaking Byzantine readers of the story, this would have appeared as a clearly imaginary mountain; Thrace and Ethiopia are occasionally mentioned in close proximity in Byzantine texts (in *Apocalypses,* for example), but they are never joined together in this way—nor are they linked with the Hittites, as in the title of our story. For an ingenious interpretation of these names, see Angelidi, "Ὁ Βίος," 37–38, with a perspective from the Greek literary tradition. More probable, however, is the possibility that we are dealing with rough translations of names into Greek; "Thrace" thus likely renders the name "Tarmaqa" of the Arabic (likely from the Coptic) and Syriac versions, which make no reference to the Hittites. Emile Amélineau, *Contes et romans de l'Egypte chrétienne* (Paris, 1888), vol. 1, p. xli, places the mountain in Sudan. See further the relevant discussion in the Introduction.

in the land of the living: Psalms 114(116):9. That is, in heaven.

3   *the dust of the earth*: Amos 2:7; compare 2 Samuel 22:43 and Ecclesiastes 44:21.

into the land of Ethiopia . . . Hittites: See the note to section 1, "the mountain of Thrace in Ethiopia," above.

5   *desert gum*: The gum arabic (*acacia arabica* or *vachellia nilotica*), a tree native to Egypt.

Take, eat: Compare Matthew 26:26.

6   *the height of heaven*: Odes 11:14, Isaiah 38:14, and elsewhere.

   I looked . . . behold: Revelation 4:1, 6:2, and elsewhere.

7   *it shall be well*: 2 Kings 25:24 and Psalms 127(128):2.

8   *Because a thousand . . . passed*: Psalms 89(90):4.

   Blessed is your soul . . . Blessed are your hands: The series of beatitudes that follow and which echo Christ's relevant section from his Sermon on the Mount (Matthew 5:1–12) underscores Markos's association with "the Blessed," the *Makares,* of the ancient and medieval tradition. On this tradition and, in reference to the protagonist of the next text in the volume, saint Makarios, see the discussion in the Introduction. For the literary history of beatitudes of the saint's body in Ethiopic, Syriac, and Greek and in relation to the story of Markos, see Basile Lourié, "S. Alypius Stylite, S. Marc de Tharmaqa et l'origine des *malkə* éthiopiennes," *Scrinium* 1 (2005): 148–60.

   have my steps been tripped up: Psalms 36(37):31.

   Bless the Lord . . . rewards: Psalms 102(103):1–2.

   An angel . . . rescue them: Psalms 33(34):7.

   Blessed is that servant: Matthew 24:46, Luke 12:43.

9   *the peace of God*: Philippians 4:7.

   Come near to me, child: Genesis 27:21, 27:26.

   he covered me with kisses: Gospel of Nicodemus 15:6. It is also a common reaction in encounters recounted in Byzantine beneficial tales.

   Come near . . . repay you: Inspired from, and partly citing, Genesis 27:21–28 (the meeting of Isaac and his son Jacob).

   that day . . . secrets of men: An adaptation of Romans 2:16.

10   *hunger . . . nakedness*: Compare 1 Corinthians 4:11.

   hair . . . heavy with it: For the motif of the hairy ascetic, see Charles Allyn Williams, *Oriental Affinities of the Legend of the Hairy Anchorite* (Urbana, 1925–1926).

   angels have . . . did not show to me: The same passage is cited at the beginning of another text (dated to the tenth century? likely from Egypt?) associated with Markos the Athenian, preserved only in Syriac translation, that carries the title *By Abba Markos of the Mountain of Tarmaqa: The Revelation Which God Showed to*

Him Regarding Human Souls; see Arnold van Lantschoot, "Révélations de Macaire et de Marc de Tarmaqā sur le sort de l'âme
après la mort," *Le Muséon* 63 (1950): 159–89, at 185. Lourié, "S.
Alypius," 152, rejects the Egyptian origins.

angels have been descending upon me: Compare Genesis 28:12, the
story of Jacob's ladder.

the tree of knowledge, from which our forefathers ate: See Genesis
2–3.

Enoch and Elijah: Enoch (compare Genesis 5:21–24) and Elijah (2
Samuel 2:11) are often listed jointly in the Byzantine tradition
as the two Old Testament figures to enter heaven alive.

in the land of the living: Compare the quotation from Psalms
114(116):9 in section 1, above. The wording in the Greek here is
slightly different.

11   *I, child, came from Athens*: Other manuscripts that transmit the
story add here the phrase "and I was educated in the school of
the philosophers" (καὶ ἐν τῇ διατριβῇ τῶν φιλοσόφων ἐπαι-
δευόμην), and similar phrases appear in the Arabic (Coptic?)
and Syriac versions. If this is a later addition, this could be re-
garded as an attempt to strengthen the identification of the
city of the original story (perhaps Tanis?) with Athens, the city
of learning. See further the relevant discussion in the Introduction.

12   *completely changed . . . corruptible body*: The Syriac version perhaps offers a better reading here: "woven within a corruptible
body"; Arnold Evert Look, *The History of Abba Marcus of Mount
Tharmaka* (Oxford, 1929), xxii.

13   *paganism*: Literally, "Hellenism."

14   *if you have faith . . . will be done*: Matthew 17:20 and 21:21.

    about five cubits: The cubit was an ancient measurement based
on the distance from the tip of the middle finger to the elbow,
around eighteen inches. Five cubits is thus around seven and a
half feet.

15   *The Lord . . . not want*: Psalms 22(23):1.

    white as snow: Compare Daniel 7:9, Matthew 28:3, Revelation
1:14.

    flowers: Again, the Arabic (Coptic?) and Syriac versions offer a

better reading here, namely "fruits"; Amélineau, *Contes,* vol. 2, p. 67, and Look, *The History,* xxiii.

than honey: Psalms 18:11(19:10) and 118(119):103.

16   *a right hand . . . from heaven*: For this notion, see Wisdom 3:1, with Sévérien Salaville, "Prière inédite de Nicolas Cabasilas à Jésus-Christ," *Échos d'Orient* 35 (1936): 43–50, at 43–49. In the Arabic (Coptic?) and Syriac versions this is "fire" (Amélineau, *Contes,* vol. 2, p. 67) or "hand of fire" (Look, *The History,* xxiii).

17   *Did you see . . . sent two*: The same motif appears also in *Life of Makarios the Roman* 34.

18   *completed all the psalms of David*: Both the Arabic (Coptic?) and the Syriac versions specify this as the office of the third hour (Amélineau, *Contes,* vol. 2, p. 69; Look, *The History,* xxiv).

20   *speaking again*: Before his farewell in both the Arabic (Coptic?) (Amélineau, *Contes,* vol. 2, p. 70) and the Syriac (Look, *The History,* xxv) versions, Markos alerts Serapion to the arrival of Archangels Michael and Gabriel.

    captives: 2 Timothy 2:26, referring to opponents of Christianity, who are described as captives of the devil.

    lavras: A type of monastery, where monks usually lived as independent solitaries in dispersed cells but also assembled regularly for liturgical gatherings and reported to an abbot.

    expiation for sins: 1 John 2:2, where the term is applied to Jesus.

    priests of the Lord: 1 Samuel 22:17, for example, among many occurrences in the Septuagint.

    who welcome strangers as Christ: Compare Matthew 25:35, Hebrews 13:2.

    kings and governors: Jeremiah 17:25.

    not fainthearted: Galatians 6:9, Hebrews 12.3.

22   *a voice . . . from heaven*: The wording reflects that of a number of biblical passages, of which John 12:28 is perhaps most likely to be in mind.

    the chosen instrument: Acts 9:15.

    faithful servant: Compare Matthew 24:45.

    white garment: Compare Revelation 6:11, and elsewhere.

    the light of righteousness: Wisdom 5:6.

a right hand: In the Arabic (Coptic?) and Syriac versions this is "fire" (Amélineau, *Contes,* vol. 2, p. 72), "hand of fire" (Look, *The History,* xxvi).

23   *to God to give me a helper*: Compare "that God would send me a helper" in the Arabic (Coptic?) and Syriac versions (Amélineau, *Contes,* vol. 2, pp. 72–73; Look, *The History,* xxvii).

of whom the world is not worthy: Hebrews 11:38. The initial prepositional phrase may also be read as "compared to which."

he said to me: That is, one of the two ascetics spoke.

25   *who works . . . without number*: Job 5:9.

Christians in name only and not at all in deed: The phrase echoes that of section 14, above.

LIFE OF MAKARIOS THE ROMAN

title   *the Roman*: This epithet could suggest that Makarios (like Alexios, the Man of God; compare section 28, below) was from Rome; however, the term could conceivably also denote "a subject of the empire of Rome," that is, what we would call a "Byzantine."

twenty miles from Paradise: A late Byzantine anonymous geographical treatise evokes Makarios the Roman as an authority on this distance from the "gate to Paradise"; Armand Delatte, "Geographica," *Byzantinische Zeitschrift* 30 (1929/30): 512–18, at 516.

was discovered: or, alternatively, "found himself."

2   *Asklepios the abbot*: Not a historical figure, but a name encountered in early Byzantine narratives about ascetics; see, for example, *BHG* 176.

the ninth hour: Midafternoon; for the office of the ninth hour, see Robert F. Taft, *The Liturgy of the Hours in East and West* (Collegeville, MN, 1986).

3   *the scriptures . . . pillar*: "Pillars of heaven" are mentioned in Job 26:11, yet without reference to iron. The same desire to see "the end of the earth and where the heaven bends (or rests)" also drives the Alexander the Great of the so-called *Alexander*

Romance tradition; see especially the likely fourth- or fifth-century recension L, ed. Helmut van Thiel, *Leben und Taten Alexanders von Makedonien: Der griechische Alexanderroman nach der Handschrift L* (Darmstadt, 1974), sections 2.37.4 and 2.41.8, and the likely eighth-century recension ε, ed. Jürgen Trumpf, *Anonymi Byzantini vita Alexandri regis Macedonum* (Stuttgart, 1974), chapter 2.

4   *all three*: The Greek word (ἀμφότεροι) normally means "the two, both."

holy Bethlehem . . . water: For the pilgrimage site of the early Byzantine Nativity church in Bethlehem on the very spot of the holy cave where Christ was born, along with the well of David (compare 2 Samuel 23:15) from which Mary supposedly also drew water and where the star that led the Magi was miraculously reflected, see Michele Bacci, *The Mystic Cave: A History of the Nativity Church in Bethlehem* (Brno, 2017), especially pages 84–90.

Glory to God . . . pleased: Luke 2:13.

5   *at a level plain . . . Apostate*: For the Byzantine legend of Saint Merkourios, see Christopher Walter, *The Warrior Saints in Byzantine Art and Tradition* (Aldershot and Burlington, VT, 2003), 101–8; that the killing of Julian took place on a plain called "Asia" is a detail that first appears in the *Chronicle* of Ioannes Malalas, ed. Ioannes Thurn, *Chronographia* (Berlin, 2000), 255–56.

Persis: A region of Persia (the southwest of modern Iran).

Ctesiphon: Ctesiphon was the royal capital of the Parthians and Sasanians from the second century BCE to the seventh century CE. It was situated on the banks of the Tigris some twenty miles south of Baghdad in modern Iran.

the three . . . are buried: The Three Youths, martyred together with the prophet Daniel in Babylon (book of Daniel), were celebrated in Byzantium on December 17, and a host of texts were produced in relation to that feast (see *BHG* 484v–488n for the Greek tradition). Their association with Ctesiphon occurs within the context of likely fifth-century legends preserved

in Coptic, Armenian, and Georgian; compare Basil Lourié, "The Syriac *Aḥiqar,* Its Slavonic Version, and the Relics of the Three Youths in Babylon," *Slověne* 2 (2013): 64–117, with Gérard Garitte, "L'invention georgienne des Trois Enfants de Babylone," *Le Museon* 72 (1959): 69–100, and David Frankfurter, *Christianizing Egypt: Syncretism and Local Worlds in Late Antiquity* (Princeton, 2018), 139–40. In the late fifth-century Greek *Life* of Daniel the Stylite, ed. Hippolyte Delehaye, *Les saints stylites* (Brussels, 1923), 87, we read that the emperor Leo I (457–474) had the relics of the Three Youths transferred to Constantinople from Babylon. In some versions of the *Alexander Romance,* Alexander visits, in an unspecified city, both the tomb of Nebuchadnezzar, the persecutor of the Three Youths, and "the dedicatory objects [?, in Greek ἀναθήματα] of the Jews"; see recension L, ed. van Thiel, *Leben und Taten,* section 2.18. Finally, some redactions of the *Life of Makarios* clarify the location of Ctesiphon by adding remarks such as "some distance from Babylon" (Oxford, Bodleian Library, Barocci 235, fol. 2r, eleventh century; London, British Library, Add. 14066, fol. 148r, twelfth century; and Vatic. gr. 2606, fol. 111v, late sixteenth or early seventeenth century). See further the relevant discussion in the Introduction.

7 *an androgyne*: The Greek could also be rendered as "a married couple"; however, I find it more likely that reference is being made here to yet another monstrous, humanoid creature (like the Cynocephali of section 9, below), with two heads or two sides, a male and a female one—hence the plurals that follow.

wearing on their head sharp arrows instead of crowns: The Greek is awkward and prompted corrections in version *BHG* 1004 and variation in the manuscripts of version *BHG* 1005. I decided to retain the text as it appears in the redaction of manuscript D (compare also manuscript Y) and signal the problems here. The noun ἀνδρόγυνον is in the neuter singular form, while the participle φοροῦντα (wearing), which likely points to vernacular usage, switches to the neuter plural, apparently in order to indicate the two separate creatures that make up the andro-

gyne. It could be corrected to φοροῦντες, which is the reading of Vatic. gr. 2606, fol. 111v, and thus agree in form with the participles that follow, namely ἰδόντες (when they saw), νομίζοντες (thinking), etc. Another likely correction, for which I thank Alexandros Alexakis, would be to change φοροῦντα to φοροῦν τὰ . . . βέλη (wearing the . . . arrows), in order to retain the singular form. Similarly, the participle ἔχοντα (having) could be taken as referring to the androgyne (though again in the neuter plural instead of the expected singular form), or to an implied accusative masculine singular form of the noun στέφανον ("crown," the reading of manuscript E). Finally, the proper Greek form for ὀξεῖα ("arrows," transmitted by all the manuscripts I have examined) would be ὀξέα.

9   *the land of the Cynocephali*: The description of the habitat of the Cynocephali that follows resembles a similar one in Ctesias's *Indica,* as reported in Photios's *Bibliotheke* cod. 72, sections 48a–b, ed. René Henry, *Bibliothèque* (Paris, 1959–1991), vol. 1, pp. 142–43. For the Cynocephali, see further the Introduction and note to the *Passion of Christopher* 2 in this volume.

   the land of the apes: A similar imaginary land, located in the inner regions of Libya, is mentioned in Diodorus of Sicily (first century BCE), *The Library of History* 20.58. See also the *Alexander Romance,* recension F, ed. Anastasios C. Lolos and Vasilis L. Konstantinopulos, *Zwei mittelgriechische Prosa-Fassungen des Alexanderromans,* 2 vols. (Meisenheim am Glan, 1983), sections 73–74.

   who saved . . . their mouths: Compare Psalms 21:22.

10   *asps . . . serpents*: Compare Psalms 90(91):13.

   antelopes . . . and leopards: Real and mythical animals known to the Byzantines also from the Old Testament (among other sources).

   who saved us from their mouths: Compare Psalms 21:22.

   blocked our ears with wax: Compare Homer, *Odyssey* 12.173–74 and 12.199–200.

12   *for no light . . . dark fog*: This arrival into a lightless land and the encounter with an inscribed arch built by Alexander the Great

is inspired directly from the *Alexander Romance*. See recension
ε, ed. Trumpf, *Anonymi Byzantini vita Alexandri,* chapters 2–3
(where, however, there is a different inscription), and, especially, recension L, ed. van Thiel, *Leben und Taten,* sections 2.38–
41, according to which Alexander arrives in a land "where the
sun does not shine, . . . the so-called Land of the Blessed (ἡ
καλουμένη Μακάρων Χώρα)" and then later orders an arch to
be built with the inscription "those who wish to enter the Land
of the Blessed should walk on the right side, otherwise you
may die."

Kalchedon: An alternative spelling of Chalcedon, the port city
located across from Constantinople on the Anatolian shore of
the Sea of Marmara in Bithynia, modern Kadıköy.

Started walking to the left of the arch: While according to the recension L of the *Alexander Romance* (see note above) Alexander's advice was to travel "on the right side," our text prefers
the "left," but then, in the following sections, has its fictitious
travelers encounter the dystopic landscapes predicted for the
"right" side followed by the wonders predicted for the "left."
This appears perhaps to be a confusion by a storyteller avid to
incorporate as much mythic material as possible into his tale,
or a "correction" of Alexander's advice, as argued by Stephen
Gero, "The Alexander Legend in Byzantium: Some Literary
Gleanings," in "*Homo Byzantinus:* Papers in Honor of Alexander
Kazhdan," ed. Anthony Cutler and Simon Franklin, special issue, *Dumbarton Oaks Papers* 46 (1992): 83–87.

14   *that Lake of Judgment*: A similar lake is mentioned in the *Apocalypse of Anastasia,* ed. Rudolph Homburg, *Apocalypsis Anastasiae:
Ad trium codicum auctoritatem, Panormitani, Ambrosiani, Parisini*
(Leipzig, 1903), section 3, and the *Apocalypse of the Theotokos,*
ed. Montague R. James, *Apocrypha Anecdota* (Cambridge, 1893),
section 24.

16   *Son of the most high God*: Mark 5:7, Luke 8:28 (the words of the
demons possessing a man subsequently cured by Christ).

17   *their voices were human voices*: Compare the *Alexander Romance,*
recension L, ed. van Thiel, *Leben und Taten,* section 2.40.1.

18   *four men . . . appearance*: Compare Revelation 7:1: "I saw four angels standing."

19   *surpassing honey and honeycomb*: See Psalms 18(19):10, and compare Psalms 118(119):103.

    A large crystal . . . fountain of water: Compare Revelation 21:6, "To the thirsty I will give from the fountain of the water of life," and 22:1, "Then he showed me the river of the water of life, bright as crystal, flowing from the throne of God and of the Lamb."

    The water was white like . . . milk: Compare Genesis 49:12 with the *Alexander Romance* recension L, ed. van Thiel, *Leben und Taten,* section 3.5.4, where the description is set in the Land of the Gymnosophists who "dwell in huts and caves" and consider their abodes as "tombs."

    The fountain of immortality: Compare *Alexander Romance* recension L, ed. van Thiel, *Leben und Taten,* sections 2.41.2–5.

    Attic honey: Attic honey (and in particular the honey of Mount Hymettos) was famous in antiquity for its quality.

20   *the four corners . . . winds here*: Compare again Revelation 7:1: "I saw four angels standing at the four corners of the earth, holding back the four winds of the earth."

    white like that of snow: Compare Daniel 7:9, Matthew 28:3, Revelation 1:14.

    their height . . . shorter: Compare the *Alexander Romance* recension ε, ed. Trumpf, *Anonymi Byzantini vita Alexandri,* chapter 26, and recension γ, ed. Ursula von Lauenstein, *Der griechische Alexanderroman,* chapter 31.

    about one cubit: Around a foot and a half.

21   *white like milk*: Compare Genesis 49:12.

    honey and honeycomb: Psalms 18(19):10.

22   *the straight way and safe path*: Compare Isaiah 40:3, Matthew 3:3, Mark 1:3, Luke 3:4.

    man's clothing: Sirach 19:30.

24   *white like snow*: Compare Daniel 7:9, Matthew 28:3, Revelation 1:14.

25   *Do not wish . . . this place*: The same advice not to proceed further

is found in the *Alexander Romance,* recension L, ed. van Thiel, *Leben und Taten,* section 2.40.1.

has placed . . . tree of life: Genesis 3:24.

the zones of heaven: Another type of heavenly being, like the angels, the principalities, or the powers (compare Romans 8:38).

27   *two lions . . . the desert*: Lions as companions of ascetics is a commonplace in early Byzantine ascetic literature; the most well-known example appears in Jerome's *Life* of Paul of Thebes (*BHL* 6596, *BHG* 1466).

28   *he said to us*: The story that follows closely resembles the first and, at that, more ancient, part of the story of Alexios the Man of God that circulated in the East before coming to Rome. See also a *synaxarion,* preserved in Ethiopic and being likely an elaborate transformation of the story of Markos the Athenian, according to which a Roman emperor named Markos, after reigning "in his virginity for five years," when forced "by the people" to get married, fled to an imaginary distant desert land in order to spend sixty years as a solitary hermit before dying and being buried by angels; see Ernest Alfred Wallis Budge, *The Book of the Saints of the Ethiopian Church: A Translation of the Ethiopic Synaxarium, made from the Manuscripts Oriental 660 and 661 in the British Museum* (Cambridge, 1928), vol. 4, p. 1044, and the relevant discussion in the Introduction.

incline your ears to my words: Psalms 77(78):1.

I used . . . excuse: Going to the bathroom as an excuse for disappearing is found also in the early Byzantine apocryphal *Testament of Abraham,* ed. M. R. James (Cambridge, 1892), chapter 4. There the person who uses the excuse is the archangel Michael!

a poor widow: Compare Luke 21:1–4 and the *Passion* of George, section 14.

made a great . . . lamentation: Compare, for example, Acts 8:2 (on the death of Saint Stephen).

29   *all those . . . name*: 1 Corinthians 1:2; compare Acts 9:14.

angel Raphael: See Tobit, throughout.

the way of life: Jeremiah 21:8; compare Psalms 15(16):11.

30   *the light of life*: John 8:12.

31   *onager ... stag ... serpent*: These three animals appear in very close
      sequence in some manuscripts of Jeremiah 14:5–6; see, for ex-
      ample, their citation in John Chrysostom, *Homilies on the Stat-
      ues,* PG 49:52, lines 45–47.

32   *bright cloud*: Matthew 17:5.
      come, follow me: Matthew 19:21, Mark 10:21, Luke 18:22.

34   *raven arrived . . . and left*: Ravens feed the prophet Elijah at 1
      Kings 17:4, 17:6.
      Now I know ... received half a loaf: The motif of providing more
      food for visitors appears also in the *Life of Markos the Athenian,*
      section 17, above.

36   *I, wretch that I am ... I'm going*: Maria's brief autobiography mim-
      ics — in some parts verbatim — that of Makarios, presented ear-
      lier in the story (section 28). For Makarios's encounter with
      Maria, see further Stratis Papaioannou, "Gender (and Sexual-
      ity) in Byzantine Literature," in *Routledge Handbook of Gender
      and Sexuality in Byzantium,* ed. Mati Meyer and Charis Messis
      (Abingdon and New York, forthcoming).
      I used my belly as an excuse: See above, section 28.

37   *took her by the hand*: Jeremiah 38:32, Hebrews 8:9, and elsewhere.

38   *heavy with sleep*: Luke 9:32.
      consort with her in sin: Compare *Passion of Boniphatios,* section 2.

39   *wept in utter bitterness*: See Matthew 26:75 and Luke 22:62.

40   *wept bitterly*: As above.
      earth and ashes: Genesis 18:27; compare Ecclesiastes 10:9 and
      17:32.
      the Lord was my supporter: Psalms 53(54):4. Makarios's self-burial
      is reminiscent of a similar extreme act of repentance following
      fornication, related in a tale about a monk called Jacob that is
      preserved in several versions (*BHG* 770 and 770c).

41   *I did ... repentance*: An almost exact quotation of Luke 5:32.
      Then I stretched out my hand: The text, from this point through
      the phrase "may he preserve you in peace" (at the end of sec-
      tion 44), is absent from version *BHG* 1004.
      I stooped to look into the cave: An echo of John 20:11, where Mary

Magdalene is about to witness the two angels in Christ's empty tomb.

I saw . . . golden crown: Compare Revelation 14:14.

43   *great earthquakes*: Compare Matthew 8:24, Revelation 6:12 and 11:13, and elsewhere. Compare the *Passion of Boniphatios,* section 12, and that of George, sections 11 and 13.

Holy, holy, holy, Lord: Isaiah 6:3; Revelation 4:8, 17:7.

cloud and fire: Compare the pillar of fire and cloud of Exodus 14:24.

seventy years or more: Manuscript E transmits here the reading "one hundred eighty."

45   *truly blessed Makarios*: A wordplay on the saint's name, which has roots literally meaning "blessed" (see Introduction).

PASSION OF CHRISTOPHER

1   *fourth year of Decius's reign*: Decius was Roman emperor from 249 to 251 CE: there was no "fourth year" during his reign. His persecution of the Christians, the setting of several Byzantine *Passions,* is, nevertheless, a well-documented event; it began with an edict in January 250.

2   *one of the counts*: A subaltern Roman army officer.

the blessed Reprebos: As Johann Popescu suggested, the name comes either from Syriac (*raurab* or *revvreb*: big) or from Latin (*reprobus*: wicked); see Johann Popescu, *Die Erzählung oder das Martyrium des Barbaren Christophorus und seiner Genossen* (Leipzig, 1903), 2. Christopher is described as "enormous" later on (section 5); could this suggest that the case for the Syriac origin of the word may have the edge over that for the Latin? Notably, throughout the narrative, Reprebos/Christopher is also called blessed (μακάριος), a likely link to the story world of Makarios the Roman.

enlisted him: Recruitment from among captives did occur in the Roman and then Byzantine armies.

army unit of the Marmaritai: A *cohors . . . Marmantarum* (or *Marmaritarum*) under the command of the *dux* (military leader) of

Syria is known from early Byzantine imperial army registries; according to his *Passion* (*BHG* 1761), the very popular saint Theodore the Recruit was also enlisted in "the legion of the Marmaritai"; see John Haldon, *A Tale of Two Saints: The Martyrdoms and Miracles of Saints Theodore "the Recruit" and "the General"* (Liverpool, 2016), 83. This is perhaps the inspiration for Christopher's designation. David Woods has, furthermore, suggested that the reference to this army unit may explain the original designation of Christopher as coming "from the land of the dog-headed" people, since the *Marmaritai* were North Africans associated already by Herodotus with the dog-headed people; "St. Christopher, Bishop Peter of Attalia, and the Cohors Marmaritarum: A Fresh Examination," *Vigiliae Christianae* 48 (1994): 170–86, at 172.

rewards: Hebrews 11:6.

Cynocephali . . . Anthropophagi: *Anthropophagi,* or "Man-eaters," are glossed as synonymous to the *Cynocephali* (literally, "Dog-Headed people") in lists of exotic human races encountered by Alexander the Great in several recensions of the *Alexander Romance;* see, for example, the likely eighth-century recension ε, ed. Trumpf, *Anonymi Byzantini vita Alexandri,* chapter 39.

4   *Bachthious*: This character is left anonymous in some versions of the legend, including the likely earliest Latin version (*BHL* 1764).

6   *your three servants in the fire*: See the note to section 5 of the *Life of Makarios,* above.

twenty-four . . . creatures: Revelation 4:4, 4:6, and elsewhere.

8   *Listen . . . eat good things*: See Isaiah 55:2.

you who . . . large crowd: See Matthew 14:13–21, Mark 6:31–44, Luke 9:12–17, John 6:1–14.

at this hour: Compare John 12:27.

God sent his blessing: In *BHG* 310c and other Greek versions, the miracle is performed by the archangel Raphael; notably, the same archangel appeared to Makarios the Roman: compare the relevant note to *Life of Makarios,* section 29, above.

Antioch in Syria: Later in the text (section 24), it appears that the Antioch in question is the Pisidian Antioch, a city in

southwestern Asia Minor; I have left the inconsistency uncorrected.

Saint Babylas: According to his Greek hagiographical dossier (*BHG* 205–206), Babylas, bishop of Antioch, was martyred under the emperor Numerian (283–284 CE).

Perge: A city near the southwestern coast of Asia Minor, capital of the Roman region of Pamphylia, roughly northwest from the island of Cyprus. Christopher's journey to Perge, a detail also present in the Syriac version, is omitted in all other Greek versions. We may nevertheless add that Perge—along with two cities mentioned later in the text, the Pisidian Antioch and Attaleia (see section 24)—features as a site where Saint Paul preached, according to *Acts* 13:13–14 and 14:25.

9   *let gods . . . sky*: See Jeremiah 10:11.

demons who are like you: Compare Psalms 113:16(114:8) and 133(134):18.

12   *live forever*: Compare John 6:51, and elsewhere.

what we were enlisted to do: The connotation is that the two women were prostitutes, as made explicit in other Greek versions. It may be noted that the names of the two women, Akylina and Kallinike (mentioned later in the text), come from Latin and Greek, respectively.

13   *so that he could burn it to ashes*: Thus avoiding the preservation of any relics.

14–15   *He then ordered Kallinike . . . died in peace*: The same fake submission to pagan sacrifices described in sections 14 and 15 here is also found in the *Passion* of George, with several similar images and phrases (sections 16–19, below). That episode likely provided the inspiration for the text on Christopher. For other similar examples, see Hippolyte Delehaye, *Les Passions des martyrs et les genres littéraires* (Brussels, 1966), 190.

14   *golden image*: Compare Daniel 3:1.

To which gods are you ordering me to sacrifice: Compare the *Passion of George*, section 3, below.

Apollo, and Herakles: The two deities are often listed together in the *Passion of George* (sections 3, 11, 14, 18).

The emperor was overjoyed: For this phrase and the surrounding

327

episode (namely, the temporary deluded joy of the persecuting emperor), see the *Passion* of George, sections 6 and, especially, 16, which perhaps provided the model for our passage here. Compare also the *Passion of Niketas,* section 7, below.

neither sound nor hearing: 2 Kings 4:31. See also the *Life of the Man of God, Alexios,* section 21, above.

15 *reduced them to dust*: Compare 2 Samuel 22:43, etc.

16 *Decius . . . tie beam*: In Greek there is a wordplay (Δέκιος/δοκός) that has remained untranslated in English. An equivalent rendering, for which I thank Richard Greenfield, might be along these lines: "You've rightly been called Decius, because you're the deck of the devil, the one on which your father Satan stands. . . ."

17 *bread from heaven*: Compare Exodus 16:4, Psalms 77(78):24, John 6:31, 6:41, 6:50, and so on.

good shepherd: John 10:11 and 10:14 (in reference to Christ).

19 *I saw*: Luke 10:18 (Christ witnessing the fall of Satan), and elsewhere.

face shone . . . garments like: Matthew 17:2 (in reference to Christ's transfiguration); compare Mark 9:3, Luke 9:29.

20 *you alone are . . . wonders*: Psalms 76:15(77:14) and 85(86):10.

21 *stood on the high places*: An Old Testament expression for the sanctuaries of the pagan gods.

they surrounded the saints in three groups: Compare Job 1:17.

Ninth of July: Or, rather, ninth of April as in the other versions of the *Passion,* and thus exactly a month before Christopher's death.

22 *like dust*: Daniel 2:35 and Deuteronomy 9:21; compare Job 21:18. Compare also the *Passion* of Saint George, section 10, below.

23 *the following prayer*: For this final prayer of the saint and God's direct confirmation of the saint's cult that follows, both patterned partly on a similar prayer and divine response in the *Passion* of George (section 20, below), see Bernard Flusin, "Le contrat de Marina: Passions épiques et culte des saints," in *Culte des saints et littérature hagiographique,* ed. Vincent Déroche, Bryan Ward-Perkins, and Robert Wiśniewski (Paris, 2020), 39–53, at 40–46.

not made by human hands: The same invocation appears in a
   prayer cited in the early Byzantine *Passion* of Saint Barbara; see,
   for example, *BHG* 215, ed. A. Wirth, *Danae in christlichen Legenden* (Vienna, 1892), p. 110, line 133. On this prayer, see also *Passion* of George, section 8, below.

my memory: Or, literally, "commemorative texts."

a voice . . . saying: Matthew 3:17; compare Mark 1:11, Luke 3:22.

child: Compare a similar utterance in the *Passion* of George, section 7, below.

24 *Peter . . . Attaleia*: Attaleia is a city (modern Antalya) in Pamphylia, Asia Minor. Its bishop Peter is only mentioned in versions
   of Christopher's *Passion*. David Woods ("St. Christopher," 175),
   who considers this present tale as refracting an earlier and historically more accurate Alexandrian legend, has suggested that
   this Peter should be identified with Peter, bishop of Alexandria
   (d. 311).

Pisidia: A Roman region in southwestern Asia Minor, corresponding roughly to the modern-day province of Antalya in
   Turkey. The region lay to the northwest of Pamphylia.

Antioch: This is Antioch, capital of Pisidia, and not the more famous city of Syria—compare section 8, above.

25 *the man of God*: For this expression, see the *Life of the Man of God,
   Alexios,* section 1, above.

the fringe . . . touch: Compare Matthew 14:36; see also Matthew
   9:20, Mark 6:56, and Luke 8:44.

amen: Right after the end of the text, the scribe has added the
   following note, signaling its completion: "Ἐπλήσθη σὺν Θεῷ
   τὸ μαρτύριον τοῦ ἁγίου Χριστοφόρου" (The Passion of Saint
   Christopher was completed with God's help).

GEORGE, THE GREAT MARTYR

Passion

1 *At that time*: A phrase that is very similar to a very common for-
   mula added to the beginning of Gospel readings in Byzantine
   lectionaries and that thus would add authority to the story;

compare the relevant note to the *Passion of Niketas,* section 1, below. See also *Miracles,* sections 2 and 6, below.

Dadian the apostate was king: "Apostate" (παραβάτης), used here of Dadian, was a common epithet for the emperor Julian in Byzantine texts after the fifth century. The Latin version uses the term *imperator* in reference to Dadian but the term *rex* for all other kings mentioned in the text (similarly, Alexandra is called *regina*); I have chosen to retain the translation "king" for the Greek βασιλεύς throughout. For Dadian, see also the *Passion of Niketas* 6.

abysmal dragon: The same expression appears in the likely apocryphal fourth-century *Gospel of Bartholomew* 4:46 (*BHG* 228), ed. N. Bonwetsch, "Die apokryphen Fragen des Bartholomäus," *Nachrichten von der königlichen Gesellschaft der Wissenschaften zu Göttingen: Philologisch-historische Klasse* (1897): 9–29. See also *Passion of Niketas,* section 7.

2   *eparch*: Senior army officer.

count: Subaltern army officer.

Let those gods . . . perish: Jeremiah 10:11.

3   *Christian is my principal . . . called*: The same phrase is repeated verbatim by Saint Carpus in the ancient *Acts of Carpus, Papylus, and Agathonike* (*BHG* 293), ed. Herbert Musurillo, *The Acts of the Christian Martyrs* (Oxford, 1972), 22. Compare also the *Passion of Niketas,* section 13. For detailed commentary as well as the recording of motifs that George's *Passion* shares with other Christian martyrdom texts, but also Greco-Roman and Near Eastern mythology, see Karl Krumbacher, *Der heilige Georg in der griechischen Überlieferung,* ed. Albert Ehrhard (Munich, 1911), 109–26 and 312–14, as well as François Cumont, "La plus ancienne légende de saint Georges," *Revue de l'histoire des religions* 114 (1936): 5–51, and Wolfgang Haubrichs, *Georgslied und Georgslegende im frühen Mittelalter: Text und Rekonstruktion* (Königstein, 1979), 406–73.

Apollo, the perdition . . . Herakles: The list of names from Ancient Greek mythology in this passage is somewhat awkward. Apart from the well-known god Apollo, the hero Herakles (together

with the giant Antaios whom Herakles defeated in one of his famous Labors), and the princess Medea (known from the story of the Argonauts and, famously, the main character in a tragedy by Euripides), we find rather obscure references to the personified river god Skamandros (known mainly from Homer's *Iliad* as the river that surrounded Troy) and the otherwise unknown "Pontic fighters" Arath and Zareth, both Hebrew names (the former attested also in magical papyri).

Jezebel: Phoenician princess who had "the prophets of the Lord" killed (1 Samuel 18:3–4, 18:13).

mother of God: The Greek term *theotokos* (mother of God) could possibly suggest that the text postdates the Council of Ephesus (431 CE).

6   *The king became overjoyed*: For echoes of this phrase and the surrounding episode (namely, the temporary deluded joy of the persecuting emperor), see section 16, below, and the *Passion of Christopher*, section 14, above, and *Passion of Niketas*, section 7, below.

the magician restored . . . into two bulls: Similar episodes are attributed in Byzantine *apocrypha* to various magicians competing with Christian saints; see, for example, Cumont, "La plus ancienne légende," 19–26.

7   *child*: An interesting appellation coming from George, who is supposedly only twenty-two at this point. Perhaps he is here assuming a fatherly figure in contrast to the failed paternal stance of Dadian.

the kings: These are "the kings who sit beside" Dadian (see section 3, above).

8   *the enemy to say 'I overpowered him'*: A slight modification of Psalms 12(13):4.

Then, raising . . . who rebuked: This entire passage as preserved in O (see the Notes to the Texts) could be translated as follows: Then, raising his eyes toward his benefactor, he said, "You, without beginning or succession, victor, crown of those who are martyred on behalf of your name, you who created heaven and earth and rest upon the waters, you whose repose the hu-

man race has never comprehended, and when you created the vault of the perceptible heaven, you ordered the rain-bringing clouds to be filled with waters, so as *to rain on the just and on the unjust.* Lord, *you who have weighed the mountains with a scale and the valleys with a balance,* you who rebuked. . . ." As already observed by Ehr. 1, p. 73, this prayer is repeated, with some variation, in the ancient versions of the *Passion* of Barbara; see, for example, *BHG* 215, ed. Wirth, *Danae,* p. 110, lines 132–39. The most ancient version of Saint Barbara's *Passion,* written after George's legend, remains still unedited.

You who, before heaven . . . rested upon the waters: Compare Genesis 1:1–2.

to rain on the just and the unjust: Matthew 5:45.

you who have weighed . . . with a balance: Isaiah 40:12.

rebuked the swollen mass . . . calmed the waves: Compare Matthew 8:26.

delivered the angels . . . Tartaros: an expression that is encountered both in Byzantine *Euchologia* and in prayers in later hagiographic texts. Tartaros, a concept inherited from Ancient Greek cosmology, is used in Christian literature to refer to the abyss in which souls were judged and both the demons and the wicked people punished after death.

You who walked . . . without polluting your feet: See Matthew 14:25–33.

rebuked the winds and the sea: A slight modification of Matthew 8:26.

9   *through whom kings reign, and tyrants rule the earth*: Compare Proverbs 8:15–16.

bring his blood upon our heads: Compare Ezekiel 33:4 and Acts 18:6.

the sea stood still fifteen cubits high: Compare Jonas 1:12 with Genesis 7:20; the latter passage is describing the depth by which the great flood covered the mountains. Fifteen cubits is around twenty-two and a half feet.

the archangel Michael . . . chariot of cherubim: Compare the *Life of Adam and Eve (Revelation of Moses)* 22 (*BHG* 24), ed. D. Bertrand, *La Vie grecque d'Adam et d'Eve* (Paris, 1987).

his horn trumpet: Compare Psalms 97(98):6.

the hand that fashioned you: Compare Psalms 118(119):73.

breathed into him . . . and he lived: Compare Genesis 2:7.

Magnentios: A fictive king but with of the name of a real Roman emperor (r. 350–353 CE).

It looks like him: Compare John 9:9.

10   *like dust*: Daniel 2:35 and Deuteronomy 9:21; compare Job 21:18. Compare also, the *Passion of Christopher,* section 22, above.

Be manly . . . be frightened . . . be strong: Deuteronomy 31:6 and Joshua 1:9.

11   *Herakleios*: Herakles is obviously meant, and that is the name used in the likely earliest Latin manuscript, X-lat; on which, see the Note on the Texts).

the Galileans: This appellation, often used derogatorily for Christians in the writings of Julian the Apostate, suggests that the story postdates Julian's reign; compare note to section 1, above, and see Amélineau, *Contes,* vol. 1, pp. xlv–xlvi.

fifteen cubits: See the note on section 9, "the sea stood still fifteen cubits high," above.

and there was a great earthquake: Matthew 8:24, Revelation 6:12 and 11:13, etc. Compare below, sections 13 and 19, and the *Passion of Boniphatios,* section 12, above.

came upon the clouds: See Daniel 7:13; compare Matthew 24:30 and 26:64, Mark 14:62, and Revelation 1:7.

Be manly and strong: Deuteronomy 31:6–7 and 31:23; Joshua 1:6, 1:7, 1:9, and 1:18; 1 Chronicles 22:13, 28:20; and Daniel 10:19.

you shall join Abraham and Isaac and Jacob: Compare Matthew 8:11.

13   *Trakylinos*: Or Tranquillinus, as in the Latin version.

If you have faith . . . nothing shall be impossible for you: An almost exact quotation of Matthew 17:20.

everything is possible for my God: See Matthew 19:26.

And there was a great earthquake: Matthew 8:24, Revelation 6:12 and 11:13, and elsewhere. Compare sections 11, above, and 19, below, and the *Passion of Boniphatios,* section 12, above.

the river of fire and the sleepless worm: Compare Isaiah 66:24, Daniel 7:10, and Mark 9:48.

gets some respite . . . holy Sunday: This motif is found also in the apocryphal *Revelation of Paul* 44 (*BHG* 1460), ed. Constantinus Tischendorf, *Apocalypses apocryphae* (Leipzig, 1866), 63.

14   *the poorest widow*: Compare Luke 21:1–4 and the *Life of Makarios,* section 28, above.

entered the house of the widow: The entire chapter from this point on is inspired by the episode of the prophet Elijah and the widow of Zarephath, recorded in 1 Kings 17:9–24. In X-lat and other early versions, George's healing miracle takes places on a Saturday.

fifteen cubits high: See the relevant note on section 9, above.

felt stronger: Acts 9:19.

she fell upon his feet: The wording parallels the description of the behavior of Mary, the sister of Lazaros, at John 11:32.

Tears fell from his eyes, and he was immediately able to see: The wording echoes the restoration of Paul's sight as recounted in Acts 9:18, where, however, something "like scales" (ὡς λεπίδες) are said to have fallen from his eyes, which is what we read in other versions of George's *Passion* in Greek, as well as other languages (see, for example, X-lat, ed. Haubrichs, *Georgslied,* 441–42).

15   *birds of the air*: Matthew 6:26.

the mountain: In several versions of the *Passion,* this mountain carries a name likely originating from a lost Greek name "of the Assyrians" (in X-lat, for instance, it is called Asinaris), as proposed in Cumont, "La plus ancienne," 29.

about thirty stades: The Greek *stadion,* or stade, measured around six hundred feet, so the distance envisaged here is, very roughly, three and a half miles.

the Lord came upon the clouds: Daniel 7:13.

16   *The king became overjoyed*: See section 6, above.

Alexandra: In other versions (as, for example, X-lat), her name is given as Alexandria.

17   *Who is as great as our God? . . . wonders*: Psalms 76:14–15(77:13–14) with minor modifications.

Why did nations . . . against his anointed: Psalms 2:1–2. The term translated as "his anointed" is, in fact, "Christ."

You who sit upon the cherubim . . . come to save us: Psalms 79:2(80:1).

Before the sun I brought you forth . . . gave birth to you: Compare Proverbs 8:22–25.

He shall come down like rain upon the mown grass: Psalms 71(72):6.

Lord, I have heard . . . astonished: Habakuk 3:2, Odes 4:2.

18   *created paradise in Eden toward the east*: Genesis 2:8.

the third heaven: See 2 Corinthians 12:2.

19   *there was a great earthquake*: Matthew 8:24, Revelation 6:12 and 11:13, and elsewhere. Compare sections 11 and 13, above, and the *Passion of Boniphatios,* section 12, above.

I sacrificed the gods: Instead of "I sacrificed *to* the gods," retaining the somewhat anomalous syntax of the Greek (compare *Niketas,* sections 3, 4, 5, again with θύω, "sacrifice," and an accusative) and George's likely sarcasm; θύω consistently governs a dative in the rest of the text on George.

tore his garment: Compare Matthew 26:65.

Theognios: According to some versions, the fictional Theognios is said to be "king of Egypt."

Strangulinos: Instead of Trakylinos as in section 13, above.

two cubits long: About three feet.

on April the fifteenth: Alexandra, in the guise of Diocletian's wife, is celebrated separately (and together with her three servants Isaakios, Apollo, and Kodratos), on April 21 (or alternatively April 20 or 22) in Byzantine *Synaxaria.*

20   *How great are your works . . . created them all*: Psalms 103(104):24.

his mother: In some versions an account is also given of George's early years, and he is presented as the offspring of a pagan father, often named Gerontios (absent from our version), and a Christian mother, named Polychronia (as below); indeed, in one late Byzantine and quite widely circulating tale in George's dossier (BGH 680b), Gerontios is said to be a Persian foreigner who "walked about the land of the Romans" and impregnated Polychronia, a beautiful Cappadocian virgin, out of wedlock.

God, who accepted Abraham's sacrifice . . . Isaac: See Genesis 22.

as he accepted Abel's gifts: Genesis 4:4. Abel is said to have brought

the firstborn of his flock, earning God's approval in comparison to the offering made by his brother, Cain.

as he loved Enoch, his servant: See Genesis 5:22–24.

Polychronia: The name literally means "the one of many years."

golden image: Daniel 3:1.

set his lot to be with the wild beasts . . . recognized you Lord: See Daniel 4:32–33. The "wicked king" is Nebuchadnezzar.

brought down his son . . . kingship: Belshazzar, see Daniel 5:32.

brought down Holofernes the destroyer: See Judith 13.

subjected the murderer's son to him: See 2 Kings 6:32.

this favor: For this part of George's final request and the divine confirmation that follows, see Flusin, "Le contrat," 40–46; compare also the *Passion of Christopher,* section 23, above.

God of Abraham . . . Jacob: Acts 7:32.

sent down fire to the five-city league of Sodom: See Genesis 19:24.

sent down fire through your prophet . . . fifty men: Compare 2 Kings 1:9–12.

kill King Dadian, and the kings that are with him: The fulfillment of this curse, recorded in most other versions of the *Passion,* is omitted in *BHG* 670a.

cut off George's holy head: The Latin text adds here (X-lat, ed. Haubrichs, *Georgslied,* 831): "and water and milk came forth from his body."

twenty-third of the month of April: It is notable that there has been an accumulation of feast days assigned to the twenty-third day of months; compare chapters 7 (January 23) and 9 (February 23), above.

amen: The earliest Latin version of George's *Passion* continues with one more concluding paragraph, whose beginning reads as follows (X-lat, ed. Haubrichs, *Georgslied,* 838–44): "I, Pasikrates, a slave of my lord George, was present at all his sufferings during the seven years during which he was tried by the emperor Dacian [the spelling of Dadian in the Latin versions] and the seventy-two kings; for each of the years and months and days, I recorded what he suffered. And I wrote all the acts of my lord George in the order in which they were performed.

The Lord of heaven and earth, who shall judge the living and the dead, knows that I neither added to nor subtracted from his passion, but I wrote about it exactly as he was martyred." This mention of "Pasikrates" (alternative spellings include Pasikratios and Pankratios, a significant name that likely denotes the "best among <the slaves>"), a supposed firsthand witness and author of George's story, most likely belonged to the original Greek *Passion* and is attested in some Greek versions (*BHG* 670b–d, 671–672c, 675) as well as in many early Byzantine translations, but is missing from *BHG* 670a, the version in this volume.

George the Great Martyr

Miracles

1   *who has . . . such*: Isaiah 66:8.

2   *Yet the Lord . . . deeds*: See Psalms 102(103):10, and also 27:4.

    a wicked dragon: On dragons in Byzantium, see Anthony Kaldellis, "Draconic Demons and Ogres: Dragons in Byzantium," in *The Penguin Book of Dragons,* ed. Scott G. Bruce (New York, 2021), 117–40.

4   *in purple and fine linen*: Luke 16:19.

    the fruit of your womb: Luke 1:42.

5   *does not wish . . . live*: Ezekiel 18:23, 33:11; compare 1 Timothy 2:4. See also the *Passion of Boniphatios,* section 1, above.

6   *Saint George . . . own fatherland*: Echoing the *Passion* of George, section 2, above.

7   *The saint said to her*: In most of the other manuscript redactions of the story, the first exchange presented here is preceded by one in which the girl praises George's "beauty" and "manliness."

    I shall die . . . abandon you: Compare Matthew 26:38.

9   *Herakles . . . Artemis*: Compare the *Passion* of George, sections 3, 9, 11, 14, 16, and 19, above, for this somewhat awkward list of pagan divinities.

10 *enthroned . . . the depths*: Daniel 3:55, Odes 8:54.

   make with me a sign for good: Psalms 85(86):17.

   making . . . beneath my feet: Compare Psalms 8:7 and 1 Corinthians 15:27.

12 *Do not be afraid . . . of God*: Compare Exodus 14:13.

   and I shall kill the dragon: Compare Bel and the Dragon 25 (Daniel 14:25).

   We believe . . . undivided: The pagan Lasians speak as if they already know the Byzantine Creed.

13 *the archbishop of Alexandria*: Most other redactions offer the likely more correct reading "the (arch)bishop Alexander."

   there was great joy in that place: Compare Acts 8:8.

14 *When Saint George left the city of Lasia*: Here begins the second miracle, an encounter with a demon. It belongs to the tradition of encounters with the devil, most of them apocryphal in nature, for which see the relevant note to the *Passion of Niketas,* section 14, below.

   angel of light: 2 Corinthians 11:14.

   come follow me: Matthew 19:21, Mark 10:21, Luke 18:22.

15 *when God . . . waters*: See Genesis 1:1–2 and the *Passion* of George, section 8, above.

   bound up the clouds: Job 26:8, speaking of the power of God.

   legions of the angels: Matthew 26:53.

16 *I shall not . . . to me*: John 6:37.

   who knows hearts: Acts 1:24 and 15:8.

   the image . . . fashioned: In other words, human beings, who were fashioned in God's own image in the Byzantine conception, based on Genesis 1:26–27.

PASSION OF NIKETAS

1 *In those days*: Matthew 3:1, Mark 1:9 and 8:1, and Luke 2:1; also, a very common phrase added to the beginning of Gospel readings in Byzantine lectionaries.

   Maximian: In a very large number of Greek *Passions,* the name Μαξιμιανός usually refers to Galerius (ca. 260–311 CE), whose full list of names included Maximianus, and who, between 293

and 305, served as Caesar under Diocletian in the Eastern Roman empire, before becoming Augustus from 305 to 311. In most of these *Passions* (as also in our text), the relation of "Maximian" (presented as a relentless persecutor of the Christians, second only to Diocletian) to the historical Galerius is tenuous—if any relation indeed exists at all. See Papaioannou, *Christian Novels,* 300–301; and Charis Messis, "'Maximien' chez les Martyrs: Lectures du passé romain dans l'hagiographie byzantine," in *L'histoire comme elle se présentait dans l'hagiographie byzantine et médiévale Byzantine and Medieval History as Represented in Hagiography,* ed. Anna Lampadaridi, Vincent Déroche, and Christian Høgel (Uppsala, 2022), 105–31. In manuscript F, Niketas has two additional brothers, Aimilianos and Alexandros.

the way of life: Jeremiah 21:8; compare Psalms 15(16):11. See also the *Life of Makarios,* section 29, above.

In the fullness of time: Compare Galatians 4:4. The demotic form πληρωμένου χρόνου is found in, for example, the late fourteenth-century *Story of Belisarios,* ed. Willem Frederik Bakker and Arnold F. van Gemert, Ἱστορία τοῦ Βελισαρίου (Athens, 1988), recension χ, line 25, and recension N², line 30.

that entire city: The name of the city remains unmentioned throughout the text.

around midnight: A common time for apparitions in Byzantine hagiography.

the archangel Michael . . . forever: In F, it is Christ himself who appears to Niketas holding the sign of the cross. In some sense, the vision mimics (and chronologically would precede) the famous vision of Constantine the Great. For Byzantine crosses with the depiction of Niketas (and the archangel Michael), see Angeliki Katsioti, "Χάλκινος λιτανικός σταυρός από τη Νίσυρο με παράσταση του αρχαγγέλου Μιχαήλ: Η πιθανή προέλευσή του," in *Χάρις Χαῖρε, Μελέτες στη μνήμη της Χάρης Κάντζια,* vol. 1 (Athens 2004), 471–85; and Miodrag Marković, "St. Niketas the Goth and St. Niketas of Nikomedeia: Apropos depictions of St. Niketas the Martyr on Me-

dieval Crosses," *Zbornik za likovne umetnosti Matice srpske* 36 (2008): 19–42.

2   *destitute woman named Iouliane*: A similarly positive female character appears in the *Life of Makarios,* section 28, above, and the *Passion* of George, section 14, above. Her name here perhaps anticipates the mention of the evil Julian (Ioulianos) introduced later in the narrative (section 4).

   do not be frightened . . . be brave: Deuteronomy 31:6 and Joshua 1:9.

3   *Taxiarch*: A common attribute of Michael as the leader of the heavenly host; *taxis* refers to an army unit in Greek.

   you who fly swiftly: The Greek term γοργοπέταστος is a hapax.

   who makes . . . ministers: Psalms 103(104):4; compare Hebrews 1:7.

4   *Julian the Apostate*: An ahistorical reference to the emperor Julian (331–363 CE), perhaps the most famous early Byzantine denier of Christianity in Byzantine religious imagination.

   Artemes: In the confused understanding of pagan deities evident in our text, Artemes (and not Artemis) is a male divinity.

   the emperor heard these words: In manuscripts A and J, Maximian promises his daughter to Julian as a bride.

5   *church of . . . Michael*: In manuscripts A and J, the church is of the Theotokos (mother of God).

   the martyr: It is noteworthy that Niketas is called a martyr before his actual martyrdom—a practice not uncommon in Byzantine *Passions*.

   ears they have . . . in them: See Psalms 113:5–8(115:13–16) and 134(135):16–18.

   they are unable . . . help themselves: Compare Job 4:20.

6   *the emperor became overjoyed*: For this phrase and the surrounding episode (namely, the temporary deluded joy of the persecuting emperor), see the *Passion* of George, sections 6 and, especially, 16, above, which perhaps provided the model for our passage here. Compare also the *Passion of Christopher,* section 14, above. For the influence of the *Passion* of George on the story of Niketas, see A. Kirpichnikov, *Св. Георгий и Егорий Храбрый: Исследование литературной истории христианской легенды* (Saint Petersburg, 1879), 47, and Alex-

ander N. Veselovskii, "Св. Георгий в легенде, песне и обряде," *Sbornik Otdeleniia russkago iazyka i slovesnosti Imp. akademii nauk* 21, no. 2 (1881): 12–19.

into dust: Daniel 2:35 and Deuteronomy 9:21; compare Job 21:18. See also the *Passion of Christopher,* section 22, above, and the *Passion* of George, section 10, above.

George . . . Kerykos . . . Blasios: Both Kerykos and George were commonly included in Orthodox lists of prohibited tales. See notes 44 and 56 in the Introduction.

I have believed: 2 Corinthians 4:13.

7   *abysmal dragon*: An expression that appears often in the *Passion* of George; see the note to section 1 there.

evil thoughts: Compare Matthew 9:4.

may you not abandon me: A frequent invocation in the Psalms; see, for example, 26(27):9. Compare Ecclesiastes 23:1.

8   *an angel of the Lord*: In manuscripts V, P, A, and J, it is specifically the archangel Michael who, here as well as later in the story, appears to Niketas. In general, in these other versions, Michael is much more prominent, like a second protagonist, present or invoked in almost all episodes. For the association of the two holy figures in Byzantine cult, see Katsioti, "Χάλκινος"; for the cult of Michael in Byzantium, see Bernadette Martin-Hisard, "Le culte de l'archange Michel dans l'empire byzantin (VIIIe–XIe siècles)," in *Culto e insediamenti micaelici nell'Italia meridionale fra tarda antichità e medioevo: Atti del Convegno internazionale, Monte Sant'Angelo, 18–21 novembre 1992*, ed. C. Carletti (Bari, 1994), 351–73.

Be brave and strong: Deuteronomy 31:6–7, 31:23, and a number of other Old Testament passages. Compare *Passion* of George, section 11, above.

destroyer of demons: This appellation appears also in other Byzantine *Passions;* here, it evokes a specific quality ascribed to Niketas (see sections 14–16, below).

Look up to heaven: Genesis 15:5 and Job 35:5.

like a dove: Matthew 3:16.

pillar of fire: Nehemiah 19:19.

9   *beautiful virgin girl*: In other versions this description is amplified: the maiden is "noble and beautiful" in manuscript C, "most beautiful" in V, J, and A, and "most beautiful in stature and appearance" in P. In contrast, W somewhat tones down the description; the girl is simply "noble and acclaimed."

with her clothes all perfumed up: Manuscripts A and J omit this detail; in V the girl is naked, while in P she is said to come to him "shamelessly."

deeply moved: John 11:38 of Christ in front of Lazaros's tomb.

with his: Μὲ τοὺς in the original Greek, which points to modern Greek usage.

threw it to a dog . . . dog, and eat it!: In our version it is mistakenly assumed that Niketas throws his tongue to an actual dog. In the related versions represented by manuscripts V and P, the appellation "dog" could be inferred as an insulting address to the girl (something made clear in A and J, where the tongue is thrown "to the ground"). In C and W, however, Niketas throws his tongue at his father and calls *him* "flesh-eating dog." For the history of this whole episode, that ultimately goes back to Jerome's *Life* of Paul of Thebes (itself inspired by earlier Greek stories), see Stratis Papaioannou, "The Philosopher's Tongue: *Synaxaria* between History and Literature, with an Excursus on the Recension M of the *Synaxarion of Constantinople* and an Edition of BHG 2371n," in Lampadaridi, Déroche, and Høgel, *L'histoire comme elle se présentait,* 151–97, at 168–69.

freely: Manuscript V and *BHG* 1344 link this word with the extreme "disgust" that the girl feels. In a related fashion, A and J offer the variant, "she saw the blood gushing freely and was disgusted."

10   *four wheels*: The wheels are nine in manuscripts V, J, and A, and seven hundred in P!

Blessed be the Lord God, who does wondrous things: Psalms 71(72):18.

soldiers: These are numbered at five hundred in the other redactions.

11   *four cubits long*: About six feet. For a similar torture device, see the *Passion* of George, section 19, above. In other redactions (including the Slavonic ones), the spit is twelve cubits long.

to earth it will return: Genesis 3:19.

12   *teeth pullers*: By using the accusative (instead of the correct dative), the scribe of manuscript M seems to understand ὀδο-ντάγραι as agents—dentists of sorts!—and not as tools for drawing teeth, which is the dictionary meaning of the Greek word.

why have you forsaken me: Psalms 21:2(22:1), with Matthew 27:46 and Mark 15:34 (Christ's desperate call while on the cross).

do not abandon: A relatively common phrase in the Old Testament. See, for example, Numbers 10:31 or Psalms 26(27):9.

hear the petition: Esther 4:17.

send your angel: 2 Maccabees 15:23.

dew . . . scorching heat: See Sirach 18:16.

dew came down from heaven: Compare Judges 6:36–40 and Genesis 27:28.

13   *Chamel and Abenagor*: Their names are Chagbel and Abdenago (for the latter name, compare Daniel 1:7) in manuscript V; Chamomelos and Abdenagoin P; not named in A and J. The entire passage is more elaborate in V, as well as in A and J. For a similar episode that results in the conversion of a magician, see the *Passion* of George, sections 6 and 7, above.

'Artemes' . . . darkness: Pseudoetymologies of the ancient divine names. "Artemes" is explained through ἄρτι (*art-i*: right now), and "Apollo" through ἀπώλεια (*apol-eia*: destruction). In the other versions of Niketas's *Passion*, "Artemes" is explained through ἄρτι and ἀπο-τέμ-νω (*apo-tem-no*: cut off).

in my name . . . hurt them: Mark 16:17–18.

Christian . . . Christ: Compare the *Passion* of George, section 3, above.

14   *The devil transformed . . . Niketas*: The dialogue that follows is somewhat shortened in comparison to the other related versions. Original readers would probably catch a parody of the Annunciation, Luke 1:28. As the episode unfolds, it becomes clear that this is not *the* devil (who, later in the text, is called "Satan"), but one of his servant spirits; the other versions usually call this evil spirit a "demon." For the apocryphal demon literature to which our text may be associated, see, for

example, Vasilij M. Istrin, *Апокрифическое мучение Никиты*
(Odessa, 1899), 29–30; Pascal Boulhol, "Hagiographie antique
et démonologie: Notes sur quelques Passiones grecques (*BHG*
962z, 964 et 1165–1166)," *Analecta Bollandiana* 112 (1994): 255–
303; and Nikolaos Kälviäinen, "'Not a Few of the Martyr Accounts Have Been Falsified from the Beginning': Some Preliminary Remarks on the Censorship and Fortunes of the Demonic
Episode in the Greek Passion of St. Marina (BHG 1165–1167c),"
in *Translation and Transmission,* ed. Jaakko Hämeen-Anttila and
Ilkka Lindstedt (Münster, 2019), 107–37 (with further bibliography). See also the *Passion* of George, section 18, above, and
the *Miracles* of George, sections 14–17, above.

angel of light: 2 Corinthians 11:14.

threw the devil to the ground: The related versions add "and
stepped on his neck"; see the continuation of the passage.

strike him fiercely: Manuscript V adds "against his head."

15   *lifted*: The Greek ἀναστείλας is, syntactically, a so-called hanging nominative, a usage that points to Modern Greek.

My father, Satan: For this expression, compare the *Passion of
Christopher,* section 16, above.

Beelzebul: See Matthew 10:25, 12:24, 12:27; Mark 3:22, 11:15, 11:18–
19; and Karel van der Toorn, Bob Becking, and Pieter W. van
der Horst, eds., *Dictionary of Deities and Demons in the Bible* (Leiden and Boston, 1999), 154–56. For a text with a similar encounter and discussion with the devil, see the apocryphal *Testament of Solomon* (*BHG* 2389–2391), trans. D. C. Duling, in *The
Old Testament Pseudepigrapha,* vol. 1, *Apocalyptic Literature and
Testaments,* ed. J. H. Charlesworth (Garden City, NY, 1983),
935–87.

And I'm the one who . . . lead them astray: Manuscripts M and (less
so) P offer us a somewhat shortened version of this list of
sins inspired by the devil, while manuscripts V, J, and A preserve a more extensive account, which includes things like
turning people to "sweet sleep" and showing "strange and ex-
quisite dreams" so as to prevent them from going to church

and making people avoid Communion because the priest is a sinner.

enmity . . . slander: Compare 2 Corinthians 12:20 and 1 Peter 2:1.

holy Sunday: Manuscript V adds "as well as on the feast days of the Lord."

17   *Lord, God of Abraham, Isaac, and Jacob*: The same form of address appears in the saint's last prayer in the *Passion* of George, section 20, above.

the cherubim . . . your glory: A phrase from the Byzantine divine liturgy attributed to John Chrysostom, inspired by Isaiah 6:2–3.

with four elements: Manuscripts V, J, and A add the idea that God also supported the world by a "purple column."

with your mighty hand: A common Old Testament expression. See, for example, Exodus 6:1.

are blessed forever, amen: Romans 1:25 and 9:5; 2 Corinthians 11:31.

18   *the dead people*: Manuscript V specifies that these were "a man, a woman, and two children." A similar episode appears in the *Passion* of George, section 13, above, where the resurrected dead were "five men, nine women, and three children."

the light of the world: John 8:12; compare Matthew 5:14.

heirs of his kingdom: James 2:5.

the delight of Paradise: Compare Genesis 3:23–24, Joel 2:3, and Ezekiel 28:13.

19   *The emperor's wife*: Manuscript P specifies that she is the "mother of the saint."

they seized him: Manuscript V adds the detail that "they slaughtered him with knives and scattered his body parts on the ground"; the latter detail is present also in A and J.

20   *Athanarichos, ruler of a heathen nation*: This detail (absent from manuscripts C, W, J, and A) alludes to the conflation of this Niketas with the more famous (and canonical) saint of the same name, Niketas the Goth (also celebrated on September 15), who, according to the *Passions* dedicated to his story (*BHG* 1339–1340), died at the hands of Athanarichos, ruler of the

Goths; see Marković, "St. Niketas." In manuscript V, the reference to Athanarichos continues with an entire episode about how this king who "lived by the Danube River" learned about the slaughter of Maximian and the conversion of his city, and thus came, arrested Niketas, and put him to death by throwing him into a furnace, once the martyr refused to venerate the pagan gods. In C and W, Niketas is beheaded by his own father, Maximian.

the holy City: In a Byzantine context, this locution normally referred to Jerusalem; the mention of Boniphatios and Alexios that follows, however, could suggest that the implied city is Rome. In manuscripts V, P, J, and A, a sentence follows in which it is specified that the head (not the body) of Niketas was deposited in Nicomedia, which is also said to be the place of Niketas's death. In relation to this, Hippolyte Delehaye raised the possibility that Niketas's story might have originated in honor of a Nicomedian saint; see Hippolyte Delehaye, "Saints de Thrace et de Mésie, *Analecta Bollandiana* 31 (1912): 161–300, at 286–87.

hanging stone: This sacred site (present also in manuscripts V, P, J, and A) is not mentioned elsewhere in Byzantine texts, as far as I can tell.

Saints Paphnoutios and Charalampos, Parakletos and Boniphatios, Alexios and Euphemianos: For the significance of this list of saints, see the Introduction. Paphnoutios (*BHG* 1419) and Charalampos (*BHG* 298) are martyrs of the Diocletian and Severan persecutions, respectively. Parakletos normally denotes the Holy Spirit in Byzantine texts, though here it refers to a saint, unknown otherwise, as far as I can tell.

21   *with the fear of God and with faith*: The same phrase is used in Byzantine liturgy when the faithful are called to receive the holy Communion.

Bibliography

Baun, Jane. *Tales from Another Byzantium: Celestial Journey and Local Community in the Medieval Greek Apocrypha.* Cambridge, 2007.

Delehaye, Hippolyte. *Les légendes hagiographiques.* 4th ed. Brussels, 1955. First edition published Brussels, 1905. English translation, *The Legends of the Saints: An Introduction to Hagiography.* Translated by V. M. Crawford. Notre Dame, 1961.

Dagron, Gilbert. "Frontières et marges: Le jeu du sacré à Byzance." *Corps écrit* 2 (April 1982): 159–66.

———. "Le merveilleux sous haute surveillance: Quelques exemples byzantins." In *Démons et merveilles au Moyen Âge,* edited by Denis Menjot and Benoît Cursente, 55–67. Nice, 1990.

Efthymiadis, Stephanos, ed. *The Ashgate Research Companion to Byzantine Hagiography.* 2 vols. Farnham, UK, and Burlington, VT, 2011–2014.

Greenfield, Richard P. H. *Traditions of Belief in Late Byzantine Demonology.* Amsterdam, 1988.

Johnson, Scott Fitzgerald. "Christian Apocrypha." In *The Oxford Handbook to the Second Sophistic,* edited by Daniel S. Richter and William A. Johnson, 669–86. Oxford and New York, 2017.

Jouanno, Corinne. *Naissance et metamorphoses du "Roman d'Alexandre": Domaine grec.* Paris, 2002.

Magdalino, Paul. "Apocryphal Narrative: Patterns of Fiction in Byzantine Prophetic and Patriographic Literature." In *Medieval Greek Storytelling: Fictionality and Narrative in Byzantium,* edited by Panagiotis Roilos, 87–102. Wiesbaden, 2014.

Maguire, Eunice Dauterman, and Henry Maguire. *Other Icons: Art and Power in Byzantine Secular Culture*. Princeton, NJ, 2007.

Maltezou, Chrysa A., ed. *Οἱ περιθωριακοὶ στὸ Βυζάντιο (Πρακτικὰ ἡμερίδας, 9 Μαΐου 1992)*. Athens, 1992.

Papaioannou, Stratis, ed. *The Oxford Handbook of Byzantine Literature*. Oxford and New York, 2021.

Poliakova, Sofia V. "Византийские легенды как литературное явление." In *Византийские легенды,* 245–73. Saint Petersburg, 1972; repr., 2004.

Index

Abel, *Pass. George* 20

Abenagor (saint), *Niketas* 13

Abgar (king of Edessa), *Alexios* 7

Abraham, *Pass. George* 11, 20; *Niketas* 17

Adam, *Makarios* 25

Aeikon (martyr), *Pass. George* 15

Aetios (*chartoularios* of the church of Rome), *Alexios* 22

Aglaïs (mistress of Boniphatios), *Boniphatios* 2–3, 14–15

Aglaïs (wife of Euphenianos), *Alexios* 3

Akakios (father of Aglaïs), *Boniphatios* 2

Akylina (martyr), *Christopher* 12–13, 15

Alexander the Great: *Makarios* 12; arch of, *Makarios* 12, 46

Alexandra (queen; wife of the fictive king Dadian), *Pass. George* 16–17, 19–20

Alexandria, *Markos* 3; archbishop of, *Mir. George* 13

Alexios, *Niketas* 20

Ananias (one of the three holy youths), *Makarios* 5

Anastasis (church in Jerusalem), *Makarios* 4, 48

Anatolios (martyr), *Pass. George* 9

Antaios (mythological giant), *Pass. George* 3

Anthropophagi, *Christopher* 2

Antioch, *Christopher* 8, 24

Apollo, *Pass. George* 3, 9, 11–14, 16, 18–19; *Mir. George* 9; spirit of, *Pass. George* 18; *Niketas* 4, 13; statue of, *Pass. George* 18

Arath (mythological figure), *Pass. George* 3

Arcadius (emperor), *Alexios* 1, 27

Artemes (male deity), *Niketas* 4, 13

Artemis (deity), *Pass. George* 11, 16; *Mir. George* 9

Asia, *Makarios* 5

Asklepios (abbot), *Makarios* 2, 49

Athanarichos (ruler of the Goths), *Niketas* 20

Athanasios (magician), *Pass. George* 6–7

349

Athens, *Markos* 11

Attaleia, *Christopher* 24

Azarias (one of the three holy youths), *Makarios* 5

Babylas (saint), *Christopher* 8

Bachthious, *Christopher* 4–5

baptism, *Markos* 20; *Christopher* 8–9; *Pass. George* 7, 13, 15, 19; *Mir. George* 13; *Niketas* 13, 19

Beelzebul, *Niketas* 16. *See also* devil; Satan

Bethlehem, *Makarios* 4

Blasios (saint), *Niketas* 6

bones (of a martyr), *Boniphatios* 9; *Christopher* 22; *Pass. George* 9, 11, 13, 15. *See also* relics

Boniphatios (saint and martyr), *Boniphatios* 1–3, 5, 7–14, 16; *Niketas* 20; church of, *Alexios* 6, 27

Capitolium, *Alexios* 7

Cappadocia, *Pass. George* 2–3; *Mir. George* 6

cave: of Jesus, *Makarios* 4; of Makarios, *Makarios* 22, 29, 41; of Markos, *Markos* 8, 15, 20, 23

Chalcedon. *See* Kalchedon

Chamel (magician), *Niketas* 13

Charalampos (saint), *Niketas* 20

cherubim, *Makarios* 25; *Pass. George* 9; *Mir. George* 10; *Niketas* 17

childlessness, *Alexios* 1–3

Christ, icon of, *Alexios* 7. *See also* Nazarene

Christians, *Boniphatios* 3, 7–8, 10, 12; *Markos* 13–14, 22, 25, 47; *Christopher* 1–5, 17, 19–20; *Pass. George* 1–2, 6, 9, 11, 13–17, 19–20; *Niketas* 6, 13, 18. *See also* souls

Christopher, *Christopher* 9, 15, 17–25. *See also* Reprebos

cross: sign of the, *Markos* 16; *Makarios* 8, 22, 35–37; *Christopher* 23; *Pass. George* 18–20; *Mir. George* 11, 14, 17; *Niketas* 1–3, 10, 15

Ctesiphon (Persia), *Makarios* 5–6, 47

Cynocephali, *Makarios* 9; *Christopher* 2

Dadian (fictive king of the Persians), *Pass. George* 1–2, 6–7, 9, 11–12, 14–15, 20–21; *Niketas* 6

Darios (Persian king), *Makarios* 12

David (Israelite king), *Markos* 8, 18; *Pass. George* 17

Decius (Roman emperor), *Christopher* 1, 5, 16, 25

demon, *Boniphatios* 8, 14–15; *Markos* 8, 10, 17, 22; *Christopher* 6, 9, 23; *Pass. George* 2–3, 7, 14, 17, 20; *Mir. George* 14–17; *Niketas* 8, 14–16, 21

devil, *Boniphatios* 3, 6–7; *Alexios* 16; *Markos* 8; *Makarios* 23, 36, 39, 44; *Christopher* 16, 18; *Pass. George* 16, 18; *Niketas* 14. *See also* Beelzebul; Satan

dragon, *Boniphatios* 12; *Pass. George*

1, 3, 8–9, 15; *Mir. George* 2, 8, 11–12, 16; *Niketas* 7. *See also* serpent

drunkenness, *Boniphatios* 2, 4, 13

East, *Boniphatios* 3
Eden, *Pass. George* 18
Edessa (Syria), *Alexios* 7, 9, 12
Elijah, *Markos* 10; *Pass. George* 3, 20
Elisha, *Pass. George* 20
Enoch, *Markos* 10; *Pass. George* 20
Ethiopia, *Markos* 1, 3
Euphemianos (father of Alexios), *Alexios* 1, 5–6, 19–22; *Niketas* 20
Euphrates, *Makarios* 2
Eve, *Makarios* 25

foreigner, *Boniphatios* 2, 13
fountain of immortality, *Makarios* 19

Galileans, *Pass. George* 11, 14–16, 18–20
George, *Pass. George* 1, 3–5, 7–20; *Niketas* 6; *Mir. George* 1, 5–6, 12, 14–16; church of, *Mir. George* 13
gladiators, *Boniphatios* 2
Glykades (martyr), *Pass. George* 15
Gospels, *Markos* 14

Habbakuk, *Pass. Georg*e 17
Hades, *Markos* 8; *Pass. George* 13
Hellenes, *Christopher* 19; *Pass. George* 20; god of the, *Pass. George* 18–19; temple of the, *Pass. George* 18

Herakleios (deity; misreading for Herakles), *Pass. George* 11
Herakles (deity), *Christopher* 14; *Pass. George* 3, 9, 14, 19; *Mir. George* 9
Hittites, *Markos* 3
Holofernes, *Pass. George* 20
Holy Spirit, *Boniphatios* 16; *Alexios* 11; *Makarios* 8; *Christopher* 25; *Pass. George* 13, 15; *Mir. George* 12; *Niketas* 8, 10, 19
Honorius (emperor), *Alexios* 1, 27
Hygienos (monk), *Makarios* 1, 3

icon: of Christ, *Alexios* 7; of Mary, *Alexios* 11
India, *Makarios* 6
Iouliane (destitute woman), *Niketas* 2
Isaac, *Pass. George* 11, 20; *Niketas* 17

Jacob, *Pass. George* 11, 20; *Niketas* 17
Jerusalem, *Makarios* 4, 48–49
Jezebel, *Pass. George* 3
John (abbot), *Markos* 1–2, 23, 25; church of, *Markos* 24
John (father of Makarios), *Makarios* 28
judgment: divine, *Boniphatios* 3; *Pass. George* 20; imperial, *Pass. George* 9; Lake of Judgment, *Makarios* 14; Pit of Judgment, *Makarios* 14
Julian the Apostate (Roman emperor), *Makarios* 5; *Niketas* 4
Juves, *Pass. George* 13

Kalchedon (Chalcedon), *Makarios* 12

Kallinike (martyr), *Christopher* 14–15

Kerykos (saint), *Niketas* 6

Laodicea (Syria), *Alexios* 7, 12

Lasia (fictive city), *Mir. George* 2, 13–14

Lasterinos (martyr), *Pass. George* 15

law court, *Boniphatios* 8

Lazaros, *Pass. George* 11

Macedonians, *Makarios* 12

Magnentios (fictive king), *Pass. George* 9, 11, 19–20

Makarios, *Makarios* 1, 22, 25–26, 28, 32, 34, 45–46, 49

Man of God, *Alexios* 11, 18–19, 21–22; *Christopher* 25; *Niketas* 13, 19

Maria (daughter of a Roman, demonic apparition), *Makarios* 36

Markianos (archbishop), *Alexios* 18

Markos (abbot), *Markos* 1, 7–8, 22, 24–25

Marmaritai (Roman army unit), *Christopher* 2

marriage, *Alexios* 5; *Makarios* 28. *See also* wedding

Mary (Mother of God), *Pass. George* 3; church of, *Alexios* 8, 11; icon of, *Alexios* 11

Maximian (Roman emperor), *Niketas* 1, 3

Medea, *Pass. George* 3

Merkourios (saint), *Makarios* 5

Mesopotamia, *Alexios* 7, 9; *Makarios* 2, 49

Michael, *Pass. George* 9, 13–14; *Niketas* 1, 3

Misael (one of the three holy youths), *Makarios* 5

Moses, *Pass. George* 17; *Mir. George* 10

Mount of Olives, *Makarios* 4, 48

multiplication of loaves, *Christopher* 8

Nazarene (Jesus Christ), *Pass. George* 18

Niketas, *Niketas* 1–21

Olives, Mount of, *Makarios* 4, 48

only begotten son: Alexios, *Alexios* 10, 14, 23–24; Jesus, *Boniphatios* 5, 12, *Pass. George* 8, 20

Palestine, *Pass. George* 3

Paphnoutios (saint), *Niketas* 20

Paradise, *Markos* 10; *Makarios* 25; *Christopher* 21; *Pass. George* 18–19; *Niketas* 18

Parakletos (unknown saint), *Niketas* 20

Paul, temple of, *Alexios* 12

Perge (Pamphylia), *Christopher* 8

Persians, *Makarios* 5–6, 12, 47

Persis (Persia), *Makarios* 5

Peter (apostle), *Pass. George* 3

Peter (bishop of Attaleia), *Christopher* 24

Philistines, *Pass. George* 20

Pisidia, *Christopher* 24

Polychronia (mother of George), *Pass. George* 20

Poseidon, *Pass. George* 9

Raphael, *Makarios* 29–30, 32

relics, *Boniphatios* 4–5, 13, 19. *See also* bones

Reprebos (pre-Christian name of Christopher), *Christopher* 2–3, 5–7, 9, 11, 13, 16–17, 20, 22–23. *See also* Christopher

resurrection, *Markos* 20; *Pass. George* 9–13, 15; *Niketas* 18

Roman, *Makarios* 1, 28, 36

Rome, *Boniphatios* 2, 13; *Alexios* 1, 7, 9, 12, 18

Sabaoth, Lord of, *Niketas* 17

Sacrifice, refusal to, *Boniphatios* 8–9; *Christopher* 4, 14–16; *Pass. George* 1, 19; *Niketas* 6

Satan, *Makarios* 35–36; *Christopher* 4, 16; *Pass. George* 2; *Mir. George* 15; *Niketas* 15. *See also* Beelzebul; demon; devil

Scholastike (recipient of miracle), *Pass. George* 12

Selvios (fictive king of Lasia), *Mir. George* 2

seraphim, *Mir. George* 10; *Niketas* 17

Serapion (abbot), *Markos* 1, 7, 9, 15–16, 18–19, 21, 25

Sergios (monk), *Makarios* 1, 3

serpent, *Makarios* 10, 16, 18, 31–33;

Christopher 7; *Niketas* 13. *See also* dragon

Skamandros (sorcerer), *Pass. George* 3, 9; *Mir. George* 9

Solomon, *Pass. George* 17

son. *See* only begotten son

souls, of Christians, *Pass. George* 18

Strangulinos (fictive king), *Pass. George* 19. *See* Trakylinos

Sun (deity), *Pass. George* 11, 16

Syria, *Alexios* 7; *Makarios* 2, 49; *Christopher* 8–9

Tarsos (in Cilicia), *Boniphatios* 6; *Alexios* 12

Tartaros (Tartarus), *Pass. George* 8

Theognios (fictive king), *Pass. George* 13, 19

Theophilos (monk and narrator), *Makarios* 1, 3, 20

Thrace, mountain of, *Markos* 1–3

Tigris (river), *Makarios* 1, 5, 47

torture, *Boniphatios* 6, 9–11; *Christopher* 5, 9–10, 13, 15, 18, 20, 23; *Pass. George* 1, 4–5, 7, 10–11, 15, 19–20; *Niketas* 9–12, 16

Trakylinos (fictive king), *Pass. George* 13. *See also* Strangulinos

Trinity, *Mir. George* 12

wedding, *Alexios* 6, 10, 17; *Makarios* 36; *Mir. George* 4

Zareth (mythological figure), *Pass. George* 3